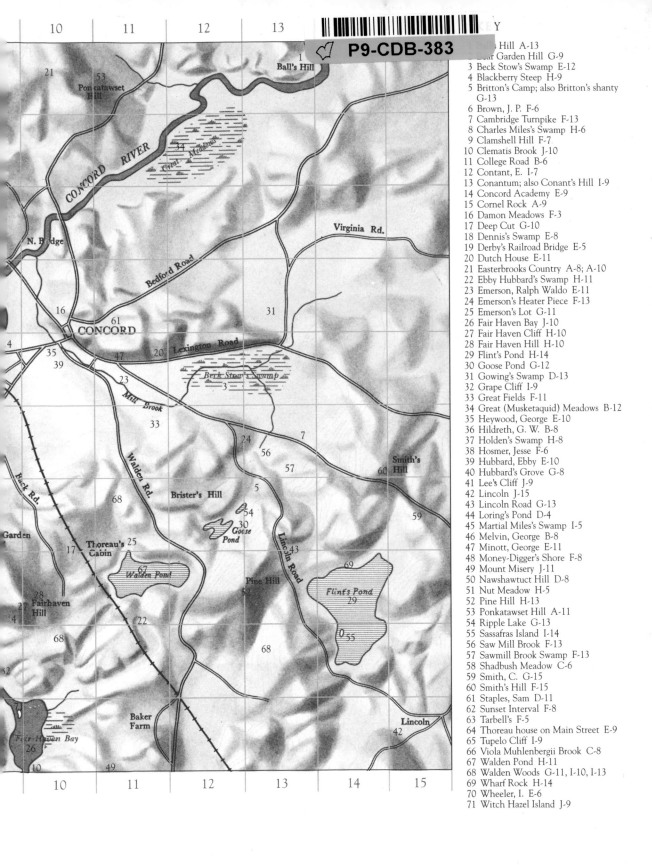

WILD FRUITS

Thoreau's Rediscovered Last Manuscript

WILD FRUITS

Henry David Thoreau

Edited and Introduced by
Bradley P. Dean

Illustrations by Abigail Rorer

W. W. NORTON & COMPANY
New York • London

The text and display of this book are composed in Goudy.
Composition by Allentown Digital Services Division.
Manufacturing by the Haddon Craftsmen, Inc.
Book design by Charlotte Staub

Library of Congress Cataloging-in-Publication Data

Thoreau, Henry David, 1817–1862.
Wild fruits : Thoreau's rediscovered last manuscript / Henry David
Thoreau ; edited and introduced by Bradley P. Dean ; illustrations
by Abigail Rorer.
p.   cm.
Includes bibliographical references (p.   ) and index.
ISBN 0-393-04751-2
1. Wild plants, Edible.   2. Fruit.   I. Dean, Bradley P.
II. Title.
QK98.5.T48   1999
581.6'32—dc21   99-31377   CIP

W. W. Norton & Company, Inc., 500 Fifth Avenue, New York, N.Y. 10110
www.wwnorton.com

W. W. Norton & Company Ltd., 10 Coptic Street, London WC1A 1PU

1 2 3 4 5 6 7 8 9 0

I THINK THAT each town should have a park, or rather a primitive forest, of five hundred or a thousand acres, either in one body or several, where a stick should never be cut for fuel, nor for the navy, nor to make wagons, but stand and decay for higher uses—a common possession forever, for instruction and recreation. All Walden Wood might have been reserved, with Walden in the midst of it....

—Thoreau, *Wild Fruits*

The editor dedicates his labor
on this project to the poet Debra Kang Dean
for her love and support, and to humanitarians Don Henley
and Kathi Anderson of the Walden Woods Project
for their efforts to save Thoreau's beloved
woods and their help in revitalizing
Thoreau studies by establishing
the Thoreau Institute in
the midst of Walden
Woods.

CONTENTS

INTRODUCTION

Henry David Thoreau died peacefully in the front parlor of his mother's home on Main Street in Concord, Massachusetts, on the morning of May 6, 1862. Tuberculosis, a common killer of the time, took him at just forty-four years of age. Among the mass of papers he left behind was the manuscript of *Wild Fruits*, published here for the first time. The final harvest of a great writer's last years, *Wild Fruits* presents Thoreau's sacramental vision of nature—a vision compelling in part because it grew out of an approach to the natural world at once scientific and mystical.

Although Thoreau began writing *Wild Fruits* in the autumn of 1859, the manuscript was part of a much larger project begun early in that decade. In the summer of 1850, he had moved into the third-floor attic of the newly remodeled house in Concord that he shared with his parents and younger sister. There he established a productive daily routine of morning and evening study separated by a long afternoon walk. He found himself at loose ends because he had completed the two books he had been working on for the preceding five years. (He had published his first book, *A Week on the Concord and Merrimack Rivers*, at his own expense in May 1849, and had announced in that book the forthcoming publication of his second book, *Walden; or, Life in the Woods*.) On November 16, 1850, he remarked in his journal, "I feel ripe for something, yet do nothing, can't discover what that thing is."

Also during this period, at least in part because his book was not selling, he started a surveying business. Most important, though, he began cultivating an interest in science, particularly botany. He built a "scaffold" inside the crown of his hat to hold plant specimens and started carrying a botanical guide with him on his afternoon walks. By mid-November 1850 he was regularly dating his journal entries and had stopped culling pages from his journal notebooks—both changes that ensured a complete and accurate record of his field observations. Prior to that time he had dated his entries very sporadically and had cut pages out of the notebooks to save himself the labor of copying passages into literary drafts. The following month he was elected a corresponding member to the Boston Society of Natural History, an honor that included lending privileges at that organization's impressive library. Six years later Thoreau himself reflected back on this period when his interests had taken such a dramatic shift toward scientific concerns:

> I remember gazing with interest at the swamps about those days and wondering if I could ever attain to such familiarity with plants that I should know the species of every twig and leaf in them. . . . Though I knew most of the flowers, and there were not in any particular swamp more than half a dozen shrubs that I did not know, yet these made it seem like a maze to me, of a thousand strange species, and I even thought of commencing at one end and looking it faithfully and laboriously through till I knew it all. I little thought that in a year or two I should have attained to that knowledge without all that labor. . . . I soon found myself observing when plants first blossomed and leafed, and I followed it up early and late, far and near, several years in succession, running to different sides of the town and into the neighboring towns, often between twenty and thirty miles in a day. I often visited a particular plant four or five miles distant, half a dozen times within a fortnight, that I might know exactly when it opened, beside attending to a great many others in different directions and some of them equally distant, at the same time.

The spring of 1851 marks the middle of this important transitional period for Thoreau. He began reading books on natural history and purchased a blank book, which he called his "Common Place Book," for recording passages from his natural history readings. Although he still had not settled on a large literary project, he did assemble from passages in his journal a lecture titled "Walking, or the Wild," which he delivered before a hometown audience on April 23. Within the next couple of months he compiled the first of what would become many hundreds of phenological lists and charts on every conceivable seasonal phenomenon, such as the migration cycles of birds or the leafing, flowering, fruiting, and seeding of plants. Interestingly, that same spring the Smithsonian Institute sent to scientists across the country a circular titled "Registry of Periodical Phenomena," which invited "all persons who may have it in their power, to record their observations [of "periodical phenomena of Animal and Vegetable life"], and to transmit them to the Institution." The circular lists 127 species of plants, using in most cases both common and Latin names, and asks observers to mark opposite each species its date of flowering.

The Smithsonian list bears a striking resemblance to the phenological lists Thoreau began assembling at that time. Although his lists and charts have never been studied carefully, they are almost certainly the foundation for the large project that eventually included *Wild Fruits*. After reading John Evelyn's *Kalendarium Hortense, or Gardener's Almanack* (1664) in the spring of 1852, Thoreau occasionally referred to this large project as his "Kalendar." Apparently he intended to write a comprehensive history of the natural phenomena that took place in his hometown each year. Although he planned to base his natural history of Concord upon field observations recorded in his journal over a period of several years, he would synthesize those observations so that he could construct a single "archetypal" year, a technique he had used to wonderful effect in *Walden*. The observations he recorded in his journal ranged from the most purely objective and scientific to the aesthetic and highly subjective. He would supplement his own wide-ranging observations in his "Kalendar" project, as he does in *Wild Fruits*, with extracts from his extensive reading.

This important period in Thoreau's life culminates in a long and quite remarkable journal entry written September 7, 1851. He began the entry with the same complaint he had voiced in his journal almost a year earlier: "I feel myself uncommonly prepared for *some* literary work, but I can select no work." He continued writing for another sixteen pages, alternately criticizing the way most people misspend their lives on trivial employments and envisioning how he might best spend his life. As the following brief selection makes clear, while writing the entry he formulates a resolve to pursue what he realizes is his life's work:

> The art of spending a day! If it is possible that we may be addressed, it behooves us to be attentive. If by watching all day and all night, I may detect some trace of the Ineffable, then will it not be worth the while to watch? Watch and pray without ceasing? . . .
>
> I am convinced that men are not well employed—that this is not the way to spend a day. If by patience, if by watching I can secure one new ray of light, can feel myself elevated for an instant upon Pisgah, the world which was dead prose to me become living and divine, shall I not watch ever—shall I not be a watch-

man henceforth? If by watching a whole year on the city's walls I may obtain a communication from heaven, shall I not do well to shut up my shop and turn a watchman? Can a youth, a man, do more wisely than to go where his life is to be found? As if I had suffered that to be rumor which may be verified. We are surrounded by a rich and fertile mystery. May we not probe it, pry into it, employ ourselves about it—a little? To devote your life to the discovery of the divinity in Nature or to the eating of oysters: would they not be attended with very different results? . . .

To watch for, describe, all the divine features which I detect in Nature.

My profession is to be always on the alert to find God in nature—to know his lurking places.

With the realization that his remaining life's work was to probe the "rich and fertile mystery" of nature and describe the "divine features" he discovered, Thoreau's great period of transition came to an end. Prior to that period he had written several works relating to natural history, but in each of them he was himself invariably center stage, with nature serving as a backdrop, albeit often an important one. He wrote in those earlier works of *his* excursions *into* nature, but commencing with "Walking, or the Wild" in 1851 his natural history writings were *about* nature *itself*: moonlight, seeds, autumn leaves, and, of course, wild fruits. Henceforth he would write a "literature which gives expression to Nature," as he put it in the 1851 lecture, and he would do so by impressing "the winds and streams into his service, to speak for him." This important shift of perspective is what he had in mind when he wrote on the title page of his 1852 draft of "Walking, or the Wild," "I regard this [lecture] as a sort of introduction to all that I may write hereafter."

THOREAU HAS BEEN ONE of the most insufficiently understood men in American letters, partly because he was so good at what he did best. For many years the popular mind has known him as a querulous hermit who lived half his life in a cabin on the shore of a pond, and who spent the other half of his life in jail to protest injustice. Recently the popular mind has had to expand itself to include, as it were, a third half of his life: the one spent closely observing and eloquently reporting on natural phenomena—Thoreau the protoecologist.

The common denominator in all three of these popular perspectives on

Thoreau is his writing. We read him because he is a great writer, indisputably one of America's best prose stylists. But we also read him because he has much to say on an astonishingly diverse range of topics of particular interest to many different people. A student of belles lettres might study the intricate interplay of metaphors in one of his essays, a historian might examine his attitude toward the fiery abolitionist John Brown, a philosopher might try to ascertain the basis for his insights on the reformist impulse, and a botanist might shed light on global warming by comparing his data with current data.

Thoreau would certainly have encouraged us to read *Wild Fruits* with an appreciation of its many dimensions—for instance, as an ecological declaration and a useful compendium of New England fruits. But he would have been most interested in our reading the work as a uniquely American scripture. On October 16, 1859, while assembling the first draft of *Wild Fruits*, he wrote in his journal of seeing a muskrat house on the river, an "annual phenomenon" that he said would have "an important place in my Kalendar." He continues, "There will be some reference to it, by way of parable or otherwise, in *my* New Testament. Surely, it is a defect in our Bible that it is not truly ours, but a Hebrew Bible. The most pertinent illustrations for us are to be drawn, not from Egypt or Babylonia, but from New England."

Although Thoreau's claim to be writing scripture in mid-nineteenth century New England may seem surprising, such an activity was in fact the natural consequence of his vocation as a transcendentalist author. Emerson had published the transcendentalist credo, *Nature,* in the fall of 1836 when Thoreau was just a few months short of his graduation from Harvard University. At the beginning of the book Emerson claims that "foregoing generations beheld God and nature face to face; we through their eyes." He then articulates in the form of a question the Transcendentalist Imperative: "Why should not we also enjoy an original relation to the universe?" As though to reinforce this simple but profoundly revolutionary idea, he immediately paraphrases: "Why should not we have a poetry and philosophy of insight and not of tradition, and a religion by revelation to us, and not the history of theirs?" Rather than experiencing God at second hand, in the usual fashion, by reading about Him in scriptures written long ago by unknown prophets in faraway places, a transcendentalist must behold God directly, here and now, without intermediaries of any kind. Likewise, a transcendentalist must resist the tendency to filter his or her perceptions of the natural world through one or another preconceptual lens, must strive for a wholly unmediated experience of nature.

The effect on Thoreau of reading *Nature* was profound and immediate. Phrases and images Emerson used in the book began appearing throughout Thoreau's college essays and continued to appear in his writings for several years. He remained something of an apprentice of Emerson's, a sort of transcendentalist poet-critic in training, until the mid-1840s, when he decided to clear a space for himself and truly settle in the world. The Walden period (1845–47) was for him a time of testing the limits of personal freedom and rethinking old assumptions. While at Walden Pond he also assessed the Transcendentalist Imperative. Was it possible, really, to practice what Emerson had preached in *Nature?* It is fine and well and even fairly easy to *say* that we should "have a poetry and philosophy of insight . . . and a religion by revelation to us," but how does one *live* in a manner that will generate insight and revelation? And once one enjoys "an original relation to the universe," how ought one to communicate that experience? How might a transcendentalist write scripture?

Thoreau addressed this crucial constellation of questions in the wonderful book that grew out of his experiment at Walden Pond, but indirectly, metaphorically, almost mythologically. In one of the most famous paragraphs in *Walden* he provides a hint of where we can locate his "true account" of life:

> I went to the woods because I wished to live deliberately, to front only the essential facts of life, and see if I could not learn what it had to teach, and not, when I came to die, discover that I had not lived. I did not wish to live what was not life, living is so dear; nor did I wish to practice resignation, unless it was quite necessary. I wanted to live deep and suck out all the marrow of life, to live so sturdily and Spartan-like as to put to rout all that was not life, to cut a broad swath and shave close, to drive life into a corner, and reduce it to its lowest terms, and . . . if it were sublime, to know it by experience, and be able to give a true account of it in my next excursion.

The "next excursion" he refers to was his essay "Ktaadn," a straightforward account of a two-week trip to the wilderness of Maine taken in the fall of 1846, exactly halfway through his twenty-six month sojourn at the pond. While there he climbed Mount Ktaadn (now spelled "Katahdin"), the state's highest peak, and encountered a landscape so strange to him, so otherworldly, that he lost himself in beholding it:

> I stand in awe of my body, this matter to which I am bound has become so strange to me. I fear not spirits, ghosts, of which I am one,—*that* my body might,—but I fear bodies, I tremble to meet them. What is this Titan that has possession of me? Talk of mysteries!—Think of our life in nature,—daily to be shown matter, to come in contact with it,—rocks, trees, wind on our cheeks! the *solid* earth! the *actual* world! the *common sense*! *Contact! Contact! Who* are we? *where* are we?

Some readers might mistake the frenzied prose of this passage for Thoreau's trauma after experiencing an alien, hostile world. But Thoreau did not write this passage extemporaneously, while reeling atop Mount Katahdin; instead, he wrote it later, while comfortably and deliberatively ensconced in his one-room house on the shore of Walden Pond. The carefully crafted prose of the *"Contact!"* passage reflects not emotional turmoil but the finer frenzy of Thoreau the transcendentalist prophet straining the capabilities of language to describe the "original relation to the universe" he experienced atop the mountain. This important passage is his attempt to articulate the ineffable, for Thoreau on Mount Katahdin, like Moses on Mount Sinai, had beheld God (spirit) and nature (matter) face to face.

The revelation Thoreau achieved on Mount Katahdin, a revelation he clearly believed was one of life's "essential facts," stemmed from his acute sense of the inherent strangeness, the fundamental "otherworldliness" of matter. A seemingly paradoxical sentence in *Walden* precisely explains his experience on the mountain: "Not till we are lost, in other words, not till we have lost the world, do we begin to *find ourselves*, and realize *where we are* and the infinite extent of our relations" (my emphases). The mountain taught him what he clearly believed all of nature teaches if properly perceived: that each of us is a *spirit* in a world of *matter* that we have contact with through the agency of a *body*. This trinity of spirit, matter, and body—and "the infinite extent" of the relations between them—comprises for Thoreau the Great Mystery that he expounds in his scriptures, including *Wild Fruits*.

If you would be a great prophet, history suggests that your first act should be to journey into a remote wilderness, where you must subsist for a goodly time (say, forty days and forty nights) on the fruits of the land (locusts and honey, say). While there you must achieve insights into the great mysteries of life, and then you are obliged to return to civilization and teach the import of those mysteries to others. Thoreau felt the prophetic impulse very keenly, as we have seen. But in *Wild Fruits* his brand of prophecy manifests itself in a unique manner: by bringing wildness out of the wilderness; or, more properly, by locating wildness within civilization, in "little oases," as he terms them in the book's "European Cranberry" section. In these holy places, these natural temples, each of us is able to implement the Transcendentalist's Imperative by learning life's great lessons ourselves, becoming our own prophet, and not having to rely on the mediated testimony of prophets from preceding generations.

When Thoreau introduced the concept of wildness in his lecture of 1851, he simply asserted that "in Wildness is the preservation of the world." But it is clear from his development of the concept in *Wild Fruits* that wildness preserves the world by prompting us to alter our perspective of who and where we are. Like Elizabeth Bishop's "grand, otherworldly" moose, which steps out of "the impenetrable wood / and stands there, looms, rather, / in the middle of the road," wildness can prompt us to a self-recognition that invariably results in a "sweet / Sensation of joy." If we can realize that we are mysteriously related to matter, we will act to preserve the world because human beings protect what we love or feel related to. Thus, a proper perception of wildness can lift us "out of the slime and film of our habitual life," as Thoreau suggests in the "European Cranberry" section, and enable us to "see the whole globe to be an ærolite" that we can "reverence" and "make pilgrimages to. . . ." Wildness helps us to understand that heaven is in fact "under our feet as well as over our heads," as he expressed the idea in *Walden*. In short, wildness for Thoreau is the key to unlocking the miraculous in the commonplace. His perspective on the redemptive potential of wildness explains the enormous importance he places near the end of *Wild Fruits* on the need to set aside "primitive forest" and wild spaces generally "for instruction and recreation."

DESPITE ITS LONG PERIOD of gestation, *Wild Fruits* remained unfinished at Thoreau's death. I have edited the manuscript as he left it, making no effort whatever to complete what he began. Even so, the intended form and scope of *Wild Fruits*, as well as at least some of Thoreau's ambitions for the work, are apparent enough to inspire admiration, and perhaps even awe. We may never know his plans for the large "Kalendar" project that *Wild Fruits* is part of, but with the publication of this important manuscript we know enough to appreciate what Emerson meant when speaking at Thoreau's funeral of his friend's "broken task":

The scale on which his studies proceeded was so large as to require longevity, and we were the less prepared for his sudden disappearance. The country knows not yet, or in the least part, how great a son it has lost. It seems an injury that he should leave in the midst of his broken task which none else can finish, a kind of indignity to so noble a soul that he should depart out of Nature before yet he has been really shown to his peers for what he is.

Bradley P. Dean
Thoreau Institute
Lincoln, Massachusetts

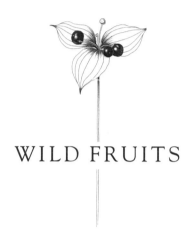

WILD FRUITS

WILD FRUITS

MOST OF US ARE STILL related to our native fields as the navigator to undiscovered islands in the sea. We can any afternoon discover a new fruit there which
will surprise us by its beauty or sweetness. So long as I saw in my walks one or two
kinds of berries whose names I did not know, the proportion of the unknown
seemed indefinitely, if not infinitely, great.

As I sail the unexplored sea of Concord, many a dell and swamp and wooded
hill is my Ceram and Amboyna. Famous fruits imported from the East or South
and sold in our markets—as oranges, lemons, pine-apples, and bananas—do not
concern me so much as many an unnoticed wild berry whose beauty annually
lends a new charm to some wild walk or which I have found to be palatable to an
outdoor taste. We cultivate imported shrubs in our front yards for the beauty of
their berries, while at least equally beautiful berries grow unregarded by us in the
surrounding fields.

The tropical fruits are for those who dwell within the tropics. Their fairest and
sweetest parts cannot be imported. Brought here, they chiefly concern those
whose walks are through the marketplace. It is not the orange of Cuba but rather
the checkerberry of the neighboring pasture that most delights the eye and the
palate of the New England child. For it is not the foreignness or size or nutritive
qualities of a fruit that determine its absolute value.

We do not think much of table fruits. They are especially for aldermen and
epicures. They do not feed the imagination as these wild fruits do, but it would
starve on them. The bitter-sweet of a white-oak acorn which you nibble in a
bleak November walk over the tawny earth is more to me than a slice of imported
pine-apple. The South may keep her pine-apples, and we will be content with our
strawberries, which are, as it were, a pine-apple with "going-a-strawberrying"

stirred into them, infinitely enhancing their flavor. What are all the oranges imported into England to the hips and haws in her hedges? She could easily spare the one, but not the other. Ask Wordsworth, or any of her poets who knows, which is the most to him.

The value of these wild fruits is not in the mere possession or eating of them, but in the sight and enjoyment of them. The very derivation of the word "fruit" would suggest this. It is from the Latin *fructus*, meaning "that which is *used* or *enjoyed*." If it were not so, then going a-berrying and going to market would be nearly synonymous experiences. Of course, it is the spirit in which you do a thing which makes it interesting, whether it is sweeping a room or pulling turnips. Peaches are unquestionably a very beautiful and palatable fruit, but the gathering of them for the market is not nearly so interesting to the imaginations of men as the gathering of huckleberries for your own use.

A man fits out a ship at a great expense and sends it to the West Indies with a crew of men and boys, and after six months or a year it comes back with a load of pine-apples; now, if no more gets accomplished than the speculator commonly aims at, if it simply turns out what is called a successful venture, I am less interested in this expedition than in some child's first excursions a-huckleberrying, in which it is introduced into a new world, experiences a new development, though it brings home only a gill of berries in its basket. I know that the newspapers and the politicians declare otherwise—other arrivals are reported and other prices quoted by them—but that does not alter the fact. Then I think that the fruit of the latter's expedition was finer than that of the former. It was a more fruitful expedition. What the editors and politicians lay so much stress upon is comparatively moonshine.

The value of any experience is measured, of course, not by the amount of money, but the amount of development we get out of it. If a New England boy's dealings with oranges and pine-apples have had more to do with his development than picking huckleberries or pulling turnips have, then he naturally and rightly thinks more of the former; otherwise not. No, it is not those far-fetched fruits which the speculator imports that concern us chiefly, but rather those which you have fetched yourself in the hold of a basket from some far hill or swamp, journeying all the long afternoon, the first of the season, consigned to your friends at home.

Commonly, the less you get, the happier and the richer you are. The rich man's son gets cocoa-nuts and the poor man's pignuts, but the worst of it is that the former never goes a-cocoa-nutting and so never gets the cream of the cocoa-nut, as the latter does the cream of the pignut. That on which commerce seizes is always the very coarsest part of a fruit—the mere bark and rind, in fact, for her hands are very clumsy. This is what fills the holds of ships, is exported and imported, pays duties, and is finally sold in the shops.

It is a grand fact that you cannot make the fairer fruits or parts of fruits matter of commerce; that is, you cannot buy the highest use and enjoyment of them. You cannot buy that pleasure which it yields to him who truly plucks it. You cannot buy a good appetite, even. In short, you may buy a servant or slave, but you cannot buy a friend.

The mass of men are very easily imposed on. They have their runways in which they always travel and are sure to fall into any pit or trap which is set there. Whatever business a great many grown-up boys are seriously engaged in is considered respectable, and great even, and as such is sure of the recognition of the churchman and statesman. What, for instance, are the blue juniper berries in the pasture, considered as mere objects of beauty, to church or state? Some cowboy may appreciate them—indeed, all who really live in the country do—but they do not receive the protection of any community; anybody may grab up all that exist; but as an article of commerce, they command the attention of the civilized world. Go to the English government, which of course represents the people, and ask, "What is the use of juniper berries?"—and it will answer, "To flavor gin with." I read that "several hundred tons of them are imported annually from the Continent" into England for this purpose; "but even this quantity," says my author, "is quite insufficient to meet the enormous consumption of the fiery liquid, and the deficiency is made up by spirits of turpentine." This is not the *use*, but the gross *abuse*, of juniper berries, with which an enlightened government, if ever there shall be one, will have nothing to do. The cowboy is better informed than the government. Let us make distinctions and call things by their right names.

Do not think, then, that the fruits of New England are mean and insignificant while those of some foreign land are noble and memorable. Our own, whatever they may be, are far more important to us than any others can be. They educate us and fit us to live here. Better for us is the wild strawberry than the pine-apple, the wild apple than the orange, the chestnut and pignut than the cocoa-nut and almond, and not on account of their flavor merely, but the part they play in our education.

If it is of low tastes only that you speak, then we will quote to you the saying of Cyrus, the Persian king, that "it is not given to the same land to produce ex-cellent fruits and men valiant in war."

I mention these phenomena in the order in which they are first observed.

E L M

Before the tenth of May (from the seventh to the ninth), the winged seeds or samaræ of the elms give them a leafy appearance, or as if covered with little hops, before the leaf buds are opened. This must be the earliest of our trees and shrubs to go to seed. It is so early that most mistake the fruit before it falls for leaves, and we owe to it the first deepening of the shadows in our streets.

D A N D E L I O N

About the same time, we begin to see a dandelion gone to seed here and there in the greener grass of some more sheltered and moist bank, perhaps before we had detected its rich yellow disk—that little seedy spherical system which boys are wont to blow to see if their mothers want them. If they can blow off all the seeds at one puff, then their mothers do not want them. It is interesting as the first of that class of fuzzy or downy seeds so common in the fall. It is commonly the first of the many hints we get to be about our own tasks, those our Mother has set us, and bringing something to pass ourselves. So much more surely and rapidly does Nature work than man. By the fourth of June they are generally gone to seed in the rank grass. You see it dotted with a thousand downy spheres, and children now make ringlets of their crispy stems.

WILLOWS

By the thirteenth of May the earliest willows (*Salix discolor*) about warm edges of woods show great green wands a foot or two long, consisting of curved worm-like catkins three inches long. Like the fruit of the elm, they form conspicuous masses of green before the leaves are noticeable, and some have now begun to burst and show their down—and thus it is the next of our trees and shrubs to shed its seeds after the elm.

Three or four days later the *Salix humilis* and the smallest of our willows, *Salix tristis*, commonly on higher and drier ground than the ash and the early aspen, *begin* to show their down. The *Salix tristis* is *generally* gone to seed by the seventh of June.

SWEET FLAG

As early as the fourteenth of May, such as frequent the riverside pluck and eat the inner leaf of the sweet flag and detect small critchicrotches, which are the green fruit and flower buds. The old herbalist Gerarde thus describes them: "The flower is a long thing resembling the cattails which grow on hazel; it is about the thickness of an ordinary reed, some inch and a half long, of a greenish yellow color, curiously checkered, as if it were wrought with a needle with green and yellow silk intermixt."

By the twenty-fifth of May this bud, before it has blossomed and while yet tender, is in condition to be eaten and would help to sustain a famished traveller. I often turn aside my boat to pluck it, passing through a dense bed of flags recently risen above the surface. The inmost tender leaf near the base of the plant is quite palatable, as children know. They love it as much as the musquash does. Early in June I see them going a-flagging even a mile or two and returning with large

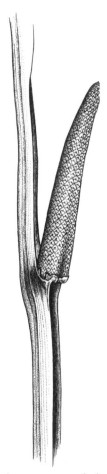

bundles for the sake of this blade, which they extract at their leisure. After the middle of June, the critchicrotch, going to seed, becomes unfit to eat.

How agreeable and surprising the peculiar fragrance of the sweet flag when you first bruise it in the spring! That this plant alone should have extracted this odor surely for so many ages from the moist earth!

Gerarde says that the Tartars hold the root "in such esteem that they will not drink water (which is their usual drink) unless they have just steeped some of this root therein." Sir John Richardson tells us that "the Cree name of this plant is *watchuske-mitsu-in*, or 'that which the muskrat eats,'" and that the Indians of British America use the root of this plant as a cure for colic: "About the size of a small pea of the root, dried before the fire or in the sun, is a dose for an adult. . . . When administered to children, the root is rasped, and the filings swallowed in a glass of water." Who has not when a child had this same remedy administered to him for that complaint—though the medicine came recommended by a lump of sugar, which the Cree boys did not get—which perhaps was longest in use thus by the Indians. Thus, we begin our summer like the musquash. We take our first course at the same table with him. These are his greens, while we are also looking for dandelions. He is so much like us; we are so much like him.

MOUSE-EAR

About the twentieth of May I see the first mouse-ear going to seed and beginning to be blown about the pastures and whiten the grass, together with bluets, and float on the surface of water. They have now lifted themselves much higher above the earth than when we sought for their first flowers. As Gerarde says of the allied English species, "These plants do grow upon sandy banks and untoiled places that lie open to the sun."

MAPLES

I begin to see the white-maple keys on the water as early as the twenty-eighth of May. Gerarde's account of the seeds of the "Great maple" of European mountains applies to these. Having described the flowers, he says, "After them cometh up long fruit fastened together by couples, one right against another, with kernels bumping out near to the place in which they are combined; in all the other parts flat and thin like unto parchment, or resembling the innermost wings of grasshoppers."

About the twentieth the similar large green keys of our white maple are conspicuous. They are nearly two inches long and half an inch wide, with waved inner edges to the wings, like green moths ready to bear off their seeds. By the sixth of June they are about half fallen, and I notice that their fall takes place about the time that the great emperor moth (*Attæus cecropia*) comes out of its chrysalis, and it is sometimes found in the morning wrecked on the surface of the river amid them.

The red-maple keys are not half so large as the white, but many times as beautiful. You notice the little fruit just formed early in May, while some trees are still in flower. As it increases in size, the maple tops acquire a browner red, almost a birch red. About the middle of May, the red maples along the edges of swamps, their fruit being nearly ripe, are among the most beautiful objects in the landscape, and more interesting than when in flower, especially if seen in a favorable light.

I stand now on a knoll in the midst of a swamp and observe a young red maple at its base a few rods off, on one side with respect to the sun. The keys are high-colored, a sort of pink scarlet, and hang down three inches or more. Masses of these double samaræ with their peduncles gracefully rising a little before they curve downward, and only a little darker shade than the fruit, are unequally dispersed along the branches and trembling in the wind.

Like the flower of the shad bush, this handsome fruit is seen for the most part against bare twigs, it is so much in advance of its own and of other leaves. It is fairly ripe about the first of June, and much of it is conspicuously light-colored instead of scarlet. It is in the midst of its fall about the seventh of June. By the first of June most trees have bloomed and are forming their fruit. Green berries also begin to be noticed.

STRAWBERRY

The strawberry is our first edible fruit to ripen. I begin to find them as early as the third of June, but commonly about the tenth or before the cultivated kinds are offered. They are in their prime the last of June. In meadows they are a week later, and they linger there till late in July.

Even old Tusser, who confines himself mostly to the coarser parts of husbandry, sings in his homely strain under "September":

> Wife, into the garden, and set me a plot,
>> with strawberry roots, of the best to be got:
> Such growing abroad, among thorns in the wood,
>> well chosen and pricked, prove excellent good.

The old herbalist Gerarde, writing before 1599, gives us this lively account of the English strawberry, which is sufficiently applicable to our own. He says:

The strawberry hath leaves spread upon the ground, somewhat snipt about the edges, three set together upon one slender footstalk, like the trefoil, green on the upper side and on the nether side more white; among which rise up slender stems, whereon do grow small flowers, consisting of five little white leaves, the middle part somewhat yellow, after which cometh the fruit, not unlike to the mulberry, or rather the raspis, red of color, having the taste of wine, the inner pulp or substance whereof is moist and white, in which is contained little seeds. The root is threaddy, of long continuance, sending forth many strings, which disperse themselves far abroad, whereby it greatly increaseth.

Of the fruit he adds, "The nourishment which they yield is little, thin and waterish, and if they happen to putrify in the stomach, their nourishment is naught."

By the thirtieth of May I notice the green fruit; and two or three days later, as I am walking, perhaps, over the southerly slope of some dry and bare hill, or where there are bare and sheltered spaces between the bushes, it occurs to me that strawberries have possibly set; and looking carefully in the most favorable places, just beneath the top of the hill, I discover the reddening fruit, and at length, on the very driest and sunniest spot or brow, two or three berries which I am forward to call ripe, though generally only their sunny cheek is red. Or else I notice one half-turned on the sand of the railroad causeway, or even on sand thrown out of a ditch in a meadow. They are at first hard to detect in such places amid the red lower leaves, as if Nature meant thus to conceal the fruit, especially if your mind is unprepared for it. The plant is so humble that it is an unnoticed carpet. No edible wild fruit, except the bog cranberry (*Vacciniæ oxycoccus*), and that requires to be cooked, lies so close to the ground as these earliest upland strawberries. Hence, Virgil with propriety refers to the strawberry as *"humi nascentia fraga"*— "strawberries growing on the ground."

What flavor can be more agreeable to our palates than that of this little fruit, which thus, as it were, exudes from the earth at the very beginning of the summer, without any care of ours? What beautiful and palatable bread! I make haste to pluck and eat this first fruit of the year, though they are green on the underside, somewhat acid as yet, and a little gritty from lying so low. I taste a little strawberry-flavored earth with them. I get enough to redden my fingers and lips at least.

The next day, perhaps, I get two or three handfuls of ripe berries, or such as I am willing to call ripe, in a similar locality, the largest and sweetest where the vines hang over the sand; and at the same time, commonly, I get my first smelling—aye, even tasting—of that remarkable bug (one of the *Scutellaridæ*) which we are wont to say tastes exactly as a certain domestic bug smells—and thus I am set up for the season. This bug, as you know, "has only to pass over a fruit to impart to it" its peculiar odor. Like the dog in the manger, he spoils a whole mouthful for you, without enjoying them himself. It is wonderful by what affinity this fellow can find out the first strawberry.

You seek the early strawberries on any of the most favorable exposures, as the sides of little knolls or swells, or in and near those little sandy hollows where cows have pawed in past years, when they were first turned out to pasture, settling the question of superiority and which should lead the herd. Sometimes the berries have been dusted by their recent conflicts.

I perceive from time to time in the spring and have long kept a record of it, an indescribably sweet fragrance, which I cannot trace to any particular source. It is, perchance, that sweet scent of the earth of which the ancients speak. Though I have not detected the flower that emits it, this appears to be its fruit. It is natural that the first fruit which the earth bears should emit and be, as it were, a concentration and embodiment of that vernal fragrance with which the air has lately teemed. Strawberries are the manna found, ere long, where that fragrance has been. Are not the juices of each fruit distilled from the air?

This is one of the fruits as remarkable for its fragrance as its flavor, and it is said to have got its Latin name, *fraga*, from this fact. Its fragrance, like that of the checkerberry, is a very prevalent one. Wilted young twigs of several evergreens, especially the fir-balsam, smell very much like it.

Only one in a hundred know where to look for these early strawberries. It is, as it were, a sort of Indian knowledge acquired by secret tradition. I know well what has called that apprentice, who has just crossed my path, to the hillsides this Sunday morning. In whatever factory or chamber he has his dwelling-place, he is as sure to be by the side of the first strawberry when it reddens as that domestic-smelling bug that I spoke of, though he lies concealed all the rest of the year. It is an instinct with him. But the rest of mankind have not dreamed of such things as yet. The few wild strawberries that we have will have come and gone before the mass know it.

I do not think much of strawberries in gardens, nor in market baskets, nor in quart boxes, raised and sold by your excellent hard-fisted neighbor. It is those little natural beds or patches of them on the dry hillsides that interest me most, though I may get but a handful at first—where, however, the fruit sometimes reddens the ground and the otherwise barren soil is all beaded with them, not weeded or watered or manured by a hired gardener. The berries monopolize the lean sward now for a dozen feet together, being the most luxuriant growth it supports, but they soon dry up unless there is a great deal of rain.

Sometimes it is under different circumstances that I get my first taste of strawberries. Being overtaken by a thundershower as I am paddling up the river, I run my boat ashore where there is a hard-sloping bank, turn it over, and take shelter under it. There I lie for an hour in close contact with the earth and in a fair way to find out what it produces. As soon as the rain begins to hold up, I scramble out, straighten my legs, and stumble at once on a little patch of strawberries within a rod, the sward all red with them, and these I pluck while the last drops are thinly falling.

But it is not without some misgivings that we accept this gift. The middle of June is past, and it is dry and hazy weather. We are getting deeper into the mists of earth; we live in a grosser element, further from heaven these days, methinks. Even the birds sing with less vigor and vivacity. The season of hope and promise is passed, and already the season of *small fruits* has arrived. We are a little saddened because we begin to see the interval between our hopes and their fulfillment. The prospect of the heavens is taken away by the haze, and we are presented with a few small berries.

I find beds of large and lusty strawberry plants in sproutlands, but they appear to run to leaves and bear very little fruit, having spent themselves in leaves by the time the dry weather comes. It is those earlier and more stunted plants which grow on dry uplands that bear the early fruit formed before the drought.

In many meadows, also, you find dense beds of rank leaves without fruit, yet some meadows produce both leaves and fruit, and these are they whose clusters are handsomest. In July these ranker meadow strawberries are ripe, and they tempt many to trample the high grass in search of them. They would not be suspected for aught that appears above, but you spread aside the tall grass and find them deep in little cavities at its roots, in the shade, when elsewhere they are dried up.

But commonly it is only a taste that we get hereabouts, and then proceed on

our way with reddened and fragrant fingers till that stain gets washed off at the next spring. The walker in this neighborhood does well if he gets two or three handfuls of this fruit in a year, and he is fain to mix some green ones and leaves with them, making a sort of salad, while he *remembers* the flavor of the ripe ones. But it is not so up-country. There they are prosaically abundant, for this plant loves a cool region. It is said to be "a native of the Alps and the forests of Gaul," but to have been "unknown to the Greeks." A hundred miles north from here, in New Hampshire, I have found them in profusion by the roadside and in the grass and about the stumps on the adjacent hillsides in newly cleared land everywhere. You can hardly believe with what vigor they grow and bear there. They are not far off, commonly, from where trout lurk, for they love the same sort of air and water, and the same hut commonly offers the traveller amid the New Hampshire mountains strawberries and trout rods. In the vicinity of Bangor, as I am told, they are found at the roots of grass where it is up to your knees, and they are smelled before they are seen, in hot weather—also on mountains whence you see the Penobscot fifteen miles off and the white sails of a hundred schooners flapping. There, sometimes, where silver spoons and saucers are scarce but everything else is plentiful, they empty countless quarts into a milk pan, stir in cream and sugar, while the party sits around with each a big spoon.

Hearne, in his *Journey to the Northern Ocean*, says that "strawberries [the *Oteagh-minick* of the Indians is so called because it in some measure resembles a heart], and those of a considerable size and excellent flavor, are found as far north as Churchill River," especially where the ground has been burned over. According to Sir John Franklin, the Cree name is *Oteimeena*, and Tanner says that the Chippeway name is *O-da-e-min*—all evidently the same word, as they have the same meaning. Tanner says that the Chippeways frequently dream of going to the other world, but when one gets to "the great strawberry, at which the *Ie-bi-ug* [or spirits of the dead] repast themselves on their journey," and takes up the spoon to separate a part of it, he finds it turned to rock, the soft red-sand rock which is said to prevail about Lake Superior. The Dakotahs call June *Wazuste-casa-wi*, "the moon when the strawberry is red."

From William Wood's *New England's Prospect*, printed about 1633, it would appear that strawberries were much more abundant and large here before they were impoverished or cornered up by cultivation. "Some," as he says, "being two inches about, one may gather half a bushel in a forenoon." They are the first blush of a country, its morning red, a sort of ambrosial food which grows only on Olympian soil.

Roger Williams says, in his *Key*, "One of the chiefest doctors of England was wont to say, that God could have made, but God never did make, a better berry. In some parts, where the natives have planted, I have many times seen as many as would fill a good ship, within a few miles' compass. The Indians bruise them in a mortar, and mix them with meal, and make strawberry bread . . . having no other food for many days." Boucher, in his *Natural History of New France*, printed in 1664, tells us that all the land is filled with an incredible and inexhaustible quantity of raspberries and strawberries; and in Loskiel's *History of the Mission of the United Brethren among the Indians of North America, especially the Delawares* (1794), it is said, "Strawberries grow so large and in such abundance, that whole plains are covered with them as with a fine scarlet cloth." In the year 1808 a Mr. Peters, a Southerner, wrote to a Philadelphia society to confirm the statement that a tract of forest containing some eight hundred acres somewhere in Virginia, as it appears, having been burned in the last century, strawberries came up profusely. "The old neighbors," says he, "dwelt much on the exuberant plenty, and general cover of the strawberries; which, they said, could be scented, when perfectly ripe, from a great distance. Some of them described the vast surface and waste of flowers, when the plants bloomed, in a style that, if the fact had not been well attested, would have appeared fiction. This inimitable gala dress of nature, and the immense number of bees, with their busy hum, frequenting the blossoms and fruit, with the rugged and diversified mountains on the borders [of the tract], would have furnished a scene of pastoral imagery, for poetic description."

The historians of New Hampshire towns tell us that "strawberries are less abundant than in former days, when the land was first cultivated." In fact, hereabouts the strawberries and cream of the country are gone. That ineffable fragrance which gives to this berry its Latin name can never exhale from our manured fields. If we would behold this concentrated perfume and fruit of virgin and untoiled regions in perfection, we must go to the cool banks of the North, where perhaps the parhelion scatters the seeds of it; to the prairies of the Assineboin, where by its abundance it is said to tinge the feet of the prairie horses and the buffaloes; or to Lapland where, as one reads, the gray rocks that rise above the lowly houses of the Laps "blush literally crimson with the wild strawberries—those wondrous strawberries that spring up everywhere in Lapland, whose profusion is such that they stain the hoofs of the reindeer, and the sledge of the traveller, yet are so delicate and matchless in flavor, that the Czar himself sends for them, by *estaffettes*, all the long way to his summer palace of Tsazkoy Chèlè." In Lapland, that twilight region where you would not expect that the sun had power enough to paint a strawberry red, still less mature it! But let us not call it by the mean name of "strawberry" any longer because in Ireland or England they spread straw under their garden kinds. It is not that to the Laplander or the Chippewayan; better call it by the Indian name of heart-berry, for it is indeed a crimson heart which we eat at the beginning of summer to make us brave for all the rest of the year, as Nature is.

You occasionally find a few ripe ones of a second crop in November, a slight evening red, answering to that morning one.

GALLS AND PUFFS

Not to mention the various beautiful fruit-like galls which form on oaks as soon as the leaves start—huckleberry apples, and so on. I notice by the sixth of June (and after) great baggy, light-green puffs on the panicled andromeda, some with a reddish side, two and a half or three inches through. They resemble those abortions to which the Canada plum is apt to turn in muggy weather, and they hang on black and shrivelled till winter. You also see now very light and whitish, but more solid juicy, puffs on the swamp pinks, which have a fungus-like smell when broken.

A peculiarly sluggish and mephistic character whom I used to know informed me that he called these "swamp apples." He said that he liked them, and he judged that he "ate as much as three bushels of them when he was a boy"! I thought as much. That is what he was raised on, then.

WILLOWS

About the tenth of June the fertile specimens of the white willow are conspicuous at a distance on the causeways, their fruit being yellowish and drooping. And by the fifteenth the black willow which borders our river goes to seed, and its down begins to fall on the water and continues to fall for a month. About the twenty-fifth it is most conspicuous on the trees, like a fruit, giving them a parti-colored or spotted white-and-green look, quite interesting to those who are pad-dling on the stream.

SHAD BUSH

The shad bush or June berry begins to be ripe by the twenty-first of June, is in its prime the twenty-fifth of June to the first of July, and lasts till August. We have two varieties: *botryapium* and *oblongifolium*. The first a taller and smoother shrub growing on higher ground. The second but six feet high, more downy, and grow-ing on low ground. The first, according to Loudon, is called the "Canadian Med-lar . . . wild Pear Tree; Alisier de Choisy . . . Alisier à Grappes, *Fr.*; Traubenbirne, *Ger.*" This is a little earlier than the other.

This is the second berry or edible wild fruit of the year, coming next after strawberries and a little before early blueberries, being at height when blueberries are just beginning. It is the very earliest borne by any tree or shrub.

By the fifteenth of May some of these shrubs have lost their blossoms and show minute fruit, which is the first sign of all edible wild fruit, except critchicrotches and possibly strawberries, for green gooseberries and currants are not noticed so soon. By the thirtieth it is as big as small peas or larger than any bush berry. A week later you will be surprised at the size of the green berries, as well as of low blueberries, choke cherries, and so on. It is but a step from flowers to fruit.

By the seventeenth of June they begin to be red, soft, and edible, though not quite ripe; and so they go on reddening till, by the twenty-first, I see some purple or dark-blue ones amid the bright-red ones. These are quite ripe. They are a dull, dark purple—or often a red purple. But they are handsomer when red, before they are ripe. In color, size, and consistency they are like a blueberry, though not so hard, but in form oblong, like little apples or pears with long stems and persis-tent calyx leaves. They are for the most part injured by worms and insects, or ap-parently pecked and deformed by birds, hereabouts, but judging from the few perfectly sound and ripe ones that we get, I should pronounce them a delicious berry, nearly equal to blueberries and huckleberries. They are perhaps the sweet-

est *bush* berry, and they need only to be more abundant to be generally appreciated. Those of the *botryapium* have a soft skin, of the *oblongifolia* a tough one.

They do not bear abundantly here and are not distinguished by many. On the
twenty-fifth of June 1853 I found an unusual quantity of these berries growing
about the edges of a long, narrow, glade-like meadow in the woods, parallel with
the Assabet River, on the Colburn Farm, as it were an ancient bed of the river. It
was a very agreeable surprise to me and must have been owing to some peculiar-
ity in the season. I picked a quart of them, and meanwhile heard many cherry-
birds and others about me, no doubt attracted by this fruit. I felt all the while I
was picking them—in the low, light-waving, shrubby wood which the bushes
make—as if I were in some remote, wild northern region where they are said to
abound, maybe on the banks of the Saskatchewan, with a long batteau voyage and
many portages between me and the village. The next day I had them made into
a pudding. It was very much like a rather *dry* cherry pudding without the stones.
They are better uncooked. Several old farmers, hearing of this, expressed surprise. One said, "Well, though I have lived seventy years, I never saw nor heard
of them."

Again, July thirtieth, 1860, one led me to a frosty hollow in the woods, southwest of Martial Miles's Swamp, where he had found a patch of the shad bush

(probably *oblongifolia*) full of fruit then in perfection. It was an open sedge-hollow, not absolutely low, surrounded by woods, with some shrub in it which had been formerly killed by frost, rising above the sedge. Here grew a pretty, thick patch about a rod and a half long, the bushes being about three feet high. It was a very interesting sight, both for its novelty and its intrinsic beauty. They were a size or two larger than huckleberry bushes, with firm dark-green leaves, somewhat like a narrow aspen leaf, with short and broad irregular racemes of red and dark-purplish berries intermixed, producing a considerable variety in the color. These conspicuous red berries—for most were red—on rather high and thin-leaved bushes, growing open and airy, reminded me a little of the wild holly, the berry so contrasted with the dark leaf. The ripest and largest dark-purple berries were just half an inch in diameter. You were surprised and delighted to see this handsome profusion in hollows so dry and usually so barren, and on bushes commonly so fruitless. These berries are peculiar in that the red are nearly as palatable as the more fully ripe dark-purple ones. I think that this crop was due to the wetness and coolness of the summer.

Though an agreeable berry for a change, they are hardly so grateful to my palate as huckleberries and blueberries. On Cape Cod they bear more abundantly and are called "Josh Pears," which a Cape man suggested to me was a corruption of "juicy."

But it is in British America that they come to perfection. They are the "service berries" which the Indians of the north and the Canadians use. Richardson says that the *"Amelanchier Canadensis (botryapium et ovalis)*, shad bush, and service berry is *La Poire* of the voyageurs, the *Misass-ku-tu-Mina* of the Crees, and the *Tchè-ki-eh* of the Dog-ribs. This shrub extends along the banks of rivers nearly as far northward as the woods go, and produces fruit up to the 65th parallel on the Mackenzie. It is common in the Northern States, in Nova Scotia, Newfoundland and Labrador, and westward to the Pacific. The black fruit is about the size of a pea, is well tasted, dries well, and in that state is mixed with pemmican, or used for making puddings, for which purpose it nearly equals the Zante currant." It is said to be the finest fruit in that country. If the strawberry is associated with the trout in our thoughts, so may this berry be with the shad, which are caught in New England when its blossoms whiten the shores and hillsides.

I frequently see some of the first variety in this town twenty feet high. Mr. George B. Emerson describes one in Chester in this state "five feet seven inches in circumference, at five feet from the ground." I have seen a small variety (*oligocarpa*) on Monadnock mountain.

EARLY LOW BLUEBERRY

The early low blueberry or dwarf blueberry, called by botanists the Pennsylvanian blueberry (*Vaccinium pennsylvanicum*), begins to be ripe June twenty-second, is brought to market by the middle of July, and is at its height about the twenty-fifth of July. In the shade and covered by other bushes it lingers far into August, and on mountains a month or two later.

The earlier European botanists called many of our more northern plants *Canadian* and more southern ones *Virginian* or *Pennsylvanian*—but very few if any of them from New England or New York—and this, apparently, not only for the sake of making a broad distinction but because the name of Virginia sounded most in their ears on account of her tobacco trade. They even attributed to her the potato, which was not found there. There would be some propriety and convenience in trivial names taken from the different states if they indicated where a plant was most abundant.

First, then, there is the early dwarf blueberry, the smallest of the whortleberry shrubs with us and the first to ripen its fruit; not commonly an erect shrub, but more or less reclined and drooping, often covering the earth with a sort of dense matting. The twigs are green, the flowers commonly white. Both the shrub and its fruit are the most tender and delicate of any of the kind that we have.

By the first of June I notice the young berries forming, and by the fifteenth green blueberries as well as huckleberries are generally noticed and remind us of the time when their berries will be ripe. Even now some of the first are prematurely turning. This is the *ante-huckleberry* season, when fruits are green. By the twenty-second I taste one or two on some high hillside, where they droop over a rock, and the next day, perhaps, I hear that somebody who is ambitious has already had a blueberry pudding.

Nature offers us fruits now as well as flowers.

One who walks in the woods daily, expecting to see the first berry that turns, will be surprised at last to find them ripe and thick, in some favorable place, before he is aware of it, ripenened he cannot tell how long before. It is impossible to say what day, almost what week, the low blueberries and huckleberries begin to be ripe, unless you are acquainted with and daily visit every bush in the town— at least every place where they grow. They, at any rate, have been minding their business, while you, we trust, have minded yours—and hence we find them in good time.

They ripen first on the tops of hills, before they who walk in the valleys suspect it. When old folks find only one turned here and there, children, who are best acquainted with the localities of berries, bring pailsful to sell at their doors.

They follow hard upon the first red *amelanchier* or shad berries.

Strawberries may almost be considered a fruit of the spring, for they have depended chiefly on the freshness and moisture of spring, and on high lands are already dried up—a soft fruit, a sort of manna which falls in June, and in the meadows lurks at the shady roots of the grass. Now the blueberry, a somewhat firmer fruit, is beginning. Nuts, the firmest, will be the last.

These berries have a very innocent ambrosial taste, as if made of the ether itself, as they plainly are colored with it. There are two kinds, very distinct in color: the one a rich, light blue with a bloom, and yellowish-green leaves, which is most common; the other a glossy black with dark-green leaves, though you would think at first that they were the same as the former, only the bloom rubbed off. I can easily see still in my mind's eye the beautiful clusters of these berries as they appeared to me twenty or thirty years ago, when I came upon an undiscovered bed of them behind some higher bushes in a sproutland—the rich clusters drooping in the shade there and bluing all the ground, without a grain of their bloom disturbed. It was a thrilling discovery to find such ethereal fruits under the still, fresh green of oaks and hickory sprouts.

This early low blueberry, which I will call "bluet," adapting the name from the Canadians, is probably the prevailing kind of whortleberry in New England, for the high blueberry and huckleberry are unknown in many sections. They love a cool atmosphere and bear in great profusion on mountains. Many years ago, when camping on Wachusett mountain, having carried up milk for drink because there was no water there, I picked blueberries enough through the holes in the buffalo skin on which I lay in my tent to have berries and milk for supper. But they are far more abundant on Monadnock mountain. They do not get ripe so early there as below, but at any rate they last much longer on account of the greater coolness of the atmosphere; and though the plants are humble, like several other shrubs there, they are very productive. On September seventh, 1852, I found an abundance between the rocks on the summit—large, fresh, and cooling to eat, supplying the place of water. I left the mountain at one in the afternoon, walked to Troy four miles distant, took the cars, and reached Concord at a quarter after five—or four hours from the time that I was picking blueberries on the summit of the mountain—with specimens of the plants and berries perfectly fresh in my hat. Indeed, this and the *Vaccinium canadense* are the ordinary refreshment of those who climb our mountains in the fall. The mountaintops of New England, often

lifted above the clouds, are covered with this beautiful blue fruit in greater profusion than the fruit of any garden.

In many New Hampshire towns a neighboring mountaintop is the common
berry field of many villages, and in the berry season such a summit will be swarm-
ing with pickers. A hundred at once will rush thither from the surrounding villages with pails and buckets of all descriptions, especially on a Sunday, which is
their leisure day. When camping on such ground, thinking myself quite out of the
world, I have had my solitude very unexpectedly invaded by an army of this description—some even making their way up there thro' the morning fog before
sunrise, shouting and thumping on their pails in order that they might keep together—and I found that the weekdays were the only sabbath days there at that
season.

For a mile or more on such a rocky summit this will be the prevailing shrub,
occupying every little shelf from several rods to a few inches only in width, and
there the berries droop in short wreaths over the rocks, often with bright scarlet
bunchberries interspersed—sometimes the thickest and largest blueberries growing along a seam in a steep shelving rock—either light, mealy blue or a shining
black or an intermediate blue without bloom. When at that season I look from
Concord toward the blue mountaintops in the northwest horizon, I am reminded
that near at hand they are equally blue with berries. These berries have grown on
all our hills in succession, whenever the woods were cut off. I remember gathering ten quarts in two hours, filling a flour kit, on Pine Hill between this town and
Lincoln, some thirty years ago, where now there is a thick and high wood.

With these what you may call the berrying season begins. The Indian marked
the midsummer as the season when berries were ripe. By the middle of July many
berries are ripening, and children are planning expeditions after them. I have seen
their shrivelled blossoms again later in the fall full of fine, whole, bell-shaped flowers contrasting with crimson berries.

When the woods on some hillside are cut off, the little Pennsylvania blueberry, so called, being exposed to the light and air, puts forth fresh shoots of a livelier green; and by the second or third year its stems, which in the shade of the
forest had scarcely yielded the walker a berry, are weighed to the ground with the
clusters of berries, which are much larger than they usually grow and also of a livelier taste, as if remembering some primitive mountainside given up to them anciently. Such places supply the villagers with the earliest berries for several years,

or until the rising wood overgrows them and they withdraw into the bosom of Nature again. They flourish during the few years between one forest's fall and another's rise.

Before you had prepared your mind or made up your mouth for berries of this description—thinking only of crude green ones—earlier by ten days than you had expected, some child of the woods is at your door with ripe blueberries, for didn't you know that Mr. Blood cut off his woodlot on Pomciticut Hill winter before last? This act has more results than he wots of. It is an ill wind that blows nobody any good; and thus it happens that when the owner lays bare and deforms a hillside, and he alone appears to reap any advantage from it by a crop of wood, all the villagers and the inhabitants of distant cities obtain some compensation in the crop of berries that it yields. They glean after the woodchopper, not faggots, but full baskets of blueberries. Let alone your garden, cease your cultivation—and in how short a time will blueberries and huckleberries grow there! This provision of Nature, by which the earth is immediately reclothed with a new but miniature forest which in the order of her economy has its turn also secured to it, goes as far as anything toward reconciling me to the cutting down of the larger forest.

These and closely allied species and varieties of whortleberries, with tender, drooping, commonly blue fruit on very low bushes, are the prevailing ones on our mountains and in British America rather than the black huckleberries and the blueberries, which grow on larger bushes with us. They are called "bluets" by the voyageurs, and some kinds, very far north, keep fresh all winter under the snow and may be gathered the following June.

As you go northward from here, when you get about one hundred miles, you begin to leave behind your own kind, the *Pennsylvania* blueberry, with smooth and glossy leaves, and to find the Canada blueberry with downy leaves and twigs, though very few notice the difference. The prevailing blueberry in some places fifty miles apart north and south will be thus distinct, though commonly taken to be the same.

On the headwaters of the St. John and Penobscot Rivers in Maine I have found the Canada blueberry in great abundance, instead of our kind, occupying the more bare and barren ridges, where the *Pinus resinosa* and *banksiana* grow, and the rocky portages. Also on the side of Katadn mountain, where quite late in the season they had a decidedly spicy taste. They are a favorite food of the bears in those parts, and you are most likely to meet with bears where these berries abound at the season when they are ripe. The traveller Mackenzie says that gooseberries and raspberries, as well as "hortle berries" springing up amid the fallen trees in the almost bare country north of Lake Superior, attract the bears in great numbers. The same kind is common on Red Hill in New Hampshire, and they also grow on *Monadnock* mountain mingled with the Pennsylvania blueberry. Indeed, they pass into one another there by insensible degrees, so that it appears as if the seeds of the downy Canada blueberry carried far enough south would at length produce the smooth Pennsylvania one, and vice versa—just as men wear furs in the north, but linen in the south. At any rate, for all practical purposes we will consider the Canadian a more northern form of the other.

On the White Mountains several more allied kinds are found: the bog bilberry (*Vaccinium uliginosum*) and dwarf bilberry (*Vaccinium cæspitorum*). The former is the prevailing blueberry of their summits, but eating many of them is said to produce a headache.

RED LOW BLACKBERRY

A rare berry, distinguished by botanists alone, *Rubus triflorus*— what I call the red low blackberry—is the the first bramble (or *rubus*) to ripen its fruit with us, being the fourth berry of the year. By the twenty-fourth of May they are nearly out of bloom and have already some green fruit as big as small peas, and they are ripe from June twenty-sixth to the middle of July. I find it *only* in meadows, sometimes where I can thrust down a pole a dozen feet into the mud beneath, yet Gray says it grows on "Wooded hill sides." It runs over the ground like the common low blackberry, but unlike that its stems are of annual growth, short, and without prickles. Its leaves are much wrinkled. The vines are scattered and beside bear very sparingly, so that you can never collect any quantity. I have noticed the vines and plucked the fruit in the wild meadows in the forest in the extreme north of Maine, where they grow thinly and bear sparingly, just as they do here. The berries are middle-sized, of a dark, shining, red color, consisting of a few (six to ten or twelve) large semi-transparent grains *in* which you see the seed. They are of a lively acid but pleasant taste, with somewhat of the raspberry's spirit. They both taste and look like a cross between a raspberry and a blackberry.

CULTIVATED CHERRY

The cultivated cherry is ripe by the twenty-second of June. Family tradition says that my grandmother, who lived in Weston, brought over the first ripe cherries of the year to her brother, Simeon Jones, who was confined in Concord Jail as a Tory, on the day of the Battle of Bunker Hill, the seventeenth of June, 1775. Pliny, writing about the middle of the first century of our era, says, "there were no cherry trees in Italy before the victory of Lucullus over Mithridates. In the year of the city 680, he first brought them out of Pontus, and in 120 years, they have penetrated [*pervernire*] across the ocean even to Britain"—and I may add that they have now crossed a far wider ocean even to America, where the birds are still carrying on the work which Lucullus is said to have begun and bearing the seed further and further westward every year. Saint Pierre says, "I have seen in Finland, near Wiburg, beyond the 61st degree of latitude, cherry trees entirely exposed to the weather, though these trees are natives of the 42d degree." Some, however, think that Lucullus only introduced a few superior kinds and that most now cultivated are indigenous in Europe. Among others cultivated in his day, Pliny names one called "the Julian, of an agreeable taste, but almost only under the tree, it being so tender as not to bear transporting."

RASPBERRY

Wild raspberries begin to be ripe by the twenty-fifth of June, and last into August, being at their height about the fifteenth of July.

The sight of these light red berries on a comparatively large and leafy bush—as, perchance, winding our way through the little groves which they make, we pluck the fruit dripping with rain—surprises us while it reminds us of the progress of the year.

This seems to me one of the simplest, most innocent, and ethereal of fruits. One European species is well named "*Idæus*." Hereabouts it grows chiefly in open swamps, though also on hilltops, but rarely bears enough fruit to be of much ac-

count. In wet summers, however, like those of 1859 and 1860, it bears quite abundantly in some places in this neighborhood and is gathered for the table. Like the strawberry, it loves a new country, or one recently burnt or cleared, where the soil is still moist, and it was far more common here formerly.

Both Indians and whites, ancients and moderns, have turned aside to pluck this little fruit. Raspberries, as appear from the recent stories, made part of the food of that unknown primitive people whose traces have been found in piles at the bottom of the Swiss lakes, probably before the foundation of Rome. The English botanist Lindley says, "I have before me three plants of raspberries, raised from seeds which were taken from the stomach of a man whose skeleton was found thirty feet below the surface of the earth [in England]. He had been buried with some coins of the emperor Hadrian, and it is therefore probable that the seeds were 1,600 to 1,700 years old." The correctness of this statement has, however, been questioned.

I sometimes see a few berries still fresh in the swamps in the middle of September, and I have heard of a second crop being found in some localities much later in the fall.

Pliny, after observing how the European species at length bends down and takes root at the extremity, so that it would occupy all places if it were not for cultivation, says that therefore "men seem to have been made to take care of the earth" and, alas, that "thus a thing most noxious and to be execrated has taught us the art of multiplying by layers and quicksets."

MULBERRY

I see the red mulberry ripe the twenty-eighth of June, and still a few the twenty-sixth of July. I know of one or two trees in the fields, but they have probably spread from cultivation. Pliny says of mulberry trees, "They are among the latest to blossom, but among the first to ripen their fruit. Ripe, they stain the hands with their juice; sour, they take out the stain. Art has effected least of all in this tree—whether in its names [that is, varieties], or by grafting, or by any other mode, except in the size of the fruit," which appears to be true still.

Early in July the early blueberry, raspberry, and thimbleberry are all beginning to be ripe together.

THIMBLEBERRY

Black thimbleberries begin June twenty-eighth and last through July, being at their height about the fifteenth of July. I notice the green ones by the nineteenth of June. They grow along walls where the mowers pluck the fruit at the end of each swath, and in sproutlands.

This is an honest and homely berry, without much flavor, but wholesome and firm. I used to have a pleasant time when young ranging the wall-sides for them, competing with the birds, gathering the large black and blackening ones, and stringing them on herd's-grass culms, the most convenient way of bringing them home if you have no dish.

They commonly begin to dry up by the middle of July. I have seen a second crop of large and perfectly ripe berries, with others still unripe, as late as the eighth of October, when there had been an abundance of rain the previous six weeks.

Henry David Thoreau

HIGH BLUEBERRY

Some ten days later comes the high blueberry, swamp blueberry, or bilberry. We have two common varieties: the blue and the black (*Vaccinium corymbosum* and its variety, *atrocarpum*). The latter, which is the least common, is small and black, without bloom, more acid, and a day or two earlier than the other, as early or earlier than the thimbleberry, beginning the first of July; and *both* last till September. I notice the green berries by the thirtieth of May, and between the first and fifth of July begin to see a few ripe ones. They are at their height from the first to the fifth of August.

They are said to be found as far north as Newfoundland and Quebec. They grow in swamps, or if they are very wet, about their edges, and about the edges of ponds, and occasionally you meet with a bush even on a hillside. It loves the water so much that though it may grow about the edge of a pond with steep and hard shores, like Walden and Goose Pond, it is confined strictly to the shoreline, and it will not bear well except in seasons when the water is high. By the sight of these bushes, as of button bushes and some others, in a hollow, you may know when you have got down to the water-level. Let the ground in the woods sink to a certain depth so that water or considerable moisture is reached, and sphagnum and other water plants spring up there; and if man does not interfere, a dense hedge of high-blueberry bushes will commonly spring up all around the edge, curving over it, or perhaps will extend through it, and this whether it is a mere hollow a rod across or a swamp of a hundred acres.

This is the commonest stout shrub of our swamps, of which I have been compelled to cut down not a few when running lines on a survey or in low woods. When I see their dense curving tops ahead, I expect a wet foot. The flowers have an agreeable, sweet, and berry-promising fragrance, and a handful of them plucked and eaten have a sub-acid taste, agreeable to some palates. The fruit has a singularly cool and refreshing, slightly acid flavor; yet the botanist Pursh says of his (*Vaccinium corymbosum*, which must be another kind) simply, "berries black, insipid." In the Duc d' Aremberg's garden at Enghien, it is said to be "cultivated in the peat border for its fruit, which is used like that of the cranberry"—so slow are they to find out what it is good for! Rarely I find some which have a peculiar and decided bitter taste, which makes them almost inedible. They are of various sizes, colors, and flavors, but I prefer the large and more acid blue ones with a bloom. These embody for me the essence and flavor of the swamp. When they are thick and large, bending the bushes with their weight, few fruits are so handsome a sight.

Some growing sparingly on recent shoots are half an inch or more in diameter, or nearly as big as cranberries. I should not dare to say now how many quarts I once picked from a single bush which I actually climbed.

These are not all that tempt most into the swamp. Annually we go on a pilgrimage to these sacred places, in spite of dogwood and bilberry bumps. There are Beck Stow's and Gowing's and the Damon Meadows and Charles Miles's and others, which all have heard of, and there is many a preserve concealed in the midst of the woods known only to a few.

I remember years ago breaking through a thick oak wood east of the Great Fields and descending into a long, narrow, and winding blueberry swamp which I did not know existed there. A deep, withdrawn meadow sunk low amid the forest, filled with green waving sedge three feet high, and the low andromeda, and hardhack, for the most part dry to the feet then, though with a bottom of unfathomed mud, not penetrable except in midsummer or midwinter, and with no print of man or beast in it that I could detect. Over this meadow the marsh-hawk circled undisturbed, and she probably had her nest in it, for flying over the wood she had long since easily discovered it. It was dotted with islands of blueberry bushes and surrounded by a dense hedge of them, mingled with the panicled andromeda, high chokeberry, wild holly with its beautiful crimson berries, and so on—these being the front rank to a higher wood. Great blueberries, as big as old-fashioned bullets, alternated or were closely intermingled with the crimson hollyberries and black chokeberries, in singular contrast yet harmony, and you hardly knew why you selected those only to eat, leaving the others to the birds. From this meadow I entered southward by a passage hardly a foot wide, stooping close to the ground and brushing off the berries with my pack, into another yet larger swamp or meadow of a similar character; for it was a twin meadow. Thus hedged about, it is only in some late year that you stumble on some of these places in your neighborhood and stand surprised on the edge of a blueberry preserve, as retired and novel as if it were a thousand miles removed from your ordinary walks, as far off as Persia from Concord.

The timid or ill-shod confine themselves to the land side, where they get comparatively few berries and many scratches; but the more adventurous—making their way through the open swamp which the bushes overhang, wading amid the water andromeda and sphagnum, where the surface quakes for a rod around, and wetting their feet at least with the contents of many an upset and rent pitcher plant—obtain access to the great drooping clusters which no hand has disturbed. There is no wilder and richer sight than is afforded from such a point of view of the edge of a blueberry swamp, when various wild berries are intermixed.

There was Charles Miles's Swamp also, where you might get more than the value of the berries in the beauty of the spruce trees with which it was beset, though not the less wildly rich and beautiful—the cool blueberries hung high over your head there. I remember years ago picking blueberries in that swamp, before it began to be *redeemed,* when from its very depths I could hear the trembling strains of Mr. Miles's bass viol, from the unseen house, for he was a famous timist and held the choir to harmony on the sabbath. I am not sure but some echo of those strains "touched my trembling ears" and reminded me about those times what true fame was, for it did not seem a "mortal soil" where I stood.

Thus, any summer, after spending the forenoon in your chamber reading or writing, in the afternoon you walk forth into the fields and woods, and turn aside, if you please, into some rich, withdrawn, and untrodden swamp, and find there bilberries large and fair awaiting you in inexhaustible abundance. This is your real garden. Perhaps you press your way through thickets of chokeberry bushes higher than your head, with many of their lower leaves already red, attenuating with young birch; raspberries; andromeda, high and low; and great, dense, flat beds of the evergreen swamp blackberry (*Rubus sempervirens*)—and ever and anon you come to a cool opening in which stands an island or two of great dark-green high-blueberry bushes, dotted with the big, cool berries. Or they rise far above your head in the shade of the swamp, retaining their freshness and coolness a long time—little blue sacks full of swampy nectar and ambrosia commingled, whose bonds you burst by the pressure of your teeth. This reminds me that according to Gerarde, whortleberries are "called in Low Dutch *Crakebesien*, because they make a certain crack whilst they be broken between the teeth."

Some large swamps consist almost exclusively of blueberry bushes growing in large clumps, whose spreading tops are closely intermingled above the countless narrow winding paths, or such they *seem*, which separate their bases, forming thus a perfect labyrinth to which there is no clue, but you must steer by the sun—paths which can be convenient only to rabbits, where you make your way with difficulty, stooping low and straddling from tussock to tussock in order to keep out of water, guided perhaps by the accidental rattling of your companion's tin pail.

The gray blueberry bushes, venerable as oaks—why is not their fruit poisonous? It has the wildest flavor of any of the huckleberry tribe that I pluck. It is like eating a poisonous berry which your nature makes harmless. I derive some of the same pleasure from it as if I were eating arum berries and musquash root with impunity, as if I were a Mithridates among the berries.

Sometimes copious rains early in August will cause those masses of small green berries, of which commonly but few get ripe, to swell and ripen every one so that their harvest fulfills the promise of their spring, even in swamps where a fortnight before you had despaired of them, and nobody can believe what sights you have seen.

Here they hang for many weeks unchanged, in dense clusters, half a dozen berries touching each other—black, blue, and intermediate colors. But our appreciation of their flavor commonly prevents our observing their beauty, though we admire the color of the holly berries, which are their neighbors. If they were poisonous, we should hear more of their beauty to the eye.

They hang on into September. Once, when Walden Pond was high, I found perfectly fresh high blueberries overhanging the south side of the pond which I gathered from a boat on the fifteenth of September, and there were many still green among them, though in swamps they were all shrivelled. Commonly they begin to wilt after the middle of August, though they may still be pretty thick, lose their raciness or wild and sprightly taste, and acquire a dead and flat one.

I sometimes see a variety two or three feet high with large, rather oblong black berries, with little or no bloom, narrow leaves, and a conspicuous calyx, which appears to be intermediate between this and the *Vaccinium vacillans* or *Vaccinium pennsylvanicum*.

Many swamps in this neighborhood are considered quite valuable for the blueberries, they being made private property, and I have heard of damages being allowed by referees on account of blueberry bushes that were burnt. I believe that the most peculiar dish made with these berries is the "blueberry hollow," which is a pudding with a distinct crust inclosing the berries, and the same disposition is made of blackberries.

When their leaves have fallen, they are scraggy, gray, dead-looking bushes, and the oldest have quite a venerable appearance; indeed, they are much older than you would suspect, for since they grow on the edges of swamps and ponds, and on islets in swamps, they frequently escape being cut with the wood and so are older than one growth of wood. There are many growing quite on the edge of Goose Pond, occupying a strip only some three or four feet wide entirely around it, between the steep hillside and the pond, which have accordingly escaped being cut. This is the whole extent of their territory there, not one growing above or below this line. They are a kind of eyelashes to the pond. They have all the appearance of age, being gray and covered with lichens, commonly crooked, zigzag, and intertwisted with their neighbors, so that when you have cut one off, it is hard to extract it from the mass.

The winter season, when you can stand on the ice, is a good time to examine them. They bend over nearly to the ice, literally bowed with the weight of many winters' snows, yet with lusty young shoots running up perpendicularly by their sides, like erect young men destined to perpetuate the family by the side of their stooping sires. They have a gray, flat, scaly bark split into long, fine, closely adhering scales, the inner bark being dull reddish. I find that many of these bushes have attained half the age of man. On one which measured eight and a half inches in circumference at the butt, I counted pretty accurately forty-two rings. From another I cut a straight and round club four feet long, and six and a half inches in circumference at the smaller end, a heavy and close-grained wood, and nobody could tell me what it was.

But the largest and handsomest that I ever saw is on what I call Sassafras Island in Flint's Pond. It, in fact, makes a small tree or clump of trees, about ten feet high and spreading the same or more, and is perfectly sound and vigorous. It divides at six inches above the ground into five stems, which, at the height of three feet, measure respectively eleven, eleven and a half, eleven, eight, and six and a half inches in circumference, or an average nine and a half inches; and near the ground, where they form one solid trunk, they are thirty-one inches in circumference, or more than ten inches in diameter; but probably they have grown together there—indeed, they look as if they had sprung from the different seeds of one berry. The branches spread a little as they rise in their usual zigzag and half-spiral manner, one sometimes resting in the forks of its neighbor, and the finely divided reddish bark is at intervals handsomely clothed with large yellow and gray lichens (the prevailing ones being *Parmelia caperata* and *saxatilis*, the sulfur and rock lichens), which extend quite around them. Next the ground, the bark is quite reddish. The top, which is spreading, is somewhat flattish or corymbose, consisting of a great many fine twigs, which give it a thick and dark appearance against the sky even in winter, compared with the more open portion beneath. In these fine twiggy tops the catbird oftenest builds her nest and the black snake loves to rest—with or without a view to the young birds. Judging from those whose rings I have counted, the largest of these stems must be about sixty years old.

I climbed up this tree and found a comfortable seat with my feet four feet from the ground, and there was room for three or four persons more there, but unfortunately it was not the season for berries.

This blueberry grove must be well known to the partridges. No doubt they distinguish its peculiar tops from afar and launch themselves in bullet-like flight toward it. In fact, I noticed in the ice the tracks of those which had been there to feed on its large red buds during a previous thaw.

These have not been cut because they stand on that rather inaccessible little island; above, there is little woodbine, and therefore they have attained their full size. Perhaps yet larger ones were to be seen here before the whites came to cut down the woods. They are often older than many whole orchards of cultivated fruit trees and may have borne fruit before the writer was born.

LATE LOW BLUEBERRY

About the same time, the late or second kind of low blueberry, the common low blueberry (*Vaccinium vacillans*), the firm berry which is generally found with huckleberries on a bush of the same size, begins to be ripe. This is an upright, slender shrub with a few long wand-like branches, with green bark and crimson-colored recent shoots and glaucous green leaves. The flowers have a considerably rosy tinge of a delicate tint. They grow either on open hillsides or pastures, or in sproutlands, or in thin woods, and are from one and a half to two feet high.

This glaucous-leaved bush ripens its fruit somewhat in advance of huckleberries, and it is sweeter than they (if not than the fruit of any of our *Vacciniums*). Both this and the high blueberry are more densely flowered than our other whortleberries, and accordingly the berries are not scattered like huckleberries, but in dense clusters, raceme-like, so that you can strip off a handful at once of various sizes and qualities. At first you find the ripest ones, not on the very top nor on the lower slopes, but on the brows or what is called the "pitch" of a hill, or the southeast or southerly side where they get most light and heat.

This is the only kind of *low blueberry* known to many who are belated in their observations and expeditions. The earlier low blueberry, which we might for convenience call bluets (*Vaccinium pennsylvanicum*) (which we now presume to be a little in the rear and out of bearing), is mountain- and spring-like with its fine light-blue bloom—very handsome, simple, and ambrosial, to be sure, but, we must admit, soft and rather thin and tasteless. But this second kind is more like solid food, hard and bread-like, though at the same time more earthy.

Some years they are particularly large, as well as abundant. By the twentieth of August they begin to be a little wilted, though still good, when huckleberries are getting to be suspected. By the first of September they are more or less shriv-elled and, if it is a wet season, spoiling; but otherwise they are half dried, many as hard as if dried on a pan—yet they are still very sweet and good, and not wormy like huckleberries. This is a great recommendation, and you can accordingly pluck and eat with confidence that they are still vegetable food. They are often very abundant in this state when there has been a drought. I gather them some-times as late as the middle of September quite sound, in fact, after all the rest of the plant has turned to a deep crimson, which is its autumnal tint. These almost spicy, lingering clusters of blueberries contrast strangely with the bright leaves.

BLACK HUCKLEBERRY

Black huckleberries begin to be ripe July third (or generally the thirteenth), are thick enough to pick about the twenty-second, at their height about the fifth of August, and last fresh till after the middle of that month.

This, as you know, is an upright shrub, more or less stout depending on the ex-posure, with a spreading, bushy top, a dark-brown bark, red recent shoots, and thick leaves. The flowers are smaller and much more red than those of the other species. It is said to range from the Saskatchewan to the mountains of Georgia, and from the Atlantic to the Mississippi in this latitude; but it abounds over but a small part of this area, and there are large tracts where it is not found at all.

By botanists it is called of late, but I think without good reason, *Gaylussacia resinosa,* after the celebrated French chemist. If he had been the first to distill its juices and put them in this globular bag, he would deserve this honor; or if he had been a celebrated picker of huckleberries, perchance paid for his schooling so, or only notoriously a lover of them, we should not so much object. But it does not appear that he ever saw one. What if a committee of Parisian naturalists had been appointed to break this important news to an Indian maiden who had just filled her basket on the shore of Lake Huron! It is as if we should hear that the daguerreotype had been *finally* named after the distinguished Chippeway conjurer, The-Wind-that-Blows. By another it has been called *Andromeda baccata,* the berry-bearing andromeda, but he evidently lived far away from huckleberries and milk.

I observe green huckleberries by the nineteenth of June, and perhaps three weeks later, when I have forgotten them, I first notice on some hillside exposed to the light, some black or blue ones amid the green ones and the leaves, always sooner than I had expected, and though they may be manifestly premature, I make it a point to taste them and so inaugurate the huckleberry season. In a day or two the black are so thick among the green ones that they no longer incur the suspicion of being worm-eaten, and perhaps a day later I pluck a handful from one bush, and I do not fail to make report of it when I get home, though it is rarely believed, most people are so behind-hand in their year's accounts.

Early in August in a favorable year the hills are black with them. At Nagog Pond I have seen a hundred bushels in one field, the bushes drooping over the rocks with the weight of them, and a very handsome sight they are, though you should not pluck one of them. They are of various forms, colors, and flavors: some round, some pear-shaped, some glossy black, some dull black, some blue with a tough and thick skin (though they are never of the peculiar light blue of blueberries with a bloom), some sweeter, some more insipid, and so on—more varieties than botanists take notice of.

Today, perhaps, you gather some of those large, often pear-shaped, sweet blue ones which grow tall and thinly amid the rubbish where woods have been cut. They have not borne there before for a century, being over-shadowed and stinted by the forest, but they have the more concentrated their juices and profited by the new recipes which Nature has given them, and now they offer to you fruit of the very finest flavor, like wine of the oldest vintage. And tomorrow you come to a strong, moist soil where the black ones shine with such a gloss, every one its eye on you, and the blue are so large and firm that you can hardly believe them to be huckleberries at all or edible; but you seem to have travelled into a foreign country or else are dreaming. They are a firmer berry than most of the whortleberry family and hence are the most marketable.

If you look closely at a huckleberry you will see that it is dotted, as if sprinkled over with a yellow dust or meal which looks as if it could be rubbed off. Through a microscope it looks like a resin which has exuded, and on the small green fruit is of a conspicuous light-orange or lemon color, like small specks of yellow lichens. It is apparently the same with that shining resinous matter which so conspicuously covers the leaves when they are unfolding, making them sticky to the touch—whence this species is called *resinosa* or "resinous."

There is a variety growing in swamps, a very tall and slender bush drooping or bent like grass to one side, commonly three or four feet high, but often seven feet; the berries, which are later than the former, are round and glossy black, with resinous dots as usual, and grow in flattish-topped racemes, sometimes ten or twelve together, though generally more scattered. I call it the swamp huckle-berry.

But the most marked variety is the red huckleberry, the *white* of some (for the less ripe are whitish), which ripens at the same time with the black. It is red with a white cheek, often slightly pear-shaped, semi-transparent with a luster, very finely and indistinctly white dotted. It is as easily distinguished from the common in the green state as when ripe. I know of but three or four places in the town where they grow. It might be called *Gaylussacia resinosa* var. *erythrocarpa*.

I once did some surveying for a man, who remarked, but not till the job was nearly done, that he did not know when he should pay me. I did not at first pay much heed to this observation, though it was unusual, supposing that he meant to pay me within a reasonable time. Nevertheless, it occurred to me that if he did not know when he should pay me, still less did I know when I should be paid. He added, however, that I was perfectly secure, for there were the pigs in the stye (and as nice pigs as ever were seen), and there was his farm itself which I had surveyed and knew was there as well as he. All this had its due influence increasing my sense of security, as you may suppose. After many months he sent me a quart of red huckleberries, for they grew on his farm, and this I thought was ominous; he distinguished me altogether too much by this gift, since I was not his particular friend. I saw that it was the first installment of my dues—and that it would go a great way toward being the last. In the course of years he paid a part of the debt in money, and that is the last that I have heard of it. I shall beware of red-huckleberry gifts in future.

Huckleberries are very apt to dry up and not attain their proper size, unless rain comes to save them before the end of July. They will be dried quite hard and black by drought even before they have ripened. On the other hand, they frequently burst open and so are spoiled in consequence of copious rains when they are fully ripe. They *begin* to be soft and wormy as early as the middle of August, and generally about the twentieth the children cease to carry them round to sell, as they are suspected by the purchasers.

How late when the huckleberries begin to be wormy and the pickers are deserting the fields! The walker feels very solitary now.

But in woods and other cool places they commonly last quite fresh a week or more longer, depending on the season. In some years, when there are far more berries than pickers or even worms, and the birds appear to pass them by, I have found them plump, fresh, and quite thick, though with a somewhat dried taste, the fourteenth of October, when the bushes were mostly leafless, and the leaves that were left were all red, and they continued to hold on after the leaves had all fallen, till they were softened and spoiled by rain.

Sometimes they begin to dry up generally by the middle of August—after they are ripe, but before spoiling—and by the end of that month I have seen the bushes so withered and brown owing to the drought that they appeared dead, like those which you see broken off by the pickers, or as if burnt. I have seen the hills still black with them, though hard and shrivelled as if dried in a pan, late in September. And one year I saw an abundance of them still holding on the eleventh of December, they having dried ripe prematurely, but these had no sweetness left. The sight of them thus dried by nature may have originally suggested to the Indians to dry them artificially.

High blueberries, the second kind of low blueberries, huckleberries, and low blackberries are all at their height generally during the first week of August. In the dog-days (or the first ten of them) they abound and attain their full size.

Huckleberries are classed by botanists with the cranberries (both bog and mountain), snowberry, bearberry, mayflower, checkerberry, the andromedas, clethra, laurels, azaleas, rhodora, ledum, pyrolas, prince's pine, Indian pipes, and many other plants; and they are called all together the Heath Family, they being in many respects similar to and occupying similar ground with the heaths of the Old World, which we have not. If the first botanists had been American this might have been called the Huckleberry Family, including the heaths. Plants of this order (*Ericaceæ*) are said to be among the earliest ones found in a fossil state, and one would say that they promised to last as long as any on this globe. George B. Emerson says that the whortleberry differs from the heath proper "essentially only in its juicy fruit surrounded by the calyx segments."

The genus to which the whortleberries belong is called by most botanists *Vaccinium*, which I am inclined to think is properly derived from *bacca*, a berry, as if these were the chief of all berries, though the etymology of this word is in dispute. Whortle- or hurtleberry, bilberry, and blæ- or blea-, that is *blue*berry, are the names given in England originally to the fruit of the *Vaccinium myrtillus*, which we have not in New England, and also to the more scarce and local *Vaccinium uliginosum*, which we have. The word "whortleberry" is said to be derived from the Saxon *heort-berg* (or *heorot-berg*), the hart's berry. "Hurts" is an Old English word used in heraldry, where, according to Bailey, it is "certain balls resembling hurtleberries." The Germans say *Heidel-beere*, that is "heath berry."

"Huckleberry," this first is used by Lawson in 1709, appears to be an American word derived from "whortleberry" and applied to fruits of the same family, but for the most part of different species from the English whortleberries. According to the dictionary the word "berry" is from the Saxon *beria*, a grape or cluster of grapes. A French name of whortleberry is *raisin des bois*, "grape of the woods." It is evident that the word "berry" has a new significance in America. We do not realize how rich our country is in berries. The ancient Greeks and Romans appear not to have made much account of strawberries, huckleberries, melons, and so on because they had not got them.

The Englishman Lindley, in his *Natural System of Botany*, says that the *Vaccinieæ* are "Natives of North America, where they are found in great abundance as far as high northern latitudes; sparingly in Europe; and not uncommonly on high land in the Sandwich Islands." Or as George B. Emerson states it, they "are found chiefly in the temperate, or on mountains in the warmer regions of America. Some are found in Europe; some on the continent and islands of Asia, and on islands in the Atlantic, Pacific and Indian Oceans." "The whortleberries and cranberries," says he, "take the place, throughout the northern part of this continent, of the heaths of the corresponding climates of Europe; and fill it with no less of beauty, and incomparably more of use."

According to the last arrangement of our plants, we have fourteen species of the Whortleberry Family *(Vaccinieæ)* in New England, eleven of which bear edible berries—eight, berries which are eaten raw, and five of the last kind are abun-

Henry David Thoreau

dant; to wit: the huckleberry, the bluet or Pennsylvania blueberry, the Canada blueberry (in the northern part of New England), the second or common low blueberry, and the high or swamp blueberry (not to mention the dangleberry, which is common in some seasons and localities). On the other hand, I gather from Loudon and others that there are only two species growing in England, which are eaten raw, answering to our eight; to wit: the bilberry (*Vaccinium myrtillus*) and the blea-berry or bog whortleberry (*Vaccinium uliginosum*), both of which are found in North America, and the last is the common one on the summit of the White Mountains; but in Great Britain it is found only in the northern part of England and in Scotland. This leaves only one in England to our five which are abundant. In short, it chances that of the thirty-two species of *Vaccinium* which Loudon describes, all except the above two and four more are referred to North America alone, and only three or possibly four are found in Europe. Yet the few Englishmen with whom I have spoken on this subject love to think and to say that they have as many huckleberries as we. I will therefore quote the most which their own authorities say, not already quoted, about the abundance and value of their only two kinds which are eaten raw.

Loudon says of the bog whortleberry (*Vaccinium uliginosum*), "The berries are agreeable, but inferior in flavor to those of *Vaccinium myrtillus* [the bilberry]; eaten in large quantities, they occasion giddiness, and a slight headache." And of their only common whortleberry (*Vaccinium myrtillus*), he says, "It is found in every country in Britain, from Cornwall to Caithness, least frequently in the southeastern countries, and increases in quantity as we advance northward." It "is an elegant and also a fruit-bearing plant." The berries "are eaten in tarts or with cream, or made into a jelly, in the northern and western countries of England; and, in other parts of the country, they are made into pies and puddings." They "are very acceptable to children either eaten by themselves, or with milk" or otherwise. They "have an astringent quality."

Coleman in his *Woodlands, Heaths, and Hedges,* says:

> The traveller in our upland and mountain districts can hardly have failed to notice, as his almost constant companion, this cheerful little shrub . . . it flourishes best in a high airy situation, only the summits of the very loftiest mountains of which this country can boast being too elevated for this hardy little mountaineer. . . .
>
> In Yorkshire, and many parts of the north, large quantities of bilberries are

brought into the market, being extensively used as an ingredient in pies and puddings, or preserved in the form of jam. . . . Much, however, of the relish of these wilding fruits must be set down to the exhilarating air, and those charms of scenery that form the accessories of a mountain feast. . . .

One of the prettiest sights that greet one's eye in the districts where it abounds, is that of a party of rustic children "a-bilberrying" (for the greater portion of those that come to market are collected by children); there they may be seen, knee deep in the "wires," or clambering over the broken gray rocks to some rich nest of berries, their tanned faces glowing with health, and their picturesque dress (or undress)—with here and there bits of bright red, blue, or white—to the painter's eye contrasting beautifully with the purple, gray and brown of the moorland, and forming altogether rich pictorial subjects.

These authorities tell us that children and others eat the fruit, just as they tell us that the birds do. It is evident from all this that whortleberries do not make an important part of the regular food of the Old English people in their season, as they do of the New Englanders. What should we think of a summer in which we did not taste a huckleberry pudding? That is to Jonathan what his plum pudding is to John Bull.

Yet Dr. Manasseh Cutler, one of the earliest New England botanists, speaks of the huckleberry lightly as being merely a fruit which children love to eat with their milk. What ingratitude thus to shield himself behind the children! I should not wonder if it turned out that Dr. Manasseh Cutler ate his huckleberry pudding or pie regularly through the season, as many his equals do. I should have pardoned him had he frankly put in his thumb and pulled out a plum, and cried, "What a Great Doctor am I?" But probably he was lead astray by reading English books— or it may be that the Whites did not make so much use of them in his time.

Widely dispersed as their bilberry may still be in England, it was undoubtedly far more abundant there once. One botanist says that "This is one of the species that, if allowed, would overrun Britain, and form, with *Calluna vulgaris* [heather] and *Empetrum nigrum* [crowberry, which grows on our White Mountains], much of the natural physiognomical character of its vegetation." The genus *Gaylussacia*, to which our huckleberry belongs, has no representative in Great Britain, nor does our species extend very far northward in this country. So I might say of edible berries generally, that there are far fewer kinds in Old than in New England.

Take the *rubuses* or what you might call bramble berries, for instance, to which genus our raspberries, blackberries, and thimbleberries belong. According to Loudon there are five kinds indigenous in Britain to our eight. But of these five only two appear to be at all common, while we have four kinds both very common and very good. The Englishman Coleman says of their best, the English raspberry, which species we also cultivate, that "the wilding is not sufficiently abundant to have much importance." And the same is true of wild fruits generally. Hips and haws are much more important comparatively there than here, where they have hardly got any popular name.

I state this to show how contented and thankful we ought to be.

It is to be remembered that the vegetation in Great Britain is that of a much more northern latitude than where we live, that some of our alpine shrubs are found on the plain there; and their two whortleberries are alpine or extreme northern plants with us.

If you look closely you will find blueberry and huckleberry bushes under your feet, though they may be feeble and barren, throughout all our woods, the most persevering Native Americans, ready to shoot up into place and power at the next election among the plants, ready to reclothe the hills when man has laid them bare and feed all kinds of pensioners. What though the woods be cut down; it appears that this emergency was long ago anticipated and provided for by Nature, and the interregnum is not allowed to be a barren one. She not only begins instantly to heal that scar, but she compensates us for the loss and refreshes us with fruits such as the forest did not produce. As the sandal wood is said to diffuse a perfume around the woodman who cuts it, so in this case Nature rewards with unexpected fruits the hand that lays her waste.

I have only to remember each year where the woods have been cut just long enough to know where to look for them. It is to refresh us thus once in a century that they bide their time on the forest floor. If the farmer mows and burns over his overgrown pasture for the benefit of the grass or to keep the children out, the huckleberries spring up there more vigorous than ever, and the fresh blueberry shoots tinge the earth crimson. All our hills are, or have been, huckleberry hills, the three hills of Boston and no doubt Bunker Hill among the rest. My mother remembers a woman who went a-whortleberrying where Dr. Lowell's church now stands.

In short, the whortleberry bushes in the Northern States and British America are a sort of miniature forest surviving under the great forest, and reappearing when the latter is cut, and also extending northward beyond it. The small berry-bearing shrubs of this family, as the crowberry, bilberry, and cranberry, are called by the Esquimaux in Greenland "berry grass"; and Crantz says that the Greenlanders cover their winter houses with "bilberry bushes," together with turf and earth. They also burn them, and I hear that somebody in this neighborhood has invented a machine for cutting up huckleberry bushes for fuel.

It is remarkable how universally, as it respects soil and exposure, the whortleberry family is distributed with us—almost we may say a new species for every thousand feet of elevation—one kind or another, of those of which I am speaking, flourishing in every soil and locality. There is the high blueberry in swamps; the second low blueberry, with the huckleberry, on almost all fields and hills; the Pennsylvania and Canada blueberries, especially in cool and airy places, in openings in the woods, and on hills and mountains; while we have two kinds confined to the alpine tops of our highest mountains—the family thus ranging from the lowest valleys to the highest mountaintops and forming the prevailing small shrubbery of a great part of New England.

The same is true *hereabouts* of a single species of this family, the huckleberry proper. I do not know of a spot where any shrub grows in this neighborhood but one or another variety of the huckleberry may also grow there. It is stated in Loudon that all the plants of this order "require a peat soil, or a soil of a close cohesive nature," but this is not the case with the huckleberry. It grows on the tops of our highest hills; no pasture is too rocky or barren for it; it grows in such deserts as we have, standing in pure sand; and at the same time it flourishes in the strongest and most fertile soil. One variety is peculiar to quaking bogs, where there can hardly be said to be any soil beneath, to say nothing of another but unpalatable species, the hairy huckleberry, which is found there. It also extends through all our woods more or less thinly, and a distinct species, the dangleberry, belongs especially to moist woods and thickets.

Such care has Nature taken to furnish to birds and quadrupeds, and to men, a palatable berry of this kind, slightly modified by soil and climate, wherever the consumer may chance to be. Corn and potatoes, apples and pears, have comparatively a narrow range, but we can fill our basket with whortleberries on the summit of Mount Washington, above almost all other shrubs with which we are familiar, the same kind which they have in Greenland, and again when we get home, with another species in our lowest swamps, such as the Greenlanders never dreamed of.

The berries *which I celebrate* appear to have a range, most of them, very nearly coterminous with what has been called the Algonquin Family of Indians, whose territories embraced what are now the Eastern, Middle, and Northwestern States, and the Canadas, and surrounded those of the Iroquois in what is now New York. These were the small fruits of the Algonquin and Iroquois Families.

Of course, the Indians made a much greater account of wild fruits than we do, and among the most important of these were huckleberries. They taught us not only the use of corn and how to plant it, but also of whortleberries and how to dry them for winter. We should have hesitated long before we tasted some kinds if they had not set us the example, knowing by old experience that they were not only harmless but salutary. I have added a few to my number of edible berries by walking behind an Indian in Maine and observing that he ate some which I never thought of tasting before.

To convince you of the extensive use which the Indians made of huckleberries, I will quote at length the testimony of the most observing travellers on this subject, as nearly as possible in the order in which it was given us; for it is only after listening patiently to such reiterated and concurring testimony, of various dates and respecting widely distant localities, that we come to realize the truth.

But little is said by the discoverers of the use which the Indians made of the fresh berries in their season, the hand-to-mouth use of them, because there was little to be said, though in this form they may have been much the most important to them. We have volumes of recipes, called cookbooks, but when a fruit or a tart is ready for the table, nothing remains but to eat it without any more words. We therefore have few or no accounts of Indians going a-huckleberrying, though they had more than a six-week's vacation for that purpose, and probably camped on the huckleberry field.

I will go far enough back for my authorities to show that they did not learn the use of these berries from us whites.

In the year 1615, Champlain, the founder of Quebec, being far up the Ottawa spying out the land and taking notes among the Algonquins, on his way to the fresh-water sea since called Lake Huron, observed that the natives made a business of collecting and drying for winter use a small berry which he called blües, and also raspberries; the former is the common blueberry of those regions, by some considered a variety of our early low blueberry (*Vaccinium pennsylvanicum*); and again when near the lake he observes that the natives make a kind of bread of pounded corn sifted and mixed with mashed beans which have been boiled—and sometimes they put dried blueberries and raspberries into it. This was five years before the Pilgrims crossed the Atlantic and is the first account of huckleberry cake that I know of.

Gabriel Sagard, a Franciscan Friar, in the account of his visit to the Huron Country in 1624, says, "There is so great a quantity of blües, which the Hurons call *Ohentaqué*, and other little fruits which they call by a general name *Hahique*, that the savages regularly dry them for the winter, as we do prunes in the sun, and that serves them for comfits for the sick, and to give taste to their *Sagamité* [or gruel, making a kind of plum porridge], and also to put into the little loaves [or cakes, "*pains*"] which they cook under the ashes." According to him they put not only blueberries and raspberries into their bread, but strawberries and "wild mulberries" (*meures champestres*) and other little fruits dry and green." Indeed the gathering of blueberries by the savages is spoken of by the early French explorers as a regular and important harvest with them.

Le Jeune, the Superior of the Jesuits in Canada, residing at Quebec, in his *Relation* for 1639, says of the savages that "Some figure to themselves a paradise full of *bluets*."

Roger Williams, who knew the Indians well, in his account of those in his neighborhood, published in 1643, tells us that "*Sautaash* are these currants [grapes and whortleberries] dried by the natives, and so preserved all the year, which they beat to powder and mingle it with their parched meal, and make a delicate dish which they call *Sautauthig*, which is as sweet to them as plum or spice cake to the English."

But Nathaniel Morton, in his *New England's Memorial*, printed in 1669, speaking of white men going to treat with Canonicus, a Narraghanset Indian, about Mr. Oldham's death in 1636, says, "Boiled chestnuts is their white bread, and because they would be extraordinary in their feasting, they strove for variety after the English manner, boiling puddings made of beaten corn, putting therein great stores of blackberries, somewhat like currants," no doubt whortleberries. This *seems* to *imply* that the Indians imitated the English, or set before their guests dishes to which they themselves were not accustomed or which were extraordinary. But we have seen that these dishes were not new or unusual to them, and it was the whites who imitated the Indians rather.

John Josselyn, in his *New England's Rarities*, published in 1672, says under the fruits of New England, "Bill berries, two kinds, black and sky colored, which is more frequent. . . . The Indians dry them in the sun and sell them to the English by the bushel, who make use of them instead of currence, putting of them into puddens, both boyled and baked, and into water gruel."

The largest Indian huckleberry party that I have heard of is mentioned in the life of Captain Church, who, it is said, when in pursuit of King Phillip in the summer of 1676 came across a large body of Indians, chiefly squaws, gathering whortleberries on a plain near where New Bedford now is, and killed and took prisoner sixty-six of them, some throwing away their baskets and their berries in their flight. They told him that their husbands and brothers, a hundred of them, who with others had their rendezvous in a great cedar swamp nearby, had recently left them to gather whortleberries there, while they went to Sconticut Neck to kill cattle and horses for further and more substantial provisions.

La Hontan in 1689, writing from the Great Lakes, repeats what so many French travellers had said about the Indians drying and preserving blueberries, saying, "The savages of the north make a great harvest of them in summer, which is a great resource especially when the chase fails them." They were herein more provident than we commonly suppose.

Father Rasles, who was making a *Dictionary of the Abenaki Language* in 1691, says that their word for blueberries was: fresh, *Satar*; dry, *Sakisatar*—and the words in their name for July meant "when the blueberries are ripe." This shows how important they were to them.

Father Hennepin, who writes in 1697, says that his captors, Naudowessi (the Sioux!), near the falls of St. Anthony, feasted on wild rice seasoned with blueberries, "which they dry in the sun during the summer, and which are as good as raisins of Corinth"—that is, the imported currants.

The Englishman John Lawson, who published an account of the Carolinas in 1709, says of North Carolina, "The hurts, huckleberries or blues of this country are four sorts. . . . The first sort is the same blue or bilberry that grows plentifully in the North of England. . . . The second sort grows on a small bush," the fruit being larger than the last. The third grows three or four feet high in low land. "The fourth sort grows upon trees, some ten and twelve foot high, and the thickness of a man's arm; these are found in the runs and low grounds. . . . The Indians get many bushels, and dry them on mats, whereof they make plum bread, and many other eatables." He is the first author that I remember who uses the word "huckleberry."

The well-known natural botanist John Bartram, when returning to Philadelphia in 1743 from a journey through what was then the wilderness of Pennsylvania and New York to the Iroquois and Lake Ontario, says that he "found [when in Pennsylvania] an Indian squaw drying huckleberries. This is done by setting four forked sticks in the ground, about three or four feet high, then others across, over them the stalks of our common *Facea* or *Saratula*, on these lie the berries, as malt is spread on the hair cloth over the kiln. Underneath she had kindled a smoke fire, which one of her children was tending."

Kalm, in his travels in this country in 1748–49, writes, "On my travels through the country of the Iroquois, they offered me, whenever they designed to treat me well, fresh maize bread, baked in an oblong shape, mixed with dried huckleberries, which lay as close in it as the raisins in a plumb pudding."

The Moravian missionary Heckewelder, who spent a great part of his life among the Delawares toward the end of the last century, states that they mixed with their bread, which was six inches in diameter by one inch thick, "whortleberries green or dry, but not boiled."

Lewis and Clarke in 1805 found the Indians west of the Rocky Mountains using dried berries extensively.

And finally in Owen's *Geological Survey of Wisconsin, Iowa and Minnesota,* published in 1852, occurs the following: "*Vaccinium Pennsylvanicum* (Lam.) [that is, our early low blueberry]. Barrens on the upper St. Croix. This is the common Huckleberry, associated with the characteristic growth of the *Pinus Banksiana,* covering its sandy ridges with a verdant undergrowth, and an unsurpassed luxuriance of fruit. By the Indians these are collected and smoke-dried in great quantities, and in this form constitute an agreeable article of food."

Hence you see that the Indians, from time immemorial down to the present day, all over the northern part of America, have made far more extensive use of the whortleberry at all seasons and in various ways than we, and that they were far more important to them than to us.

It appears from the above evidence that the Indians used their dried berries commonly in the form of a cake, and also of huckleberry porridge or pudding.

What we call huckleberry cake, made of Indian meal and huckleberries, was evidently the principal cake of the aborigines, though they also used other berries and fruits in a similar manner, and often put things into their cake which would not have been agreeable to our palates, though I do not hear that they ever put any soda or pearl-ash or alum into it. We have no national cake so universal and well known as this was in all parts of the country where corn and huckleberries grew. They enjoyed it all alone ages before our ancestors heard of their Indian corn or their huckleberries, and probably if you had travelled here a thousand years ago it would have been offered you alike on the Connecticut, the Potomac, the Niagara, the Ottawa, and the Mississippi.

The last Indian of Nantucket, who died a few years ago, was very properly represented in a painting which I saw there with a basket full of huckleberries in his hand, as if to hint at the employment of his last days. I trust that I may not outlive the last of the huckleberries.

Tanner, who was taken captive by the Indians in 1789 and spent a good part of his life as an Indian, gives the Chippeway names of at least five kinds of whortleberries. He gives "*meen*—blue berry, *meenun*—blue berries," and says that "this is a word that enters into the composition of almost all words which are used as the names of fruits," that is, as a terminal syllable. Hence, this would appear to have been the typical berry—or berry of berries—among the Chippeway, as it is among us.

I think that it would be well if the Indian names were as far as possible restored and applied to the numerous species of huckleberries by our botanists, instead of the very inadequate Greek and Latin or English ones at present used. They might serve both a scientific and popular use. Certainly it is not the best point of view to look at this peculiarly American family, as it were, from the other side of the Atlantic. It is still in doubt whether the Latin word for the genus *Vaccinium* means a berry or a flower.

Botanists, on the look out for what they thought a respectable descent, have long been inclined to trace this family backward to Mount Ida. Tournefort does not hesitate to give it the ancient name of "Vine of Mount Ida." The common English raspberry also is called *Rubus Idæa*, or the Mount Ida bramble, from the old Greek name. The truth of it seems to be that blueberries and raspberries flourish best in cool and airy situations, on hills and mountains, and I can easily believe that something *like* these, at least, grows on Mount Ida. But Mount

Monadnock is as good as Mount Ida, and probably better for blueberries, though its name is said to mean "Bad rock." But the worst rocks are the best for poets' uses. Let us then exchange that oriental uncertainty for this western certainty.

We have in the northern states a few wild plums and inedible crab apples, a few palatable grapes, and many tolerable nuts; but I think that the various species of berries are our *wild fruits* which are to be compared with the more celebrated ones of the tropics, and for my part I would not exchange fruits with them; for the object is not merely to get a ship-load of something which you can eat or sell, but the pleasure of gathering it is to be taken into the account.

What is the pear crop as yet to the huckleberry crop? Horticulturists make a great ado about their pears, but how many families raise or buy a barrel of pears in a year all told? They are comparatively insignificant. I do not taste more than half a dozen pears annually, and I suspect that the majority fare worse even than I. (This was written before my neighbor's pear-orchard began to bear. Now he frequently fills my own and others' pockets with the fruit.) But Nature heaps the table with berries for six weeks or more. Indeed, the apple crop is not so important as the huckleberry crop. Probably the apples consumed in this town annually do not amount to more than one barrel per family. But what is this to a month or more of huckleberrying to every man, woman, and child—and the birds into the bargain. Even the crop of oranges, lemons, nuts, raisins, figs, quinces, and so on is of little importance to us compared with these.

They are not unprofitable in a pecuniary sense; I hear that some of the inhabitants of Ashby sold two thousand dollars' worth of huckleberries in 1856.

In May and June all our hills and fields are adorned with a profusion of the pretty little more or less bell-shaped flowers of this family, commonly turned toward the earth and more or less tinged with red or pink, and resounding with the hum of insects, each one the forerunner of a berry, the most natural, wholesome, and palatable that the soil can produce. I think to myself, these are the blossoms of the *Vacciniæ* or Whortleberry Family, which affords so large a portion of our berries; the berry-promising flower of the *Vacciniæ!* This crop grows wild all over the country—wholesome, bountiful, and free, a real ambrosia. And yet men, the foolish demons that they are, devote themselves to the culture of tobacco, inventing slavery and a thousand other curses for that purpose, with infinite pains and inhumanity go raise tobacco all their lives, and that is the staple instead of huckleberries. Wreaths of tobacco smoke go up from this land, the only incense which its inhabitants burn in honor of their gods. With what authority can such as we distinguish between Christians and Mahometans? Almost every interest, as the codfish and mackerel interest, gets represented at the General Court, but not the huckleberry interest. The first discoverers and explorers of the land make report of this fruit, but the last make comparatively little account of them.

Blueberries and huckleberries are such simple, wholesome, and universal fruits that they concern our race much. It is hard to imagine any country without this kind of berry, on which men live like birds—still covering our hills as when the red men lived here. Are they not the principal wild fruit?

What means this profusion of berries at this season only? Nature does her best to feed her children, and the broods of birds just matured find plenty to eat now. Every bush and vine does its part and offers a wholesome and palatable diet to the wayfarer. He need not go out of the road to get as many berries as he wants, of various kinds and qualities according as his road leads him over high or low, wooded or open ground: huckleberries of different colors and flavors almost everywhere, the second kind of low blueberry largest in the moist ground, high blueberries with their agreeable acid when his way lies through a swamp, and low blackberries of two or more varieties on almost every sandy plain and bank and stone heap.

Man at length stands in such a relation to Nature as the animals which pluck and eat as they go. The fields and hills are a table constantly spread. Diet drinks, cordials, wines of all kinds and qualities are bottled up in the skins of countless berries for the refreshment of animals, and they quaff them at every turn. They seem offered to us not so much for food as for sociality, inviting us to a picnic with Nature. We pluck and eat in remembrance of her. It is a sort of sacrament, a communion—the *not* forbidden fruits, which no serpent tempts us to eat. Slight and innocent savors which relate us to Nature, make us her guests, and entitle us to her regard and protection.

When I see, as now, in climbing one of our hills, huckleberry and blueberry bushes bent to the ground with fruit, I think of them as fruits fit to grow on the most Olympian or heaven-pointing hills. It does not occur to you at first that where such thoughts are suggested is Mount Olympus, and that you who taste these berries are a god. Why, in his only royal moments, should man abdicate his throne? You eat these berries in the dry pastures where they grow not to gratify an appetite, but as simply and naturally as thoughts come into your mind, as if they were the food of thought, dry as itself, and surely they nourish the brain there.

Occasionally there is an unusual profusion of these fruits to compensate for the scarcity of a previous year. I remember some seasons when favorable moist weather had expanded the berries to their full size, so that the hillsides were literally black with them. There were infinitely more of all kinds than any and all creatures could use. One such year, on the side of Conantum Hill, they were literally five or six species deep. First, if you searched low down in the shade under all, you found still fresh the great, light-blue, earliest blueberries, bluets, in heavy clusters—that most Olympian fruit of all—delicate-flavored, thin-skinned, and cool; *then*, next above, the still denser masses or clusters of the second low blueberry of various varieties, firm and sweet food; and rising above these, large blue and black huckleberries of various qualities; and over these ran rampant the low blackberry, weighing down the thicket with its wreaths of black fruit and binding it together in a trembling mass—while here and there the high blackberry, just beginning to be ripe, towered over all the rest. Thus, as it were, the berries hung up lightly in masses or heaps, separated by their leaves and twigs so that the air could circulate through and preserve them; and you went daintily wading through this thicket, picking perhaps only the finest of the high blackberries, as big as the end of your thumb, however big that may be, or clutching here and there a handful of huckleberries for variety, but never suspecting the delicious, cool, blue-bloomed ones, which you were crushing with your feet under all. I have in such a case spread aside the bushes and revealed the last kind to those who had never in all their lives seen or heard of it before. Each such patch, each bush, seems fuller and blacker than the last as you proceed, and the huckleberries at length swell so big, as if aping the blackberries, that you mark the spot for future years.

There is all this profusion, and yet you see neither birds nor beasts eating them—only ants and the huckleberry-bug. It seems fortunate for us that those cows in their pasture do not love them, but pass them by. We do not perceive that birds and quadrupeds make any use of them because they are so abundant we do not miss them, and they are not compelled to come where we are for them. Yet they are far more important to them than to us. We do not notice the robin when it plucks a huckleberry as we do when it visits our favorite cherry tree, and the fox pays his visits to the fields when we are not there.

I once carried my arms full of these bushes to my boat, and while I was rowing homeward, two ladies, who were my companions, picked three pints from these alone, casting the bare bushes into the stream from time to time.

Even in ordinary years, when berries are comparatively scarce, I sometimes unexpectedly find so many in some distant and unfrequented part of the town, between and about the careless farmers' houses and walls, that the soil seems more fertile than where I live. Every bush and bramble bears its fruit. The very sides of the road are a fruit garden. The earth there teems with blackberries, huckleberries, thimbleberries, fresh and abundant—no signs of drought nor of pickers. Great shining blackberries peep out at me from under the leaves upon the rocks. Do the rocks hold moisture? or are there no fingers to pluck these fruits? I seem to have wandered into a land of greater fertility, some up-country Eden. These are the Delectable Hills. It is a land flowing with milk and huckleberries, only they have not yet put the berries into the milk. *There* the herbage never withers, *there* are abundant dews. I ask myself, What are the virtues of the inhabitants that they are thus blessed?

> *O fortunatos nimium, sua si bona norint Agricolas—*
> O too fortunate husbandmen, if they knew their own happiness.

These berries are further important as introducing children to the fields and woods. The season of berrying is so far respected that the school children have a vacation then, and many little fingers are busy picking these small fruits. It is even a pastime, not a drudgery, though it often pays well beside. The First of August is to them the anniversary of Emancipation in New England.

Women and children who never visit distant hills, fields, and swamps on any other errand are seen making haste thither now with half their domestic utensils in their hands. The woodchopper goes into the swamp for fuel in the winter; his wife and children for berries in the summer. Now you will see who is the thorough country-woman, who does not go to the beach, conversant with berries and nuts, a masculine, wild-eyed woman of the fields.

Now for a ride in the hay-rigging to that far off Elysium that Zechariah Seeall alighted on, but has not mentioned to any person, in the hay-rigging without springs—trying to sensitive nerves and to full pails, for all alike sit on the bottom; such a ride is favorable to conversation, for the incessant rumble hides all defects and fills the otherwise awful pauses—to be introduced to new scenes more mem-

orable than the berries; but to the old walker the straggling party itself, half concealed amid the bushes, is the most novel and interesting feature. If hot, the boys
break up the bushes and carry them to some shady place where the girls can pick
them at their ease. But this is a lazy and improvident way, and gives an unsightly
look to the hill. There are many events not in the program. If you have an ear for
music, perhaps one is the sound of a cow bell, never heard before, or a sudden
thunder shower, putting you to flight, or a breakdown.

I served my apprenticeship and have since done considerable journeywork in
the huckleberry field. Though I never paid for my schooling and clothing in that
way, it was some of the best schooling that I got, and paid for itself. Theodore
Parker is not the only New England boy who has got his education by picking
huckleberries, though he may not have gone to Harvard thereafter nor to any
school more distant than the huckleberry field. *There* was the university itself,
where you could learn the everlasting Laws and Medicine and Theology, not
under Story and Warren and Ware, but far wiser professors than they. Why such
haste to go from the huckleberry field to the college yard?

As in old times, they who dwelt on the heath, remote from towns, being
backward to adopt the doctrines which prevailed in towns, were called "heathen" in a bad sense, so I trust that we dwellers in the huckleberry pastures, which
are our heath-lands, shall be slow to adopt the notions of large towns and cities,
though perchance we may be nicknamed "huckleberry people." But the worst of
it is that the emissaries of the towns come more for our berries than they do for
our salvation.

Occasionally, in still summer forenoons—when perhaps a mantua-maker was
to be dined and a huckleberry pudding had been decided on—I, a lad of ten, was
despatched to a neighboring hill alone. My scholastic education could be thus far
tampered with, and an excuse might be found. No matter how scarce the berries
on the near hills, the exact number necessary for a pudding could surely be collected by eleven o'clock—and all ripe ones, too, though I turned some round
three times to be sure they were not premature. My rule in such cases was never
to eat one till my dish was full, for going a-berrying implies more things than eating the berries. They at home got nothing but the pudding, a comparatively
heavy affair, but I got the forenoon out of doors—to say nothing about the appetite for the pudding. They got only the plums that were in the pudding, but I
got the far sweeter plums that never go into it.

At other times, when I had companions, some of them used to bring such remarkably shaped dishes that I was often curious to see how the berries disposed of themselves in them. Some brought a coffeepot to the huckleberry field, and such a vessel possessed this advantage at least, that if a greedy boy had skimmed off a handful or two on his way home, he had only to close the lid and give his vessel a shake to have it full again. I have seen this done all round when the party got as far homeward as the Dutch House. It can probably be done with any vessel that has much side to it. There was a Young America, then, which has become Old America, but its principles and motives are still the same, only applied to other things. Sometimes, just before reaching the spot, every boy rushed to the hillside and, hastily selecting a spot, shouted, "I speak for this place," indicating its bounds, and another "I speak for that," and so on; and this was sometimes considered good law for the huckleberry field. At any rate, it is a law similar to this by which we have taken possession of the territory of Indians and Mexicans.

I once met with a whole family—father, mother, and children—ravaging a huckleberry field in this wise. They cut up the bushes as they went and beat them over the edge of a bushel basket till they had it full of berries, ripe and green,

leaves, sticks, and so forth; and so they passed along out of my sight like wild men.

I well remember with what a sense of freedom and spirit of adventure I used to take my way across the fields with my pail, some years later, toward some distant hill or swamp, when dismissed for all day, and I would not now exchange such an expansion of all my being for all the learning in the world. Liberation and enlargement—such is the fruit which all culture aims to secure. I suddenly knew more about my books than if I had never ceased studying them. I found myself in a schoolroom where I could not fail to see and hear things worth seeing and hearing, where I could not help getting my lesson, for my lesson came to me. Such experience, often repeated, was the chief encouragement to go to the Academy and study a book at last.

But, ah, we have fallen on evil days! I hear of pickers ordered out of the huckleberry fields, and I see stakes set up with written notices forbidding any to pick there. Some let their fields or allow so much for the picking. *Sic transit gloria ruris*. I do not mean to blame any, but all—to bewail our fates generally. We are not grateful enough that we have lived a part of our lives before these things occurred. What becomes of the true value of country life—what, if you must go to market for it? It has come to this, that the butcher now brings round our huckleberries in his cart. Why, it is as if the hangman were to perform the marriage ceremony. Such is the inevitable tendency of our civilization, to reduce huckleberries to a level with beef-steaks; that is, to blot out four-fifths of it or the going a-huckleberrying, and leave only a pudding, that part which is the fittest accompaniment to a beef-steak. You all know what it is to go a-beef-steaking. It is to knock your old fellow laborer Bright on the head to begin with, or possibly to cut a steak from him running, in the Abyssinian fashion, and wait for another to grow there. The butcher's item in chalk on the door is now "Calf's head and huckleberries."

I suspect that the inhabitants of England and the continent of Europe have thus lost in a measure their natural rights with the increase of population and monopolies. The wild fruits of the earth disappear before civilization, or only the husks of them are to be found in large markets. The whole country becomes, as it were, a town or beaten common, and almost the only fruits left are a few hips and haws.

What sort of a country is that where the huckleberry fields are private property? When I pass such fields on the highway, my heart sinks within me. I see a

blight on the land. Nature is under a veil there. I make haste away from the ac-
cursed spot. Nothing could deform her fair face more. I cannot think of it ever
after but as the place where fair and palatable berries are converted into money,
where the huckleberry is desecrated. It is true, we have as good a right to make
berries private property as to make wild grass and trees such; it is no worse than
a thousand other practices which custom has sanctioned; but that is the worst of
it, for it suggests how bad the rest are and to what result our civilization and division of labor naturally tend.

It has come to this, that A——, a professional huckleberry picker, has hired
B——'s field, and, we will suppose, is now gathering the crop with a patent huckleberry horse-rake. C——, a professed cook, is superintending the boiling of a
pudding made of some of the berries, while Professor D——, for whom the pudding is intended, sits in his library writing a book—a work on the *Vacciniæ*, of
course. And now the result of this downward course will be seen in that work,
which should be the ultimate fruit of the huckleberry field. It will be worthless.
It will have none of the spirit of the huckleberry in it, and the reading of it will
be a weariness of the flesh. I believe in a different kind of division of labor: that
Professor D—— should be encouraged to divide himself freely between his library
and the huckleberry field.

What I chiefly regret in this case is the, in effect, dog-in-the-manger result;
for at the same time that we exclude mankind from gathering berries in our field,
we exclude them from gathering health and happiness and inspiration and a hundred other far finer and nobler fruits than berries which are found there, but
which we have no notion of gathering and shall not gather ourselves nor ever
carry to market, for there is no market for them, but let them rot on the bushes.
We thus strike only one more blow at a simple and wholesome relation to nature.
I do not know but this is the excuse of those who have lately taken to swinging
bags of beans and ringing dumb-bells. As long as the berries are free to all com-
ers, they are beautiful, though they may be few and small; but tell me that this is
a blueberry swamp which somebody has hired, and I shall not want even to look
at it. We so commit the berries to the wrong hands; that is, to the hands of those
who cannot appreciate them. This is proved by the fact that if we do not pay them
some money, these parties will at once cease to pick them. They have no other
interest in berries but a pecuniary one. Such is the constitution of our society that

we make a compromise and permit the berries to be degraded—to be enslaved, as it were.

Accordingly, in laying claim for the first time to the spontaneous fruit of our pastures, we are inevitably aware of a little meanness, and the merry berry party which we turn away naturally looks down on and despises us. If it were left to the berries to say who should have them, is it not likely that they would prefer to be gathered by the party of children in the hay-rigging, who have come to have a good time merely?

This is one of the taxes which we pay for having a railroad. All our improvements, so called, tend to convert the country into the town. But I do not see clearly that these successive losses are ever quite made up to us. This suggests, as I have said, what origin and foundation many of our institutions have. I do not say this by way of complaining of this custom in particular, which is beginning to prevail—not that I love Cæsar less, but Rome more.

RED AND FETID CURRANTS

Common red currant, say July third.

July 7, 1860. Three or four days.

Many old writers on New England speak of the wild red currant, as well as black, though they are rarely seen now; and no doubt these, like strawberries, gooseberries, and raspberries, were far more abundant here then. Red currants, like the garden ones, are said to be found on the Island of Anticosti. Roger Williams describes an Indian dish made of dried currants, grapes, and whortleberries.

Between Loudon and Canterbury, New Hampshire, I saw the fetid currant (*Ribes prostratum*) by the roadside already red. I gathered it in the hollow between the rocks on Monadnock on September seventh, 1852. The berries have the odor of skunk cabbage, but a not quite disagreeable wild flavor. I have gathered it also in the White Mountains. Its fruit is covered with little bristles.

RED ELDERBERRY

I saw the red elderberry ripe—that is, red—between Loudon and Canterbury, July fourth, 1858. I saw it only in the northern part of New Hampshire. But I have seen it in Worcester County. The fruit is quite handsome.

NORTHERN WILD RED CHERRY

The northern wild red cherry begins to be ripe July fourth. Do not last long. Handsome, bright red, but scarcely edible.

Find them on Monadnock, September seventh, 1852 and August fourth, 1860.

June 2, 1858. An abundance of wild red cherry in bloom between Fitchburg and Troy, especially in burnt lands and on hillsides. Common down cut or burnt grounds, and old campsites and carries. Rather scarce in Concord.

SARSPARILLA

Some sarsaparilla berries are ripe by July seventh.

October 14, 1859. I had not noticed any for some weeks.

June 10, 1852. Green ones begin to show.

June 19, 1860. Green berries make quite a show as you catch sight of them under the leaves.

August 1, 1860. Mixed black and green berries in bush.

LOW BLACKBERRY

The low blackberry (*Rubus canadensis*) begin to be ripe July ninth, berrying commences about the twenty-second, in prime about August first to fourth, last in shade till near end of August.

August 4, 1856. Softening already; multiplying July nineteenth, 1851.

July 21, 1856. Thick enough to pick in some places; done August twenty-eighth, 1856. In shade fresh August twenty-third.

"There is a delicious berry now abundant in the woods, growing on a very low plant, scarcely rising above the ground: it is called here the Dewberry (*Rubus procumbens*). In appearance it is much like the berry of that name in England, but is superior in taste, being of a pleasant tartness."

By July ninth it bears already a few ripe ones on sandy banks, like the railroad causeway, exposed to the sun. By the seventeenth I *begin* to see children a-blackberrying in the Great Fields.

July 21, 1853. Am surprised by the abundance of large shining blackberries on the hillsides.

July 17, 1856. Going up the hillside between J. P. Brown's and the rough-cast house, am surprised to see great plump, ripe low blackberries. How important their acid (as well as that of currants) this warm weather!

July 19, 1856. On the sand thrown out by the money-diggers (near the river beyond Clamshell Hill) I find the first ripe blackberries thereabouts. The heat reflected from the sand had ripened them earlier than elsewhere. It did not at first occur to me what sand it was, nor that I was indebted to the money-diggers, or their Moll Pitcher, for those berries. I am probably the only one who has got any fruit out of that hole, for the farmer only complains that they do not fill up the holes. It is an ill wind that blows nobody any good. The result of some idler's folly, probably some spiritualist's nonsense, is that I get my blackberries a few days the earlier. Looking up, I observed that they had dug another hole a rod higher up the hill last spring, for the blackberries had not yet spread over it.

They begin to soften early in August, but in cool and shady places keep quite fresh till near the end of that month.

August 12, 1854. I see some great low blackberries on long peduncles lifted above the huckleberries, composed of great grains, as large as the largest high blackberries.

August 23, 1859. I gathered perfectly fresh and large low blackberries, peculiarly sweet and soft, in the shade of the pines at Thrush Alley long after they are done in open fields. They appear to be a different variety from the common, they are so much sweeter, tenderer, and larger. They do not grow densely, but sparingly, now resting on the ground in the shade of their leaves, perfectly ripe. These that have ripened slowly and perfectly in the shade are the sweetest and tenderest of all, and have the least of the brambleberry about them.

August 27, 1860. Gather some of those large and late low blackberries which run over the thin herbage, green moss, and so on in open pitch-pine woods.

July 31, 1852. Can that low blackberry—which has, I think, a rather wrinkled leaf and bears dense masses of lively berries now, commonly in cool, moist ground—be the same with the common?

July 22, 1853. It (?) does not bear large fruit but very dense clusters (especially by wall sides shaded by its vines and other plants often) of clammy and strong-tasted berries.

August 5, 1856. I now find an abundance of the last ripe. It is not large and has a clammy, sub-acid taste, but some are very sweet; clusters generally drooping.

August 19, 1856. What countless varieties of low blackberries! Here in this open pine grove I pluck some large, fresh, and very sweet ones when they are mostly gone without. So they are continued a little longer to us.

WILD GOOSEBERRY

I have gathered the wild gooseberry the tenth of July, *Ribes hirtallum*.

July 22, 1860. *Almost* northeast base of Annursnack.

May 27, 1854. The young are as big as small green peas.

July 30, 1853. I find some in J. P. Brown's land. It is globular, smooth, red, marked by internal meridional lines, and inclined to be flattened at the poles. (This does not blossom as early as our earliest in gardens, but its fruit is more like that in color—though more smooth and glossy—than like the later one of the garden, which is dark purple or blue.) This is rather acid and wild tasted.

July 10, 1854. Most of the wild gooseberries are dried up and blackened.

July 19, 1856. Plucked a handful of gooseberries at J. P. Brown's bush, probably ripe some time. It is of fair size, red, purple, and greenish. Has not so much flavor or agreeable tartness as the first in garden.

Josselyn says, "The gooseberry bush, the berry of which is called Grosers or thorn Grapes, grow all over the country, the berry is but small, of a red or purple color when ripe."

Lindley says of the *Grosenlaceœ* (gooseberries and currants), "In North America they are particularly abundant."

HYPERICUMS

Even the red capsules of the hypericums are a pleasing sight to me. Those of the *Hypericum ellipticum* begin to show in low grounds by the tenth of July.

GRAINS

I am annually surprised by the rapid growth of the rye.

Tradition says that on the day of Concord Fight, 1775, the apple tree was in blossom and the grain was waving in the fields. One old man of whom I inquired about this said that he supposed that the grain was not up very high, but only a few inches, just that you could see it wave. Looking about, I have observed this phenomenon in rye fields the fourteenth of May, earlier than it is observed in the grass.

By the eleventh of July reaping has begun, and I hear, perchance as I am paddling unseen quietly up the river, the reaper's cradle crunching the rye behind some fringe of bushes.

By the thirty-first of July I hear the distant sound of the flail, and the sights of autumn occupy my mind, and the memory of past years, and I shall hear it at intervals all the fall—aye, and occasionally in the winter, which agrees with Tusser's verse:

> Keep threshing for thresher, till May be come in,
> to have to be sure, fresh chaff in the bin:
> And somewhat to scamble for hog and for hen,
> and work when it raineth, for loitering men.

October 8, 1851. Farmers gathering their corn and apples and threshing.
November 1. Gathering corn.
September 13, 1858. Hear the sound of the flail separating the chaff from the wheat, some two hundred years old here—to be heard how long?

July 30, 1860. Hear the sound of the first flail; some farmer, perchance, wishes to make room in his barn—or else wants the grain. Is it wheat or rye? It may be either.

Saint Pierre thinks that if we had better impression of fruits we should have placed our principal crops on trees, and not on simple grasses, but "Had our harvests been the produce of the forests, in the event of these being destroyed by war, or set on fire through our own imprudence, or rooted up by the winds, or ravaged by inundations, whole ages would have been requisite to reproduce them in a country."

Alphonse De Candolle says, "Some observations of M. Esprit Fabre had made many persons believe that *Ægilops tritcoides*, Req., can become by culture a sort of *blé*, and yet this *Ægilops tritcoides* itself appears to be a modification of *Ægilops ovata*, so common in the south of Europe. One owes it to M. Godron, to have demonstrated that these changes of forms in excessive sowings [*semis*] take place simply in the case of hybrids which spring up between the wild *Ægilops* and cultivated wheat." He says wheat is found wild in Asia, especially Asia Minor and Mesopotamia.

TOUCH-ME-NOT

July 14, 1856. The touch-me-not (*noli-me-tangere*) seeds already spring.

September 27, 1852. Its seeds vessels go off like pistols—shooting their seeds like shot. They explode in my hat.

July 30, 1850. Some quite seedy and spring on a slight touch, and startling you: striped, stomate, *light-* and dark-green.

WILD HOLLY

Wild holly (*Nemopanthis canadensis*), the imp-eyed, red, velvety-looking berry of the swamps, *begins* by the fourteenth of July. This is perhaps the most beautiful of our berries, hanging by slender threads from its light and open bushes amid its delicate leaves.

TURNIP

Raw turnips. July fifteenth.

Another finger-cold evening, which I improve in pulling my turnips—the usual amusement of such weather—before they shall be frozen in. It is worth the while to see how green and lusty they are yet, still adding to their stock of nutriment for another year; and between the green and also withering leaves it does me good to see their great crimson, round or scalloped tops, sometimes quite above ground, they are so bold. They remind you of rosy cheeks in cool weather, and indeed there is a relationship. All kinds of harvestry, even pulling turnips when the first cold weather numbs your fingers, are interesting if you have been the sower and have not sown too many.

SCHEUCHZERIA

July fifteenth. *Scheuchzeria.*

July 3, 1860. The scheuchzeria is full of green fruit fully grown at Gowing's. It forms the upright grass-like plant next the more open pool, rising amid the floating sphagnum, with the spatulate sundew interspersed with it, and a very little of the leaden-sheathed eriophorum and a sprig or two of cassandra.

January 10, 1855. At European Cranberry Swamp, I saw great quantities of the seeds of that low three-celled rush or sedge, *Scheuchzeria palustris*, about the edge of the pool on the ice, black and elliptical, looking like the droppings of mice, this size: ∘∘,* so thick in many places that by absorbing the sun's heat they had melted an inch or more into the ice. No doubt they are the food of some creatures.

June 13, 1858. The *Scheuchzeria palustris*, now in flower and going to seed, grows at Ledum Pool, as at Gowing's Swamp.

---

*Thoreau included sketches in his *Wild Fruits* manuscript to illustrate his observation. These drawings are reproduced from the manuscript.

CHOKEBERRY

The chokeberry (*Pyrus arbutifolia* var. *melanocarpa*) begins to be ripe July six-teenth, in prime after huckleberries or say the latter part of August, and begins to be stale early in September.

These occasionally get into the baskets of young huckleberry pickers by mis-take and are deemed their biggest and finest berries. They are particularly com-mon in the blueberry swamps and are ripe at the same time with the blueberries. Fair to the eye but scarcely palatable, they hang far above your head there, weigh-ing down the bushes. Some of the bushes are eight feet high and black with berries, some twelve feet high, at least, and you see no creatures eating them. These are among the berries which men do not use. In some swamps they grow in great profusion three to five feet high and blacken the bushes. How much richer we feel for this unused abundance and superfluity. Nature would not appear so rich if we knew a use for everything.

August 31, 1852. At Weir Hill are great pyrus berries, as big as small cherries, in dense clusters falling over in wreaths, and actually blackening the ground. I have rarely seen any kind of berry so thick.

August 12, 1858. I *eat* the high blueberry, but I am also interested in the rich-looking, glossy-black chokeberries, which nobody eats and which bend down the bushes on every side—sweetish berries, with a dry and so choking taste.

August 28th, 1856. Now the black chokeberries are in their prime, just after huckleberries and blueberries. The bushes are weighed down with these berries, which no creature appears to gather. This crop is as abundant as the huckleber-ries have been. They have a sweet and pleasant taste enough at first, but leave a mass of dry pulp in the mouth. Nevertheless, it is worth the while to see their pro-fusion, if only to know what Nature can do, but she can do some things as well as others and has other children to feed beside us.

Sometimes, though abundant, they are mostly *dried black* by the twenty-fifth of August.

September 4, 1853. They are stale. They hold on, many of them, till winter on low bushes in open swamps.

December 19, 1850. The dried chokeberries so abundant in the swamps, are now quite sweet.

January 28, 1853. Tasted some black shrivelled ones in a spruce swamp—rather sweet.

January 29, 1858. The dried still common in swamps.

August 26, 1860. But there is far the greatest show of chokeberries there (Martial Miles's Swamp; that is, greater than blueberries), rich to see. I wade and press my way thro' endless thickets of these untasted berries, their lower leaves now fast reddening. Yet they have an agreeable juice, though the pulp may be rejected, and perhaps they might be made into wine.

August 28, 1856. Black chokeberries in prime (and black cherries) just after huckleberries and blueberries, both very abundant this year.

TRIENTALIS

By the sixteenth of July I begin to notice the small, bluish-white or ash-colored fruit of the trientalis in the woods.

SKUNK CABBAGE

The skunk cabbage fruit, July seventeenth. Now and in August and September, where the grass is cut in low grounds, I begin to notice the black, checkered fruit of the skunk cabbage, rough as a nutmeg grater, barely rising above the level of the ground—lying flat on it, indeed—a large oval fruit, shaped somewhat like a strawberry, but emitting a different fragrance. You often see where it has been cut in two by the mowers, revealing its large hut-like seeds, green inside, but most of them in the uneven ground lie below the plane in which the scythe traverses and so are uninjured. Its fruit, too, lies in the lap of the meadow. The largest fruit we have had yet—our northern pine-apple; some are three inches long. When the mower lays bare the ground in some low meadow in the latter part of July, he is surprised to find that Nature has already matured so sizeable a fruit there—before he has anything ripe or so large to show in his garden at home. It is that little infant that we detected under its hood in the spring, now come to maturity—what is called the spadix of the plant. All parts of the flower but the anthers left and enlarged. It turns black when ripe.

I had quite forgotten the promise of this earliest spring flower, which—unremembered by us, deep in the grass which has sprung up around it, its own leaves for the most part decayed—has been steadily maturing its fruit. How far we have wandered, in our thoughts at least, since we heard the bee humming in its spathe! I can hardly recall or believe now that for every such black and rather unsightly fruit (pericarp) there was, in the spring, a pretty, freckled horn, which attracted our attention. When I carry it home my friends can scarcely guess what fruit it is, but think of pine-apples and the like. After being in the house a week, and becoming wilted and softened, it emits, on being broken open, an agreeable sweetish scent, perchance like a banana, which suggests that it may be edible. But a good while after I have tasted it, it bites my tongue. I do not know that any of mankind but invalids use it, but I often find, even in the spring, twenty or thirty of its little brown nuts collected on some shelf or in some hole of a bank, I suspect by mice.

SAND CHERRY

The sand cherry (*Cerasus pumila*) begins to be ripe about the eighteenth of July, perhaps in prime about August first or later.

June 10, 1852. I see it in puffs, like some Canada plums.

August 10, 1860. Some of it is *well* ripe.

It is a handsome fruit, but scarcely palatable, though some call it "eatable." Yet I find it sometimes tolerable—better than red or choke cherry (*Cerasus pennsylvanica* or *Cerasus virginiana*). The fruit droops in umbel-like clusters, two to twenty peduncles together, on each side the axil of a branchlet or leaf. Emerson and Gray call it dark red. It is black when ripe. Emerson, Gray, and Bigelow speak of it as rare in this state. It is common enough in Concord, both on high and dry ground, and (another variety) in meadows. The cherry is three-eighths of an inch in diameter on a peduncle seven-sixteenths of an inch long.

Hind, in *Report for 1857*, says he found this, the *Cerasus pumila*, abundant on an island in the Lake of the Woods, "the favorite Nekaumina of the Savages." It is probably a more palatable fruit there, where it thrives better.

CLINTONIA

The clintonia or dracæna berries, first seen about July twentieth and last through August.

July 30, 1860. Beautiful.

This plant grows in the shade about the edges of swamps. The berries, which are of a peculiar dark, indigo blue (also like some kinds of blue china—some say "Amethystine blue") grow in umbels of two or five on the summits, very brittle stems eight or ten inches high, which break with a snap, and on erectish stemlets or pedicels. They are of singular form, oblong or squarish round, the size of large peas with a dimple atop. Seen above these very regular and handsome green leaves—which are still perfect in form and color, and which, growing close together, checker the ground—and also in the dense shade of the copse, there is something peculiarly celestial about them. They are rather rare and known to few—like poetry. This is the plant's true flower, to set off which, it has preserved its leaves fresh and unstained so long.

Toward the end of August they are mostly fallen.

GNAPHALIUM ULIGINOSUM

Gnaphalium uliginosum gone to seed, say July twentieth—or how long?

POLYGONATUM PUBESCENS

Polygonatum pubescens is seen by July twenty-second. A month later the leaves are eaten up. They seem in prime September fourth, 1853, or say September first.

This is a delicate plant with a handsome leafy stem recurved over the hillside, with generally two bluish-green (that is, dark-green with a bluish bloom) berries, about the size of a pea, dangling from the axils of the leaves. There are eight or nine of these slender axillary peduncles to a plant, hanging straight down three-quarters of an inch, each two dividing into two short pedicels at the end, and the berries are necessarily smaller—from below upwards along the stem—from three-eighths to hardly more than one-eighth of an inch in diameter.

H I G H   B L A C K B E R R Y

I pluck the very earliest high blackberry by July twenty-second, commonly noticed about the beginning of August, at their height about the eighteenth of August, and last into September.

Surely the high blackberry is the finest berry that we have—whether we find their great masses of shining black fruit, mixed with red and green, bent over amid the sweet fern and sumac on sunny hillsides, or growing more rankly and with larger fruit in low ground and by rich roadsides. But especially you go over to them when now the season is rather late (say the twenty-fifth of August) and low blackberries and huckleberries are generally spoiled; and you come across these not by dusty roadsides, but in some moist, rocky sproutland, far from any road, fully ripe, having escaped the pickers, weighing down their stems and half hidden amid the green leaves of the plants—their great shining wreaths of fruit often flat on the moist earth amid the thorny, bracing-scented, brittle dicksonia fern, which you crush with your feet. There they are perfectly fresh, black, and shining, ready to drop, with a spirited juice. Who will pretend that, plucked and eaten there, they are the same with those offered at the tea table? These are among the berries that are eaten by men.

Yet even by roadsides they are sweet, though covered with dust.

Along the up-country roads in New Hampshire and Maine they seem to be mainly confined to the roadside, growing in its wash—the long, sweet, mulberry-shaped kind, as if expressly for the foot traveller, who often turns aside into groves higher than his head and gathers vigor to renew his journey.

I find them still abundant in certain localities the very last of August and first of September, vines which have been overlooked. (I know what routes are peculiar to me by the state of the berries.) At a little distance you would not suspect that there were any vines, for the racemes are bent down out of sight amid the dense sweet ferns, sumacs, and so on. The berries are still not more than half of them ripe or black, keeping fresh in the shade, while those in the sun are a little wilted or insipid.

We have two varieties in Concord beside the common: namely, that which is the common in New Hampshire, with long mulberry-shaped berries; and the variety *frondorus*, whose berries are globular, of good size, of a very few large grains, very glossy, and of a lively flavor—when young, of a peculiar light pink.

Gerarde says of the "Common Bramble," "The ripe fruit is sweet and containeth in it much juice of a temperate heat, therefore it is not unpleasant to be eaten."

CHOKE CHERRY

The choke cherry (*Cerasus virginiana*) begins to be ripe July twenty-third, at height about August twentieth. I see them as big as small peas the twenty-third of June.

Wood, in his *New England's Prospect,* says of our cherries, "They be much smaller than the English cherry, nothing near so good, if they be not very ripe; they so furr the mouth that the tongue will cleave to the roof, and the throat wax hoarse with swallowing those red bullies (as I may call them) being little better in taste; English ordering may bring them to an English cherry, but they are as wild as the Indians."

It is no mere shrub here, growing along the fences and hedgerows. The bushes, about as high as your head, are loaded with full racemes two or three inches long, of shining dark-red berries, the size of a pea, slightly oblong or oval, but as yet (July 30), at least, very astringent—puckering the mouth for a long time. They are no doubt frequently mistaken at sight for the rum-cherry. Even a month later they actually fur the mouth, and the juice of those taken into the mouth mixed with the saliva is feathered, like tea into which sour milk has been poured. They are a rich, fatty-looking fruit. However, though they are scarcely edible, their beauty, especially when they are half ripe, atones for it. See those handsome racemes of ten or twelve cherries each—dark, glossy, red; semi-transparent? You love them not the less because they are not quite palatable. However, finding some once near the end of August dead, ripe, and a little wilted, they were tolerable eating—much better than I had ever tasted—yet the stones are much in the way.

This is said to be ever a small tree, never twenty feet high, on the

Saskatchewan, where its fruit, though "not very edible in a recent state . . . forms a desirable addition to pemmican when dried and bruised."

May 22, 1854. The dense cylindrical racemes of the choke cherry, some blasted into a puff.

Lindley says the "*Cerasus virginiana . . .* is known in North America to be dangerous" to cattle.

YEW

The yew, *Taxus americana,* is ripe probably about the twenty-fifth of July and lasts till September twelfth, at least.

I find this interesting undershrub in but one place in Concord. It fruits very sparingly, the berries growing singly here and there on last year's wood, and hence four or five inches below the extremities of the upturned twigs. It is the most wax-like and artificial looking and altogether surprising berry that we have. First, because it is borne by an ever-green, hemlock-like shrub, with which we do not associate a soft and bright-colored berry, and hence its deep scarlet contrasts the more strangely with the pure, dark, ever-green needles (as surprising as it would be to find currants on hemlocks). Secondly, because of its form, so like art, which

could be easily imitated in wax—a very thick, scarlet cup shaped like a little mortar, with a dark-purple seed set at the bottom. My neighbors are not prepared to believe that such a berry grows in Concord.

WILD APPLES

Early apples begin to be ripe about the first of August, but I think that none of them are so good to eat as some to smell. One is worth more to scent your handkerchief with than any perfume which they sell in the shops. The fragrance of some fruits is not to be forgotten, along with that of flowers. Some gnarly apple which I pick up in the road reminds me by its fragrance of all the wealth of Pomona—carrying me forward to those days when they will be collected in golden and ruddy heaps in the orchards and about the cider-mills.

A week or two later, as you are going by orchards or gardens, especially in the evenings, you pass through a little region possessed by the fragrance of ripe apples, and thus enjoy them without price and without robbing anybody.

There is thus about all natural products a certain volatile and ethereal quality which represents their highest value, and which cannot be vulgarized, or bought and sold. No mortal has ever enjoyed the perfect flavor of any fruit, and only the god-like among men begin to taste its ambrosial qualities. For nectar and ambrosia are only those fine flavors of every earthly fruit which our coarse palates fail to perceive—just as we occupy the heaven of the gods without knowing it. When I see a particularly mean man carrying a load of fair and fragrant early apples to market, I seem to see a contest going on between him and his horse on the one side, and the apples on the other, and, to my mind, the apples always gain it. Pliny says that apples are the heaviest of all things and that the oxen begin to sweat at the mere sight of a load of them. Our driver begins to lose his load the moment he tries to transport them to where they do not belong, that is, to any but the most beautiful. Though he gets out from time to time and feels of them and thinks they are all there, I see the stream of their evanescent and celestial qualities going to heaven from his cart, while the pulp and skin and core only are going to market. They are not apples, but pomace. Are not these still Iduna's apples, the taste of which keeps the gods forever young? and think you that they will let Loki or Thjassi carry them off to Jötunheim, while they grow wrinkled and gray? No, for Ragnarök, or the destruction of the gods, is not yet.

There is another thinning of the fruit, commonly near the end of August or in September, when the ground is strewn with windfalls; and this happens especially when high winds occur after rain. In some orchards you may see fully three-quarters of the whole crop on the ground, lying in a circular form beneath the trees, yet hard and green—or, if it is a hillside, rolled far down the hill. However, it is an ill wind that blows nobody any good. All the country over people are busy picking up the windfalls, and this will make them cheap for early apple-pies.

In October, the leaves falling, the apples are more distinct on the trees. I saw one year in a neighboring town some trees fuller of fruit than I remembered to have ever seen before, small yellow apples hanging over the road. The branches were gracefully drooping with their weight, like a barberry bush, so that the whole tree acquired a new character. Even the topmost branches, instead of standing erect, spread and drooped in all directions; and there were so many poles supporting the lower ones that they looked like pictures of banyan trees. As an Old English manuscript says, "The mo appelen the tree bereth, the more sche boweth to the folk."

Surely the apple is the noblest of fruits. Let the most beautiful or the swiftest have it. That should be the "going" price of apples.

Between the fifth and twentieth of October I see the barrels lie under the trees. And perhaps I talk with one who is selecting some choice barrels to fulfill an order. He turns a specked one over many times before he leaves it out. If I were to tell what is passing in my mind, I should say that every one was specked which he had handled; for he rubs off all the bloom, and those fugacious ethereal qualities leave it. Cool evenings prompt the farmers to make haste, and at length I see only the ladders here and there left leaning against the trees.

It would be well if we accepted these gifts with more joy and gratitude, and did not think it enough simply to put a fresh load of compost about the tree. Some old English customs are suggestive at least. I find them described chiefly in Brand's *Popular Antiquities*. It appears that "on Christmas eve the farmers and their men in Devonshire take a large bowl of cider, with a toast in it, and carrying it in state to the orchard, they salute the apple trees with much ceremony, in order to make them bear well the next season." This salutation consists in "throwing some of the cider about the roots of the tree, placing bits of the toast on the branches," and then, "encircling one of the best bearing trees in the orchard, they drink the following toast three several times":

> Here's to thee, old apple tree,
> Whence thou mayst bud, and whence thou mayst blow;
> And whence thou mayst bear apples enow!
> Hats full! caps full!
> Bushel—bushel—sacks full!
> And my pockets full, too!
> Huzza!

Also what was called "apple-howling" used to be practised in various counties of England on New-Year's eve. A troop of boys visited the different orchards, and, encircling the apple trees, repeated the following words:

> Stand fast, root! bear well, top!
> Pray God send us a good howling crop:
> Every twig, apples big;
> Every bough, apples enow!

"They then shout in chorus, one of the boys accompanying them on a cow's horn. During this ceremony they rap the trees with their sticks." This is called "wassailing" the trees and is thought by some to be "a relic of the heathen sacrifice to Pomona."

Herrick sings,

> Wassaile the trees that they may beare
> You many a plum and many a peare;
> For more or less fruits they will bring
> As you so give them wassailing.

Our poets have as yet a better right to sing of cider than of wine, but it behoves them to sing better than English Phillips did, else they will do no credit to their Muse.

So much for the more civilized apple trees (*urbaniores*, as Pliny calls them). I love better to go through the old orchards of ungrafted apple trees, at whatever season of the year—so irregularly planted, sometimes two trees standing close together, and the rows so devious that you would think that they not only had grown while the owner was sleeping, but had been set out by him in a somnambulic state. The rows of grafted fruit will never tempt me to wander amid them like these. But I now, alas, speak rather from memory than from any recent experience, such ravages have been made!

Some soils, like a rocky tract called the Easterbrooks Country in my neighborhood, are so suited to the apple, that it will grow faster in them without any care, or if only the ground is broken up once a year, than it will in many places with any amount of care. The owners of this tract allow that the soil is excellent for fruit, but they say that it is so rocky that they have not patience to plow it, and that, together with the distance, is the reason why it is not cultivated. There are, or were recently, extensive orchards there standing without order. Nay, they spring up wild and bear well there in the midst of pines, birches, maples, and oaks. I am often surprised to see rising amid these trees the rounded tops of apple trees glowing with red or yellow fruit, in harmony with the autumnal tints of the forest.

Going up the side of a cliff about the first of November, I saw a vigorous young apple tree which, planted by birds or cows, had shot up amid the rocks and open woods there and had now much fruit on it, uninjured by the frosts, when all cultivated apples were gathered. It was a rank, wild growth, with many green leaves on it still, and made an impression of thorniness. The fruit was hard and green, but looked as if it would be palatable in the winter. Some was dangling on the twigs, but more half buried in the wet leaves under the tree or rolled far down the hill amid the rocks. The owner knows nothing of it. The day was not observed when it first blossomed nor when it first bore fruit, unless by the chickadee. There was no dancing on the green beneath it in its honor, and now there is no hand to pluck its fruit—which is only gnawed by squirrels, as I perceive. It has done double duty—not only borne this crop, but each twig has grown a foot into the air. And this is *such* fruit! bigger than many berries, we must admit, and, carried home, will be sound and palatable next spring. What care I for Iduna's apples so long as I can get these?

When I go by this shrub thus late and hardy, and see its dangling fruit, I respect the tree, and I am grateful for Nature's bounty, even though I cannot eat it. Here on this rugged and woody hillside has grown an apple tree, not planted by man, no relic of a former orchard, but a natural growth, like the pines and oaks. Most fruits which we prize and use depend entirely on our care. Corn and grain, potatoes, peaches, melons, and so on, depend altogether on our planting; but the apple emulates man's independence and enterprise. It is not simply carried but, like him, to some extent, it has migrated to this New World and is even, here and there, making its way amid the aboriginal trees, just as the ox and dog and horse sometimes run wild and maintain themselves.

Even the sourest and crabbedest apple growing in the most unfavorable position suggests such thoughts as these, it is so noble a fruit.

Nevertheless, *our* wild apple is wild only like myself, perchance, who belong not to the aboriginal race here, but have strayed into the woods from the cultivated stock. Wilder still, as I have said, there grows elsewhere in this country a native and aboriginal crab apple, *Malus coronaria*, "whose nature has not yet been modified by cultivation." It is found from western New York to Minnesota and southward. Michaux says that its ordinary height "is fifteen or eighteen feet, but it is sometimes found twenty-five or thirty feet high," and that the large ones "exactly resemble the common apple tree." "The flowers are white mingled with rose-color, and are collected in corymbs." They are remarkable for their delicious odor. The fruit, according to him, is about an inch and a half in diameter and is intensely acid. Yet they make fine sweetmeats and also cider of them. He concludes that "if, on being cultivated, it does not yield new and palatable varieties,

it will at least be celebrated for the beauty of its flowers, and for the sweetness of its perfume."

I never saw the crab apple till May 1861. I had heard of it through Michaux, but more modern botanists, so far as I know, have not treated it as of any peculiar importance. Thus it was a half-fabulous tree to me. I contemplated a pilgrimage to the "Glades," a portion of Pennsylvania where it was said to grow to perfection. I thought of sending to a nursery for it, but doubted if they had it, or would distinguish it from European varieties. At last I had occasion to go to Minnesota, and on entering Michigan I began to notice from the cars a tree with handsome rose-colored flowers. At first I thought it some variety of thorn, but it was not long before the truth flashed on me—that this was my long-sought crab apple. It was the prevailing flowering shrub or tree to be seen from the cars at that season of the year—about the middle of May. But the cars never stopped before one, and so I was launched on the bosom of the Mississippi without having touched one, experiencing the fate of Tantalus. On arriving at St. Anthony's Falls, I was sorry to be told that I was too far north for the crab apple. Nevertheless, I succeeded in finding it about eight miles west of the Falls; touched it and smelled it, and secured a lingering corymb of flowers for my herbarium. This must have been near its northern limit.

But though these are indigenous, like the Indians, I doubt whether they are any hardier than those backwoodsmen among the apple trees, which, though descended from cultivated stocks, plant themselves in distant fields and forests, where the soil is favorable to them. I know of no trees which have more difficulties to contend with and which more sturdily resist their foes. These are the ones whose story we have to tell. It oftentimes reads thus:

> Near the beginning of May we notice little thickets of apple trees just springing up in the pastures where cattle have been—as the rocky ones of our Easterbrooks Country or the top of Nobscot Hill in Sudbury. One or two of these perhaps survive the drought and other accidents—their very birthplace defending them against the encroaching grass and some other dangers, at first.

> In two years' time 't had thus
> Reached the level of the rocks,
> Admired the stretching world,
> Nor feared the wandering flocks.

> But at this tender age
> Its sufferings began:
> There came a browsing ox
> And cut it down a span.

This time, perhaps, the ox does not notice it amid the grass; but the next year, when it has grown more stout, he recognizes it for a fellow emigrant from the old country, the flavor of whose leaves and twigs he well knows; and though at first he pauses to welcome it and express his surprise and gets for answer, "The same cause that brought you here brought me," he nevertheless browses it again, reflecting, it may be, that he has some title to it.

Thus cut down annually, it does not despair; but, putting forth two short twigs for every one cut off, it spreads out low along the ground in the hollows or between the rocks, growing more stout and scrubby, until it forms, not a tree as yet, but a little pyramidal, stiff, twiggy mass, almost as solid and impenetrable as a rock. Some of the densest and most impenetrable clumps of bushes that I have ever seen, as well on account of the closeness and stubbornness of their branches as of their thorns, have been these wild-apple scrubs. They are more like the scrubby fir and black spruce on which you stand, and sometimes walk, on the tops of mountains, where cold is the demon they contend with, than anything else. No wonder they are prompted to grow thorns at last, to defend themselves against such foes. In their thorniness, however, there is no malice, only some malic acid.

The rocky pastures of the tract I have referred to—for they maintain their ground best in a rocky field—are thickly sprinkled with these little tufts, reminding you often of some rigid gray mosses or lichens, and you see thousands of little trees just springing up between them with the seed still attached to them.

Being regularly clipped all around each year by the cows, as a hedge with shears, they are often of a perfect conical or pyramidal form, from one to four feet high, and more or less sharp, as if trimmed by the gardener's art. In the pastures on Nobscot Hill and its spurs, they make fine dark shadows when the sun is low. They are also an excellent covert from hawks for many small birds that roost and build in them. Whole flocks perch in them at night, and I have seen three robins' nests in one which was six feet in diameter.

No doubt many of these are already old trees, if you reckon from the day they were planted, but infants still when you consider their development and the long life before them. I counted the annual rings of some which were just one foot high, and as wide as high, and found that they were about twelve years old, but quite sound and thrifty! They were so low that they were unnoticed by the walker, while many of their contemporaries from the nurseries were already bearing considerable crops. But what you gain in time is perhaps in this case, too, lost in power—that is, in the vigor of the tree. This is their pyramidal state.

The cows continue to browse them thus for twenty years or more, keeping them down and compelling them to spread, until at last they are so broad that they become their own fence, when some interior shoot, which their foes cannot reach, darts upward with joy—for it has not forgotten its high calling, and bears its own peculiar fruit in triumph.

Such are the tactics by which it finally defeats its bovine foes. Now, if you have watched the progress of a particular shrub, you will see that it is no longer a simple pyramid or cone, but that out of its apex there rises a sprig or two, grow-ing more lustily perchance than an orchard tree since the plant now devotes the whole of its repressed energy to these upright parts. In a short time these become a small tree, an inverted pyramid resting on the apex of the other, so that the whole has now the form of a vast hour-glass. The spreading bottom, having served its purpose, finally disappears, and the generous tree permits the now harmless cows to come in and stand in its shade, and rub against and redden its trunk, which has grown in spite of them, and even to taste of part of its fruit, and so dis-perse the seed.

Thus the cows create their own shade and food; and the tree, its hourglass being inverted, lives a second life, as it were.

It is an important question with some nowadays, whether you should trim young apple trees as high as your nose or as high as your eyes. The ox trims them up as high as he can reach, and that is about the right height, I think.

In spite of wandering kine and other adverse circumstances, that despised shrub, valued only by small birds as a covert and shelter from hawks, has its blos-som week at last and in course of time its harvest—sincere, though small.

By the end of some October, when its leaves have fallen, I frequently see such a central sprig, whose progress I have watched, when I thought it had forgotten its destiny, as I had, bearing its first crop of small green or yellow or rosy fruit, which the cows cannot get at over the bushy and thorny hedge which surrounds it, and I make haste to taste the new and undescribed variety. We have all heard of the numerous varieties of fruit invented by Van Mons and Knight. This is the system of Van Cow, and she has invented far more and more memorable varieties than both of them.

Through what hardships it may attain to bear a sweet fruit! Though somewhat small, it may prove equal, if not superior, in flavor to that which has grown in a

garden—will perchance be all the sweeter and more palatable for the very difficulties it has had to contend with. Who knows but this chance wild fruit, planted
by a cow or a bird on some remote and rocky hill side, where it is as yet unobserved by man, may be the choicest of all its kind, and foreign potentates shall
hear of it, and royal societies seek to propagate it, though the virtues of the perhaps truly crabbed owner of the soil may never be heard of—at least beyond the
limits of his village? It was thus the Porter and the Baldwin grew.

Every wild-apple shrub excites our expectation thus, somewhat as every wild
child. It is, perhaps, a prince in disguise. What a lesson to man! So are human beings, referred to the highest standard, the celestial fruit which they suggest and as-
pire to bear, browsed on by fate; and only the most persistent and strongest genius
defends itself and prevails, sends a tender scion upward at last, and drops its perfect fruit on the ungrateful earth. Poets and philosophers and statesmen thus
spring up in the country pastures and outlast the hosts of unoriginal men.

Such is always the pursuit of knowledge. The celestial fruits, the golden apples of the Hesperides, are ever guarded by a hundred-headed dragon which never
sleeps, so that it is an Herculean labor to pluck them.

This is one, and the most remarkable way, in which the wild apple is propagated; but commonly it springs up at wide intervals in woods and swamps and by
the sides of roads, as the soil may suit it, and grows with comparative rapidity.
Those which grow in dense woods are very tall and slender. I frequently pluck
from these trees a perfectly mild and tamed fruit. As Palladius says, *"Et injussu con-
sternitur ubere mali"*: And the ground is strewn with the fruit of an unbidden
apple tree.

It is an old notion that if these wild trees do not bear a valuable fruit of their
own, they are the best stocks by which to transmit to posterity the most highly
prized qualities of others. However, I am not in search of stocks, but the wild fruit
itself, whose fierce gust has suffered no "inteneration." It is not my

> highest plot
> To plant the Bergamot.

The time for wild apples is the last of October and the first of November. They
then get to be palatable, for they ripen late, and they are still perhaps as beautiful as ever. I make a great account of these fruits, which the farmers do not think

it worth the while to gather—wild flavors of the Muse, vivacious and inspiriting. The farmer thinks that he has better in his barrels, but he is mistaken, unless he has a walker's appetite and imagination, neither of which can he have.

Such as grow quite wild and are left out till the first of November, I presume that the owner does not mean to gather. They belong to children as wild as themselves—to certain active boys that I know—to the wild-eyed woman of the fields, to whom nothing comes amiss, who gleans after all the world—and, moreover, to us walkers. We have met with them, and they are ours. These rights, long enough insisted upon, have come to be an institution in some old countries, where they have learned how to live. I hear that "the custom of grippling, which may be called apple gleaning, is, or was formerly, practised in Herefordshire. It consists in leaving a few apples, which are called the gripples, on every tree, after the general gathering, for the boys, who go with climbing-poles and bags to collect them."

As for those I speak of, I pluck them as a wild fruit, native to this quarter of the earth—fruit of old trees that have been dying ever since I was a boy and are not yet dead, frequented only by the woodpecker and the squirrel, deserted now by the owner, who has not faith enough to look under their boughs. From the appearance of the treetop, at a little distance, you would expect nothing but lichens to drop from it, but your faith is rewarded by finding the ground strewn with spirited fruit—some of it, perhaps, collected at squirrel holes, with the marks of their teeth, by which they carried them—some containing a cricket or two silently feeding within, and some, especially in damp days, a shell-less snail. The very sticks and stones lodged in the treetop might have convinced you of the savoriness of the fruit which has been so eagerly sought after in past years.

I have seen no account of these among the *Fruits and Fruit Trees of America*, though they are more memorable to my taste than the grafted kinds; more racy and wild American flavors do they possess, when October and November, when December and January, and perhaps February and March even, have assuaged them somewhat. An old farmer in my neighborhood, who always selects the right word, says that "they have a kind of bow-arrow tang."

Apples for grafting appear to have been selected, commonly, not so much for their spirited flavor, as for their mildness, their size, and bearing qualities—not so much for their beauty, as for their fairness and soundness. Indeed, I have no faith in the selected lists of pomological gentlemen. Their "Favorites" and "Nonesuches" and "Seek-no-farthers," when I have fruited them, commonly turn out very tame and forgettable. They are eaten with comparatively little zest and have no real *tang* nor *smack* to them.

What if some of these wildings are acrid and puckery, genuine *verjuice?* do they not still belong to the *Pomaceæ*, which are uniformly innocent and kind to our race? I still begrudge them to the cider mill. Perhaps they are not fairly ripe yet.

No wonder that these small and high-colored apples are thought to make the best cider. Loudon quotes from the *Herefordshire Report* that "Apples of a small size are always, if equal in quality, to be preferred to those of a larger size, in order that the rind and kernel may bear the greatest proportion to the pulp, which affords the weakest and most watery juice." And he says that "To prove this, Dr. Symonds of Hereford, about the year 1800, made one hogshead of cider entirely from the rinds and cores of apples, and another from the pulp only, when the first was found of extraordinary strength and flavor; while the latter was sweet and insipid."

Evelyn says that the "Red-strake" was the favorite cider apple in his day, and he quotes one Dr. Newburg as saying, "In Jersey 't is a general observation, as I hear, that the more of red any apple has in its rind, the more proper it is for this use. Pale-faced apples they exclude as much as may be from their cider-vat." This opinion still prevails.

All apples are good in November. Those which the farmer leaves out as unsalable and unpalatable to those who frequent the markets, are choicest fruit to the walker. But it is remarkable that the wild apple, which I praise as so spirited and racy when eaten in the fields or woods, being brought into the house, has frequently a harsh and crabbed taste. The Saunterer's Apple not even the saunterer can eat in the house. The palate rejects it there, as it does haws and acorns, and demands a tamed one; for there you miss the November air, which is the sauce it is to be eaten with. Accordingly, when Tityrus, seeing the lengthening shadows, invites Melibœus to go home and pass the night with him, he promises him *mild* apples and soft chestnuts—*mitia poma, castaneæ molles.* I frequently pluck wild apples of so rich and spicy a flavor that I wonder all orchardists do not get a scion from that tree, and I fail not to bring home my pockets full. But, perchance, when I take one out of my desk and taste it in my chamber, I find it unexpectedly crude—sour enough to set a squirrel's teeth on edge and make a jay scream. These apples have hung in the wind and frost and rain till they have absorbed the qualities of the weather or season, and thus are highly *seasoned*, and they *pierce* and *sting* and *permeate* us with their spirit. They must be eaten in *season*, accordingly—that is, out of doors.

To appreciate the wild and sharp flavors of these October fruits, it is necessary that you be breathing the sharp October or November air. The outdoor air and exercise which the walker gets give a different tone to his palate, and he craves a fruit which the sedentary would call harsh and crabbed. They must be eaten in the fields, when your system is all aglow with exercise, when the frosty weather nips your fingers, the wind rattles the bare boughs or rustles the few remaining leaves, and the jay is heard screaming around. What is sour in the house a bracing walk makes sweet. Some of these apples might be labelled, "To be eaten in the wind."

Of course, no flavors are thrown away; they are intended for the taste that is up to them. Some apples have two distinct flavors, and perhaps one half of them must be eaten in the house, the other outdoors. One Peter Whitney wrote from Northborough in 1782, for the *Proceedings of the Boston Academy*, describing an apple tree in that town "producing fruit of opposite qualities, part of the same apple being frequently sour and the other sweet"; also some all sour and others all sweet, and this diversity on all parts of the tree.

There is a wild apple on Nawshawtuct Hill in my town which has to me a peculiarly pleasant bitter tang, not perceived till it is three-quarters tasted. It remains on the tongue. As you eat it, it smells exactly like a squash-bug. It is a sort of triumph to eat and relish it.

I hear that the fruit of a kind of plum tree in Provence is "called *prunes sibarelles*, because it is impossible to whistle after having eaten them, from their sourness." But perhaps they were only eaten in the house and in summer, and if tried out of doors in a stinging atmosphere, who knows but you could whistle an octave higher and clearer?

In the fields only are the sours and bitters of Nature appreciated; just as the woodchopper eats his meal in a sunny glade in the middle of a winter day with content, basks in a sunny ray there, and dreams of summer in a degree of cold which, experienced in a chamber, would make a student miserable. They who are at work abroad are not cold, but rather it is they who sit shivering in houses. As with temperatures, so with flavors; as with cold and heat, so with sour and sweet. This natural raciness, the sours and bitters which the diseased palate refuses, are the true condiments. Let your condiments be in the condition of your senses. To appreciate the flavor of these wild apples requires vigorous and healthy senses, *papillæ* firm and erect on the tongue and palate, not easily flattened and tamed.

From my experience with wild apples, I can understand that there may be reason for a savage's preferring many kinds of food which the civilized man rejects. The former has the palate of an outdoor man. It takes a savage or wild taste to appreciate a wild fruit. What a healthy out-of-door appetite it takes to relish the apple of life, the apple of the world, then!

> Nor is it every apple I desire,
> > Nor that which pleases every palate best;
> 'T is not the lasting Deuxan I require,
> > Nor yet the red-cheeked Greening I request,
> Nor that which first beshrewed the name of wife,
> Nor that whose beauty caused the golden strife:
> No, no! bring me an apple from the tree of life!

So there is one *thought* for the field, another for the house. I would have my thoughts, like wild apples, to be food for walkers and will not warrant them to be palatable if tasted in the house.

Almost all wild apples are handsome. They cannot be too gnarly and crabbed and rusty to look at. The gnarliest will have some redeeming traits even to the eye. You will discover some evening redness dashed or sprinkled on some protuberance or in some cavity. It is rare that the summer lets an apple go without streaking or spotting it on some part of its sphere. It will have some red stains, commemorating the mornings and evenings it has witnessed; some dark and rusty blotches, in memory of the clouds and foggy, mildewy days that have passed over it; and a spacious field of green reflecting the general face of Nature—green even as the fields; or a yellow ground, which implies a milder flavor—yellow as the harvest or russet as the hills.

Apples, these I mean, unspeakably fair—apples not of Discord, but of Concord! Yet not so rare but that the homeliest may have a share. Painted by the frosts, some a uniform, clear, bright yellow, or red, or crimson, as if their spheres had regularly revolved and enjoyed the influence of the sun on all sides alike; some with the faintest pink blush imaginable; some brindled with deep red streaks like a cow or with hundreds of fine blood-red rays running regularly from the stem dimple to the blossom end, like meridional lines on a straw-colored ground; some touched with a greenish rust like a fine lichen here and there, with crimson blotches or eyes more or less confluent and fiery when wet; and others gnarly and freckled or peppered all over on the stem side with fine crimson spots on a white ground, as if accidentally sprinkled from the brush of Him who paints the autumn leaves. Others, again, are sometimes red inside, perfused with a beautiful blush, fairy food, too beautiful to eat—apple of the Hesperides, apple of the evening sky! But like shells and pebbles on the seashore, they must be seen as they sparkle amid the withering leaves in some dell in the woods, in the autumnal air, or as they lie in the wet grass, and not when they have wilted and faded in the house.

It would be a pleasant pastime to find suitable names for the hundred varieties which go to a single heap at the cider mill. Would it not tax a man's invention— no one to be named after a man and all in the *lingua vernacula?* Who shall stand godfather at the christening of the wild apples? It would exhaust the Latin and Greek languages, if they were used, and make the *lingua vernacula* flag. We should have to call in the sunrise and the sunset, the rainbow and the autumn woods and the wild flowers, and the woodpecker and the purple finch and the squirrel and the jay and the butterfly, the November traveller and the truant boy, to our aid.

In 1836 there were in the garden of the London Horticultural Society more than fourteen hundred distinct sorts. But here are species which they have not in their catalogue, not to mention the varieties which our crab might yield to cultivation.

Let us enumerate a few of these. I find myself compelled, after all, to give the Latin names of some for the benefit of those who live where English is not spoken—for they are likely to have a worldwide reputation.

There is, first of all, the Wood Apple (*Malus sylvatica*); the Blue-jay Apple; the apple which grows in dells in the woods (*Malus sylvestrivallis*), also in hollows in pastures (*Malus campestrivallis*); the apple that grows in an old cellar hole (*Malus cellaris*); the Meadow Apple; the Partridge Apple; the Truant's Apple (*Malus cessatoris*), which no boy will ever go by without knocking off some, however *late* it may be; the Saunterer's Apple—you must lose yourself before you can find the way to that; the Beauty-of-the-air (*Malus decus-æris*); December-eating; the Frozen-thawed (*Malus gelato-soluta*), good only in that state; the Concord Apple, possibly the same with the *Malus musketaquidensis*; the Assabet Apple; the Brindled Apple; Wine of New England; the Chickaree Apple; the Green Apple (*Malus viridis*), this has many synonyms: in an imperfect state it is the *Cholera morbifera aut dysenterifera, puerulis dilectissima*; the apple which Atalanta stopped to pick up; the Hedge Apple (*Malus sepium*); the Slug Apple (*Malus limacea*); the Railroad Apple, which perhaps came from a core thrown out of the cars; the apple whose fruit we tasted in our youth; our Particular Apple, not to be found in any catalogue, *Malus pedestrium-solatium*; also the apple where hangs the forgotten scythe; Iduna's Apple; the apple which Loki found in the wood; and a great many more I have on my list, too numerous to mention—all of them good. As Bodæus exclaims, referring to the cultivated kinds and adapting Virgil to his case, so I, adapting Bodæus:

> Not if I had a hundred tongues, a hundred mouths,
> An iron voice, could I describe all the forms
> And reckon up all the names of these *wild apples*.

By the middle of November the wild apples have lost some of their brilliancy and have chiefly fallen. A great part are decayed on the ground, and the sound ones are more palatable than before. The note of the chickadee sounds now more distinct as you wander amid the old trees, and the autumnal dandelion is half closed and tearful. But still, if you are a skillful gleaner, you may get many a pocketful even of grafted fruit long after apples are supposed to be gone out of doors. I know a blue-pearmain tree growing within the edge of a swamp almost as good as wild. You would not suppose that there was any fruit left there, on the first survey, but you must look according to system. Those which lie exposed are quite brown and rotten now, or perchance a few still show one blooming cheek here and there amid the wet leaves. Nevertheless, with experienced eyes I explore amid the bare alders and the huckleberry bushes and the withered sedge, and in the crevices of the rocks, which are full of leaves, and pry under the fallen and decaying ferns, which, with apple and alder leaves, thickly strew the ground. For I know that they lie concealed, fallen into hollows long since and covered up by the leaves of the tree itself—a proper kind of packing. From these lurking places anywhere within the circumference of the tree I draw forth the fruit, all wet and glossy, maybe nibbled by rabbits and hollowed out by crickets, and perhaps with a leaf or two cemented to it (as Curzon an old manuscript from a monastery's mouldy cellar), but still with a rich bloom on it, and at least as ripe and well kept, if not better than those in barrels, more crisp and lively than they. If these resources fail to yield anything, I have learned to look between the bases of the suckers which spring thickly from some horizontal limb, for now and then one lodges there, or in the very midst of an alder clump, where they are covered by leaves, safe from cows which may have smelled them out. If I am sharp set, for I do not refuse the blue pearmain, I fill my pockets on each side; and as I retrace my steps in the frosty eve, being perhaps four or five miles from home, I eat one first from this side and then from that to keep my balance.

I learn from Topsell's *Gesner,* whose authority appears to be Albertus, that the following is the way in which the hedgehog collects and carries home his apples. He says, "His meat is apples, worms, or grapes: when he findeth apples or grapes on the earth, he rolleth himself upon them, until he have filled all his prickles, and then carrieth them home to his den, never bearing above one in his mouth; and if it fortune that one of them fall off by the way, he likewise shaketh off all the residue, and walloweth upon them afresh, until they be all settled upon his back again. So, forth he goeth, making a noise like a cartwheel; and if he have any young ones in his nest, they pull off his load wherewithal he is loaded, eating thereof what they please, and laying up the residue for the time to come."

Toward the end of November, though some of the sound ones are yet more mellow and perhaps more edible, they have generally, like the leaves, lost their beauty and are beginning to freeze. It is finger cold, and prudent farmers get in their barrelled apples, and bring you the apples and cider which they have engaged; for it is time to put them into the cellar. Perhaps a few on the ground show their red cheeks above the early snow, and occasionally some even preserve their color and soundness under the snow throughout the winter. But generally, at the beginning of the winter they freeze hard and soon, though undecayed, acquire the color of a baked apple.

Before the end of December, generally, they experience their first thawing. Those which a month ago were sour, crabbed, and quite unpalatable to the civilized taste, such at least as were frozen while sound, let a warmer sun come to thaw them, for they are extremely sensitive to its rays, are found to be filled with a rich, sweet cider, better than any bottled cider that I know of and with which I am better acquainted than with wine. All apples are good in this state, and your jaws are the cider press. Others, which have more substance, are a sweet and luscious food—in my opinion of more worth than the pine-apples which are imported from the West Indies. Those which lately even I tasted only to repent of it—for I am semi-civilized—which the farmer willingly left on the tree, I am now glad to find have the property of hanging on like the leaves of the young oaks. It is a way to keep cider sweet without boiling. Let the frost come to freeze them first, solid as stones, and then the rain or a warm winter day to thaw them, and they will seem to have borrowed a flavor from heaven through the medium of the air in which they hang. Or perchance you find, when you get home, that those which rattled in your pocket have thawed, and the ice is turned to cider. But after the third or fourth freezing and thawing they will not be found so good.

What are the imported half-ripe fruits of the torrid South, to this fruit matured by the cold of the frigid North? These are those crabbed apples with which I cheated my companion and kept a smooth face that I might tempt him to eat. Now we both greedily fill our pockets with them—bending to drink the cup and save our lappets from the overflowing juice—and grow more social with their wine. Was there one that hung so high and sheltered by the tangled branches that our sticks could not dislodge it?

It is a fruit never carried to market, that I am aware of—quite distinct from the apple of the markets, as from dried apple and cider—and it is not every winter that produces it in perfection.

The era of the wild apple will soon be past. It is a fruit which will probably become extinct in New England. You may still wander through old orchards of native fruit of great extent, which for the most part went to the cider mill, now all gone to decay. I have heard of an orchard in a distant town on the side of a hill where the apples rolled down and lay four feet deep against a wall on the lower side, and this the owner cut down for fear they should be made into cider. Since the temperance reform and the general introduction of grafted fruit, no native apple trees, such as I see everywhere in deserted pastures and where the woods have grown up around them, are set out. I fear that he who walks over these fields a century hence will not know the pleasure of knocking off wild apples. Ah, poor man, there are many pleasures which he will not know. Notwithstanding the prevalence of the Baldwin and the Porter, I doubt if so extensive orchards are set out today in my town as there were a century ago, when those vast, straggling cider-orchards were planted, when men both ate and drank apples, when the pomace heap was the only nursery, and trees cost nothing but the trouble of setting them out. Men could afford then to stick a tree by every wall side and let it take its chance. I see nobody planting trees today in such out-of-the-way places, along the lonely roads and lanes, and at the bottom of dells in the wood. Now that they have grafted trees and pay a price for them, they collect them into a plat by their houses and fence them in—and the end of it all will be that we shall be compelled to look for our apples in a barrel.

ALTERNATE CORNEL

Alternate cornel. I see it beginning as early as July twenty-first.

This is an interesting small tree, often with a flat top, with a peculiarly spotted bark, yellow when dead, and peculiarly ribbed and green leaves, and pretty red stems supporting its harmless blue berries, which are inclined to drop off. It grows along walls, as between Holden Swamp and Miles's. The berries, which are the earliest of our cornels, are in open cymes, dark, dull-blue, depressed, globular, tipt with the persistent styles, but fall very soon *or are eaten by birds* as soon as they ripen, are mostly gone by the twenty-eighth of August; but the red peduncles and pedicels which are left bare are the handsomest far, like fairy fingers spread. These, being arranged in cymes, make a show at the distance of a dozen rods even. There is something light and open about this *tree*, but it is witch-like nevertheless.

RUBUS SEMPERVARIENS

The *Rubus sempervariens* begins July twenty-sixth in open and higher ground, but not common till the middle of August, and is in prime toward the end of August, say the twenty-fifth. Have seen them abundant September seventh and I know not how much later.

This a small, late blackberry growing in low ground, as at the bottom of hollows in the woods and along the edges of meadows, in maple swamps, and so on, with small, glossy, and ever-green leaves which are much indented along the veins. In open hollows it forms dense beds, like a matting covering the ground seven or eight inches deep. It bears a very small black fruit not abundant till the common low blackberries are for the most part gone. They are a peculiar and hardly agreeable acid. Yet, though not commonly eaten, they are quite edible; some call them snake blackberries—I know not for what reason except that snakes must have some things named after them as well as other things, and men can afford to give them these, and moreover that snakes are common in the moist and cool places where they grow. The berries are especially abundant where the vines lie over a stump.

STAGHORN SUMAC

Staghorn sumac, July twenty-sixth, 1860, just out of bloom and fruit as handsome as ever.

BRISTLY ARALIA

The bristly-aralia berries begin about July twenty-eighth, in their prime in August, and are getting stale by September fourth.

This plant grows often in *dense* patches on sandy banks and by the edges of woods in sproutlands, bearing its fruit in numerous umbels, perfect hemispheres of dark-blue or blue-black berries about the size of a huckleberry, and much like the sarsaparilla berry in color, on slender pedicels of equal length, forming a dense, hemispherical umbel two inches in diameter. I counted one hundred and thirty berries in one umbel. The central ones ripen first.

SOLANUM DULCAMARA

The *Solanum dulcamara*, bitter-sweet, or nightshade berries begin July twenty-eighth; are in their prime in August and September; but last in and over water even through November, but more or less shrivelled.

These bright-red berries are still handsomer than the flowers. This is one of the kinds that grow in *drooping clusters,* and I do not know of any more graceful and beautiful clusters than these. Those in the water at the bend of the river are peculiarly handsome, they are so long an oval or ellipse. (A drooping berry should always be of an oval or pear shape, drop-like.) No berries that I am acquainted with are so agreeably arrayed, somewhat hexagonally, like a small wasp nest. The cymes are of singular yet regular form, not too crowded, but elegantly spaced, not stiff and flat, but in different stages above and around—finding ample room in the universe.

Then what variety of color! The peduncle and its branches are green, the pedicels and sepals only a rare steel-blue purple, and the berries scarlet or translucent cherry-red.

They hang more gracefully over the river's brim than any pendants in a lady's ear. Yet they are considered poisonous! Not to look at, surely. Is it not a reproach that so much that is beautiful is poisonous to us? But why should they not be poisonous to eat? Would it not be *in bad taste* to eat those berries which are ready to feed another sense?

Gerarde thus describes the "Bitter-sweet, or Woody Nightshade," our *dulcamara,* but not the Deadly Nightshade:

Bitter-sweet bringeth forth woody stalks as doth the Vine, parted into many slender creeping branches, by which it climbeth and taketh hold of hedges and shrubs next unto it. The bark of the oldest stalks is rough and whitish, of the color of ashes, with the outward rind of a bright green color, but the younger branches are green as are the leaves; the wood brittle, having in it a spongie pith; it is clad with long leaves, smooth, sharp pointed, lesser than those of the Binde-weed. At the lower part of the same leaves doth grow on either side one small or lesser leaf like unto two ears. The flowers be small and somewhat clustered together, consisting of five little leaves apiece, of a perfect blue color, with a certain prick or yellow pointall in the middle; which being past, there do come in place fair berries, more long than round, at the first green, but very red when they be ripe; of a sweet taste at the first, but after very unpleasant, of a strong savor, growing together in clusters like burnished coral. The root is of a mean bigness and full of strings.

The juice [of the plant] is good for those that have fallen from high places, and have been thereby bruised or dry beaten: for it is thought to dissolve blood congealed or cluttered any where in the intrals, and to heal the hurt places.

This is a fair example of Gerard's style of description. Since it grows in the crevices of bank walls, we are likely to be "dry-beaten" sometimes in climbing to it.

TRILLIUM

Trillium berries are already pink by the twenty-second or twenty-fourth, begin to be *ripe* say the thirtieth, in prime the middle of August, and last till September.

Most who know the flower of this plant are unacquainted with the fruit. The trillium berry is very handsome and large; six-sided or angled; three-fourths or even an inch in diameter nearing the puff and seeds; drooping, with the red anthers surrounding it, under its green leaves in shady swamps. It is glossy red or the color of stained and varnished cherry wood, growing darker red with age. Later in August the plant lies prostrate on the ground, revealing its fruit; or those which stood on the brink of rills, falling over, bathe their red berries in the cold water just from the bowels of the earth and wave in the stream.

Perhaps fruits are colored like the trillium berry and the scarlet thorn to attract birds to them.

Sagard, in his *Grand Voyage*, describing the small fruit of the Huron country, says, "There are some red, which seem almost of coral, and which *viennent quasi contre terre* in little bouquets, with two or three leaves, resembling the laurel, and seem very beautiful bouquets, and would serve for such if there were any here."

DWARF CORNEL

Dwarf cornel or bunchberry begins say July thirtieth, lasts long on mountains, rarely bears here—the bright scarlet fruit arranged in little "bunches" in the center of its whorl of leaves. All who have climbed on mountains must remember it and have eaten it, though it is of no consequence as food. But in more northern latitudes, where edible fruits are scarce, they make an account of haws and bunchberries. You commonly cross a zone of their scarlet clusters not far below the summit of our higher mountains.

SUMMER SQUASH

Summer squash, July thirtieth, 1860, notice them yellow.

BLACK CHERRY

The wild black cherry begins to be ripe by July thirty-first. It is in prime the latter part of August *in sproutlands* and lasts till the middle of September *at least*.

Michaux says that "The wild cherry tree is one of the largest productions of the American forests." The very young trees which grow in sproutlands bear much the largest and finest fruit, and some of it is very juicy and agreeable, though it varies much—that is, some much better than others—very superior to the small and bitter ones on large trees. They are in their prime in such places about the twenty-eighth of August and are sometimes quite abundant, the branches drooping with them. By the first of September, when the huckleberries are dried up or wormy, these are almost the only small fruit which the walker finds to pluck.

The birds make much account of them, and about the first of September that locality where a wild cherry stands will be all alive with them, coming and going, though the rest of the country may appear silent and deserted.

They bear so abundantly that you can strip off more than your hands can hold from their great black wreaths—green, ripe, and imperfect—and their astringency is very grateful at that season. Some, I hear, make a spiritous drink with them, which they disguise under such names as "cherry-bounce." The common way of gathering them is to shake them down upon sheets spread beneath the tree. I remember once shaking a tree in this wise, and when I came to gather up the edges of the cloth, I found an old cent of the last century among the cherries.

September 1, 1859. Wild red cherry and elderberry for *birds* the two prevailing fruits now.

BLACK CURRANT

Black currants are ripe about the first of August.

I find them wild in only three or four localities. Josselyn speaks of "red and black currants."

HOUND'S-TONGUE

I notice hound's-tongue seeds about August first; at height perhaps the middle of August.

I thoughtlessly put a handful of the nutlets in my pocket with my handkerchief, but it took me a long time to pick them out of my handkerchief when I got home, and I pulled out many threads in the process. I know of but one place in this town where it is naturalized. In the spring of 1857 I gave some of the above-named seeds (gathered the previous August) to a young lady who cultivates a flower garden and to my sister—wishing to spread it, it is so rare. Their expectations were excited and kept on the *qui vive* for a long time, for it does not blossom till the second year. The flower and peculiar odor were sufficiently admired in due time, but now and for a long time it has been regarded as a pest in the garden on account of its seeds clinging to your clothes. I have spent twenty minutes at one time in clearing myself of it, and that young gardener's mother, who frequently takes a turn in the flower garden, found that she had carried an abundance to Boston thus on her dress.

So it is in a fair way to be dispersed, and my purpose is accomplished.

THISTLE

I begin to see thistledown in the air about the second of August, and thenceforward till winter. We notice it chiefly in August and September.

What is called the Canada thistle is the earliest, and the goldfinch or thistlebird *(Carduelis tristis)*, for he gets his name from his food *(carduus* being the Latin for "a thistle"), knows when it is ripe sooner than I. So soon as the heads begin to be dry, I see him pulling them to pieces and scattering the down, for he sets it a-flying regularly every year all over the country, just as I do once in a long while.

The Romans had their *Carduelis* or thistle-bird also, which Pliny speaks of as the smallest of their birds, for eating thistle seeds is no modern or transient habit with this genus. The thistle seed would oftener remain attached to its receptacle till it decayed with moisture or fell directly to the ground beneath if this bird did not come like a midwife to release it—to launch it in the atmosphere and send it to seek its fortune, taking toll the while by swallowing a few seeds.

All children are inspired by a similar instinct and, judging from the results, probably for a similar purpose. They can hardly keep their hands off the opening thistle-head. Mudie, speaking of the food of the English goldfinch, observes that it is especially the winged seeds of those *compositæ* which "keep the air powdered all summer over with the excess of their productiveness" and that of these "there is a constant succession all the year through, for the wind has not shaken the autumnal thistles bare by the time that the early groundsels are in flower; and to these the dandelion and many other species are soon added."

The thistles have a grayish-white and a much coarser pappus than the milkweeds, and it begins to fly earlier. The first sight of it floating through the air is interesting and stimulating to me as an evidence of the lapse of the season, and I make a note of the first which I see annually.

It is remarkable how commonly you see the thistledown sailing low over water, and quite across such ponds as Walden and Fair Haven. For example, at five o'clock one afternoon last year, just after rain, being on the middle of Walden, I saw many seedless thistledowns (sometimes they are seeded) sailing about a foot above the surface, yet there was little or no wind. It is as if they were attracted to the pond and there were a current just above the surface which commonly prevented their falling or rising while it drove them along. They are probably wafted to the water from the neighboring hollows and hillsides where they grow because the currents of air tend to the opening above the water as their playground.

Here is a wise balloonist for you, crossing its Atlantic, perhaps going to plant a thistle seed on the other side; and if it comes down in a wilderness, it will be at home there.

Theophrastus, who lived three hundred and fifty years before Christ, has this among his weather signs, that "when many thistledowns [*spinarum lanugines*, says the old translation] are borne dispersed over the sea, they announce that there will be a very high wind"; and Phillips, in his *History of Cultivated Vegetables*, says, "The shepherd when he sees the thistledown agitated without an appearance of wind,

'And shakes the forest leaf without a breath,'

drives his flocks to shelter and cries, Heaven protect yon vessel from the approaching tempest!"

COHOSHES

Cohosh, white and red (*Actæa spicata*, var. *alba* and *rubra*), both begin about August sixth. The fruit is in prime about August thirty-first and lasts till September twenty-third at least.

About the first of September the white cohosh startles the intruder into moist and shaded grounds with its remarkable spike of ivory-white berries, which contrast singularly with the greenness around. The berries are wax-white, as if they contained a pearly venom, tipped with a very dark-brown or black spot, imp-eyed, on stout red pedicels.

The *red* variety is rarer hereabouts. In this, the berries are red, on slender pedicels. (One which I pluck has a round conical spike two and a half inches long by one and three-quarters wide, and contains about thirty cherry-red berries. The

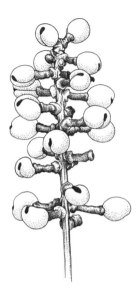

berries are oblong, seven-sixteenths of an inch by six-sixteenths, with a seam on one side, on slender pedicels about five-eighths of an inch long.) I have seen the berries ripe in Maine earlier than here.

Cornutus evidently describes and figures the two cohoshes as *"Aconitum baccis niveis et rubris."*

COMMON CRANBERRY

It may be a question when the common cranberry is *ripe*. Perhaps it never gets fairly ripe, or ceases growing, before the frosts come. It is not edible raw till softened by the frost and turned a crimson red quite late in the fall. It acquires its full color as early as August sixth in some places, and some begin to rake them before the first of September even, some years, for fear of frosts; and I see them raking them as late as September twenty-fourth. They commonly rake them from the fifth to the twentieth of September.

In the middle of July the green berries are as big as peas and remind me of the advancing season. Early in August their cheeks begin to redden, especially if they grow on rather dry and elevated or sandy ground along the edge of the meadows, and they are then a very fair fruit to behold. Some are already wholly red, like varnished cherry wood.

Cranberries are very often frostbitten in the latter part of August and the crop much reduced. They are also *softened* and spoiled by the water standing over them in a flood at that season. Some think it depends on the warmth of the water how much they are injured. I perceive that in *some* places the greatest injuries done by the water is that it prevents their ripening. Sometimes the water is still high when they are raked. They carry them home, spread and dry them, and pick out the spoilt ones.

By the middle of September, as I sail up our river, I perceive that, instead of haying, they are raking cranberries all along the river. The raker moves slowly along with a basket before him, into which he rakes the berries, and his wagon stands on one side. I see others far away squatting in the meadows where they are picking them by hand. These are perhaps women and children who glean after the rakers.

Some regard the pear-shaped cranberries, which are not uncommon, as a different species from the round ones. And I have seem one picking over his cran-

berries in the house and putting by themselves those of a peculiar and, as he thought, better kind than the rest. They were very dark red, shaded with lighter—harder and more oblong, somewhat like a sweet-briar hip or a Canada plum. He said that they grew apart from the others.

In the fall of 1853 there was an unusual flood on our meadows which washed up great quantities of cranberries which had been loosened by the rake, and the shore on the lee side was lined with them, mixed with wrecked grass and weeds, and peppered with myriads of snow fleas. As I paddled over the meadows November fifteenth, I saw a great many cranberries on the vines at the bottom, making a great show.

The twentieth of November that year I had my first experience in raking cranberries. Being up the river in my boat, I met with and saved a broken cranberry rake on its way to the sea, and soon after I saw that all the lee shore of some meadow was reddened with the berries mixed with chaff so that I could see them fifteen or twenty rods off coloring it. I got a boat-load—chaff, water, and all—but it was a good deal of trouble to cleanse them, and going again I sent two and a half bushels to Boston and got four dollars for them.

Raking so many cranberries out of the water made me quite conversant with the materials which compose the river wrack. There was an abundance of chaff—that is, broken meadow grass and cranberry leaves with little bugle-shaped snails and middle-sized black daw bugs and bits of yellow-lily roots which the musquash had gnawed, and occasionally a frog or a painted tortoise in it—and these all were peppered over and alive with skipping snow fleas. This chaff and so on was an assistance in getting the cranberries into my boat with an iron rake.

I found that the best way to get them would be to go forth in time of flood, just before the water began to fall and after strong winds had driven them to the shore; then, choosing the thickest places, let one with an instrument like a large coarse dung fork hold down the floating grass and other coarser parts of the wrack mingled with it, while the other with a common rake rakes the berries and chaff into the boat, there being just enough chaff left to enable you to raise them.

I once came near speculating in cranberries. Being hard pushed to get my living and having occasion to go to New York to peddle pencils, it occurred to me that perhaps I might export cranberries thither to my advantage. So as I passed thro' Boston I went to Quincy Market and inquired the price of cranberries. One dealer took me down-cellar, asked if I wanted wet or dry, and showed me what he had. I gave them to understand that I might want an indefinite quantity. It made a considerable sensation among the sellers and for aught I know raised the price of this berry for a time. I then visited various New York packets and was told by the masters what would be the freight of cranberries on deck and in the hold (wet and dry), and one skipper was very anxious for my freight. When I got to New York (for I was prudent enough to go first without the cranberries), I visited the markets there as a purchaser, and "the best of eastern cranberries" were offered me at a cheaper rate than I could buy them at in Boston.

I was over picking cranberries in Merriam's pasture thirty years ago, when suddenly I saw and heard one whom we boys amicably called Old Foster come after me with great strength. I caught my pail and, being young and active, as most boys are at twelve, I soon distanced him, though he steadily pursued; but I climbed the walls nimbly and at length reaching the village I dodged among the houses, and then I lost him and he at the same time lost me. I did not know till then that cranberries were private property.

In the *Geological Survey of Canada for 1853, 1854, 1855, and 1856:* At Lake Nipissing "I was informed by an Indian, that he and his family, which consisted of his wife and two small children, could easily gather from four to five barrels of cranberries [does not say which species] in a day, for which they were paid, on delivery at Shi-bah-ah-mah-ming, at the rate of $5 the barrel; and that the only difficulty which they had in making the trade a very profitable one, was the small amount their canoes were capable of conveying at a time, together with the shortness of the season previous to the formation of the ice."

About the middle of November, when some are frostbitten ere having fully ripened, I discover again that cranberries are good to eat in small quantities as you are crossing the meadows. They have the pleasant taste of spring cranberries. If the water is high enough they generally begin to wash up at this season, and this you might consider their true ripening. I sometimes find a few, however, in December, quite hard and not touched by the frost. Though many are decayed and spoiled, many more are merely mellowed and ripened by the cold and wet, and are preserved in the best condition all winter. We country people give the preference to these spring cranberries.

It might in some cases be worth the while to flood a meadow before the severe frosts come, and so preserve the berries plump and fresh till spring.

No sooner has the river broken up and the meadows partially cleared in March than I see someone whose palate requires to be humored and provoked out in his boat looking for this salad or sauce to relieve the monotony of his winter fare. At the least the gunner makes sure of these when no musquash shows himself. But no doubt we are all in a measure renovated and more surely keep pace with the season by tasting this wholesome native acid, with which lime juice is not to be compared. In the Musketaquid meadows is our acetarium and vinegar cruet. I always make it a point to taste a few if only that I may be acclimated. A little later, when the spring freshet and the wind have collected them along the shore of the meadows and the river, mixed with the coarse river wrack—these, and those frozen in—the children make a business of gathering them and selling them by the quart, and the ducks going northward dive for those which are still attached to the vines.

We require just so much acid as the cranberries afford in the spring. No tarts that I ever tasted at any table possessed such a refreshing, cheering, encouraging acid that literally put the heart in you and set you on edge for this world's experiences, bracing the spirit, as the cranberries I have plucked in the meadows in the spring. They cut the winter's phlegm, and now you can swallow another year of this world without other sauce. Even on the Thanksgiving table they are comparatively insipid, have lost as much flavor as beauty. They are never so beautiful as in water. In the markets and aboard ships they ask if you will have wet or dry, if they shall be transported on deck or in the hold, but to my mind the only wet cask in which to get them is the flooded meadows in the spring. I remember a little boy who was said to have been killed by eating too many cranberries found about the shore, but surely he died because he did not eat them every day of his life.

Frequently, when sailing over the middle sea of our meadows with the helm tied up, looking over the side, I have a vision of a cranberry bed which has escaped the rake, deep under my keel, with a thousand bright-red berries stirring upward as far as their vines will permit—a desirable place to loiter if you can go about quietly enough to find the place again.

I have seen some handsome patches of cultivated cranberries in Harwich and Provincetown on Cape Cod, some containing ten or twelve acres in one piece. They occupy a reclaimed meadow adjoining a pond or swamp, just sand enough being carted on to raise the surface a few inches above the level of the water, and then the plants are set in the coarse white sand, in perfectly straight rows which

are eighteen inches apart, and what with the runners and the moss and so on between, they soon form a perfectly level and uniform green bed, very striking and
handsome.

WATERMELONS

Watermelons. The first are ripe from August seventh to twenty-eighth
(though the last is late), and they continue to ripen till they freeze; are in their
prime in September.

John Josselyn, an old resident in New England, speaks of the watermelon as
one of the plants "proper to the country." He says that it is "of a sad grass-green
color, or more rightly sap green; with some yellowness admixed when ripe."

September is come with its profusion of large fruits. Melons and apples seem
at once to feed my brain.

How differently we fare now from what we did in winter! We give the butcher
no encouragement now, but invite him to take a walk in our garden.

I have no respect for those who cannot raise melons or who avoid them as unwholesome. They should be spending their third winter with Parry in the arctic
regions. They seem to have taken in their provisions at the commencement of the
cruise, I know now how many years ago, and they deserve to have a monument
erected to them of the empty cans which held their preserved meats.

Our diet, like that of the birds, must answer to the season. This is the season
of west-looking, watery fruits. In the dog-days we come near to sustaining our lives
on watermelon juice alone, like those who have fevers. I know of no more agreeable and nutritious food at this season than bread and butter and melons, and you
need not be afraid of eating too much of the latter.

When I am going a-berrying in my boat or other carriage, I frequently carry
watermelons for drink. It is the most agreeable and refreshing wine in a convenient cask, and most easily kept cool. Carry these green bottles of wine. When you
get to the field you put them in the shade or in water till you want them.

When at home, if you would cool a watermelon which has been lying in the
sun, do not put it in water, which keeps the heat in, but cut it open and place it
on a cellar bottom or in a draught of air in the shade.

There are various ways in which you can tell if a watermelon is ripe. If you have had your eye on the patch much from the first, and so know the history of each one and which was formed first, you may presume that those will ripen soonest. Or else you may incline to those which lie nearest to the center of the hill or root, as the oldest.

Next, the dull, dead color and want of bloom are as good signs as any. Some *look* green and livid, and have a very fog of bloom on them, like a mildew. These are as green as a leek through and through, and you'll find yourself in a pickle if you open one. Others have a dead dark-greenness, the circulations coming less rapid in their cuticles and their blooming period passed, and these you may safely bet on.

If the vine is quite lively, the death of the quirl at the root of the stem is almost a sure sign. Lest we should not discern it before, this is placed for a sign that there is redness and ripeness within. Of two, otherwise similar, take that which yields the lowest tone when struck with your knuckles, that is, which is hollowest. The old or ripe ones ring bass; the young, tenor or falsetto. Some use the violent method of pressing to hear if they crack within, but this is not to be allowed. Above all no tapping on the vine is to be tolerated, suggestive of a greediness which defeats its own purpose. It is very childish.

One man told me that he couldn't raise melons because his children *would cut them all up*. I think that he convicted himself out of his own mouth. It was evident that he could not raise children in the way they should go and was not fit to be the ruler of a country, according to Confucius's standard. I once, looking by a special providence through the blinds, saw one of his boys astride of my earliest watermelon, which grew near a broken paling, and brandishing a case-knife over it, but I instantly blowed him off with my voice before serious damage was done— and I made such an ado about it as convinced him that he was not in his father's dominions, at any rate. This melon, though it lost some of its bloom then, grew to be a remarkably large and sweet one, though it bore, to the last, a triangular scar of the tap which the thief had designed on it.

The farmer is obliged to hide his melon patch far away in the midst of his corn or potatoes. I sometimes stumble on it in my rambles. I see one today where the watermelons are intermixed with carrots in a carrot bed and so concealed by the general resemblance of the leaves at a little distance.

It is an old saying that you cannot carry two melons under one arm. Indeed, it is difficult to carry one far, it is so slippery. I remember hearing of a lady who had been to visit her friends in Lincoln, and when she was ready to return on foot, they made her the rather onerous present of a watermelon. With this under her arm she tript it glibly through the Walden Woods, which had a rather bad reputation for goblins and so on in those days. While the wood grew thicker and thicker, and the imaginary dangers greater, the melon did not grow any lighter, though frequently shifted from arm to arm; and at length, it may have been through the agency of one of those mischievous goblins, it slipt from under her arm, and in a moment lay in a dozen pieces in the middle of the Walden road. Quick as thought the trembling traveller gathered up the most luscious and lightest fragments with her handkerchief, and flew rather than ran with them to the peaceful streets of Concord.

If you have any watermelons left when the frosts come, you may put them into your cellar and keep them till Thanksgiving time. I have seen a large patch in the woods frozen quite hard, and when cracked open they had a very handsome crystalline look.

Watermelons, said to be unknown to the Greeks and Romans. It is said to be one of those fruits of Egypt which the Jewish people regretted in the desert under the name of *abbattichim*.

The English botanists may be said to know nothing about watermelons. The nearest that Gerarde gets to our watermelon is in his chapter on "Citrull Cucumbers," where he says, "The meat or pulp of Cucumer Citrill which is next unto the bark is eaten."

In Spence's *Anecdotes* it is said that Galileo used to compare Ariosto's *Orlando* to a melon field. "You may meet with a very good thing here and there in it, but the whole is of very little value." Montaigne says, quoting Aurelius Victor, "The emperor Dioclesian, having resigned his crown and retired to 'private life,' was some time after solicited to resume his charge, but he announced, 'You would not offer to persuade me to this, had you seen the fine condition of the trees I have planted in my orchard, and the fair melons I have sowed in my garden.' " Gosse, in his *Letters from Alabama,* says of the watermelon, "I am not aware that it is known in England; I have never seen it exposed in the London markets," but it is abundant all over the United States; and in the South:

The very negroes have their own melon "patches," as well as their peach orchards, and it is no small object of their ambition to raise earlier or finer specimens than their masters. . . . [It] may be considered as the best realization of the French princess's idea of "ice with the chill taken off." . . . A cart-load is brought home from the field nearly every evening, to supply the demand of the family for the next day; for during this torrid weather, very little business but the eating of watermelons is transacted. If a guest call, the first offering of friendship is a glass of cold water as soon as seated; then there is an immediate shout for watermelons, and each taking his own, several are destroyed before the knife is laid down. The ladies cut the hard part, near the rind, into stars, and other pretty shapes, which they candy as a conserve for winter.

ELDERBERRIES

Elderberries begin to be ripe by August seventh, have fairly begun August twenty-fifth, and are in prime September fourth and twelfth. I notice the green berries the latter part of July.

On the twenty-second of August I have seen the elderberry bushes weighed down with fruit partially turned and *still in bloom* at the extremities of their twigs. The great black cymes begin to be conspicuous, weighing down the bushes along fences near the end of August. The clusters swell and become heavy and there-

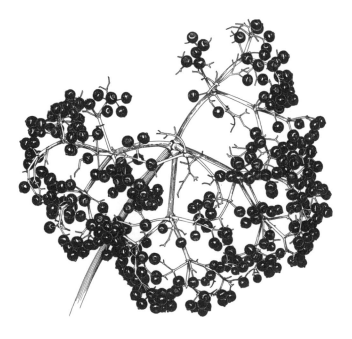

fore droop, bending the bushes down, just in proportion as they ripen. Hence, you see the green cymes perfectly erect, the half ripe more or less drooping, and the perfectly ripe commonly hanging straight down on the same bush. The terminal cyme, when it chances to be held erect, is of a very regular form: four principal divisions drooping toward each quarter around an upright central one, as the lower cymes droop around the upper one.

These berries fill your basket quickly, the cymes are so large and lie up so light. They are said to make a good dye.

About the first of September, excepting the vacciniums, which are then past prime and drying up, the wild cherries and elderberries are the two prevailing wild fruits; and, accordingly, we find the berry-eating birds assembled where they grow. By the twentieth of September the birds (young of robins, blue-birds, and so on) have greatly thinned their cymes, and it is too late to gather them.

LATE WHORTLEBERRY

Then there is the late whortleberry, dangleberry, or blue tangle, whose fruit does not begin to be ripe until about August seventh and is in its prime near the end of August.

This is a tall and handsome bush about twice as high as a huckleberry bush, with altogether a glaucous aspect, growing in shady copses where it is rather moist, and to produce much fruit it seems to require wet weather. The fruit is one of the handsomest of berries: smooth, round, and blue, larger than most huckleberries and more transparent, on long stems dangling two or three inches, and more or less tangled. By the inexperienced it is suspected to be poisonous and so avoided, and perhaps is the more fair and memorable to them on that account. Though quite good to eat, it has a peculiar, slightly astringent, and compared with most huckleberries, not altogether pleasant flavor, and a tough skin. At the end of the first week of September, they are commonly the only edible whortleberries which are quite fresh. They are rare hereabouts, however, and it is only in certain years that you can find enough for a pudding.

VIBURNUM DENTATUM

The *Viburnum dentatum* berries begin about August seventh, are in their prime say September first, and last, some of them, through September. I notice them green toward the end of July.

This is the earliest of the viburnums to ripen its fruit and the smallest berried, more remarkable for the leaves than fruit. Their fruit, beginning to turn or ripen on one side, is a dark spot which looks like decay. By the middle of August their flattish cymes are seen overhanging the side of the river amid the cornels, willows, and button bushes, occupying any crevice on the bushy brink. The berries are small, depressed, globular, three-sixteenths of an inch in diameter, and quite unpalatable. They are of a dull or dead light-blue or lead color, though held close in some lights they are glossy.

PLUMS

Canada plum (and introduced), say August eighth.

William Wood, in his *New England's Prospect*, says, "The plumbs of the country be better for plumbs than the cherries be for cherries [referring to choke cherries]; they be black and yellow, about the bigness of dawsons, of a reasonable good taste." Cartier speaks of the Indians of Canada drying prunes for the winter as the French do. Josselyn found round white, yellow, and black plums in New England different from those in England. Nuttall, in his *North American Sylva*, says of the *Prunus americana*, wild plum:

> Few plants in North America have a more extensive range than this species of Plum: it is met with from the Saskatchewan towards Hudson's Bay, and through all the intermediate country to Georgia, Louisiana, and Texas. In the western part of the State of New York it is very common, and, in some instances, (as it appeared to me in 1810,) it has been cultivated by the aborigines around their dwellings, in the same manner as the Chickasaw Plum. . . . [The fruit is] in some instances almost wholly yellow, but commonly vermilion red on one side, or a mixture of both colors.

HAIRY HUCKLEBERRY

The hairy huckleberry (*Gaylussacia dumosa*, var. *hirtella*) is ripe about August eighth.

It is quite rare, growing only in the wildest and most neglected places, such as cold, sphagnous swamps where the *Andromeda polifolia* and *Kalmia glauca* are found, and in some almost equally neglected but firmer low ground. The berries are oblong and black, and, with us, roughened with short hairs. It is the only species of *Vacciniæ* that I know of in this town whose fruit is inedible, though I have seen another kind of whortleberry, the *deer-berry* or squaw huckleberry, growing in another part of the state, whose fruit is said to be equally inedible. The former is merely insipid, however. Some which grow on firmer ground have a little more flavor, but the thick and shaggy-feeling coats of the berries left in the mouth are far from agreeable to the palate. Both these and dangle-berries are placed in the same genus (or section) with the common huckleberry.

August 30, 1860. Am surprised to find on Minott's hard land where he once raised potatoes an abundance of hairy huckleberry, the prevailing if not only one there, now in prime, which before I had seen in swamps only. Here, too, they are more edible, not so insipid, yet not quite edible generally. They are improved, you would say, by the firmer ground. The berries are in longer racemes or clusters than any other huckleberries. They are *oblong* and black, and the thick shaggy-feeling coats left in the mouth are far from agreeable to the palate.

I think that they grow here still, together with some kind of native grass (*Muhlenberghia*), because Minott is an old-fashioned man and has not scrubbed up and improved his land, as most have. It is in a wilder and more primitive condition. The very huckleberries are shaggy there.

MUSKMELONS

Muskmelons begin to be ripe by August tenth, and the late green citrons are ripened by the frosts, often after the vines are killed. I plucked the first one on August tenth in 1854, August twenty-third another year, and August twelfth in 1853.

The ripeness of the yellow kinds is at once indicated by their color and also their fragrance. It is surprising how rapidly they turn—as much as to say, "Pluck me." You gather all the ripe ones in the morning, but when you go into your patch at night, one or two more will perhaps be peeping out from unexpected nooks. As the sun makes his way from east to west through the sky, so yellow spreads over the surface of the melon. Those which are ripening are, however, betrayed by their fragrance first. The roughest skinned are commonly the best, and the green citrons the most uniformly good. Plums and grapes, about which gardeners make such an ado, are, in my opinion, low fruits compared with melons.

It is uncertain what the ancients had for melons, but their muskmelons, I suspect, were no better than gourds. The *cucumis* and *cucushita* appear to have been commonly associated in their thought, as in their gardens. Theophrastus speaks of what his translator Gaza calls *pepones*, *cucumeres*, and *cucushita*; and Theophrastus calls the skin of the *cucumeris* "bitter." This seems to be a cucumber. He says that "the *megarenses* when the etesian-winds blow raise with a hoe a dust about their *pepones*, *cucumeres*, and *cucushita*, and so make them sweeter and tenderer without watering." He mentions these fruits, especially the last two, very often; says that to make the second tender they soaked the seed in milk, to which Columella adds that to make it (the *cucumis*) sweet they soaked the seed in *musa*, and Palladius says that to make *melones* high-scented the seeds were buried for some time amid dry rose leaves. It will appear from these verses of Columella's to what uses the *cucumis* and *cucushita* were put:

> if the longest pleases most, which grows
> Suspended by its own head's slender top,
> Then from its slender neck select ten seeds;
> But if that with a globe-like body please,
> Which with too huge a belly swells, then choose
> The seed which in its womb inclosed lies;
> This will an offspring bring, fit to contain
> Hymethian honey, or Narycian pitch:
>
> •　　　•　　　•
>
> And boys in rapid streams will teach to swim.

These were evidently gourds.

De Candolle, speaking of the evening melo or muskmelon, quotes Olivier de Serres (1629) thus: "Pliny takes oftenest the cucumber for the melon, confounding these two fruits under the same appellation." De Candolle says the Spaniard Herrera said in 1513, "If the melon is good it is one of the best fruits which exists, and even none is preferable to it. If it is bad, it is bad indeed"—and in this he likens it to women.

Of muskmelon Gerarde writes, "in Greek μῆλον, which doth signify an apple; and therefore this kind of cucumber is more truly called μηλοπέπων, or *Melopepon*; by reason that *Pepo* hath the smell of an apple, whereto the smell of this fruit is like; having withal the smell as it were of musk: which for that cause are also named *Melones Muschatellini*, or musk melons."

September 13, 1858. Muskmelons and squashes are turning yellow in the gardens and ferns in the swamps.

Saint Pierre, after saying that "our fruit trees are easily scaled" and that soft fruits which would be injured by felling are borne near the ground, adds, "There is no less marvelousness of adaptation in the forms and sizes of fruits. Many of them are moulded for the mouth of man, such as cherries and plums; others for his hand, such as pears and apples; others much larger, such as melons, have the subdivisions marked, and seem destined to be a social family repast: nay, there are some in India, as the jacq, and with ourselves the pumpion, large enough to be divided among a neighborhood." I may add that in the watermelon, though these divisions are not revealed by the form or to the touch, they are by the coloring: the breadth is a reasonable slice. Perchance the divisions of this fruit are thus faintly indicated to suggest that it is so wholesome, though an individual may safely consume alone what would commonly suffice for a whole family.

Often, owing to copious and protracted rains, the muskmelons crack open before they are sweet.

POTATOES

They begin to dig early potatoes by the eleventh of August.

July 16, 1851. My neighbor put his hand in a hill some days ago and extracted some new potatoes, as big as walnuts, then covered them up again. Now they will need, or will get, no more weeding.

Some dig the earliest by the eleventh of August, and *toward the end of* August (August twentieth and twenty-third) they begin to dig in earnest. I see them at it with cart and barrels in the fields on all hands before they are fairly ripe, for fear of rot or a fall in the price. They now carry these and their onions to market, starting very early in the morning or at midnight. I see them returning in the afternoon with the empty barrels.

In the last of August and in September we observe the balls lying ripe in the fields.

We love to see Nature fruitful in whatever kind. It assures us of her vigor and that she may in equal profusion bring forth the fruits which we prize. I love to see the acorns plenty even in the shrub oaks. I love to see the potato balls numerous and large as I go through the low fields, poisonous though they look—the plant thus, as it were, bearing fruit at both ends—as much as to say, I offer you not only these tubers for the present, but, if they do not satisfy you, and you will have new varieties, plant these seeds. What bounty—what beauty even! These balls which are worthless to the farmer combine to make the general impression of the year's fruitfulness. It is as cheering to me as the rapid increase of the population of New York. One of these drooping clusters of potato balls would be as good a symbol of our year's fertility as anything I know of—better as yet, surely, than a bunch of grapes.

July 28, 1860. A man shows me in the street a single bunch of potato balls— that is, on one stem—just twenty in number, several of them quite an inch in diameter and the whole cluster nearly five inches in diameter as it hangs, to some extent emulating a cluster of grapes. The very sight of them supplies my constitution with all the needful potash. I see them afterward suspended at the post office.

July 30, 1860. As I come through Cyrus Hosmer's potato field, I see the great clusters of potato balls lie sprawling on the sandy ground and covered with sand since the rains, on each side of the ones I see down between two rows. Owing to the wet and coolness, they are uncommonly abundant this year.

August 22, 1860. Yes, and a potato field is a rich sight to me, even when the vines are half decayed and blackened, and their decaying scent fills the air, though unsightly to many, for it speaks then more loudly and distinctly of potatoes than ever. I see their weather-beaten brows peeping out of the hills here and there, for the earth cannot contain them, when the creak of the cricket and the shrilling of the locust prevail more and more in the sunny end of summer. There the con-fident husbandman lets them lie for the present—even as if he knew not of them or as if that property were insured, had invested in these banks or on deposit there—so carelessly rich he is. He relaxes now his labors somewhat, seeing to their successful end, and takes long noonings, perchance, stretched in the shade of his ancestral trees. I had just passed him bareheaded and in his short sleeves lying at length on a buffalo skin, with his great bare feet stretched beyond it, on the grass by the roadside before his house, sleeping and reading his agricultural paper by turns while the hens and turkeys tip-toed around him.

Potatoes are so abundant this year that the very pedlar, this time without smarter mysteries, tarries to see me have out the monstrous Davis seedlings as big as robins. Perhaps he is thinking of giving up his peddling business and raising potatoes. One farmer who has to shoulder them up the steep hillside to his cellar swears soundly, they are so heavy, but I am sure he would be glad if they were heavier still.

Our vintage is come; an olive is ripe. Fruit of the strong soil, containing potash. I am glad to know that Nature has her potash works, as well as sugar house.

It seems to me that the year has nothing more worthy to brag of than these. Why not take for our crest of arms a drooping cluster of potato balls in a *potato field*, which commonly is the same as a field *d'or* or *d'argent*.

In Moore's new field, a reclaimed swamp, they grow luxuriantly and rankly, manured with ashes and sphagnum. How they take to the virgin soil! An Irish-man tells me that he took a piece of land to bog in Lincoln, cleared, turned up the stumps and roots, and burned it over, making a coat of ashes six inches deep, and then planted potatoes. He never put a hoe to it till he went to dig there one morning, and before night he and another man had dug and housed seventy-five bushels apiece.

By the middle of September the farmers are so busy on all sides digging their potatoes, so prone to their work, that they do not see me going across-lots. Toward the last of October they make haste to dig such as remain in the fields before the ground freezes hard.

October 16, 1859. Passed through the sandy potato field at Witherell's cellar-hole. Potatoes not dug look late and neglected now, the very vines almost van-ished on some sandier hills. It will soon take a plan of the field and a divining rod to find them. The farmer begins to calculate how much longer he can simply leave his potatoes out.

I remember one large field of potatoes whose owner was very particular about the plowing and planting, having some new theory to prove. The rows were of great length and mathematically straight, the admiration of all beholders, but this farmer having gone so far omitted to dig his potatoes till the ground froze, and so they were all lost.

It is commonly stated in our histories that the potato was introduced into Great Britain from Virginia by Sir Walter Raleigh, but the fact is that it is not indigenous in the United States. It came from South America. Dr. T. W. Harris told me that he, having seen a report of remarks made by the younger De Candolle in France, in which he spoke of the potato as having come from Virginia, wrote to him and set him right about it, assuring him that the common groundnut described by Harriot was the wild or Virginian potato at first and correctly referred to.

Charles Darwin, in his *Voyage round the World,* speaks of finding wild potatoes on the islands of the Chronos Archipelago in South America, the tallest plant being four feet high. The tubers, generally small, but one or two inches in diameter, "resembled in every respect and had the same smell as English potatoes; but when boiled they shrunk much and were watery and insipid, without any bitter taste."

Gerarde says:

Of Potatoes of Virginia
Battata Virginiana,
sine Virginianorum, & Pappus

Virginia Potato hath many hollow flexible branches trailing upon the ground, three square, uneven, knotted or kneed in sundry places at certain distances: from the which knots cometh forth one great leaf made of divers leaves, some smaller and others greater, set together upon a fat middle rib by couples, of a swart green color tending to redness; the whole leaf resembling those of the winter-cresses, but much larger; in taste at the first like grass, but afterward sharp and nipping the tongue. From the bosom of which leaves come forth long round slender foot-stalks, whereon do grow very fair and pleasant flowers, made of one entire whole leaf, which is folded or plaited in such strange sort, that it seemeth to be a flower made of five sundry small leaves, which cannot easily be perceived except the same be pulled open. The whole flower is of a light purple color, striped down the middle of every fold or welt with a light shew of yellowness, as if purple and yellow were mixed together. In the middle of the flower thrusteth forth a thick flat pointal yellow as gold, with a small sharp green pricke or point in the middest thereof. The fruit succeedeth the flowers round as a ball, of the bigness of a little Bullace or wild plum, green at the first, and black when it is ripe; wherein is contained small white seed lesser than those of Mustard. The root is thick, fat, and tuberous, not much differing either in shape, color, or taste from the common Potatoes [that is, scallop], saving that the roots hereof are not so great nor long; some of them are as round as a ball, some oval or egge-fashion; some longer and others shorter: the which knobby roots are fastened unto the stalks with an infinite number of threddie strings.

It groweth naturally in America, where it was first discovered, as reports C. *Clusius*, since which time I have received roots hereof from Virginia, otherwise called Norembega, which grow and prosper in my garden as in their own native country.

VIBURNUM NUDUM

Viburnum nudum berries begin to be ripe by August eleventh, are in their prime about the first of September, do not last long, generally all gone soon after the middle of September, are inevitably earlier than the *Viburnum lentago*.

This is a very handsome, though to some poisonous-looking, fruit of the swamps, remarkable and interesting for the variety of colors or shades of colors which they pass through before arriving at maturity and which a single cyme presents: light green or whitish, deep pink or some purple, dark purple or black when the bloom is scrubbed off, and also shrivelled (purple) berries all together, for they do not all ripen at once. The berries are of various sizes and forms: elliptical, oblong, or globular. They are commonly singularly elliptical, one side being longer than the other. Some are irregularly globular or apple shaped, and larger than common.

They begin to turn early in August, and you see their whiteness faintly blushing. They are generally green then, but some higher and more exposed to the light are soon of a deep fiery pink on one cheek, and light green on the other, and perhaps a very few dark purple or, if without bloom, already black. They seem to ripen one by one, though suddenly. By the middle of August you see some quite dark purple amid the red, while those clusters on the same bush are wholly green yet, and a little later you may detect a few shrivelled purple ones even amid the light green.

It is surprising how suddenly they change at last from deep pink to a very distinct dark purple when the vine which they entwine is mature. Frequently those cymes which are pink when I pluck them and put into my hat for their beauty will have half of them turned to a dark purple by the time I get home. I one evening brought home a cyme of fifty-three berries, all of them rose colored, and the next morning thirty were turned dark purple. Again, at 4:30 one afternoon I plucked a cluster all green, with very little pink tinge even. When I got home at half past six (or in two hours), nine were turned dark blue, and the next morning thirty—from which it would appear that they do not always pass thro' their deep-pink stage. And, moreover, those which before were hard and bitter, as soon as they turn dark purple are soft and edible, having somewhat of a wild-cherry flavor—but a large seed. It is a singular and sudden chemical change.

They are ever a little sweetish and raisin-like, or rather like dates.

At the end of October 1856 I found at Perth Amboy, New Jersey, that species or variety which they call the black haw (*Viburnum prunifolium*) still full of fruit long after the *Viburnum nudum* berries had fallen with us, and they held on for three or four weeks still. Such as set out about the homes were very ornamental on account of the abundance of the dark-purple berries. Walking with a gentleman there, I stepped up to a bush and ate a handful of them, at which he was surprised, not knowing that they were wholesome, and the fact being made known to a neighboring school, these shrubs soon lost their ornaments. They are called "Nanny berries" about New York. This shrub, however, differs from ours in its thorniness. I had to cut my way in this region through dense, thorny, and almost impenetrable thickets of it.

This is one of the most noticeable wild fruits toward the end of August or first of September. The numerous drooping, rich, variegated cymes seen against its handsome, firm, green leaves add to the wildness and beauty of the swampy sproutlands—and must have caught the eye of many a walker who did not know its name or dare to taste it.

September 3. Now is the season for those comparatively rare but beautiful wild berries which are not food for man. If we so industriously collect those berries which are sweet to the palate, it is strange that we do not devote an hour in the year to gathering those which are beautiful to the eye. It behoves us to go a-berrying in this sense once a year at least and gather berries which are as beautiful as flowers but far less known—the fruit of the flowers—to fill our baskets, for instance, with the neglected but beautiful fruit of the various species of cornel and viburnum—poke, arum, medeola, thorns, and so on. Now is the time for *Beautiful* Berrying, for which the children have no vacation. They should have a vacation for their imaginations as much as for their bodies. Puddings and pies are not the last or sweetest fruit of living. I take my basket and go after these berries at this season just as I gather mints and asters in their turn.

Some years the crop of *Viburnum nudum* berries is particularly abundant. September third, 1856, I gathered four or five quarts of them, then in their prime, at Shadbush Meadow, plucking the whole cymes in their different colors and stages of maturity. You would not believe the pleasing variety which different bushes offer you, as you wind from one apartment or parterre of the swamp to another. It is a fairy-like garden. You will never see them till you *go* to see them. There is also some advantage in seeing them collected into a mass, though they are handsomest on the bush. It is worth the while to bring home thus the different kinds of viburnum and cornel berries, and compare them with each other.

EUROPEAN MOUNTAIN ASH

The European mountain-ash berries begin to be ripe about August twelfth. They are in prime perhaps September first and last through September.

I see young purple finches eating them by July twenty-eighth close to the window. About the twentieth of September those trees which stand in front yards will be all alive with robins and cherry birds, stripping them of their drooping orange clusters. My neighbor complains that the birds first get most of his strawberries, which are quasi-useful, and finally, when his mountain-ash berries have got to be most ornamental to his front year, they take every one of them in a few days.

Loudon says that "In Livonia, Sweden, and Kamtschatka, the berries of the mountain ash are eaten, when ripe, as fruit." There is nothing so crabbed but somebody will eat it somewhere. They are exceedingly bitter and austere to my

taste, and I do not see how the birds can eat them, but the fact is they do not chew them.

WHITE-BERRIED CORNEL

The white-berried cornel (*Cornus alba* or *paniculata*) begins to be ripe about August twelfth, though they were in prime August second, 1852; but most of them drop and are eaten before fairly ripe, are dropping by the middle of August, and are mostly fallen early in September, though I see it still holding on abundantly, the wax-like fruit, September eleventh, 1859.

This and the alternate cornel drop prematurely or are eaten by birds. When ripe they are white. Perhaps they make the greatest show the latter part of August. They are common on College Road and by Shadbush Meadow and in Ripple Lake's frosty hollows. Love a *rather* dry soil along walls, with the *Cornus alternifolia*. It is on the whole an interesting berry, both for its white waxen color and the pretty, reddish fairy fingers of its commonly half-bare cymes, spreading their little palms to the skies. The berries are very bitter. Though its little red fingery stems are oftenest bare, they are perhaps pretty enough to take the place of the berries.

CORNUS SERICEA

Cornus sericea, August thirteenth.

July 27, 1852. Silky cornel with abundance of green berries help clothe the bank of the Assabet and fill its crevices.

August 25, 1852. The silky cornel is the most common, everywhere bordering the river and swamps, its drooping cymes of amethystine china or glass beads mingled with whitish.

August 28, 1852. Now the silky-cornel berries are very handsome along the river overhanging the water, for the most part pale blue mixed with whitish, part of the pendant jewelry of the season dangling over the face of the river and reflected in it. These and the white-berried are in their prime.

August 24, 1852. Next after the alternate cornel, the silky cornel begin to turn bright glass nearly blue green. Then the white-berried, but the round-leaved I have not seen.

August 30, 1853. Some of the berries are almost clear white on one side, the other china blue.

September 4, 1853. China-like berries of cornel along the river now abundant, some cymes wholly white.

September 11, 1853. Begin to disappear.

August 15, 1854. At the hill landing in a day or two.

September 1, 1854. Are now in prime, of different shades of blue, lighter or darker, and bluish white. They are so abundant as to be a great ornament to our causeways and riverside.

September 23, 1854. *Cornus sericea* is turned mulberry, and here is our end of its berries then. The hard frosts of twenty-first and twenty-second did it.

August 28, 1856. The bright china-colored blue berries of the *Cornus sericea* begin to show themselves along the river amid their red-brown leaves, the kinnikinnik of the Indians.

September 3, 1856. The berries of the silky cornel prematurely dropping.

August 26, 1859. Fairly begin to be ripe.

Hind writes about the "bear-berry from which the kinni-kinnik, used to mix with tobacco is made":

The Indians of the prairies generally use the inner bark of the *Cornus sericea*, the red-backed willow, as they term it. We saw them smoke the inner bark of the dog-wood, *Cornus alternifolia*.

The mode in which these barks are prepared is very simple. A few branches about three-fourths of an inch thick and four or five feel long are procured, the outer bark is scraped off, after having been warmed over a fire, a knife is then passed against the inner bark and drawn upwards, for a space of six or eight inches, until the whole of the inner bark is gathered in curly clusters round the stick, it is then thrust in the ground over the embers and roasted until quite dry, when, mixed with tobacco in equal proportions, it forms the favorite kinni-kinnik of the Northwest Indians. I often saw them smoke bark or the leaves of the bear-berry alone, when their supply of tobacco was exhausted.

GROUNDSEL

Groundsel down begins to fly, say August 13.

SMOOTH SUMAC

The smooth sumac *(Rhus glabra)* begins to be admired about August thirteenth. All turned by the last of August. As they are reddening for a week or two after July nineteenth, they are of rare beauty. Are they crimson or vermillion? I am not sure but the bunches of the smooth-sumac berries are handsomest when but partly turned, the green berries showing a velvety crimson cheek—say about August first or early in August.

August 23. Erect spearheads rising from the ample dark-green, unspotted leaves, pointing in various directions. They begin to be stale early in September.

Early in November I begin to admire again their still bright-red or crimson fruit, when not only its own but most other leaves have fallen, and there are few bright tints of any kind. It is now so distinct on its twigs. Your attention is not distracted by its brilliant leaves now.

It holds on all winter and is eaten by partridges, chickadees, and probably mice. You will see it plenty still in April.

Loudon, apparently quoting Kalm, says, "The berries are eaten by children with impunity, but they are very sour: they are red, and are made use of for dyeing that same color." Professor Rogers in *Silliman's Journal* "observes that the berries contain a large portion of the malic acid, and are used as a substitute for lemons in various preparations of domestic economy and medicine."

January 30, 1856. Some bunches quite ripe right yet.

August 27, 1860. Notice now that sour-tasting white and creamy incrustation between and on the berries of the smooth sumac, like frostwork. Is it not an exudation? or is it produced by the bite of an insect?

September 18, 1860. Are about past their beauty, and the white, creamy incrustation mostly dried up.

Eaten by partridges and mice January eleventh and by chickadees January thirtieth, 1856. From Kalm's *Travels* (at Philadelphia): "The branches boiled with the berries afford a black ink-like tincture. The boys eat the berries, there being no danger of falling sick after the repast, but they are very sour."

SAW GRASS

Saw grass (*Paspalum setaceum*) is observed by the fourteenth of August.

Its long, slender, seedy spikes, growing low and spreading almost horizontally, seen after the fields have been mowed, remind us of early autumn. Certain phenomena like this, however slight, are interesting by the regularity with which they annually occur and remind us of the progress of the seasons. About this time I am sure to notice in my walk the seedy spike of this grass, now approaching maturity. By its arrangement on its spike it produces the effect of a serration, and hence I have called it *saw grass*.

EARLY ROSES

Hips of the two early roses begin to redden about August fifteenth or generally begin to be handsome about September first.

Those of the moss rose are large, depressed, globular, and scarlet.

September 7, 1854. *Some* of the moss rose very large and handsome, very much flattened, globular.

Manasseh Cutler says of our "Wild Rose, Dog Rose. . . . Common in moist land. . . . The pulp of the berries beat up with sugar, makes the conserve of hepps of the London dispensatory."

December 14, 1850. In one place in the meadow by Loring's Pond saw the greatest quantity of wild rose hips of various forms that I ever saw. They were as thick as winterberries.

EPILOBIUM

Epilobium down, August fifteenth.

August 23, 1858. Abundantly shedding its downy seeds, wands of white and pink.

PEAR

August fifteenth. Wild pear.

Loudon quotes Pliny as saying, "All pears whatsoever are but a heavy meat unless they are well boiled or baked."

Gerarde says, "To write of pears and apples in particular, would require a particular volume: the stock or kindred of pears are not to be numbered: every country hath his peculiar fruit: myself knows one curious in grafting and planting of fruits, who hath some piece of ground, at the point of three-score sundry sorts of pears, and those exceedingly good"—just to mention the poorer ones.

September 9, 1853. Half a bushel of handsome pears on the ground under the wild pear tree on Pedrick's land—some ripe, many more on tree.

September 23, 1854. Gather pretty good there, in prime.

September 3, 1860. See on two pear trees by the Boze cellar ripe pears, some ripe for several days. Most are bitter, others mealy, but one was quite sweet and good, of middling size and prettier, with more color than most cultivated ones. It had some streaks of red and was exceedingly wax-like—so that Sophia appropriated it when I got home for her vase of fruit, and it was the handsomest fruit in it.

October 11, 1860. This season has been as favorable for pears as for apples and potatoes and white-oak acorns. Ralph Waldo Emerson's garden is strewn with them. They are not so handsome as apples nor so poetic, and he says his children complain that they cannot introduce them so well into verse. They are of more earthy and homely colors, yet they are of an agreeable and very wholesome color, many inclining to a rough russet or even ferruginous (rusty), both to touch and eye, and look as if they were proof against frost. They are commonly so dull a color that it is hard to distinguish them from the leaves, they not revealing themselves distinctly amid the leaves, as an apple by its bright color; and, accordingly, I see that my companion, who thought he had gathered all of *one* kind, has overlooked half a dozen large ones in a small tree which were concealed by their perfect resemblance to the leaves, a yellowish-green spotted with darker-green rust. Some of the wild ones that I find have more color and are handsomer than the many celebrated varieties that are cultivated. They have an unexpectedly luscious flavor, however, and are like thrushes, which conceal a sweet voice under a dull exterior. Yet some of these have a fair cheek, and generally in their form they are true pendants, as if shaped expressly to hang from the trees. Hence, we have not only the *plum* weight of the carpenter and mason, but the *poire* or "pear" of the weigher.

They are a more aristocratic fruit than apples. How much more attention they get from the proprietor! The hired man gathers the apples and barrels them. The proprietor himself plucks the pears at odd hours for a pastime, and his oldest daughter wraps them each in its paper, or they are perchance put up in the midst of a barrel of winter apples, as if they were a more precious care to those. They are spread on the floor of the best room and are a gift to the most distinguished guest. Judges and ex-judges and honorables are connoisseurs of pears and discourse of them at length between sessions.

Yet they have neither the beauty nor the fragrance of apples. Their excellence is in their flavor, which speaks to a grosser sense. They are *glout-morceaux*. Hence, while children dream of apples, ex-judges realize pears. They are named after emperors, kings, queens, dukes, and duchesses. I fear I shall have to wait till we get to pears with American names, which a republican can swallow. The next French Revolution will correct all that.

I hold in my hand a *Bonne Louise* which is covered with minute brown specks or dots, from one-twelfth to one-sixteenth of an inch apart, and are largest and most developed on the sunny side. Looking closely at them I find that they are quite regularly dispersed and formed, as if they were the termination or operculum of pores which had burst in the very thin pellicle of the fruit, producing a slight roughness to the touch as well as eye. Each of these little ruptures (so to call them) is in form a perfect star with four to six, commonly five, rays with a wart or prominence in the midst of the pellicle, having been so rent. So that if the apple is higher colored, reflecting the sun, on the duller surface of this pear (as on the sky by night) the whole firmament with its stars shines forth. They whisper of the happy stars under whose influence they have grown and matured. This is not the case with all of them, but only the more perfect specimens. It suggests a sympathy with the law by which the light of the stars bursts its way thro' the air and space to us.

PEACH

Peaches, August fifteenth, twenty-fourth fairly begun, September twenty-seventh in prime, last into October.

The Romans are said to have received the peach from Persia in the reign of Claudius, and through them it came to Britain.

September 27, 1857. I am surprised to find that, yesterday having been a very warm day, the peaches have mellowed suddenly and wilted, and there are many more fallen than there were even after previous rains. They are better when they ripen more gradually.

October 12, 1851. I hear that the Smiths have carried their last load to market.

June 9, 1852. Evelyn says, "We may read that the peach was at first accounted so tender and delicate a tree or that it was believed to thrive only in Persia; and, even in the days of Galen, it grew no nearer than Egypt, of all the Roman provinces, but was not seen in the city till about thirty years before Pliny's time." But now it is the principal crop cultivated in Lincoln in New England, and it is also cultivated extensively in the West and on lands not half a dozen years vacated by the Indians—nay, by the Indians themselves.

In Lawson's *Carolina* it is said, "A peach falling on the ground brings a peach tree that shall bear in three years, or sometimes sooner. Eating peaches in our orchards makes them come up so thick from the kernel, that we are forced to take a great deal of care to weed them out; otherwise they make our land a wilderness of peach trees"; and in Beverly's *Virginia* it is said, peaches are so easily raised "that some good husbands plant great orchards of them purposely for their hogs."

WATER DOCK

Water dock, August seventeenth.
The great shaggy, brown panicles of the water dock.

CARRION FLOWER

I see the carrion flower just beginning to turn August seventeenth, in prime say September fourth.

August 2, 1853. I observe the green fruit forming dense spherical umbrels two inches in diameter at the end of stems five or six inches long. I find *one* to be composed of eighty-four berries the size of peas, three- to six-sided, closely wedged together on pedicels three-fourths of an inch long. The whole feels hard and solid in the hand. As these balls ripen and become purple, they open a little beneath, becoming more hemispherical, and seen standing out on all sides six or eight inches from the neat-twining stem, they are quite handsome. They are covered with a blue bloom, and when this is rubbed off by leaves, they are a shining blackish. It grows in meadows.

ARUM TRIPHYLLUM

Arum triphyllum, August nineteenth, in prime September first. Have seen them still abundant September twenty-eighth. I notice the green berries July twenty-second.

The dense oval bunches of the arum berries, turning from green to scarlet, now startle the walker in swamps and on moist banks. It is one of the most remarkable and dazzling, if not the handsomest, fruits that we have. A crowded but handsome conical or ovate, cone-shaped mass of brilliant scarlet- or vermillion-colored berries (exactly the color of bright sealing wax or, I believe, the *painted-tortoise*

shell), commonly one and a half inches long, but sometimes two and a half inches long by two inches wide, rather flattish, on a short peduncle, (*some* six or eight inches long).

The individual berries, which on a large head number about a hundred, are of various sizes, between pear and mitre and club form, flattened against each other, and spring from a singular purplish case, sometimes white or variegated, hollow like a bag. (Does not this turn purple on exposure as the berries fall off?) This rich ground is seen only where the berries have fallen off or been plucked, so thoroughly does it tend to depth and brilliancy of color. This fruit often resembles a very short, thick, conical ear of *scarlet* corn, especially when the white and withered spathe invests it like a husk, and deserves better to be called "snake corn" than the fruit of the *Smilacina stellata* does.

The changed leaves (which have commonly fallen when the fruit is ripe) are delicately white, especially beneath.

This splendid scarlet fruit here and there lies prostrate on the damp leaves, and it is one of the most conspicuous and easily detected objects on the floor of the swamp, its bright scarlet cone above the fallen and decaying foliage, and amid its own brown and whitish and withering leaves, which perchance is part of the withered spathe still investing and veiling it, spotting the ground. You had quite forgotten its promise since you first detected its handsome flower in early spring, and now at last it blazes forth one of the most conspicuous fruits of the swamp, and challenges attention and admiration. What rank if not venomous luxuriance in this swamp sproutland!

It is remarkable how many fruits are scarlet now—barberries, prinos, and so on. No wonder that the Indian, after such an education, was attracted by the white-man's vermillion—so *natural* a color.

I have never tasted these berries. They are said to be exceedingly biting and caustic. Yet I often see where they have been the greater part devoured by some creatures in the latter part of August.

It is remarkable how long this fruit keeps fresh and glossy. Its own leaves and stem will commonly be soft and decaying, while it is perfectly fresh and dazzling. It has the brightest gloss of any fruit that I remember, and this makes the green part about as interesting as the scarlet.

Not only do I see it perfectly fresh and abundant in the swamps as late as the twenty-eighth of September, but a spike of the berries which I gathered quite *green* on the first of September one year had by the eighteenth turned completely scarlet, and though it lay in a dry and warm chamber all the while, the berries were as plump and fresh and glossy as ever—and *some* of them continued so even till the eighteenth of November, or for more than ten weeks after they were gathered.

R H U S   T O X I C O D E N D R O N

Rhus toxicodendron, August nineteenth. Greenish yellow and some *shrivelled* over bare rocks, but not generally till September.

Cornutus evidently represents the *Rhus toxicodendron* as the *Hedera trifolia canadensis* and the *Ampelopsis quinquefolia* as the *Hedera quinquefloria canadensis*, and they are both called ivy today.

November 15, 1850. The berries of the ivy (probably *radicans*) sere and yellowish, sand-colored, like the berries of the dogwood.

W O O L - G R A S S

Wool-grass with its brown heads, August nineteenth.

POKE

Poke begins August nineteenth, not fairly till September, in prime say September twenty-fifth, and lasts till it is killed, which for the greater part is early in *October*.

I find this oftenest and most abundant on rather elevated and rocky ground, as sides of hills in sproutlands, where they grow in a community. In such places the large, bending, tree-like plants stand close together, and their drooping racemes almost crush one another, hanging around the bright purple and, by the last of September, for the most part bare, stems. The racemes are cylindrical, six inches or more in length, tapering a little toward the end, and consist of purple berries which are large and blackish or ripe at the base, with smaller reddish ones next, and finally green ones and flowers at the tip—all on brilliant purple or crimson-purple peduncles and pedicels. I could sometimes gather bushels of them. Robins and other birds make great account of them and make the places where they grow busy with their coming and going at this season.

Their sour juice makes a better red or purple ink than I have bought. They are frequently part bitter in the latter part of September, before they are one-third of them ripe, those which stand lowest on a hillside being killed first. But I still see some of these standing higher up, which have escaped the frost, partly green even in November.

February 9, 1852. I am interested to see the seeds of the poke, ten shiny-black with a white spot, *somewhat* like a saba bean in shape. The still full granary of the birds.

GROUND NUT

Ground nuts, *Apios tuberosa*, begin August twentieth *(or earlier)*. The vines are killed by September twenty-ninth at least. I have dug them by August twenty-first and in the middle of October.

These grow in low ground along the edge of meadows, running over fences and

other plants. They are commonly from the size of a walnut to that of a hen's egg.

October 12, 1852. I dug some ground nuts with my hands in the railroad sand bank, just at the bottom of the high embankment on the edge of the meadow. These were nearly as large as hen's eggs. I had them roasted and boiled at supper time. The skins came off readily, like a potato's. Roasted they had an agreeable taste, very much like a common potato, though they were somewhat fibrous in texture. With my eyes shut I should not have known but I was eating a somewhat soggy potato. Boiled they were unexpectedly quite dry, and though in this instance a little strong, had a more nutty flavor. With a little salt a hungry man could make a very palatable meal on them.

Again, September 29, 1859. Having just dug my potatoes in the garden, which did not turn out very well, I took a basket and trowel and went forth to dig my wild potatoes or ground nuts by the railroad fence. I dug out the tubers of some half-dozen of the largest plants and found an unexpected yield. One string weighed a little more than three-quarters of a pound. There were thirteen which for size I should have put with the large potatoes which I had previously been digging. The biggest was two and three-quarters inches long and seven inches in circumference the smallest way. Five would have been called good-sized for common potatoes. Those whom I met could not tell what I had in my basket. These large ones, however, were more than usually stringy when boiled and not so agreeable to taste as common, I suspect. If they increased in size on being cultivated as much as the common potato has, they would become monstrous; however, one tells me that he planted a tuber in his garden in good soil, but they grew no bigger than a bean. He did not know but it would take more than *one* year.

It is not easy to find this plant, especially when the vines are dead, unless you know beforehand where they grow. It is but a slender vine and not promising much a yield, as I have described. But deep in the soil (it may be sandy or stony) five or six inches or sometimes a foot, you come to the string of brown and commonly knobby nuts. The cuticle of the tuber is more or less cracked longitudinally, forming meridional furrows. The ordinary roots bear a large proportion to the tubers or swollen part.

The thirty-first of August 1857, as I was wading along the edge of Flint's Pond for eight or ten rods at Wharf Rock, carrying my shoes and stockings in my hand, I was surprised to see on the bottom and washing up on the shore many little farinaceous roots or tubers, like very small potatoes in strings. I saw these at every step for more than a dozen rods and thought at first that they must have come from the deeper water. But examining very closely, I traced one long string (which was not detached) through the sandy soil to the root of a ground nut which grew on the edge of the bank and afterward saw many more whose tuberous roots were washed bare where they lay in the sand, the pond being unusually high. I never saw so many ground nuts before. I could have gathered quarts of them. One string which floated loose and was about eighteen inches long, with as usual a little greenness at one end, had thirteen nuts on it about the size of a walnut or smaller. This is an annual phenomenon. I observed it again August thirty-first, 1858.

This is the real Virginia potato, about which historians have blundered, which Raleigh's colonists found in Virginia used by the natives, which have led to the story of the common potato having been introduced at Britain from Virginia.

In case of a famine, I should soon resort to these roots.

PRINOS VERTICILLATUS

Prinos (*verticillatus*) berries, well known under the name of winterberry and black alder, begin to redden about the twentieth of August, are fairly ripe the twentieth of September, and last till February in some places. I begin to notice them reddening, commonly, early in September in sunny places. I see them, red or scarlet, clustered along the stems, amid the as yet green leaves, a cool red, and by the middle of the month they are conspicuous. About the twentieth of September they get to be fairly ripe and are in their prime perhaps October first.

The berries are scarlet, seven-sixteenths of an inch in diameter, somewhat lighter than the arum berries. How densely they cover the bushes, and how handsome, contrasting with the leaves! What adds to this effect is the darker freshness and greenness of the leaves amid which they are seen. They are very remarkable

now—so *brilliant* and fresh—when most things, flowers and berries, have withered. A very cheerful and invigorating sight.

By October tenth the leaves are falling and leaving the bright berries bare, and toward the end of the month they are seen bare of leaves but full of red berries. The robins now eat them, and I see them partly eaten by mouse holes, or tucked into crevices or holes by them.

Now especially (say about the first of November) they attract us and are more conspicuous than ever in the scarcity of leaves, their own being all fallen, and they appear the brighter scarlet for it.

Robins, partridges, mice, and probably some other creatures feed on them; and sometimes they are mostly gone early in November, though I have seen them abundant till January. Toward the end of December they are mostly consumed, only their skins for the most part left sticking to the twigs, as if our woods had had to entertain arctic visitors in unusual numbers, who have exhausted their stores. They are especially interesting when seen through a glaze in midwinter.

By February I see them turned to a dark, coppery brown, looking blackish at a little distance. Even as late as March seventh I have seen where a partridge has eaten many of them, all black and shrivelled as they are.

November 19, 1857. In Stow's sproutland west of the railroad I see where a mouse which has a hole under a stump has eaten out clean the *insides* of the *little seeds* of *Prinos verticullata* berries. What pretty fruit for the mice, these bright prinos berries! They run up the twigs in the night and gather this shining fruit, take out the small seeds, and eat their *kernels* at the entrance of their burrows. The ground is strewn with them there.

SPIKENARD

Spikenard (petty morel), about August twenty-first. I did not see them here till September twelfth one year; they probably last through September. Perhaps in prime September fifth.

July 24, 1853. I see already pretty large green berries, with a few flowers.

About the fifth of September I see occasionally their great panicles or dense cylindrical masses of berries a foot or more long projecting horizontally from some hedge, the color of varnished mahogany.

CAT-TAIL

Cat-tail, say August twenty-first.

The cat-tail down puffs and swells in your hand like a mist or the conjurer's trick of filling a hat with feathers, for when you have rubbed off but a thimbleful and can close and conceal the wound completely, the expanded down fills your hand to overflowing. Apparently there is a spring to the fine elastic threads which compose the down, which, after having been so long closely packed, on being the least relieved at the base spring open apace into the form of parachutes to convey the seed afar. Where birds on the winds or ice have assaulted them, this has spread like an eruption. Again, when I rub off the down of its spike with my thumb, I am surprised at the sensation of warmth it imparts to my hand as it flushes over it magically at the same time revealing a faint purplish crimson tinge at the base of the down as it rolls off and expands. It is a very pleasing experiment to try.

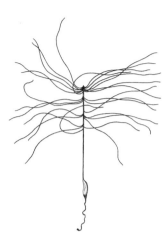

Lindley writes, "The pollen of *Typha* is inflammable, like that of *Lycopodium*, and is used as a substitute for it."

THORN

Scarlet thorn, August twenty-second. Begin to be edible the latter part of August, are at their height the middle of September. Last through October in some places. The green fruit is conspicuous as early as the nineteenth of June.

When they first ripen, the bright scarlet fruit contrasts handsomely with the green leaves, and later some of them are really a splendid fruit to look at (if you bring home a sprig) and far from inedible. They are not only large, but their beauty is enhanced by the persistent calyx relieving the clear scarlet of the fruit. It is an oblong squarish fruit, deep scarlet with yellowish specks or spaces. It bears fruit in abundance, though not the same plant every year, some of an agreeable sub-acid.

I am glad to see anything that can be eaten so abundant by the roadside or in the pastures. They must be a supply depended on by some creatures. Are rather crimson than scarlet when ripe. Perhaps fruits are colored like the trillium berry and the scarlet thorn to attract birds to them.

September 28, 1852. There is a very handsome gray-dotted thorn near Ebby Hubbard's Yellow Birch Swamp six inches in diameter, with a top large in proportion, as large as a small apple tree, bristling with many thorns from suckers about its trunk. This is a very handsome object and the largest thorn I have seen in Concord—now about bare of leaves and one mass of red fruit five-eighths of an inch in diameter, causing its slender branches to spread and droop gracefully. It reminds me of a wisp of straws tied together or a dust brush upright on its handle. \\⚹ There are similar very handsome but smaller ones on Nawshawtuct Hill. ⏐ They must be the same with those large ones which I have seen in Canada. They are probably most beautiful in fruit, not only on account of its color, but because this makes the branches to spread and curve outward gracefully. There are few handsomer objects than such a thorn—full of fruit.

The fruit continues to redden the bushes till the middle of October, but toward the end of the month they have mostly fallen, *reddening* the ground.

William Wood's *New England's Prospect*: "The white thorn affords haws as big as an English cherry, which is esteemed above a cherry [that is, probably, a choke cherry] for his goodness and pleasantness to the taste."

September 25, 1856. Some of the *Cratægus crus-galli* haws are now stale and not good at all.

October 5, 1857. See many haws still green and hard (in Shattuck's barn), though their leaves are mostly fallen. Do these ever become red and edible?

September 24, 1859. The same (nearly leafless) has hard green fruit as usual.

March 6, 1859. Measured a thorn which, at six inches from the ground, or the smallest place below the branches, for it branches soon, was two feet, three inches in circumference.

Mrs. Lincoln quotes Lord Bacon, "White thorns and dog-rose bushes. Wet summers are generally attended with an uncommon quantity of seed on these shrubs, whence their unusual fruitfulness is a sign of severe winter."

SMILACINA TRIFOLIA

Smilacina trifolia, August twenty-third.

FEVER-WORT

Fever-wort (*Triosteum*), August twenty-third. In prime say September fifth and are *fresh* in middle of October.

These are remarkable for their peculiar color, a clear "corn-yellow," and as large as a hazel nut, in whorls at the axils of the leaves of the half-prostrate plants.

I see some fresh as late as October thirteenth, when the leaves are quite withered. They grow by wall-sides on hills and rocky places.

TWO-LEAVED SOLOMON'S-SEAL

Two-leaved Solomon's-seal, August twenty-third; in prime in September.

August 1, 1860. Begin to be pretty, fine red-spotted.

About the nineteenth of July I begin to notice these small whitish berries finely peppered with red, and toward the end of August some of a clear, semilucent red, being ripe; and these are of a pleasantly sweetish taste, but have a large, hard seed.

All through the fall they spot the ground in swamps amid the dry leaves, scarcely lifted above them, but I notice them also whenever the ground is laid bare in the winter, though they are shrivelled then and even as late as April. The dry leaves in the woods just laid bare—I see these bright-red berries still here and there upon them, where they have been flatted down by the snow—affording food, no doubt, for some creatures.

BARBERRY

Barberry, August twenty-third. In prime say October first.

Go a-berrying September eighteenth, 1852; October first, 1853; September twenty-ninth, 1854; September twenty-fifth, 1855; September eighteenth, 1856; September sixteenth, 1857 (*some* gather); October fifth, 1857 (many gather); and September twenty-fourth, 1859.

July 19. They hang yellowish green.

August 20. Their drooping wreaths of fruit are now turning red.

September 12. Are pretty well reddened and handsome, though not much more than half turned. They are not fairly turned before September twentieth, if so soon, though many begin to gather them earlier—to anticipate one another. October fifth would be early enough (if they were not plucked), but October first or September twenty-fifth is the *actual* middle of the barberry season.

Few objects are so handsome as a barberry bush when the fruit is ripe—bushed up with some other shrub or tree perhaps—its pendulous wreaths of red or scarlet berries drooping over a rock. The increasing weight of the fruit adds to its gracefulness. On each one you come to the berries seem to be more abundant and plumper than on the last.

My resorts are the cedar hill south of Flint's Pond and Conantum, Nawshawtuct Hill and the Easterbrook's Country. I used formerly to go to Flint's Pond alone. There they stood half concealed amid the cedars, between which here and there I got a view of the pond, and eight or ten years ago nobody else appeared to pick them—but my half-bushel basketful grew heavy before I got home. I like best to go to Conantum, for I can bring them home in my boat.

September 25, 1855. I carry my aunts and Sophia a-barberrying to Conantum in my boat—a fine warm afternoon. We get about three pecks of barberries from

four or five bushes. (I have picked three pecks alone in less than three hours.) We get our baskets full of berries but our fingers full of prickles to pay for them. With the hands well defended it would be pleasant picking, they are so handsome and beside are so abundant, and fill up so fast.

I consider myself a dexterous barberry picker—but a pair of gloves would be convenient, for with all my knack, it will be some days before I get all the prickles out of my fingers. I take hold of the end of the drooping twigs with my left hand, raise them, and then with my right hand strip downward at once as many clusters as my hand will embrace, bending the prickles and taking as few leaves as possible—commonly bringing away with each raceme one or two small green leaves or bracts which I do not stop to pick out. When I come to a particularly thick and handsome wreath of fruit, I pluck the twig entire and bend it around the inside of the basket—to show when I get home. Some pickle these sprigs entire. Some bushes bear much larger and plumper berries than others, and some years the racemes appear uncommonly long.

How productive a barberry bush. I once picked a half-bushel basketful of barberries at Conantum from one clump which was about four feet in diameter at the base, falling over in wreaths on every side. I filled my basket standing behind it, without being seen by some of the pickers only a dozen rods off—who conversed more loudly than need was of their affairs—and then just to see what I could do, I withdrew—still unobserved—bringing the clumps between me and them—and half an hour after they may have seen my lessening sail upon Fair Haven Bay. In the meanwhile the catbird mews in the alders by my side, and the scream of the jay is heard from the woodside.

A few years ago I had scarcely any competitors—but now the case is altered. They were more to me than the apple crop, especially when apples and cranberries were scarce, for two or three pecks preserved in the fall lasted all winter, though we had them on the table daily, while the two barrels of apples which we lay up did not amount to so much.

But if you would see what nature can do in the way of barberries, go to the Easterbrook's Country! Not a cultivated, hardly a cultivatable field is it, and yet it delights all natural persons and feeds more still. Such great rocky and moist tracts which daunt the farmer, are reckoned as unimproved land, and therefore worth but little, but think of the miles of huckleberries, barberries, and wild apples—so fair both in flower and fruit—resorted to by wild men and children, quadrupeds and birds.

If you chance to be there toward the end of September, when many have improved the first fair day to come a-barberrying, those bushy fields will be all alive with their voices, though you see scarcely one. I meet a sportsman who is well acquainted with that tract and was cunning enough to go early, leaving his gun at home, now returning loaded down with barberries, in game bags and in baskets, so that he is obliged to travel by stages and is glad to stop and talk with me. It is surely better to take thus what Nature offers in her season, like a robin, than to buy an extra dinner at Parker's.

The barberry bushes are so large and numerous there that you cannot see across the field in any direction. There are clumps there behind which I could actually pick two bushels of berries without being seen by you on the other side, and they are not a quarter picked at last by all creatures together. I walk for two or three miles, and still the clumps of barberries, great sheaves with their wreaths of scarlet fruit, show themselves before me and on every side. They seem to issue from between the pines or other trees, as if it were they that were promenading and not I.

About the twentieth of October the bushes thus will be all alive with robins feeding on the berries. By December they are shrivelled—but in this state I find the seeds tucked into crevices of rocks by the mice. And in midwinter the crows and even partridges eat them. I even notice a few still hanging on in April. They are the more palatable after the frost has touched them. As the poet says:

THE BARBERRY BUSH

The bush that has most briars and bitter fruit,
Wait till the frost has turned its green leaves red,
If, sweetened berries will thy palate suit,
And thou may'st find e'en there a homely bread.
Upon the hills of Salem scattered wide,
Their yellow blossoms gain the eye in Spring;
And straggling e'en upon the turnpike's side,
Their ripened branches to your hand they bring,
I've plucked them oft in boyhood's early hour,
That then I gave such name and thought it true;
But now I know that other fruit as sour

Grows on what now thou callest *Me* and *You;*
Yet, wilt thou wait the autumn that I see,
Will sweeter taste than these red berries be.

These bushes appear to be dispersed chiefly by birds and by cows.

Late in the fall you see on many rocks in the pastures where they grow the seeds which have been raided by birds (probably robins chiefly), and in May you may often mistake dense groves of little barberries just sprung up in the droppings of the cows for apple trees—for the cows eat their fruit, sour as it is, and thus help to disseminate it, just as they do the apple. Here they find manure and an open space—for the first year, at least, if they are not killed by drought—but those which spring up single by the sides of rocks, where probably birds have dropt them, seem to succeed best; and thus new clumps are formed, and those creatures which make the most extensive use of them are employed to propogate them. They are about it for a month or two in the fall.

Loudon says, "In a wild state, the common barberry is seldom found higher than four or five feet, but in a state of culture, it may be grown nearly thirty feet high. . . . The tree will live for two or three centuries without increasing much in size." With us they average much higher than four or five feet.

PRINOS LÆVIGATUS

Prinos lævigatus, August twenty-fourth in swamps, as at Fox Castle Swamp.

RED PYRUS

Red pyrus, say twenty-fourth of August, in prime perhaps August thirty-first.
August 31, 1858. Apparently not long.
August 21, 1854. I saw it dried black in Hubbard's Swamp.
With its peculiar glossy red and squarish form it is really very handsome. I see it in Sawmill Brook Swamp and elsewhere.

CORNUS CINCINNATA

Cornus cincinnata, August twenty-seventh.

See them September sixteenth, 1852.

Sometimes each berry is half china blue, half white. Commonly very light-blue or bluish-white. These too fall early, or are eaten, like the *alternifolia* and *paniculata*.

September 4, 1857. At Cornel Rock is the handsomest and most perfect *Cornus cincinnata* that I know, now apparently its fruit in prime, hardly light-blue but delicate bluish-white. It is the richest-looking of the cornels, with its large round leaf and showy cymes; a slender bush seven or eight feet high.

SWEET VIBURNUM

Sweet viburnum (*Viburnum lentago*), August twenty-seventh; in prime September twenty-fourth, 1854; seen September twenty-ninth, 1853. I see it turning August eleventh, by August twenty-first it has fairly begun to redden on one cheek, and from the twenty-fifth of August to middle of September are at the height of their beauty (though not of their ripeness).

June 13, 1852. About out of flower and shows green berries.

September 4, 1860. Hardly yet at Conantum.

September 11. The clusters *now in prime* are exceedingly and peculiarly handsome and are edible withal. These are drooping like the *Cornus sericea* cymes. Each berry in the cyme is now a fine clear red on the exposed side and a distinct and clear green on the opposite side. Many are already purple and they turn in your hat, but they are handsomest when thus red and green.

This is the largest of our viburnums; grows along fences in rather low grounds. The berry is large, half an inch long by three-eighths of an inch by two-eighths of an inch, being somewhat flattish, grows in open, drooping clusters; and about the first of September, before many of them are ripe, they are one of the handsomest of our berries.

About the twenty-fifth of August commonly you begin to notice their sessile cymes of large, elliptic, mucronated berries, pale green on one side, and red with a purple bloom on the other or exposed side, blushing on one cheek. They are handsomest in this stage. A little later, commonly, you begin to notice a few turned blue-black and very distinct amid the rest, as if decayed. Their ripening looks like decay to one unacquainted with them. These are ripe and are rather sweet and edible, though they are dry and have a large, flat seed. They are carried to market in Canada. They turn thus in my pocket like the *Viburnum nudum*, and many of those which I bring home will turn in a single night, and from being green and red as well as hard, they become, suddenly, blue-black, soft, and edible—shrivelled like raisins—and you may eat them from day to day as they ripen in your chamber. The *Viburnum nudum* is all gone when the *lentago* are in their prime.

Sometimes they turn blue before fairly reddening, and they appear to drop off or are decreased about as soon as they turn, so that you can rarely find many ripe at once.

I have seen where squirrels have eaten them on a wall together with hazel nuts.

September 13, 1856. The *Viburnum lentago* which I left on my table not half-turned red when I went up-country a week ago are now quite black-purple and shrivelled like raisins and sweet to taste, though chiefly seed.

October 13, 1860. The *Viburnum lentago* fruit is quite sweet and reminds me of dates in their somewhat mealy pulp. It has large, flat black seeds, somewhat like watermelon seeds but not so long.

SWAMP SUMAC

Swamp sumac begins, say August twenty-eighth.

The *smooth* has crimson berries before this is in bloom.

Its berries are a hoary crimson (as if covered with dust or meal), not brilliant like those of the *smooth*. Also, they are in looser masses and are later. It appears to bear quite sparingly here.

I see no redness in them the next April, though I do in the smooth.

PUMPKINS

Pumpkins begin say August twenty-eighth, lie in field till mid-October.

August 27, 1853. Topping corn reveals the yellowing pumpkins.

August 31, 1852. From Israel Rice's hill I see some yellow pumpkins afar in the field next his house. This sight belongs to the season.

September 10, 1857. The vines are killed on the Great Fields, revealing the yellow pumpkins.

In the spring of 1857 I planted six seeds sent from the Patent Office and la-belled, I think, *Potiron Jaune Grosse*—Large Yellow Pumpkin (or Squash). Two came up, and one has become a pumpkin which weighed 123½ pounds. The other bore four weighing together 186¼ pounds. Who could have believed that there were 310 pounds of *Potiron Jaune Grosse* in that corner of my garden! These seeds were the bait I used to catch it, my ferrets which I sent into its burrow, my brace of terriers which unearthed it. A little mysterious hoeing and manuring was all the *Abracadabra-presto-change* that I used, and lo! true to the label, they found for me 310 pounds of *Potiron Jaune Grosse* there, where it never was known to be nor was before. These talismens had perchance sprung from America at first and returned to it with unabated force. Other seeds I have which will find other things there in like fashion—almost any fruit you wish, every year for ages until the crop more than fills the whole garden. (You have but little more to do than throw up your cap for entertainment these American days.) Perfect alchemists I

keep who can transmute substances without end, and thus the corner of my garden is an inexhaustible treasure chest. Here you can dig not gold, but the value which gold merely represents. The big squash took a premium at the Middlesex Show that fall, and I understood that the man who bought it intended to sell the seeds for ten cents apiece—and were they not cheap at that? But I have more hounds of the same breed. I learn that one which I despatched to a distant town, true to its instinct, points the large yellow pumpkin there, where no hound ever found it before, as its ancestors did here and in France. Yet farmers' sons will stare by the hour to see a juggler draw ribbons from his throat, though he tells them it is all deception, while in this case there is no deception—no Signor Blitz. Surely men love darkness rather than light.

By the middle of October there are but few left in the field. And in some places I see all the farmers' old coats spread over the few that are left out in piles.

As for pumpkins and squashes, Dr. T. W. Harris states in the *Patent Office Reports for 1854*:

> Accident led me, some four years ago, to undertake the investigation of the history of squashes and pumpkins, which has led to quite interesting results. Most of the older and well-known species and varieties were by modern botanists supposed to have come originally from Asia, and particularly from India. This I have proved to be an error, and have shown that these fruits were wholly unknown to the ancients, no mention being made of them in the Scriptures, nor by Greek and Latin authors. The writers of the middle ages, while they describe or take note of other cucurbitaceous plants, entirely omit pumpkins and squashes; and these did not begin to be known and noticed in Europe till after the discovery of America. Early voyagers found them in the West Indies, Peru, Florida, and even on the coast of New England, where they were cultivated by our Indians before any settlements were made here by the Europeans. The old botanists, who flourished during the first century after the discovery of the New World, or the West Indies, begin to describe them for the first time, and give to them specific names, indicating their Indian (American) origin. Hence arose the mistake of modern botanists in referring these plants to the East Indies and to Asia.
>
> From a study of the history of the plant, I went next to a study of the species, with particular reference to their botanical characters, and to this end have been cultivating and examining every year all the kinds accessible to me. I think I

have established the fact that all the fruits known by the names of "pumpkins" and "squashes" are of American origin; that there are three distinct groups of them; the first, including summer squashes, that have shells when ripe; the second, the winter squashes and pumpkins with deep, five-furrowed fruit, stems; and the third the winter pumpkins and squashes, with short, cylindrical and longitudinally wrinkled (but not five-furrowed) fruit, stems. The last group was probably originally confined to tropical and sub-tropical parts of the western side of this continent, from California to Chili. The most esteemed varieties now cultivated in New England belong to this group, and the best of them are the "autumnal," "Marrow," and "Acorn" squashes.

September 4, 1859. Topping the corn, which has been going on some days now, reveals the yellow and yellowing pumpkins. This is a genuine New England scene. The earth blazes not only with sunflowers, but with sun fruits.

WHITE ASH

White ash begins say August twenty-ninth.
Its knife-shaped fruit has strewn the paths of late.

MITCHELLA

Mitchella (partridge berry or twin berry) begins August twenty-ninth, generally ripe in October, and lasts all winter.

The last of July they show small green fruit, and in the middle of September I see many still perfectly green. It is a fruit of the damp and mossy forest floor,

ripening amid the now (September twelfth, 1854) mildewy and bracing fern scent of the damp wood.

The middle of October the little leaves of the mitchella, as big as a mouse ear, with a whitish mid-rib and veins, lying generally flat on the mossy ground, perhaps about the base of a tree, with their bright-scarlet twin berries sprinkled over them (their leaves interspersed with red berries), may properly be said to *checker* the ground, and I think that these are now correctly so called there the *Gaultheria*. Now, particularly, they are noticed amid the fallen leaves.

And when the snow goes off in the winter or the next spring on hummocks or about the insteps of trees, they appear very bright amid the still fresh green leaves.

They are an insipid berry, more important to the eye than to the palate, associated in my mind with the cool weather of the fall and spring.

POISON DOGWOOD

Poison dogwood (*Rhus venenata*) begins say August twenty-ninth.

August 29, 1854. It begins to look ripe or dry, of a pale straw color.

September 7, 1857. It is whitening.

In the swamps in winter the dry, yellowish-colored fruit of the poison dogwood hangs like jewelry on long, pricking stems. It is pleasant to meet with it, it has so much character relatively to man. The berries are pendant on long stems which hang *short down* (now, near the end of December) as if broken, and are between yellowish and greenish-white, ovoid, pearly or waxen on its few coarse branches— beautiful as Satan.

With its long fruit and stems hanging, is an agreeable object seen against the snow. ⅋ I derive a certain excitement not to be refused even from going through Dennis's Swamp by the railroad, where the poison dogwood abounds, now in mid-winter. This simple-stemmed bush is very full of fruit, hanging in loose, dry, pale-green, drooping panicles, some of them a foot long. It impresses me as the most fruitful shrub thereabouts. I cannot refrain from plucking it and carrying home some pretty sprigs.

As I am thus engaged it chances that the freight train rattles past, and some humane employee, who himself probably has no authority to stop the train, leans over with earnestness and shouts with warning voice and gesture "Dogwood!" in my ear.

January 24, 1858. With its recurved panicles of pale-greenish fruit massed together in profusion at the base of last year's store of blunt twigs, is very interesting and handsome. It is one of the chief ornaments of the swamps, dry and durable, befitting the season, and always attracts me. It might be the symbol of a vigorous swamp. The wood is very brittle to split down in the forks and, just broken, has a strong, somewhat liquorice-like scent. I do not know that any bird eats them.

RHUS RADICANS

Rhus radicans (on trees), August thirtieth.

WILD GRAPE

Wild grape *(Vitis labrusca)*, August thirtieth, in prime September twentieth or eighteenth.

Theophrastus includes the grape among the trees. Columella places it between trees and shrubs. Bohn's translators thinks Pliny wrong in making the vine indigenous to Italy and refers it to Asia.

Pliny complains that Virgil has "named only fifteen varieties of the grape" and three of the pear, and says that he does not describe all the kinds, "for there are almost as many as there are fields." He describes, for colors: purple, rosy, and green—the same variety that we have. "No sweetness anywhere," says he, "is preferred to the odor of the vine in flower. . . . The vine was justly numbered among trees by the ancients on account of its size. We see a statue of Jupiter made out of one in the city of Populonicum, in so many ages undecayed . . . nor has any wood a more durable nature." In Campania, says he, they climb so high up the poplars "that the vintager when hired stipulates that his employer shall pay for his funeral pyre and his grave" (*rogum ac tumulum*), and Numa "made it unlawful to make a libation to the gods of wine from an unpruned vine, for this reason, that the plowers might be compelled to prune, who were reluctant for fear of breaking their necks" (*circa pericula arbusto*; Bohn's translator says, "in consequence of the danger which attended climbing the trees"). Pliny says further:

> When at any time the vine has been liberated from its bonds, it should be allowed to range unconstrained for some days, and to spread abroad at pleasure, as well as to recline upon the ground which it has been looking down upon the whole year through. For in the same manner that beasts of burden when released from the yoke, and dogs when they have returned from the chase, love to roll themselves on the ground, just so does the vine delight to stretch its loins. The tree itself, too, seems to rejoice, and, thus relieved from the continuous weight which has burdened it, to have all the appearance of now enjoying a free respiration. Indeed, there is no object in all the economy of nature, that does not desire certain alternations, for the enjoyment of rest, witness the succession of night and day, for instance.

Pliny says of the wine bibbers, "They assert that they so enjoy life" (*rapere vitam*) and that "Androcides, illustrious for his wisdom, wrote to Alexander, the Great, checking his intemperance, 'About to drink wine, O king, remember that you drink the blood of the earth. . . .' "

July 15, 1854. Green grapes, as large as ripe cranberries, remind me of the advancing season.

July 28, 1852. Got green grapes to stew. There is a hearty diet for you, these stewed bullets, skins full of natural vinegar, which will make you think you've got into the country at last. Is not this the Vineland of the Northmen? How they overcome sugar!

Green grapes now found in berry time.

July 27, 1852. I observe green clusters almost fully grown hanging over the water. By the twenty-third of August I notice some turning.

August 27, 1859. The first notice I have that grapes are ripening is by the rich scent at evening from my own native vine against the house when I go to the pump, though I thought there were none on it.

August 28, 1853. Walking down the street in the evening I detect my neighbor's ripening grapes by the scent twenty rods off, though they are concealed behind his house. Every passer knows of them. Perhaps he takes me to his back door a week afterward and shows me with an air of mystery his clusters concealed under the leaves, which he thinks will be ripe in a day or two—as if it were a secret. He little thinks that I smelled them before he did.

August 30. I smell some already ripe in the fields, where they have sun enough, before I see any, so indeed detect them.

Early in September the ripening grapes begin generally to fill the air with their fragrance.

It is surprising how a single vine fastened to a house, though it bears but a cluster or two, will perfume the whole house through an open lattice. The fragrance of a single bunch which I have brought home with ripe grapes on it will also fill the house and surpasses the *flavor* of any grape.

September 8, 1858. I gather half of my own which are early and in an early place.

I find a few quite sweet, which have ripened on rocks, by the second of September.

I find the grapes in the greatest abundance from about September eighth to September twenty-eighth or for twenty days. At their height say the twentieth.

As soon as the berries are gone, grapes come.

I remember my earliest going a-graping. I got dismissed and went alone to a particular vine in Walden Woods which I can even now point out. It was a wonder that we boys ever hit upon the ripe season. There was more fun in finding and eying the big purple clusters high on the trees, and climbing to them—shinning up a vine as a sailor a rope—than in eating them. We used to take care not to chew the skins lest they should make our mouths sore.

Frequently, as I am paddling down the river at this season in the evening, I perceive the rich fragrance of ripe grapes wafted to me from this shore or that, where nothing was perceived as I ascended by day. I think that I could discover them surely thus, without the trouble of examining so many vines which have more on them.

I go a-graping, say to front of Cliffs or Fair Haven Pond, September twentieth. The grapes would no doubt be riper one week hence, but I am compelled to go now before the vines are stript. I faintly smell them out.

Some I find ripened early on a sunny rock in the meadow, sweeter than any. How handsome they lie with the bloom on them. This rubbed off, they show purple or black. They are a noble fruit to the eye. I pluck splendid great bunches of the purple ones with a rich bloom on them and the purple glowing through it like a fire. Large red ones also with light dots, and some clear green. I smell them out and, peeping, detect them under dense bowers made by their leaves, three feet above the water or the meadow. The purple clusters hang at that height and scent the air.

Sometimes I crawl under low and thick bowers where they have run over the alders only four or five feet high and see the grapes hanging from a hollow hemisphere of leaves over my head. At other times I see them dark-purple or black against the silvery undersides of the leaves, high above my head where they have run over birches or maples, and either climb or pull them down to pluck them.

Methinks the true grape trellis or arbor is a wild apple tree, its top wholly covered with the vine, like a tree caught in a net, as that near the old lime-kiln. Though quite low it is difficult to break off the large bunches without some dropping off, and if I am climbing to them, I am disappointed to see the ripest rattle off and strew the ground before I reach their clusters; or, while I am standing on tiptoe and endeavoring gently to break the tough peduncle of some particularly fair cluster, the petiole of a leaf gets entangled in the bunch, and I am compelled to strip them all off loosely. The ripest drop off at the slightest touch, and if they fall into the water they are lost, going to the bottom.

Depositing them in the bows of the boat, they filled all the air with their fragrance, as we rowed along homeward against the wind, as if we were rowing thro' an endless vineyard in its maturity. Every now and then, when their perfume was wafted to me in the stern, I thought that I was passing some richly laden vine on shore.

I have paddled far down the stream, three or four miles below the town, where no grapers had been, when the whole river was scented with them.

I love to bring some home if only to scent my chamber with them, for they are more admirable for their fragrance than their flavor. But it is impossible to get them home in a basket with all their rich bloom on them, which no less than the form of the clusters makes their beauty.

What is a whole binful that have been plucked to that solitary cluster left dangling inaccessible from some birch far away over the stream in the September air, with all its bloom and freshness?

About the last of September the grapes have begun to shrivel on their stems, though in some places still abundant, and they fall on the slightest touch. I have only to shake the birches to bring down a shower of plums. They are never better flavored than now. The vines are partly bare and the leaves yellowed or killed by frost, say October first.

Yet as late as October of 1853, being far down the river in Billerica, opposite Jug Island (which I once called Grape Island), I perceived the fragrance of ripe grapes in the air, and though I saw no vines at first, they being bare of leaves, I at last found them quite plenty, ripe, and fresh enough on the ground amid the alder leaves. It was very gratifying to detect them thus—as a hound its game. Ah! their scent is very penetrating and memorable.

September 16, 1852. I discovered a particularly sweet red grape with a soft pulp by the river in front of the Cliffs, the best wild grape that I ever tasted. I laid some down there the next day and the next fall transplanted them to my garden—where they have done well and are very early. I call it the Musketaquid grape.

Thus for the common or *Vitis labrusca*.

We have *at least* two other kinds here, smooth leaved. There is at Grape Cliff the perhaps *Vitis æstivalis* partly fallen September twenty-ninth, 1856. It is dark purple, about seven-sixteenths of an inch in diameter, very acid, and commonly hard. Should not this be called frost grape rather than that I ate in Brattleboro September sixth?

October 18, 1857. I find, halfway up Blackberry Steep, above the rock, an abundance of those small, densely clustered grapes (not the *smallest* quite) still quite fresh and full on green stems, and leaves crisp but not all fallen; so much later than other grapes, which were further advanced than this October fourth—for it was then too late to get many of them. *These* are not yet ripe, and may *fairly* be called *frost* grapes.

October 28, 1857. The last mentioned are now as ripe as ever they will be. They are sweet and shrivelled, but on the whole poor. They ripen, then, the latter part of October. It is a smooth-leaved grape. Also, October thirty-first, though shrivelled and therefore ripe, are very acid and inedible—unlike the Eagleswood grape.

I am not sure whether that very dense-bunched and small grape is distinct from the last.

October 2, 1858. I sailed to Lee's Cliff with a strong north wind and got a peck of the last-named small, long-bunched grapes, now turned purple under Lee's Cliff. One or two vines there bear very plentifully. The bunches are about six inches long by one and a half wide, and are quite dense and cylindrical, commonly. They are now apparently just in their prime (to judge from color), considerably later than the *Vitis labrusca.* They are never good raw, nor are they gathered, to my knowledge. But my mother made a very *nice tart* jelly of these. None are better for that.

We have also a rather smooth-leaved variety with a leaf of peculiar form such as described by Michaux, but I have not found the fruit.

September 6, 1856. I found at Brattleboro, on the bank of the Connecticut River, small grapes, in size one-third of an inch in diameter and clusters somewhat like our smallest (clusters three to five inches long), just fairly begun to be ripe; but they were not only thus much earlier than *ours*, but were agreeably acid and edible, evidently distinct. Are these the *Vitis cordifolia?* Perhaps they call them frost grape there.

About the tenth of November, 1856, I first noticed in a wood at Eagleswood, New Jersey, long bunches of very small dark-purple or black grapes fallen on the dry leaves in the ravine east of my host's house. Quite a large mass

of clusters remained hanging on the leafless vine thirty feet overhead there, even till I left (the twenty-fourth of November). These grapes were much shrivelled, but they had a very agreeable spicy, acid taste, evidently not acquired till after the frosts. I thought them quite a discovery and ate many from day to day, swallowing the skins and stones, and recommended them to my host, who had never noticed them. He said that they were much like a certain French grape, which he had eaten in France. This was a true frost grape; apparently *answers* to *Vitis æstivalis*.

Torrey, in *New York Reports*, says, the *Vitis cordifolia*, winter grape, frost grape, is "not uncommon in the vicinity of New York." Can the Brattleboro grape, which begins to ripen so early, be the same?

June 27, 1856. At Naushon I saw a common wild grape vine running over a beech, which was apparently flattened out by it, which vine measured at six feet from the ground, twenty-three inches in circumference. It was larger below and had already forked. At five feet from the ground (along the vine) it divided into three great branches. It did not rise directly but with a great half-spiral sweep or *anguish*. No sight could be more primæval. It was partly or chiefly dead.

This was in the midst of the woods by a path side. Just beyond we started up two deer.

November 4, 1857. I see in a wood path some rank thimbleberry shoots covered very thickly with a peculiar, hoary bloom. It is rubbed off down to the purple skin only in a few places, by some passing hunter perchance. It is a very singular and delicate outer coat, surely, for a plant to wear. I find that I can write my name in it with a pointed stick, very distinctly each stroke, however fine, going down to the purple. It is a new kind of enamelled card. What is this bloom, and what purpose does it serve? Is there anything analogous in animated nature? It is the *coup de grace,* the last touch and perfection of any work, a thin Elysian veil cast over it, through which it may be viewed. It is breathed on it by the artist, and thereafter his work is not to be touched without injury. It is the evidence of a ripe and completed work, on which the unexhausted artist has breathed out of his superfluous genius, and his work looks through it as a veil. If it is a poem, it must be invested with a similar bloom by the imagination of the reader. It is the subsidence of superfluous ripeness, like a fruit preserved in its own sugar. It is the handle by which the imagination grasps it.

Is not the bloom on fruits equivalent to that blue veil of air which distance gives to many objects, as to mountains in the horizon? The very mountains, blue and purple as they are, have a bloom on them.

Dr. Carpenter says wax "may be seen in the form of minute scales, upon the outer surface of the plum and other stone fruits, forming what is known as the bloom; and it is by the existence of a thin coating of it, that the leaves of the cabbage, Tropacolum (Sturtion) and other plants are enabled to resist moisture."

Pursh says of *Vitis labrusca,* "Berries black, large, of a disagreeable fox-smell, commonly called *Fox-grape.*"

So Beverly, in his *History of Virginia,* speaks of a very large kind of grape which has "a rank taste when ripe, resembling the musk of a fox, from whence they are called fox grapes."

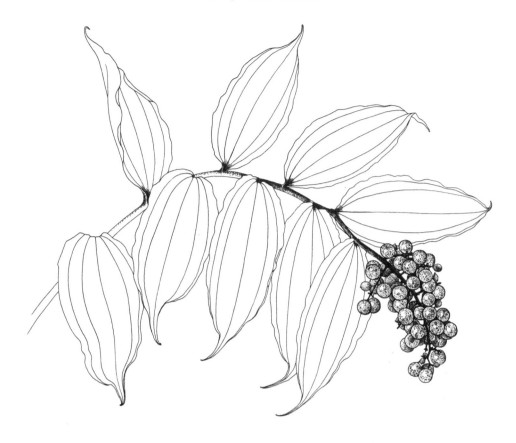

SMILACINA RACEMOSA

Smilacina racemosa berries begin to be ripe August thirty-first, in prime say September fifteenth.

In the latter part of August and in September we notice the dense clusters of Solomon-seal berries at the end of the stalk, which is bent over by their weight. It is a compound raceme four or five inches long, of whitish berries a little smaller than a pea, finely marked or dotted with vermillion or bright red. This is very conspicuous and handsome.

At length, in September, they become a clear and uniform semi-lucent red, being soft and ripe, and have a sweetish taste, but a large and hard stone. Are common September twenty-seventh, *at least*.

DESMODIUM

Desmodium, August thirty-first.

Desmodium nudiflorum in woods not ripe.

One afternoon, having landed far down the river (at Ball's Hill) with a companion and walked about through a quantity of desmodium (*marylandicum* or *rigidum*, which have roundish joints) by the shore there, we found our pantaloons covered with its seeds to a remarkable and amusing degree. These green scale-like seeds densely covering and greening our legs reminded me of the *lemna* on a ditch. It amounted to a kind of coat of mail. It was the event of our walk, and we were proud to wear this badge, regarding each other with a little envy from time to time, as if he were the most distinguished who had the most of them on his clothes. My companion betrayed a certain religion about it, for he said, reproving me, that he thought it would not be right to walk intentionally amid the desmodium in order to get more of the ticks on us, nor yet to pick them off, but they must be carried about till they were rubbed off accidentally. The consequence was that when he reappeared for a walk a day or two after, his clothes were nearly as well covered as at first. I saw that Nature's design was furthered even by his superstition.

WAX-WORK

Wax-work begins to be orange August thirty-first, but not open.

By August second I see it yellowing. By the second of September it is fairly yellow on all hands, and it is time to gather it. September twenty-third it is not open.

At length, as October fourteenth, 1860, the orange shell spreads open and reveals the red inside.

HAZEL

Hazel nuts begin to be ripe say September first. About the first of July the burrs make a show. Between July sixteenth and twenty-fourth they are fully formed and are richly, autumnally significant.

Loudon says, "According to some, from κόρυς, a helmet; the fruit, with its involucre, appearing as if covered with a bonnet." Others give a different interpretation.

This shaggy fruit now meets the eye, always an agreeable sight to me, with which when a boy I used to take the stains of berries out of my hands and mouth, as some eat a salad after a berry pudding. These and green grapes are found in berry time.

August 12, 1854. The husks have now a reddish edge, being ripe, and by the next day, or from the thirteenth to the twenty-fourth of August, I first notice when the squirrels have begun to eat hazel nuts, and I see their dry involucres on the ground, or on a stump or rock or wall, turned reddish brown. Toward the end of the month I see there dried and reddened burrs and shells under every bush where the squirrels have been, and the walls are strewn with them, though those on the bushes are still quite green. This is a peculiar rich brown which these *dried* burrs and shells have acquired, not chestnut nor yet hazel, and always excites me a little.

Thomson in his *Autumn* speaks of shaking down the nuts:

A glossy shower, and of an ardent brown.

August 24, 1858. Now and of late we are reminded of hazel bushes; we become aware of such a fruit-bearing bush. They have their turn now, and every clump and hedge seems composed of them. The burrs looking more and more red, handsome, crimson-tipt on their edges, remind us that it is time to gather them if we would anticipate the squirrels. Indeed, you cannot gather those which are most exposed to squirrels soon after the twentieth of August.

Toward the end of the month those which grow along the walls and where squirrels abound will be all stript by them while still green, and the ground and walls are strewn with their brown husks, and every nut that you can find left there will be a poor one, suggesting that they must have been very busy—when by more frequented paths the squirrels have not worked yet.

The striped squirrels begin to eat the hazel nuts early in August, or about the time the flail begins to be heard, and you must gather those which are most expanded soon after the twentieth of that month, if you would get them at all. Many a man who has observed these nuts peculiarly abundant has waited ten days before he went after them and then not found a dozen left.

Towards the end of August those bushes which grow along the walls and where squirrels abound will be all stript by them while still green, and the ground will be strewn with their brown husks. Every nut that you can find left there will be a poor one, suggesting that they must have been very busy for a fortnight past climbing to the extremities of the slender twigs. Who witnesses the gathering of the hazel nuts—the hazel harvest? Yet what a busy and important season to the striped squirrel! Now, if ever, he needs to get up a *bee*. Every nut that I could find left in that field (now hemlocks) was a poor one. By some frequented paths they did not get them so early.

When the bushes on the brink of the river are otherwise completely stript, I sometimes find some clusters left hanging over the water, as if the squirrels had been unwilling to return there for them. I sometimes see a bird's nest in a thorn or other bush half full of acorn and hazel-nut shells, where evidently some mouse or squirrel has left them.

How important the hazel nut to the ground squirrel! They grow along the walls where the squirrels have their homes. They are the oaks that grow before their doors. They have not far to go to their harvesting.

These bushes are generally stript now, but isolated ones in the middle of the fields, away from the squirrel walks, are still full of burrs. The wall is both highway and rampart to these little beasts. They are almost inaccessible in their holes beneath it, and on either side of it spring up, also defended by the wall, the hazel bushes on whose fruit the squirrels in a great measure depend.

The squirrel lives in a hazel grove. There is not a hazel bush but some squirrel has his eye on its fruit, and he will be pretty sure to anticipate you; for you think of it only between whiles, but he thinks of it all the while. As we say, "The tools to those who can use them," so we may say, "The nuts to those who can get them."

I would not be surprised to find that they have an instinct which prompts them to plant hazel nuts—regularly.

They know better than to open an unsound nut, or at most they only peep into them. I see some on the walls with a little hole gnawed in them, enough to show that they are empty.

You must gather them with burrs for the most part green and spread them in some sunny place away from mice to dry. There they will open and expose their nuts, which turn brown and will drop out in a few days. I see where farmers' boys have spread bushels of them to dry in the latter part of August.

I got a parcel along the bank of the Assabet River September third, 1858. Up that way they are chiefly confined to the drier river bank; at least they do not extend into the lower, somewhat meadowy land further inland. The bushes were mostly stript. Most of those I got were such as were left hanging over the water at the swimming ford, as if the squirrels had been unwilling to venture over the water for them. Many of the burrs were perfectly green—though others were brightly red-edged.

I sometimes see a bird's nest in a thorn or other bush half full of acorns and hazel-nut shells, where evidently some mouse or squirrel has left them.

You may gather them as late as September tenth where the squirrels have not found them. But they will all be gone soon after that date. They are worth gathering if only to see the rich color of the fruit brought together in a quantity.

The beaked hazelnut, though the only kind much further north, is comparatively scarce here. The burrs have a very long beak, and the nuts also are larger.

September 9, 1858. I find an abundance of beaked hazel nuts at Blackberry Steep (one to three burrs together). But gathering them I get my fingers full of fine, shining bristles, while the common hazel burrs are either smooth or covered with a softer, glandular down (that is, its horns are brazen tipt).

The beaked are pointed nuts, while the common are blunt (::) (⌣), and the former are much paler brown—also have a yellower and much sweeter meat. Are they not later?

Notwithstanding the abundance of hazel nuts hereabouts, very little account is made of them—partly, I think, because pain is not taken to collect them before squirrels have done so. Yet the meat is small. Loudon says of *Corylus rostrata*, "The nuts are so hard that they are said to have been used by the inhabitants as shot."

MEDEOLA

Medeola. September first, perhaps in prime September fourth, and common September twenty-seventh.

July 24, 1853. Still in flower, though with large green berries.

September 2. About three dull, glossy, dark blue-black berries on slender peduncles about one inch long, arising in the midst of the cups formed by the purple base of the whorl of three upper leaves.

By the middle of September, the upper whorl of leaves stands empty for the most part, like shallow saucers, with their purple centers and bare peduncles.

PEAS

Peas, September first.

Phillips, in his *History of Cultivated Vegetables*, says of "Pea.—Pisum.": "The English name is evidently a corruption of the Latin, as Tusser calls it 'peason'; also Gerarde, and *then* Dr. Holland, 'pease.' " *I* think it another evidence of the Roman pronunciation of the vowel *i*.

BEANS

Beans, September first.

Phillips says, "Columella notices them in his time as food for the peasants only: 'And herbs they mix with beans for vulgar fare.' "

Gerarde says, "The fruit and cods of kidney beans boiled together before they be ripe, and buttered, and so eaten with their cods, are exceedingly delicate meat, and do not ingender wind as the other pulses do." After they are boiled, "the rib or sinew that doth run along the cod is to be taken away"; so stringed beans are an old institution.

EUROPEAN CRANBERRY

European cranberry, September first.

August 23, 1854. *Vaccinium oxycoccus* has a small, now purplish-dotted fruit, flat on the sphagnum, some turned partly scarlet, on terminal peduncles, with slender thread-like stems, and small leaves, strongly resolute on the edges—of which Emerson says, the "Common cranberry of the north of Europe," cranberry of commerce there.

October 17, 1859. These interesting little cranberries are quite scarce, the vine bearing (this year at least) only amid the higher and drier sphagnum mountains amid the lowest bushes about the edge of the open swamp. There the dark red berries (quite ripe, only a few spotted still) now rest on the shelves and in the recesses of the red sphagnum. There is only enough of these berries for sauce to a botanist's Thanksgiving dinner.

I have come out this afternoon a-cranberrying, chiefly to gather some of the small cranberry, *Vaccinium oxycoccus*. This was a small object, yet not to be postponed, on account of imminent frosts—that is, if I would know this year the flavor of the European cranberry as compared with our larger kind. I thought I should like to have a dish of this sauce on the table at Thanksgiving of my own gathering. I could hardly make up my mind to come this way, it seemed so poor an object to spend the afternoon on. I kept foreseeing a lame conclusion—how I should cross the Great Fields, look into Beck Stow's Swamp, and then retrace my steps no richer than before. In fact, I expected little of this walk, yet it did pass through the side of my mind that somehow, on this very account (my small expectation), it would turn out well, as also the advantage of having some purpose, however small, to be accomplished—of letting your deliberate wisdom and foresight in the house to some extent direct and control your steps. If you would really take a position outside the street and daily life of men, you must have deliberately planned your course, you must have business which is not your neighbors' business, which they cannot understand. For only absorbing employment prevails, succeeds, takes up space, occupies territory, determines the future of individuals and states, drives Kansas out of your head, and actually and permanently occupies the only desirable and free Kansas against all border ruffians. The attitude of resistance is one of weakness, inasmuch as it only faces an enemy; it has its back to all that is truly attractive. You shall have your affairs, I will have mine. You will spend this afternoon in setting up your neighbor's stove, and be paid for it; I will spend it in gathering the few berries of the *Vaccinium oxycoccus* which Nature produces here, before it is too late, and be paid for it also, after another fashion. I have always reaped unexpected and incalculable advantages from carrying out at last, however tardily, any little enterprise which my genius suggested to me long ago as a thing to be done, some step to be taken, however slight, out of the usual course.

How many schools I have thought of which I might go to but did not go to! expecting foolishly that some greater advantage (or schooling) would come to me! It is these comparatively cheap and private expeditions that substantiate our existence and batten our lives—as, where a vine touches the earth in its undulating course, it puts forth roots and thickens its stock. Our employment generally is tinkering, mending the old worn-out teapot of society. Our stock in trade is solder. Better for me, says my genius, to go cranberrying this afternoon for the *Vaccinium oxycoccus* in Gowing's Swamp, to get but a pocketful and learn its peculiar flavor—aye, and the flavor of Gowing's Swamp and of *life* in New England—than to go consul to Liverpool and get I don't know how many thousand dollars for it, with no such flavor. Many of our days should be spent, not in vain expectations and lying on our oars, but in carrying out deliberately and faithfully the hundred little purposes which every man's genius must have suggested to him. Let not your life be wholly without an object, though it be only to ascertain the flavor of a cranberry, for it will not be only the quality of an insignificant berry that you will have tasted, but the flavor of your life to that extent, and it will be such a sauce as no wealth can buy.

Both a conscious and an unconscious life are good; neither is good exclusively, for both have the same source. The wisely conscious life springs out of an unconscious suggestion. I have found my account in travelling in having prepared beforehand a list of questions which I would get answered, not trusting to my interest at the moment, and can then travel with the most profit. Indeed, it is by obeying the suggestions of a higher light within you that you escape from yourself and, in the transit, as it were see with the unworn sides of your eye, travel totally new paths. What is that pretended life that does not take up a claim, that does not occupy ground, that cannot build a causeway to its objects? that sits on a bank looking over a bog, singing its desires?

However, it was not with such blasting expectations as these that I entered the swamp. I saw bags of cranberries, just gathered and tied up, on the banks of Beck Stow's Swamp. They must have been raked out of the water, now so high, before they should rot. I left my shoes and stockings on the bank far off and waded barelegged through rigid andromeda and other bushes a long way, to the soft open sphagnous center of the swamp.

I found these cunning little cranberries lying high and dry on the firm uneven tops of the sphagnum—their weak vine considerably on one side—sparsely scattered about the drier edges of the swamp, or sometimes more thickly occupying some little valley a foot or two over, between two mountains of sphagnum. They were of two varieties, judging from the fruit. *The one,* apparently *the ripest,* colored most like the common cranberry but more scarlet—that is, yellowish-green, blotched, or checked with dark scarlet-red, commonly pear-shaped. *The other,* also pear-shaped, or more bulged out in the middle, thickly and finely dark-spotted or peppered on yellowish-green or straw-colored or pearly ground—almost exactly like the *Smilacina* and *Convallaria* berries now, except that they are a little larger and not so spherical, with a tinge of purple. A singular difference. They both lay very snug in the moss, often the whole of the long (one and a half inch or more) peduncle buried, their vines very inobvious, projecting only one to three inches, so that it was not easy to tell what vine they belonged to, and you were obliged to open the moss carefully with your fingers to ascertain it; while the common large cranberry there, with its stiff, erect vine, was commonly lifted above the sphagnum. The grayish-speckled variety was particularly novel and pretty, though not easy to detect. It lay here and there snugly sunk in the sphagnum, whose drier parts it exactly resembled in color, just like some kind of swamp-sparrow's eggs in their nest. I was obliged with my finger carefully to trace the slender pedicel through the moss to its vine, where I would pluck the whole together, like jewels worn on or set in these sphagnous breasts of the swamp—swamp pearls, call them—one or two to a vine and, on an average three-eighths of an inch in diameter. They are so remote from their vines, on their long thread-like peduncles, that they remind you the more forcibly of eggs, and in May I might mistake them for such. These plants are almost parasitic, resting wholly on the sphagnum, in water instead of air. The sphagnum is a living soil for it. It rests on and amid this, on an acre of sponges. They are evidently earlier than the common. A few are quite soft and red-purple. I waded quite round the swamp for an hour, my bare feet in the cold water beneath, and it was a relief to place them on the warmer surface of the sphagnum. I filled one pocket with each variety, but sometimes, being confused, crossed hands and put them into the wrong pocket.

I enjoyed this cranberrying very much, notwithstanding the wet and cold, and the swamp seemed to be yielding its crop to me alone, for there are none else to pluck it or to value it. I told the proprietor once that they grew here, but he, learning that they were not abundant enough to be gathered for the market, has probably never thought of them since. I am the only person in the township who regards them or knows of them, and I do not regard them in the light of their pecuniary value. I have no doubt I felt richer wading there with my two pockets full, treading on wonders at every step, than any farmer going to market with a hundred bushels which he has raked, or hired to be raked. I got further and further away from the town every moment, and my good genius seemed to have smiled on me, leading me hither, and then the sun suddenly came out clear and bright, but it did not warm my feet. I would gladly share my gains, take one or twenty into partnership and get this swamp with them, but I do not know an individual whom this berry cheers and nourishes as it does me. When I exhibit it to them I perceive that they take but a momentary interest in it and commonly dismiss it from their thoughts with the consideration that it cannot be profitably cultivated. You could not get a pint at one haul of a rake, and Slocum would not give you much for them. But I love it the better partly for that reason even. I fill a basket with them and keep it several days by my side. If anybody else—any farmer, at least—should spend an hour thus wading about here in this secluded swamp, bare-legged, intent on the sphagnum, filling his pocket only, with no rake in his hand and no bag or bushel on the bank, he would be pronounced insane and have a guardian put over him; but if he'll spend his time skimming and watering his milk and selling his small potatoes for large ones, or generally in skinning flints, he will probably be made guardian of somebody else. I have not garnered any rye or oats, but I gathered the wild vine of the Assabet.

I see that all is not garden and cultivated field and copse, that there are square rods in Middlesex County as purely primitive and wild as they were a thousand years ago, which have escaped the plow and the axe and the scythe and the cranberry rake—little oases of wildness in the desert of our civilization, wild as a square rod on the moon, supposing it to be uninhabited. I believe almost in the personality of such planetary matter, feel something akin to reverence for it, can even worship it as terrene, titanic matter extant in my day. We are so different we admire each other, we healthily attract one another. I love it as a maiden. These spots are meteoric, ærolitic, and such matter has in all ages been worshipped. Aye, when we are lifted out of the slime and film of our habitual life, we see the whole globe to be an ærolite, and reverence it as such, and make pilgrimages to it, far off as it is. How happens it that we reverence the stones which fall from another planet, and not the stones which belong to this—another globe, not this—heaven, and not earth? Are not the stones in Hodge's wall as good as the ærolite at Mecca? Is not our broad backdoor stone as good as any corner-stone in heaven?

It would imply the regeneration of mankind if they were to become elevated enough to truly worship sticks and stones. It is the sentiment of fear and slavery and habit which makes a heathenish idolatry. Such idolaters abound in all countries, and heathen cross the seas to reform heathen, dead to bury the dead, and all go down to the pit together. If I could, I would worship the parings of my nails. If he who makes two blades of grass grow where one grew before is a benefactor, he who discovers two gods where there was only known the one (and such a one!) before is a still greater benefactor. I would fain improve every opportunity to wonder and worship, as a sunflower welcomes the light. The more thrilling, wonderful, divine objects I behold in a day, the more expanded and immortal I become. If a stone appeals to me and elevates me, tells me how many miles I have come, how many remain to travel—and the more, the better—reveals the future to me in some measure, it is a matter of private rejoicing. If it did the same service to all, it might well be a matter of public rejoicing.

The botanist refers you, for wild berries and we presume wild plants, further inland or westward to so many miles from Boston, as if Nature or the Indians had any such preferences. Perchance the ocean seemed wilder to them than the woods. As if there were primarily and essentially any more wildness in a western acre than an eastern one!

So many plants, the indigenous and the bewildering variety of exotics, you see in conservatories and nurserymen's catalogues, or read of in English books, and the Royal Society did not make one of them, and knows no more about them than you! All truly indigenous and wild on this earth. I know of no mark that betrays an introduced plant, as none but the gardener can tell what flower has strayed from its parterre; but where the seed will germinate and the plant spring and grow, there it is at home.

Loudon writes of *Oxycoccus palustris*, the marsh or common cranberry:

MOSSBERRIES, MOORBERRIES, FENBERRIES, MARSHWORTS, OR WHORTLEBERRIES, CORNBERRIES, ENG. . . .

The name of Cranberry is supposed to be given from the peduncles of the flowers being crooked at the top, and, before the expansion of the flowers, resembling the head and neck of a crane (*Smith* and *Withering*); or because they are much eaten by cranes. . . . Berries pear-shaped, globular, often spotted, crimson, of a peculiar flavor, with a strong acidity, grateful (*Don's Mill.*). . . . It is a native of turfy mossy bogs in the mountainous parts of Europe; common in Switzerland, Russia, Scotland, Ireland, and the north of England, as well as in the east [that is, of England and in America]. . . . [In Siberia] the berries remain during the whole winter under the snow; and are collected in spring, after it is thawed and gone, as well as in autumn, before it falls. In the north of Europe, as well as in Britain, cranberries have been in use from time immemorial, for supplying an acid drink during the hot summer months, for tarts, and other purposes. . . . [Now in England nearly exterminated, and she depends on Russia and Sweden, and the *Oxycoccus macrocarpus* from North America.] The Russian cranberries are considered to be superior in quality to those of America. . . .

In Russia, and in some parts of Sweden, the long filiform shoots of the *Oxycoccus* are collected in spring, after most of the leaves have dropped off, and are dried and twisted into ropes, which are used to tie on the thatch of houses and even for harnessing horses.

Of "Marish Worts or Fen Berries," Gerarde says, "The marish wortleberries grow upon the bogs in marish or moorish grounds, creeping thereupon like unto wild Time having many small limmer and tender stalks laid almost flat upon the ground, beset with small narrow leaves fashioned almost like the leaves of Time; but lesser . . . in taste rough and astringent"! "*Oxycoccon . . . Vaccinia palustria . . .* Moose berries or Moore berries."

SASSAFRAS

Sassafras, September first. Lasts through September.

September 3, 1856. I find one berry (on the hill) dark blue in its crimson cup, club-shaped. It is chiefly stone, and its taste is like that of tar, methinks, far from palatable.

September 24, 1854. On the large sassafras trees on the hill I see many of the handsome red club-shaped pedicels left, with their empty cups which have held fruit, and I *see one or two elliptical* but still *green* berries. All the rest have ripened and fallen or been gathered by birds already, unless they fall prematurely. Gray says that the berries are dark blue and ripen in September.

On Hill and trees northwest of P. Dudley's, toward Lee's, and behind A. Heywood's.

BUTTERNUT

Butternut, September first.

September 13, 1854. Many have dropt—more than walnuts.

According to Loudon, are ripe a fortnight earlier than other nuts, or in middle of September.

September 19, 1859. Alcott says his have fallen two or three weeks since. They must dry and lose their outer shell before cracking.

September 28, 1860. Still on trees and holding on all September.

July 16, 1858. Noticed the butternut, a common tree in Thornton and Campton.

Michaux says, "They are ripe in the neighborhood of New York about the fifteenth of September, a fortnight earlier than the other species of walnut."

PELTANDRA

About the first of September I see the great peduncles of the peltandra, one and a half to two feet long, curving downward along the riverside and in the meadows, with its globular mass of green fruit at the end, often two inches in diameter, looking like slung-shot. This contains a mass of viscid seeds or nuts. The fruit curves downward so close to the ground that this part annually escapes the scythe, though the leaves are closely shorn, and thus the plant is preserved and propagated. Nature gives the mower the leaves but holds back the seeds, waiting for the floods to come to get them.

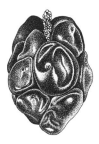

PONTEDERIA

Pontederia, September first.

September 17, 1860. Rapidly falling.

August 19, 1858. Seed vessels turned down.

Now, while other fruits are ripe or ripening (September first), it is fall and harvest by the riverside.

September 13, 1859. The pontederia spike is now generally turned downward beneath the water, though some others have flowers still at their tips. Curving down August tenth, 1860.

September 17, 1860. Shedding its seeds in a freshet.

September 26, 1859. The pontederia is fast shedding its seeds of late. I saw a parcel suddenly rise to the surface of their own accord, leaving the axis of the spike nearly bare. Many were long since bare. They float at present, but probably sink at last. There are a great many of these loose ones floating amid the pads and in the wrack washed up next to the shore, singular, green, spidery-looking seeds. Probably they are the food of returning waterfowl. They are ripe, like the seeds of different lilies, at the time the fowl return from the north.

October 7, 1859. The pontederia seeds which I dropt into a pitcher of water have now mostly sunk. As the outside decays, they become heavier than water.

LILIES

So too the yellow lily (*Nuphar advena*) is ripening its seed September first in the water and mud beneath the surface. Its fruit is now green and purplish, and of this form and size, and is full of yellow seeds . The white-lily fruit, when stript of the blackened and decaying petals and so on, is of this form .

MALLOWS

Mallows, September first.

Abounds at the Hunt cellar.

September 22, 1859. With its pretty little button-shaped fruit, which children eat green and call cheeses. 🌼 There are several such fruits discoverable and edible by children.

FLOWERING RASPBERRY

Flowering raspberry, September first.

September 6, 1856. At Brattleboro. When ripe it is red and quite agreeable. I gathered them in all my walks there and found them a pleasant taste—berry large, but never abundant.

DATURA

Datura, September first.

September 21, 1858. At Marblehead *generally* done flowering.

Gerarde says of the Thorny apple of Peru, our Jamestown weed, "There is another kind hereof, altogether greater than the former [standard thorny-apple], whose seeds I received of the right honorable, the Lord Edward Zouch; which he brought from Constantinople, and of his liberality did bestow them upon me, as also many other rare and strange seeds; and it is that thorn apple that I have dispersed thro' this land."

GREEN-BRIAR

Green-briar, September first.

August 31, 1853. Begins to turn. September 4. The same. September 11,

1851. Mostly turned dark. September 8, 1854. Not quite ripe. September 17, 1852. Ripe.

September 24, 1854. Umbelled, blue-black or purplish, ripened apparently by the frost of the twenty-first and twenty-second.

December 19, 1850. Are as pleasant as ever.

February 19, 1854. Full of shining and fresh berries. Are very persistent and durable.

January 8, 1851. Still hang on like small grapes.

VIBURNUM ACERIFOLIUM

Viburnum acerifolium, September second.

August 22, 1852. The oval berries of *Viburnum acerifolium* have got to be yellowish, and August twenty-fourth and twenty-eighth are merely yellowish, oval, and flattish.

September 2, 1853. They are dark purple, black.

September 4, 1853. Fall when ripe, like the *Viburnum dentatum*.

September 6. Are in prime at Brattleboro, or a little past; ovoid, dull, blue-black.

September 12, 1854. Blue-black with but little bloom; no full cymes, and their cymes rather less spreading than the other kinds.

September 23. Are fresh, dark bluish.

They are rather scarce hereabouts. Loudon calls them "black."

BLACK ASH

Black ash, September second.

SWEET BRIAR

Sweet-briar hips begin to redden September third, or sometimes I do not notice them fair till near the end of September.

In October they are very handsome, a very beautiful glossy, elliptical fruit, a dozen sometimes crowded in a space of two inches square. Their form is a hand-

some oval with a flat apex (is it not somewhat like an olive jar?). These are about the prettiest red berries that we have. But most are more regular, jar-shaped ⬭. What with the fragrance of its leaves, its flowers, and its fruit, it is thrice crowned.

They do not deserve to be coupled with *our* haws as articles of food, even in extremities. They are very dry, hard, seedy, and unpalatable. Yet December eighteenth, 1852, I saw a red squirrel eating them.

November 6, 1853. They were abundant and fresh and handsome, though haws had fallen and much of the prinos too. There were also some fragrant green leaves left.

February 19, 1854. They had lost their color and begun to decay.

Gerarde says:

> The Brier Bush or Hep Tree, is also called *Rosa canina* [still the same], which is a plant so common and well known, that it were to small purpose to use many words in the description thereof: for even children with great delight eat the berries thereof when they be ripe, make chains and other prettie gewgaws of the fruit: cooks and gentlewomen make tarts and such like dishes for pleasure thereof, and thereof this shall suffice for the description.
>
> The sweet Brier [ours] doth oftentimes grow higher than all the kinds of Roses; the shoots of it are hard, thick, and woody; the leaves are glittering and of a beautiful green color, of smell most pleasant: the Roses are little, five leaved, most commonly whitish, seldom tending to purple, of little or no smell at all: the fruit is long, of color somewhat red, like a little olive stone and like the little heads or berries of the others, but lesser than those of the garden: in which is contained rough cotton or hairy down and seed, folded and wrapped up in the same, which is small and hard: there be likewise found about the slender shoots hereof round, soft, and hairy spunges, which we call Brier balls, such as grow about the prickles of the Dog-rose.
>
> [Speaking of the "wild rose" generally:] The fruit when it is ripe maketh most pleasant meats and banquetting dishes, as tarts and such like; the making whereof I commit to the cunning cook, and teeth to eat them in the rich man's mouth.

WOODBINE

Woodbine, September third. Purple.

HOP

Hop picking, September sixth.

AMERICAN MOUNTAIN ASH

American mountain ash, September sixth.
August 25, 1859. Partly turned.
Old Gerarde says it is ripe "in August."
September 15, 1860. Seven or ten days—say sixth.
Nuttall says, "The mountain ash or Roan Tree of North America." In the *Geological Report on the Island of Anticosti for 1856:* "Of fruit-bearing trees and shrubs, the mountain ash or rowan, was the largest; it was most abundant in the interior"—largest forty feet high.

VIBURNUM LANTANOIDES

Viburnum lantanoides, September sixth. How long? Hobble bush, American wayfaring tree.
September sixth. Petersboro—mostly large and red, but the ripe dark-blue and black, like the *Viburnum nudum.*
September eighth. Brattleboro.

ACORNS: SHRUB OAK

Acorns, September sixth.

Osterman says, "The acorns and nuts of the primitive days have given way to all the variety of sweeter farinaceous seeds and roots."

Loudon quotes Burnet, "Oak corn, that is ac-corn, or acorn."

August 22, 1852. I am struck by the handsome and abundant clusters of yet green shrub-oak acorns. Some are whitish. How much food for some creatures!

August 28, 1853. Show now on shrub oaks.

August 30, 1859. Acorns (many kinds) have not fallen yet.

September 4, 1853. The crowded clusters of shrub-oak acorns are very handsome—the rich, wholesome brown of the cups contrasting with the now clear, green acorns, sometimes twenty-four within a breadth of three inches.

September 6, 1854. Now apparently is the time to gather the clusters of shrub-oak acorns before they drop, to adorn a shelf with. Some, however, are ready to fall on account of the late drought. I see where the squirrels have eaten them (the *Quercus ilicifolia*) and left the shells on a stump.

September 12, 1859. Some shrub-oak acorn cups are empty, but not many have fallen yet. Large yellowish caterpillars heaped on the leaves have so stripped some of the bushes as to expose and reveal the acorns.

September 12, 1854. Some black scrub-oak acorns fallen.

September 13, 1859. I see some shrub-oak acorns turned dark on the bushes, and showing their meridional lines, but *generally acorns of all kinds* are green yet.

September 22, 1854. Some shrub-oak acorns are prettily rayed green and yellowish.

September 24, 1859. The common shrub oak is apparently the most fertile of our oaks. I count two hundred sixty-six acorns on a branch just two feet long. Many of the cups are fully empty now, showing a pretty, circular, pink scar, at the bottom where the acorn adhered. They are of various forms and sizes on different bushes. Are now turning *dark brown*, leaving those converging meridional light-brown lines. Never fear for striped squirrels in a shrub-oak land.

September 30. Most shrub-oak acorns are browned.

October 1, 1859. The shrub oaks on this hill (Pine Hill) are now at their height, both with respect to their tints and their fruit. The plateaus and little hollows are crowded with them, three to five feet high, the pretty fruit—varying in size, pointedness, and downiness—being now generally turned brown with light, converging, meridional lines. Many leading shoots are perfectly bare of leaves, the effect of the frost, and on some bushes half the cups are empty; but these cups generally bear the marks of squirrels' teeth and probably but few acorns have fallen of themselves yet. However, they are just ready to fall, and if you bend back the peduncles of these bare and frost-touched shoots (or limbs) you find them just ready to come off, separating at the base of the peduncle, and the peduncle remaining attached to the fruit. The squirrel, probably striped, must be very busy here nowadays. Though many twigs are bare, these clusters of brown fruit in their grayish brown cups are unnoticed and almost invisible when you are looking for them above the ground, which is strewn with their similarly colored leaves; that is, this leaf-strewn earth has the same general gray and brown color with the twigs and fruit, and you may brush against great wreaths of fruit without noticing them. You press through dense groves full of this interesting fruit, each seeming prettier than the last. Now is the time for shrub-oak acorns there (if not for others). I see where the squirrels have left the shells on rocks and stumps. They take the acorn out of its cup on the bush, leaving the cup there with a piece bit out of its edge.

Michaux says, "The vastness of this oak enables the bears, deer, and hogs to feed on it by merely raising their heads a little, or standing upon their hind feet."

October 2, 1859. Shrub oak turned brown.

October 14, 1859. The shrub-oak acorns are now all fallen, only one or two left on, and their cups, which are still not on, are apparently somewhat incurved at the edge, as they have dried, so that probably they would not admit the acorn now.

October 15, 1859. In some places at least half the shrub-oak acorns hold on yet. The last are handsome now that they have turned so much darker.

October 21, 1859. A great many shrub-oak acorns hold on in Indigo Sproutland and are a darker brown than ever.

When Gosnold and Pring and Champlain coasted along our shores, even then the small shrub oak grew on the mainland, with its pretty acorns (if the former were here so late) striped dark and light alternately.

November 12, 1853. The shrub-oak cups which I notice today have lost their acorns.

ACORNS: RED OAK

Red oak.

August 27, 1854. Many red-oak acorns have fallen. (Were they not cast down?) The great green acorns in broad, shallow cups. Is not this a reason that the pigeons are about?

September 8, 1858. Red-oak acorns, yet green, abundantly cut off by squirrels.

September 12, 1854. Red-oak acorns began to fall before white.

September 13, 1859. Have not fallen.

October 12. Red-oak acorns (as well as white) appear to be fallen or falling.

October 14, 1859. The ground is strewn with red-oak acorns.

October 28, 1858. How handsome the great red-oak acorns now! I stand under the tree on Emerson's Lot. They are still falling. I heard one fall into the water as I approached and thought that a musquash had plunged. They strew the ground and the bottom of the river thickly, and while I stand here I hear one strike the boughs with force, as it comes down, and drop into the water. The part that was covered by the cup is whitish, woolly.

How munificent is Nature to create this profusion of wild fruits, as it were, merely to gratify our eyes! Though inedible they are more wholesome to my nobler part, and stand by me longer than the fruits which I eat. If they had been plums or chestnuts I should have eaten them on the spot and probably forgotten

them; they would have afforded me only a momentary gratification, but, being acorns, I remember and as it were feed on them still. Yet as it respects their peculiar and final flavor, they are untasted fruits, forever in store for use, and I know not of their flavors as yet. That is postponed to some yet *unimagined* winter evening. These which we admire but do not eat are the real ambrosia—nuts of the gods. When time is no more, we shall crack them.

I cannot help liking them better than horse chestnuts, which are of a similar color, not only because they are of a much handsomer form, but because they are indigenous. What hale, plump fellows they are! They can afford not to be useful to me—not know me or be known by me. They go their way, and I go mine. Yet sometimes I go *after* them.

November 5, 1858. The large shallow cup of the red-oak acorns look like some buttons I have seen which had lost their core.

May 12, 1859. Red-oak acorn has sent down radicles.

ACORNS: BLACK OAK

Black oak.

September 12, 1854. A few black-oak acorns fallen.

September 28, 1858. The black-oak acorns are slightly rayed like the shrub oak.

October 2, 1859. *Generally* turned brown.

October 11, 1859. Appear to have fallen or been abstracted.

October 15, 1859. I see some black-oak acorns on the trees still.

ACORNS: WHITE OAK

White oak.

October 12, 1858. White and red oak. They are so fair and plump and glossy. I love to handle them and am loath to throw away what I have in my hand.

September 11, 1859. The white-oak acorns are very pretty, three raying from one center.

September 12, 1854. White-oak acorns have many of them fallen. They are small and very neat light-green acorns, with small cups, commonly arranged two by two close together ⟨🌰⟩, often with a leaf growing out between them, but frequently forming a little star with three rays, looking very artificial.

September 21, 1854. Those pretty little white-oak acorn stars with three rays are quite common on the ground.

September 22, 1854. Some white-oak acorns are turned salmon color or blushing, like the leaves.

September 30, 1854. Acorns are generally now turned brown and the ground is strewn with them, and in paths they are crushed by our feet and wheels. The white-oak are dark and the most glossy.

October 2, 1859. Acorns generally, as I notice (swamp-, white-, shrub-, black-, and white-oak) are turned brown (this would be the time to notice them), but few are still green. Yet few, except of shrub oak, have fallen. I hear them fall, however, as I stand under the trees.

October 7, 1852. There must be an abundance of mast this year. I could gather up nearly a bushel of acorns under some white oak, out of their cups, and I think quite good to eat. They are earlier to fall than the walnuts. It is encouraging to see a large crop of acorns, though *we* do not use them.

Michaux says that the white-oak acorns are "rarely abundant."

October 8, 1851. Under the woodside by J. P. Brown's grain field I picked up some white-oak acorns in the path, which I found to be unexpectedly sweet and palatable, the bitterness being scarcely perceptible. To my taste, they are almost as good as chestnuts. No wonder that the first men lived on acorns. Such as these are no such mean food as they are represented. Their sweetness is like the sweetness of bread. And now that I have discovered the palatableness of this neglected nut, life has acquired a new sweetness for me, and I am related to the first men. What if I were to discover also that the grass tasted sweet and nutritious? Nature seems the more friendly to me. I have added to the number of my allies. Methinks I could easily feed myself in the woods at this season. There is mast for me, too, as well as for the pigeon and the squirrel.

I question if acorns were not intended to be the food of man. These are agreeable to the palate as the mother's milk to the babe. The sweet acorn tree is famous and well known to the boys. Surely there can be no question respecting the wholesomeness of this diet. Might we not recover some robustness by living on them? When the Lacedæmonians consulted the Oracle at Delphi about the conquest of Arcadia, the Pythian answered, "Dost thou ask of me Arcadia? Thou askest a great deal. I cannot grant it thee. There are many acorn-eating men on Arcadia, who will hinder thee."

What can be handsomer and wear better to the eye than this Dodonean fruit?—polished or varnished and colored like the leaves on which they fall? Is not the afternoon memorable when you find edible acorns?

The next day I boiled a quart of these acorns for breakfast, but I found them not so palatable as the raw, having acquired a bitterish taste—perhaps from being boiled with the shells and skins. Yet perhaps I should soon get accustomed to them, and who knows but it is a kind of tonic which we require in our diet? Have we not too much of the sweet and too little of the bitter in our food these days? The Indians used to boil them in a log. All the acorns on the same tree are not equally sweet. They appear to dry sweet.

October 8, 1860. Falling fast.

October 12, 1858. White-oak fallen or falling.

October 11, 1859. Looking under large oaks (black and white), the acorns appear to have fallen or been gathered by squirrels and so on. I see clusters on twigs cut off, the nuts abstracted.

October 17, 1857. Glossy-brown white-oak acorns strew the ground thickly, many of them sprouted. How soon they have sprouted! I find some quite edible. But they, too, like wild apples, require an outdoor appetite. I do not admit their palatableness when I try them in the house. Is not the outdoor appetite the one to be prayed for?

ACORNS GENERALLY

Acorns generally.

September 18, 1859. Acorns green generally.

September 19, 1854. Fallen acorns in a few days acquire that wholesome, shiny, dark-chestnut color.

September 18, 1859. Perhaps green acorns before they have fallen attract most attention, about the middle of September. They have been dropt sparingly, and chiefly wormy ones, ever since September first.

October and the last half of September is the time for acorns, though now (October twenty-sixth, 1853) it is too late.

October 3, 1859. It must be the frost that ripens nuts—acorns, for example—browning them. Frost and cold paint the acorn and the chestnut.

October 13, 1859. I see no acorns on the trees; they appear to have all fallen before this. Or is it a poor year?

October 14, 1859. Apparently acorns of all kinds have fallen. But they have not been abundant (on *trees*) this year.

October 21, 1855. Squirrels have eaten acorns very generally.

It is a wonder how pigeons can swallow acorns whole, yet they do.

November 27, 1852. I find an acorn which has sent a shoot down into the earth.

April 23, 1859. What proportion sound. In about five quarts of scarlet-oak acorns gathered the other day there were only some three gills that had life in them, or say one in seven. I do not know how many the squirrels had got, but as it was quite near a house, a tree by itself, I think not a great many. The rest were apparently destroyed by worms; so that I should say the worms destroyed before spring three-fourths of them. As the grub is already in the acorn, it may be just as well (except for the squirrels) to sow them now as in the fall, whatever you can get.

May 29, 1859. Oaklets springing up on all sides.

How oak woods are produced, if necessary.

March 25, 1855. See where squirrels have fed extensively on acorns exposed by melting of snow.

September 30, 1859. Some *swamp-white*-oak acorns are browned.

Michaux says that they are not abundant and that the inside of the cup is peculiarly downy.

September 26, 1854. Many swamp-white-oak acorns are turned brown on the trees.

Michaux says of scarlet oak, "it is often very difficult to distinguish them externally from those of the black oak. Their only discriminative character is in the color of the kernel, which is white in the acorn of the scarlet oak, and yellowish in those of the other species."

September 19, 1854. Scarlet-oak acorn *figured* .

November 10, 1858.

Hearing in the oak wood nearby a sound as if someone had broken a twig, I looked up and saw a jay pecking at an acorn. There were several jays busily gathering acorns on a scarlet oak. I could hear them break them off. They then flew to a suitable limb and, placing the acorn under one foot, hammered away at it busily, looking round from time to time to see if any foe was approaching, and soon reached the meat and nibbled at it, holding up their heads to swallow, while they held it very firmly with their claws. (Their hammering made a sound like the woodpecker's.) Nevertheless it sometimes dropped to the ground before they had done with it.

November 27, 1858. Some scarlet-oak shaped like black-oak . Also some with longitudinal lines .

November 10, 1856. Almost every acorn of white and chestnut oak (*Quercus montana* probably) at Perth Amboy is sprouted.

November 2, 1856. The acorn of the pin oak subglobose and very prettily marked with meridional lines.

Michaux says *Quercus prinus palustris,* chestnut white oak, next bulkiest of all in United States and hence sought after by wild animals. Also *Quercus prinus monticola* long and sought after as the last.

Michaux says the small chinquapin is very fertile.

September 30, 1854. The conventional acorn of art is of course of no particular species, but the artist might find it worth his while to study nature's varieties again. How attractive these forms. No wonder they are imitated on pumps, fences, and bed posts.

September 11, 1859. No fruit is handsomer than the acorn. I see but few fallen yet, and they are all wormy.

What is acorn color? Is it not as good as chestnut or hazel?

October 16, 1857. Melvin thinks that the summer ducks up the Assabet River are after acorns. Caught seven once by baiting his traps under water with acorns.

Wood, in his *New England's Prospect,* says, "These trees [oaks] afford much mast for hogs, especially every third year."

September 19, 1856. Fallen acorns in a few days acquire that wholesome, shining, dark-chestnut color.

April 29, 1852. The acorn among the leaves has been sprouted for a week past, the shells open and the blushing red meat exposed on the sprout end where the sprout is already turning toward the bowels of the earth, already thinking of the tempests which it is destined as an oak to withstand if it escapes worm and squirrel. Pick them up and plant them if you would make a forest.

September 26, 1860. Acorns, white-oak and so on, have fallen after *wind* and rain, just as leaves and fruit have.

October 7, 1860. See a small but spreading white oak (southeast of Hubbard's Grove) full of acorns just falling and ready to fall. When I strike a limb, great numbers rattle down. They are almost black (the effect probably of frost) amid the still green leaves, a singular but agreeable contrast. Some that have fallen upon bare earth are already split and sprouted, though far the greater part have not yet fallen.

June 30, 1852. Shrub-oak acorns as big as peas.

Sagard, *History du Canada,* says, when the inhabitants of Quebec suffered from famine in 1629, the year their town was taken by the English, they used the root of what they called *Sigillum Salomoris,* either as bread, or with acorns or barley meal. They boiled their acorns in water with ashes twice to remove the bitterness, then pounded and mixed them with barley meal and so thickened [*espessir*] their broth.

PAINTED TRILLIUM

Painted trillium *(Trillium pictum)* once here September seventh, up-country, how long?

September 7, 1852. And *Trillium erythrocarpum,* with the large red berry.

TUPELO

Tupelo, also called sour gum and black gum, begins September seventh.

September 11. Apparently in prime. October 19, 1859. All fallen; how long? Michaux says the *Nyssa aquatica* is "ripe toward the beginning of November," holds on after the leaves, and is food for "red-breasts."

September 7, 1857. What I examined was green.

September 7, 1860. Hardly yet in Hubbard's Grove; less seed than last year.

September 11, 1859. By the pool in Hubbard's Grove I see tall tupelos all dotted with and quite full of the now ripe (apparently in prime) fruit—small, oval, dark-purple berries two or three together on the end of slender peduncles amid the reddening leaves. This fruit is very acid and has a large stone, but I see several robins on the trees which appear to have been attracted by it. Neither the tree nor the fruit is generally known, and many liken the former, when small, to a pear.

September 30, 1854. That behind Sam Barrett's was (its leaves) all scarlet, had borne much fruit—small oval, bluish berries (Gray calls it "blackish-blue")—and a very little which was not ripe was left.

October 19, 1859. All fallen; how long?

A large tall one on railroad, and one in Staples's meadow wood.

WHITE PINE

White-pine cones begin to open September ninth.

January 25, 1855. Looking at the base of some which I have, I find just five rays (the number of needles in a fascicle) of scales and each goes round once.

March 6, 1855. Pick up a very handsome white-pine cone six and a half inches long by two and three-eighths near the base and two near the apex, perfectly blossomed or open. It is a very rich and wholesome acorn color of various shades as you turn it in you hand, a light ashy or gray brown, somewhat like unpainted wood, as you look down on it (or as if the lighter brown was covered with a gray lichen), seeing only those parts of the scales always exposed, with a few darker streaks or marks, and a drop of pitch at the point ofeach scale. (I hear, October 1860, that they have begun to sell them for kindling.) Within, the scales are a dark brown above (that is, as it hangs) and a light brown beneath—very *distinctly,* being marked beneath by the same darker brown down the center and near the apex, somewhat anchor like.

October 16, 1855. What has got them at handsome grove?

October 19, 1855. See at last a few, but they are open.

November 4, 1855. Have failed to find—though I began to look a month ago. The cones were fallen and open. Look September first.

June 1850. Last year's cones are now two inches long (this year's not having blossomed), curved sickle-like from the top-most branches, reminding you of those tropical trees which bear their fruit at their heads.

August 22, 1859. Squirrels have stripped quite green for a week past. September 1. Ground strewn with.

Michaux says open about first of October.

October 8, 1856. At length I discover some white-pine cones, a few on Emerson's Heater-Piece trees. They are all open, and all the sound seeds but one gone. So September is the time to gather them. The tip of each scale is covered with fresh flowing pitch.

September 9, 1857. Afternoon to the Hill for white-pine cones. Very few trees have any, and they are of course at the tops. I can manage only small trees fifteen or twenty feet high, climbing till I can reach the dangling green pickle-like fruit with my right hand while I hold to the main stem with my left (but I am in a pickle when I get one). The cones are now all flowing with pitch and my hands are soon so covered with it that I cannot easily cast down my booty when I would, it sticks to my fingers so; and when I get down at last and have picked them up, I cannot touch my basket with such hands, but carry it on my arm, nor can I pick up my coat which I have taken off, unless with my teeth, or else I kick it up and catch it on my arm. Thus I go from tree to tree rubbing my hands from time to time in brooks and mud holes in the hope of finding something that will remove pitch, as grease does, but in vain. It is the stickiest work I ever did, yet I stick to it. I do not see how the squirrels that gnaw them off and then open them scale by scale keep their paws and whiskers clean. They must possess some remedy for pitch that we know nothing of, for they can touch it and not be defiled. What would I not give for their recipe? How fast I could collect cones if I could only contract with a family of squirrels to cut them off for me—or what if I had a pair of shears eighty feet long, and a derrick to wield them with! They are far more effectually protected than the chestnut by its burr.

Some are already brown and dry and partly open, but these commonly have hollow seeds and are worm-eaten.

These cones collected in my chamber have a strong spirituous scent, almost rummy or like a molasses hogshead, which would probably be agreeable to some.

In short, I found the business far from profitable, for commonly the trees do not bear more than enough for the squirrels.

September 16, 1860. At the beautiful pine grove in John Flint's pasture, I see green and closed cones beneath branches which the squirrels have thrown down. On the trees many are already open. They have begun within a week. In one small wood all the white-pine cones are on the ground, generally unopened, evidently freshly thrown down by the squirrels, and there the greater part have already been stripped. They begin at the base of the cone, as with the pitch pine. It is evident that they have just been very busy throwing down the white-pine cones in all woods. Perhaps they have stored up the seeds separately. This they can do before chestnut burrs open.

September 24, 1857. At Meriam's pine grove, the ground is completely strewn with white-pine cones cast down by the squirrels, still generally green and closed, but many *stripped*, about the base of almost every pine, sometimes all of them. Now and for a week will be a good time to collect *such*.

October 6, 1857. Going thro' Ebby Hubbard's woods I see thousands of white-pine cones on the ground—fresh, light-brown—which lately opened and shed their seeds and lie curled up on the ground. The seeds are rather pleasant or nutritious tasting taken in quantity, like beechnuts methinks.

At length after two or three afternoons I get a bushel of them home, but I have not got at the seeds yet. They are far more effectually protected than a chestnut in its burr. I must wait till they please to open and then get pitched once more.

September 1, 1859. Ground about white pines strewn with their green cones for some time.

November 25, 1857. Quarts of scales in a heap under a white pine.

October 29, 1858. Long since open; hard to come off.

March 21, 1859. Fallen in late winds—apparently twenty-four, almost entirely.

How little observed are the fruits which we do not use! How few attend to the ripening and dispersion of the white-pine seed! In the latter part of September in a fruitful year, the tops of high trees for six or ten feet are quite browned with the cones, hanging with their points downward and just opened. They make a great show even sixty rods off, and it is worth the while to look down from some favorable height over such a forest—to observe such evidence of fertility in this which commonly we do not regard as a fruit-bearing tree. I occasionally go to the white-pine woods merely to look at their crop of cones, just as a farmer visits his orchards in October. In the fall of 1859 the white pines bore a peculiarly abundant crop, as I observed not only in this town but in all this part of the country and as far off as Worcester. I could see its burden of brown cones half a mile distant.

September 18, 1860. I see cones open, but they may be old ones. Am not sure that I see any this year, it may be because they failed (the young) last year.

September 28, 1859. Coombs has found much in his pigeons' crops.

AMPHICARPÆA

Amphicarpæa, say September tenth.

Found in drill hole.

September 29, 1856. Partly ripe, little black-dotted beans, about three in a pod.

RHEXIA

Rhexia chalices, September tenth.

It is the red chalices only that show *much* at a distance now, little pitchers of graceful forms. Some low fields are quite ruddy with them.

WITCH HAZEL

Witch hazel, say September tenth.

One September I gathered some of the peculiarly formed nuts of the witch hazel, which grow in pretty clusters—clothed, as it were, in close-fitting buckskin—amid the yellowing leaves, and laid them in my chamber. The double-fruited stone splits and reveals the two shining black, oblong seeds. Three nights afterward I heard at midnight a snapping sound and the fall of some small body on the floor from time to time. In the morning I found that it was produced by

the witch-hazel nuts on my desk springing open and casting their hard and stony seeds across the chamber. They were thus shooting their shining black seeds about the room for several days. Apparently it is not when they first gape open that the seeds fly out, for I saw many if not most of them open already with seeds in them; but the seed appears to fit close to the shell at its base, even after the shell gapes above, and when I release one with my knife, it being still held by its base, it flies, as I have said. Its slippery base appears to be compressed by the unyielding shell, which at length expels it, just as you can make one fly by pressing it and letting it slip from between your thumb and finger. Thus, it spreads itself by leaps ten or fifteen feet at a time.

October 19, 1859. Many not yet ripe.

CISTUS

Cistus, September twelfth.
September 18, 1859. Some gone to seed now, open several days.
December 6, 1856. Pin-weed.

SOLANUM NIGRUM

Solanum nigrum, September fourteenth.
September 10, 1856. Green at Walpole, New Hampshire.

September 21, 1856. Apparently just ripe here on Cliff.

September 21, 1860. Say a week or ten days at Pratt's.

CROTALARIA

Crotalaria, September fifteenth.

September 18, 1860. The rattle-pod in the Deep Cut has begun to turn black and rattle for three or four days.

October 3, 1856. Detect the crotalaria behind Wyman's site by hearing the now rattling seed in its pods as I go through the grass, like the trinkets about an Indian's leggins or a rattlesnake. Their scientific names have the same origin— the Greek κρόταλον, a rattle.

November 1, 1857. Going over the high field west of the Deep Cut, my foot strikes a rattle in the stubble, and the crotalaria was betrayed. I find it by this sound, just as I detect the desmodiums by their pods adhering to me (for they so advertise themselves to me, sticking their bills on me). From *that* faint sound I knew it must be there, and so went back and found it. (So in the winter I hear the seeds rattling, but more finely in the little black pods of the indigo weed when the wind blows, and late in the fall I sometimes detect the beans which the farmer has not gathered in some weedy or grassy field by my feet striking them and causing them to rattle. Perchance these seeds are thus betrayed to those wild creatures that feed on them.) I could have told it as well in the dark. In a similar way you find penny-royal by the fragrance it emits when bruised by your feet—as the sandal wood sheds its perfume on the chopper.

October 3, 1858. As I go thro' the Deep Cut I discover a new locality for the crotalaria, being attracted by the pretty, blue-black pods now ripe and dangling in profusion from these low plants on the bare sandy and gravelly slope of the Cut. The plants are but half a dozen times higher than the pods are long. It was the contrast of these black pods with the yellowish sand which betrayed them.

It is interesting to consider how that plant spreads itself, sure to find out the suitable soil. One year I find it on the Great Fields and think it rare; the next I find it in a new and unexpected place. Thus it flits about, as it were, like a flock of sparrows, from field to field.

I have found it only on light and sandy soil, much as are commonly devoted to beans.

ZOZANIA

Zozania, September fifteenth.

September 15, 1859. The grain of the wild rice is all green yet.

September 16, 1860. See none ripe or black, yet almost all is fallen.

September 25, 1858. Still green.

September 30, 1859. Is almost entirely fallen or eaten by some insect or grub. Yet I see some green and also black grain left.

WEEDS AND GRASSES

Sown weeds and grass seeds begin to ripen September fifteenth.

Now that the potatoes are cared for, Nature is preparing a crop of Roman wormwood, chenopodium, amaranth, and so on for the *birds*. These *late* weeds, now so rank and prevalent in cultivated fields, which were long since deserted by the hoers, now that the potatoes are for the most part ripened, are preparing a crop for the small birds of the fall and winter—those pensioners on civilization. These seeds require cultivated ground, and Nature perseveres each year till she succeeds in producing a bountiful harvest of their seeds, in spite of our early assiduity.

September 25, 1859. The very crab grass in our garden ⋎⁄⁄ is for the most part a light-straw color and withered, probably by the frosts of the fifteenth and sixteenth, looking almost as white as the corn, and hundreds of sparrows find their food amid it. The same frosts that fill and whiten the corn whiten many grasses thus.

BEECH

Beech, September fifteenth.

Springer, in his *Forest Life and Forest Trees,* says, "Impelled by hunger, bears often climb and gather the nut before it is ripe. I have frequently seen, during my backwoods excursions, the topmost limbs broken off and pulled in toward the trunk of the tree, some of them three inches in diameter, until the whole of the top branches were furled in, forming a tufted circle fifty feet in air."

November 2, 1853. I find that there have been plenty of beech nuts and there are still some empty burrs on the trees and many nuts on the ground, but I cannot find one with meat in it.

June 12, 1853. I find the nuts about fully grown where a tree overhangs Baker's hillside. Are they ever perfect here? Got sound ones in 1859.

October 1st, 1859. The little beech-nut burrs are mostly empty and abortive. Yet I pluck some apparently full-grown with meat. This fruit is apparently now at its height.

September 18, 1860. The burrs are browned but not falling. They open immediately in my chamber. The nuts are all empty.

September 1, 1859. The little beech burrs are mostly empty and abortive. Yet I pluck some apparently full grown with meat—apparently now at its height. Red beech ripe about October first according to Michaux.

LATE ROSE

Late rose, say September fifteenth.

January 30, 1854. The hips of the late rose are still abundant and perfect amid the button bushes.

October 28, 1860. Rose hips are as handsome as ever, especially on Turnpike just this side last rocky hill by Smith's.

November 11, 1853. Hips of rose still show abundantly along river.

December 14, 1850. In one place in the meadow by Loring's Pond saw the greatest quantity of wild rose hips of various forms that I ever saw. They were as thick as winterberries.

February 19, 1854. The hips of the late rose, though more or less shrivelled, are still red and handsome. It outlasts other hips. The sweet-briar hips have lost their color and begun to decay, but the former are still very abundant and showy in perfect corymbs of a dozen or so amid the button bushes.

March 4, 1854. The same abundant in some creature's droppings by the river.

UVA-URSI

Uva-ursi, September fifteenth.

May 22, 1853. Small berries formed.

August 14, 1854. Begin to turn.

July 16, 1855. Begin to redden on Cape Cod.

July 31, 1856. Many full grown.

September 18, 1859. A bearberry ripe.

September 23, 1860. Ripe.

August 1, 1860. Full size—not turned.

Loudon says, "The berries are filled with an austere mealy pulp, and serve as food for grouse and other birds in Britain; and in Sweden, Russia, and America, they form a principal part of the food of bears."

BEACH PLUM

Beach plum, September fifteenth.

June 20, 1857. Talked with a woman on Cape Cod who thought beach plums better than cherries.

July 6, 1857. The beach plums have everywhere the crescent-shaped mark made by the curculio—the few that remain on.

September 10, 1857. They are about ripe (the same September 12, 1859).

September 20, 1857. Beach plums are now perfectly ripe and unexpectedly good—as good as an average cultivated plum. I get a handful (behind Clarke's) darker purple with a bloom, as big as good-sized grapes (but little more oblong— about three-quarters of an inch broad and a very little longer).

Come up forty miles inland from the coast of Maine.

ASCLEPIAS CORNUTI

Asclepias cornuti, September sixteenth.

The earliest *Asclepias cornuti* begins to fly about the sixteenth of September, and the pods are in the midst of dispersing their seeds about the twentieth or twenty-fifth of October. (I have seen it in the air even in the spring.) Its pods are large, thick, and covered with soft prickles, and stand at various angles with the stem like a flourish. If you examine both inside and out, its pod is a fairy-like casket shape, somewhat like a canoe. As they dry, they turn upward, crack, and open by the seam along the convex or outer side—revealing the brown seeds with thin, silvery parachutes like the finest unsoiled silk closely compressed and arranged in an imbricated manner, and already right-side up. Some children call these manes of seed and silk fishes, and as they lie they somewhat resemble a plump, round, silvery fish with a brown head.

Densely packed in a little oblong chest armed with soft downy prickles and with a smooth, silky lining lie thus some two hundred (in one instance I counted one hundred thirty-four, in another two hundred seventy) of these pear-shaped seeds (or shaped like a steelyard *poire*), which have derived their nutriment through a band of extremely fine silken threads attached by their extremities to the core. (The silk is moreover divided once or twice by the raised partitions of the core.)

At length, when the seeds are matured and cease to require nourishment from the parent plant, being weaned, and the pod with dryness and frost bursts, the pretty fishes loosen and lift their brown scales, somewhat bristling a little; the extremities of the silken threads detach themselves from the core and from being the conduits of nutriment to the seed, perchance to become the buoyant balloon which, like some spiders' webs, bear the seeds to new and distant fields. Far finer than the finest thread, they will soon serve merely to buoy up the full-fed seed.

The pods commonly burst after rain—opening on the underside, away from succeeding showers. The outer part of the down of the upper seeds is gradually blown loose, while they are still retained by the ends of the middle portion, in loops attached to the core. Perchance at the tops of some more open and drier pods is already a little flock of these loosened seeds and down, held by the converging tips of the down-like meridians—just ready to float away when the wind rises, to be a vessel moored with long cables and lying in the stream, prepared to spread her sails and depart any moment. These may be blown about a long time, however, before a strong puff launches them away, and in the meanwhile they are expanding and drying their silk and becoming buoyant. These white tufts show afar as big as your fist. One of my neighbors says that the plant is now discounting.

The few seeds which I release soon come to earth, but probably if they waited for a stronger wind they would be carried far. Others, again if you wait a while, are found open and empty, except of the brown core, and you may see what a delicate, smooth, white- or straw-colored lining this casket has.

If you sit at an open attic window toward the end of September, you will see many a milkweed down go sailing by on a level with you, though commonly it has lost its freight—notwithstanding that you may not know of any of these plants growing in your neighborhood. I notice milkweed growing in hollows in the fields, as if the seed had settled there owing to the lull of the wind in such places. Thus, the quietest behaved carries off the prize while exposed plains and hills send forth violent winds to hale the seed to them. The calm hollow in which no wind blows without effort receives and harbors it.

Returning one afternoon by way of Mount Misery from a walk through Conantum and over Lee's Bridge into Lincoln, I perceive in the little open meadow on Clematis Brook that the follicles of the *Asclepias cornuti* now point upward and are already bursting. When I release some seeds, the fine silky threads fly apart at once, opening with a spring—and then ray their relics out into a hemispherical form, each thread freeing itself from its neighbor, and all reflecting prismatic tints. These seeds are besides furnished with broad, thin margins or wings, which plainly keep them steady and prevent their whirling round. I let one go, and it rises slowly and uncertainly at first, now driven this way, then that, by invisible currents, and I fear it will make shipwreck against the neighboring wood. But no; as it approaches it, it surely rises above it, and then feeling the strong north wind, it is borne off rapidly in the opposite direction, over Deacon Farrar's woods, ever rising higher and higher, and tossing and heaved about with every fluctuation of the air, till at fifty rods off and one hundred feet above the earth, steering south— I lose sight of it.

I had watched it for the time with as much interest as his friends did Mr. Lauriat, disappearing in the skies. But not in this case is the return to earth fraught with danger, but toward night perchance, when the air is moist and still, it descries its promised land and settles gently down between the woods, where there is a lull of the wind, into some strange valley—it may be by some other brook like this— and its voyage is over. Yet it stoops to rise.

Thus, from generation to generation it goes bounding over lakes and woods and mountains. Think of the great variety of balloons which at this season are buoyed up by similar means! How many myriads go sailing away thus, high over hill and meadow and river, on various tracks until the wind lulls, to plant their race in new localities—who can tell how many miles away? I do not see but the seeds which are ripened in New England may plant themselves in Pennsylvania. At any rate, I am interested in the fate or success of every such venture which the autumn sends forth. And for this end these silken streamers have been perfecting themselves all summer, snugly packed in this light chest, a perfect adaptation to this end—a prophecy not only of the fall, but of future springs. Who could believe in prophecies of Daniel or of Miller that the world would end this summer, while one milkweed with faith matured its seeds?

I brought home two of these pods which were already bursting and amused myself from day to day with releasing the seeds and watching them rise slowly into the heavens till they were lost to my eye. No doubt the greater or less rapidity with which they rise would serve as a natural barometer to test the condition of the air.

Near the end of November I sometimes see the milkweed pods by the roadside yet but half emptied of their silky contents, though we may have had snow. Thus, for months the gales are dispersing their seeds.

FEVER BUSH

Fever bush, September sixteenth.
August 2, 1854. Will not be ripe for two or three weeks on Conantum.
September 16, 1857. Some already ripe.

October 5, 1858. Being at height of change (foliage) its clear lemon-yellow leaves contrast with the scarlet berries.

September 24, 1859. The fever-bush berries are scarlet now and also green. They have a more spicy taste than any of our berries, carrying us in thought to the Spice Islands. They taste like orange peel. October 15. See no berries.

September 21, 1860. Have begun sometime, say one week, but are not yet in prime. Taste about exactly like orange peel. But few bushes bear any. I suspect that the tropical have few if any flowers—which are not represented in the temperate zone.

HIERACIUM

Hieracium down. September eighteenth.

After the middle of September, hard frosts put a period to many flowers, and we begin to see their seeds only. By the eighteenth of September two or three kinds of *Hieracium* are already going to seed. Their little yellowish globes are characteristic of autumn in the woods. And ere long in all meadows the fall dandelion with its small spheres repeats the phenomena of May.

SWEET GALE

Sweet gale, September twenty-second.

September 22, 1860. Is yet green, but perhaps it is ripe.

January 25, 1855. I find an abundance of the seeds of the sweet gale in windows frozen into the ice of the river meadows as I return (from Fair Haven Pond), which were washed out by the freshet. I color my fingers with them. And thus they are planted there, somewhat perhaps in waving lines as they wash up.

March 5, 1854. In the upper Nut Meadow the sweet gale grows rankly along the edges of the brook, slanted over the water almost horizontally, so as frequently to meet and conceal the water altogether.

It is here a dark and sluggish water, comparatively shallow, with a muddy bottom. This sweet gale is now full of fruit. This and the water andromeda—wild plants, as it were, driven to the water's edge by the white man.

December 14, 1850. On one of the islands in Loring's Pond I found a low-branching shrub frozen into the ice near its edge with a fine spicy scent, somewhat like sweet fern, and a handsome imbricated bud (staminate). When I rubbed the dry-looking fruit in my hands, it felt greasy and stained them a permanent yellow which I could not wash out. It lasted several days and my fingers smelled medicinally.

August 28, 1859. Saw sweet-gale fruit begin to yellow.

August 19, 1851. The fruit of the sweet gale by Nut Meadow Brook is now a yellowish green, and has not yet its greasy feel.

November 19, 1857. Going thro' a partly frozen meadow (J. Hosmer's or Wheeler's land), scraping thro' the sweet gale toward the Assabet River, I am pleasantly scented with its odoriferous fruit.

Gerarde says of the sweet gale, "Among the branches come forth many other little ones [that is, leaves] whereupon do grow many spokie ears or tufts, full of small flowers."

CLEMATIS

Clematis, September twenty-second.

September 21, 1860. Just beginning to be feathered, but *no show*. Feathers out next day in house.

By the last of September the clematis begins to be feathered. A month later, when the leaves had mostly fallen, I have mistaken it, draping a low tree, for a tree

full of white blossoms. It is said of the English species, in *The Journal of a Naturalist,* "I have often observed the long feathered part of the seed at the entrance of holes made by mice on the banks, and probably in hard seasons the seed may yield these creatures part of their supply."

PANICLED ANDROMEDA

Panicled andromeda, September twenty-fourth.

September 24, 1859. Begins to brown.

December 6, 1856. I am excited at the sight of the rich brown fruit of the panicled andromeda, growing about the swamps—hard, dry, inedible, suitable to the season. The dense panicles of the berries are of a handsome form, made to endure. Lasting often over two seasons, only becoming darker or gray. The enduring panicled andromeda, which belongs to the hard season.

This appears to be the plant referred to by Manasseh Cutler, L.L.D., in the *American Academy's Reports,* where he says, "White pepperbush. Blossoms white. Common in swamps. June. . . . It is used for fish flakes, and as the wood is very hard and durable, is one of the best shrubs employed for that purpose." Yet the "Andromeda. Linn. Gen. Plant. 485. *Andromeda racemis secundis nudis, corollis rotundo ovatis.* Syst. Nat." to which he refers, is *really,* according to a recent *Systema Naturæ,* Linnæus's *arborea (oxydendron)* of the South.

LESPEDEZA

Lespedeza, September twenty-fifth.

HORSE CHESTNUT

Horse chestnut, September twenty-fifth.

September 29, 1859. These nuts strew the roadside. Very handsome-colored but simply formed nuts, looking like mahogany knobs with the waved and curled grains of knots.

BAYBERRY

Bayberry, September twenty-fifth.

September 16, 1854. My sister saw much in Princeton.

September 24, 1859. They are apparently ripe, though not so gray as they will be; more lead-colored. They bear sparingly here. Leaves *not* fallen nor changed, and I the more easily find the bushes amid the changed huckleberries, brakes, and so on, by their greenness.

October 15, 1859. All gone; probably eaten by birds.

September 21, 1860. Are perhaps ripe, but not so light a gray nor so rough or wrinkled as they will be.

CICUTA MACULATA

Cicuta maculata, September twenty-fifth.

Bigelow says, "No botanist, even if in danger of starving in a wilderness, could indulge his hunger on a root or fruit taken from an unknown plant of the natural order *Luridæ*, of the *Multisiliquæ*, or the umbelliferous aquatics. On the contrary, he would not feel a moment's hesitation in regard to any of the *Gramina*, the fruit of the *Pomaceæ*, and several other natural families, which are known to be uniformly innocent in their effects."

October 2, 1859. Some of the *Umbelliferæ* have gone to seed, are very pretty to examine. The *Cicuta maculata*, for instance. The concave umbel is so well spaced. The different umbellets like so many constellations or separate systems in the firmament. They get a sympathy with the stars.

BASS

Bass, September twenty-ninth.

September 29, 1854. Dry and brown.

January 27, 1856. See what I think are bass nuts on the snow of the river at Derby's Railroad Bridge, probably from up-stream.

September 30, 1859. Some browned.

Michaux says about October first.

BUTTON BUSH

Button bush, September thirtieth.

September 27, 1860. The balls are hardly reddened.

September 30, 1860. They were fairly reddened yesterday by the frosts.

October 12, 1858. The balls stand out (on the two-thirds bare bushes), have ruddy or brown look, much blacker against the light, than a month ago.

ARBOR VITÆ

Arbor vitæ, October first.

October 4, 1860. Say first.

SUGAR MAPLE

Sugar maple, October first.

1860. Was turned brown (at least *in some measure*) by the severe frosts of October first.

October 8, 1860. Are now browned—the seed end as well as wing—the severe frosts about October first about ripened them.

October 25, 1860. It still holds on where most of the leaves on this small tree have fallen.

June 19, 1860. See apparently immature abortive ones falling.

HIBISCUS

Hibiscus, October first.

October 4, 1856. Gone to seed and pods open showing the seed.

CORN

Corn, October first.

See them *topping* corn about September first or earlier even.

Early in August we begin to have green corn.

I remember when boiled green corn was sold piping-hot on a muster field in this town, and my father says that he remembers when it used to be carried about the streets of Boston in large baskets on the bare heads of negro women, and gentlemen used to stop, buy an ear, and eat it in the street.

About the first of September they begin to top corn, and the stacks of stalks set in rows around the fields reminds you of stacks of bayonets on a muster field.

Toward the end of September (or first of October) they begin to cut up and gather in the corn, though some is left out even till after the middle of November some years.

Gerarde says:

The stalk of turkey wheat is like that of the reed, full of spongy pith, set with many joints, five or six foot high, big beneath, and now and then of a purple color, and by little and little small above: the leaves are broad, long, set with veins like those of the reed. The ears on the top of the stalk be a span long, like unto the feather top of the common reed, divided unto many plumes hanging downward, empty and barren without seed, yet blooming as rye doth. The flower is either white, yellow, or purple, that is to say, even as the fruit will be. The fruit is contained in very big ears, which grow out of the joints of the stalk, three or four from one stalk, orderly placed one above another, covered with coats or films like husks and leaves, as if it were a certain sheath; out of which do stand long and slender beards, soft and tender, like those laces that grow upon savory, but greater and longer, every one fastened upon his own seed. The seeds are great, of the bigness of common peason, cornered in that part whereby they are fastened to the ear, and in the outward part round: being of color sometimes white, now and then yellow, purple, or red; of taste sweet, and pleasant, very closely joined together in eight or ten orders or ranks. This grain hath many roots, strong and full of strings. . . .

We have as yet no certain proof or experience concerning the virtues of this kind of corn; although the barbarous Indians, which know no better, are constrained to make a virtue of necessity, and think it a good food: whereas we may easily judge, that it nourisheth but little, and is of hard and evil digestion, a more convenient food for swine than for men.

Lindley quotes from Schouw in Jameson's *Philosophical Journal*, 1825: "it appears that in respect of the predominating kinds of grain, the earth may be divided into five grand divisions, or kingdoms. The kingdom of Rice, of Maize, of Wheat, of Rye, and lastly of Barley and Oats. The first three are the most extensive; the

Maize has the greatest range of temperature; but Rice may be said to support the greatest number of the human race. . . . Asia is the native country of Rice, and America of Maize."

September 18, 1860. According to all accounts, very little corn is fit to grind before October first (though I hear of *one* kind ripe and fit to grind September first). It becomes hard and dry enough in the husk in the field by that time. But way before this, or say by the first of September, it begins to glaze (or harden on the surface), when it begins to be too hard to boil.

October 7, 1860. Looked thro' Hayden's farm and granary. He now takes pleasure in his field of corn just ready for harvesting and counts the ears on a stalk. Being early, the ears set low. The rather small ears are fully filled out and rounded at the end. He loves to estimate the number of bushels he will have, has already calculated the number of hills, some forty thousand in this field; and he exhibits some of the corn in his granary. Also his rye in barrels and his seed corn, the larger and fuller ears picked out with the husk on and tucked into the mow as he was husking (to be brought to the house when he has leisure). But all this corn will be given to his pigs and other stock; three great hogs which will dress twelve hundredweight, lie asleep under his barn, already sold. Hears of one man who sold his fat hog for $75.00.

November 22. Heard of a husking a week ago, though a little corn is still left in the field.

Brand in his *Popular Antiquities* describes "harvest home":

Macrobius tells us that, among the Heathens, the masters of families, when they had got in their harvest, were wont to feast with their servants, who had labored for them in tilling the ground. (*Patres familiarum, et fugibus et fructibus iam coætis, passim cum servis escerentur, cum quibus patrintuam laboris in colendo rure toleraverant. Macrob. Sauturnal. Diepium, Cap. 10.*) In exact conformity to this, it is common among Christians, when the fruits of the earth are gathered in and laid in their proper repositories, to provide a plentiful supper for the harvestmen and the servants of the family. At the entertainment all are, in the modern revolutionary idea of the word, perfectly equal. . . . Bourne thinks the original of both these customs is Jewish. . . . For the Jews rejoiced and feasted at the getting in of the harvest.

Vacina (or Vacuna, so called as it is said *à vocando,* the titular deity, as is were, of rest and ease,) among the ancients, was the name of the goddess to whom rustics sacrificed at the conclusion of harvest. . . .

In England anciently they used to dress up a figure of corn, when they brought home their last load, which they called a Harvest Doll or a Kern (that is, corn) Baby, "by which," says one, "perhaps they would signify Ceres . . ." " 'round which," says another, "men and women were singing promiscuously, preceded by a drum or a pipe."

At Werington, in Devonshire, the clergyman of the parish informed me that when a farmer finishes his reaping, a small quantity of the ears of the last corn are twisted or tied together in a curious kind of figure, which is brought home with great acclamations, hung up over the table, and kept till the next year. The owner would think it extremely unlucky to part with this, which is called "a knack."

Another says, "When they have cut the corn, the reapers assemble together: a knack is made which one placed in the middle of the company holds up, crying thrice, 'A Knack!' which all the rest repeat: the person in the middle then says:

Well cut! Well bound!
Well shocked! Well saved from the ground!

He afterwards cries 'Whoof!' and his companions hollow as loud as they can. . . ."

So according to Eugene Aram, what is called the "Mell-supper, Churn-supper, Harvest Supper, Harvest-Home, Feast of In-gathering, and so on" is "as old as a sense of joy for the benefit of a plentiful harvest, and human gratitude to the Creator for his munificence to men. . . ."

This "Harvest-Home Call" is the one generally made use of in the county of Devon:

We have ploughed, we have sowed,
We have reaped, we have mowed,
We have brought home every load. . . .

CORNUS FLORIDA

Cornus florida, October first.

October 27, 1856. At Perth Amboy, conspicuous with its scarlet berries, fed on by robins, amid its scarlet leaves.

QUINCE

Quince, October first.

Ours not so early in 1860; gathered about October twentieth.

October 12, 1859. See them commonly left out yet, though apples are gathered. Probably their downy coats defend them.

Their fragrance is the best part of them, and for this they may be worth raising: to scent your chamber.

Pliny says, "They drag down the bent branches, and prevent the parent from increasing." Also that they were shut up in the ante-chambers of the great and hung upon the statues of the gods in their chambers (probably for their fragrance). This was better than putting them directly into a preserve pot.

BIDENS

Bidens ticks, October second.

November 10, 1856. At Perth Amboy I used to get my clothes covered with beggar ticks in the fields—and with burrs, small and large.

HEMLOCK

Hemlock, October fifth.

March 6, 1853. The hemlock cones have shed their seeds, but there are some closed yet on the ground.

October 31, 1853. The seeds are apparently ready to drop from their cones. The cones are mostly open.

October 15, 1856. Great part of the seeds fallen.

September 6, 1860. See no new cones, but *many* old. Apparently there were so many last year that there are none this. The cone has five rays like white pine, but little twisted.

BLACK SPRUCE

Black spruce, October fifth.

May 31, 1857. Spruce cones, though now erect, at length will turn down.

November 20, 1857. See where squirrels, apparently, have eaten and stripped the spruce cones.

October 28, 1860. See no cones as yet.

LARCH

Larch, October fifth.

This, like the hemlock, had so many cones last year that I have not seen one this year (October 28, 1860).

It has five rays like the white-pine cone.

Michaux says on some "the cones are violet colored instead of green."

CELTIS

Celtis, October fifth.

September 4, 1853. Green.

September 22, 1854. Begin to yellow.

September 26, 1859. Still green.

October 15, 1859. Ripe how long?

October 6, 1860. Only copper-brown, perhaps owing to frost.

CHESTNUT

Chestnuts, October sixth.

November 22, 1850. I get nothing to eat in my walk now but wild apples, sometimes some cranberries and some walnuts.

October 11, 1852. Now the chestnuts are rattling out. The burrs are gaping and showing the plump nuts. They fill the ruts in the road and are abundant amid the fallen leaves in the midst of the wood. The jays scream and the red squirrels scold while you are clubbing and shaking the trees.

October 15. The rain of the night and morning together with the wind has strewn the ground with chestnuts. The burrs, generally empty, come down with a loud sound while I am picking the nuts in the woods. I have come out before the rain is fairly over, before there are any fresh tracks on the Lincoln road by Britton's shanty, and I find the nuts abundant in the road itself. It is a pleasure to detect them in the woods, amid the firm, crispy, crackling chestnut leaves. There is somewhat singularly refreshing in the color of this nut—the chestnut color. No wonder it gives a name to a color. One man tells me he has bought a wood-lot in Hollis to cut and has let out the picking of the chestnuts to women at the halves; as the trees will probably be cut *for them*, they will make rapid work of it.

October 23, 1852. Chestnuts have mostly fallen.

December 9, 1852. The chestnuts are about as plenty as ever, both in the fallen burrs and out of them. There are more this year than the squirrels can consume. I picked three pints this afternoon, and though some bought at a store the other day were more than half mouldy, I did not find one mouldy one among these which I picked from under the wet and mouldy leaves, where they have been snowed on once. Probably they do not heat, though wet. These are also still plump and tender. I love to gather them, if only for the sense of the bountifulness of Nature they give me.

December 27. Find chestnuts quite plenty today.

December 31, 1852. I was this afternoon gathering chestnuts at Saw Mill Brook. I have within a few weeks spent some hours thus scraping away the leaves with my hands and feet over some square rods, and have at least learned how chestnuts are planted and new forests raised. First fall the chestnuts with the severe frosts, the greater part of them at least, and then at length the rains and winds bring down the leaves which cover them with a thick coat. I have wondered sometimes how the nuts got planted which merely fell on the surface of the earth, but already I find the nuts of the present year partially mixed with the mould, as it were under the decaying and mouldy leaves, where is all the moisture and manure they want. A large proportion of this year's nuts are now covered loosely an inch deep under mouldy leaves, though they are themselves sound and are moreover concealed from squirrels thus.

January 10, 1853. Went a-chestnutting this afternoon to Smith's Grove with four ladies. I raked, and we got six and a half quarts, the ground being bare and the leaves not frozen. I found thirty-five chestnuts left by a mouse in his gallery. Many chestnuts are still in the burrs on the ground. My aunt found a twig which had apparently fallen prematurely with eight small burrs, all within the compass of five or six inches, and all but one full of nuts.

January 25, 1853. I still pick chestnuts. Some larger ones prove to contain double meats, divided as it were arbitrarily, as with a knife, each part having the common division without the brown skin transverse to them.

Chestnut—evidently because it is packed in a little chest.

March 7, 1859. I think that many of the nuts which we find in the crevices of bark, firmly wedged in, may have been placed there by jays, chickadees, and so on, to be held fast while they crack them with their bills.

October 19, 1855. Afternoon to Pine Hill for chestnuts (Indian-summer day). The chestnuts are scarce and small, apparently have just begun to open their burrs.

October 27, 1855. Afternoon a-chestnutting down the turnpike. It is high time we came a-chestnutting, for the nuts have nearly all fallen, and you must depend on what you can find on the ground, left by the squirrels, and cannot shake down any more to speak of. The trees are nearly all bare of leaves as well as burrs. The wind comes cold from the northwest, as if there were snow on the earth in that direction.

October 8, 1856. A few chestnut burrs are open and have been some days before they could have felt frost, showing that they would open without it, but a stone will not jar them down, nor a club, thrown into the tree yet. I get half a pocketful out of slightly gaping burrs at the expense of many prickles in my fingers. The squirrels have cut off some burrs. I see the marks of their teeth.

October 16. Many chestnut burrs are now open, yet a stone will not jar down many nuts. Burrs which were quite green on the eighth are now all brown and dry, and the prickles come off in your hand when you touch them; yet the nuts do not readily drop out. Many nuts have fallen within two or three days, but many squirrels have been busily picking them up.

October 18, 1856. The chestnuts are not so ready to fall as I expected. Perhaps the burrs require to be dried now after the rain. In a day or two they will nearly all come down. They are a pretty fruit thus compactly stowed away in this bristly chest—three is the regular number—and there is no room to spare. The two outside nuts having each one convex side and a flat side within; the middle nut has two flat sides. Sometimes there are several more nuts in a burr. But this year the burrs are small and there are not commonly more than two *good* nuts—very often only one, the middle one—both sides of which will then be convex, bulging out each way into a thin, abortive, mere reminiscence of a nut, all shell, beyond it. It is a rich sight, that of a large chestnut tree, with a dome-shaped top—where the yellowing leaves have became thin (for most now strew the ground evenly as a carpet throughout the chestnut woods and so save some seed), all richly rough, with great brown burrs which have opened into several segments so as to shew the wholesome-colored nuts peeping forth, ready to fall on the slightest jar.

The individual nuts are very interesting and of various forms according to the season and the number in a burr. The base of each, where it was joined to the burr, is marked with an irregular dark figure on a light ground—oblong, crescent-shaped, much like a spider or other insect with a dozen legs—while the upper or small end tapers into a little white woolly spire crowned with a star, and the whole upper slopes of the nuts are covered with the same hoary wool, which reminds you of the frosts on whose advent they peep forth. (Each nut stretches forth a little starry hand at the end of a slender arm, and by this, when mature, you may pull it out without fear of prickles.) Within this thick, prickly burr the nuts are about as safe, until they are quite mature, as a porcupine behind its spines. Yet I see where the squirrels have gnawed through many closed burrs and left the pieces on the stumps.

I forgot to say that there are sometimes two meats within one chestnut shell, divided transversely, and each covered by its separate brown-ribbed skin. ⊖ As if Nature meant to smuggle the seed of an additional tree into this chest and multiply chances.

I see where the chestnut trees have been sadly bruised by the large stones cast against them in previous years and which still lie around.

November 28. Unexpectedly find many chestnuts in the burrs which have fallen (at Smith's Grove) some time ago. Many are spoiled, but the rest being thus moistened are softer and sweeter than a month ago, very agreeable to my palate—the burrs, from some cause, having fallen without dropping their nuts.

December 1. I have seen more chestnuts in the streets of New York than anywhere else this year—large and plump ones roasting in the street, and popping on the steps of banks and exchanges. Was surprised to see that the citizens made as much of the nuts of the wild wood as the squirrels. Not only the country boys—all New York goes a-nutting. Chestnuts for cabmen and newsboys, for not only are squirrels alone to be fed.

December 12. Dug chestnut burrs out of the snow (as the squirrels have done), and though many of these nuts are softened and discolored, they have a peculiarly sweet and agreeable taste.

Loudon quotes Pliny as saying that "Chestnuts are better roasted than cooked in any other manner"—in which I agree with him.

Evelyn says, referring to the chestnut, "We give that fruit to our swine in England, which is amongst the delicacies of princes in other countries; and, being of the larger nut, is a lusty and masculine food for rustics at all times, and of better nourishment for husbandmen than cale and rusty bacon; yea, or beans to boot."

In France, according to Loudon, "The husks of the chestnuts beaten off the trees being generally attached to the nuts, they are trodden off by peasants furnished with heavy sabots, when the nuts are wanted for immediate use. . . ."

September 24. Minott tells of them finding near a bushel of chestnuts in a rock when blasting for the mill-brook ditch near Flint's Pond. He said it was the gray squirrel's work.

October 5, 1857. See a red squirrel cast down a chestnut burr.

October 6. See one or two chestnut burrs open in the woods. The squirrels, red and gray, are on all sides throwing them down. You cannot stand long in the woods without hearing one fall.

October 22. Now is just the time for chestnuts.

What a perfect chest the chestnut is packed in. I now hold a green burr in my hand—which, round, must have been two and a quarter inches in diameter—from which three plump nuts have been extracted. It has a straight stout stem three-sixteenths of an inch in diameter, set on strongly and abruptly. It has gaped in four segments or quarters, revealing the thickness of its walls (from five-eighths to three-quarters of an inch); with such wonderful care Nature has secluded and defended these nuts, as if they were her most precious fruits, while diamonds are left to take care of themselves. First, it bristles all over with sharp green prickles, some nearly half an inch long, like a hedgehog rolled into a ball. The little stars on the top of the nuts are but shorter and feebler spines which mingle with the rest. They stand up close together, three or more, erecting their feeble weapons, as an infant in the arms of its nurse might put out its own tiny hands to fend off the aggressor. The prickles rest on a thick (one-sixteenth to one-eighth of an inch), stiff, bark-like rind—which again is most daintily lined with a kind of silvery fur or velvet plush (one-sixteenth of an inch thick) even rising in a ridge between the nuts, like the lining of a casket in which the most precious commodities are kept. I see the brown-spotted white cavities where the bases of the nuts have rested and sucked up nourishment from the stem. There is no waste room; the chest is packed quite full. Half-developed nuts are the waste-paper used in the packing to fill the vacancies.

Such is the cradle, thus daintily lined, in which they have been rocked in their infancy. With what steadiness the nuts must be held within these stout arms—there can be no motion on their bases—and yet how tenderly, by a firm hold that relaxes only as they grow, the walls that confine them, superfluously strong as they seem, expanding as they grow! The chestnut with its tough shell looks as if it were able to protect itself, but see how tenderly it has been reared in its cradle, before its green and tender skin hardened into a shell.

At last frost comes to unlock this chest. It alone holds the true key. Its lids straightway gape open, and the October air rushes in, dries the ripe nuts, and then, with a sudden gust, shakes them all out in a rattling shower down upon the withered leaves. The October air comes in, as I have said, and the light too, and proceeds to paint the nuts that clear, handsome reddish brown which we call chestnut. Nowadays the brush that paints chestnuts is very active. It is entering into every open burr over the stretching forests' tops for hundreds of miles, without horse or ladder, and rapidly putting on coats of this wholesome color. Otherwise the boys would not think they had got perfect nuts. And that this may be further protected, perchance, both within the burr and afterward, the nuts themselves are partly covered toward the top, where they are first exposed, with that same soft velvety down. And then Nature drops it on the rustling leaves—a *done* nut, prepared to begin a chestnut's course again.

Within itself each individual nut is lined with a reddish velvet, as if to preserve the seed from jar and injury in falling, and perchance from sudden damp and cold, and within that a thin white skin enwraps the meat. Thus, it is lining within lining and unwearied care—not to count closely, six coverings at least—before you reach the contents!

Is it not a barbarous way, to jar the tree? I trust I *do repent of it*. Gently shake it only, or, better, let the wind shake it for you. You are gratified to find a nut that has in it no bitterness—altogether palatable.

October 24, 1857. I get a couple of quarts of chestnuts at Smith's Grove by patiently brushing the thick bed of leaves aside with my hand in successive concentric circles till I reach the trunk. More than half were under one tree. I believe that I get more by resolving, where they are reasonably thick, to pick *all* under one tree first. Begin at the tree and brush the leaves with your right hand in toward the stump while your left holds the basket, and so go round and round it in concentric circles, each time laying bare about two feet in width, till you get as far as the boughs extend. You may presume that you have got about all there are then. It is best to reduce it to a system. Of course, you will shake the tree first, if there are any on it. The nuts lie commonly two or three together as they fell.

I find my account in this long-continued monotonous labor of picking chestnuts all the afternoon, brushing the leaves aside without looking up, absorbed in *that*, and forgetting better things awhile. I rebound afterward and between whiles with fresher sense. It is as good as a journey; I seem to have been somewhere and done something. It is a slight adventure. I have been so much in the habit of looking for Indian relics that my eye is educated to discover anything on the ground—as chestnuts and so on. It is probably wholesomer to look at the ground much than at the heavens. As I go stooping and brushing the leaves aside by the hour, I am not thinking of chestnuts merely, but I find myself humming a thought of more significance. This occupation affords a certain broad pause and opportunity to start again afterward—*turn over a new leaf*.

I hear the dull thump of heavy stones against the trees from far thro' the rustling wood, where boys are ranging for nuts.

November 9, 1857. One of the company today told of George Melvin once, for a joke, directing Jonas Melvin to go to the widow Hildreth's woodlot and gather the chestnuts. They were probably both working there (at Hildreth's). He accordingly took the oxen and cart and some ladders and another hired man, and they worked all day and got half a bushel.

July 4, 1858. Saw a chestnut tree in Loudon, New Hampshire. First and frequently.

October 14, 1859. The chestnuts *generally* have not yet fallen, though *many* have. I find under one tree a great many burrs apparently *not* cast down by squirrels, for I see no marks of their teeth, and not yet so open that any of the nuts fall out. They do not all wait till frosts open the burrs before they fall, then.

Josselyn says that the Indians hereabouts used to sell chestnuts to the English for twelve pence a bushel.

March 7, 1853. Gathered a few chestnuts. A good many if not most are now turned black and soured, or spoiled and softened by the wet. Where they are less exposed to moisture—close to the base of the (or on) stumps, where the ground is more elevated, or where they are protected under a very thick heap of light lying leaves—they are perfectly sound and sweet and fresh yet, neither shrivelled nor soured. This peculiar condition is probably requisite to preserve their life for sprouting. I planted some in Sophia's pot. No doubt the mice and squirrels put many in secure, sufficiently dry, and sufficiently moist places for this purpose— and so do a service.

March 20, 1853. At Flint's Pond gathered a handful or two of chestnuts on a sloping bank under the leaves, *every one* sound and sweet, but mostly sprouting. There were none black as at C. Smith's, proving that in such places as this, somewhat warm and dry, they are all preserved the winter through. Now their new groves of chestnuts and oaks are being born.

WALNUTS

Walnuts, October thirteenth.

May 7, 1852. The ground under the walnuts (on the hill) is richly strewn with nut shells broken and gnawed by squirrels, like an unswept dining hall in early times.

August 18, 1852. Perceived today, and some weeks since (August third) the strong invigorating aroma of green walnuts, astringent and *bracing* to the spirits, the fancy and imagination, suggesting a tree that has its roots well in amid the bowels of Nature. Their shells are invigorating to smell—suggesting a strong, nutty native vigor. A fruit which I am glad that our zone produces, looking like the nutmeg of the East. I acquire some of the hardness and elasticity of the hickory when I smell them. They are among our spices; high-scented, aromatic, as you bruise one against another in your hand, almost like nutmegs, only more bracing and northern—fragrant stones which the trees bear.

October 23, 1852. See where larger boys have gathered the mockernut, though it has not fallen out of its husks.

October 24, 1852. See boys far off on the hillside gathering walnuts, and on the twenty-eighth. October is the month for barberries and walnuts.

September 23, 1852. Some acorns and hickory nuts (mockernuts) on the ground, but they have not begun to shell. The walnuts rubbed together smell like varnish.

October 27, 1853. Now is the time to look for walnuts, last and hardest nut of the year.

October 31, 1853. Now appears to be the very time for walnuts. I knock down showers with a stick, but all do not come out of the shells.

November 1, 1853. Gathered five or six quarts of pignuts, partly by clubbing the trees, thinking they might furnish entertainment some evening the coming winter. Not more than half are out of the shells, but it is pleasant shelling them to have one's fingers scented with their fine aroma (the red squirrel reproving the while).

November 2, 1853. I gather some fine large pignuts by the wall near the beeches on Asher's land. It is just the time to get these, and this seems to be quite early enough for most pig*nuts*. (Wall-nutting last of October and first of November.)

November 6, 1853. Gathered some of those fine large mockernuts which are now in their prime: *Carya tomentosa*. I am struck by the variety in the form and size of the walnuts (in shells). Some with a slight neck and slightly club-shaped, perhaps the most common. Some much longer, nearly twice as long as wide.

Some (like the mockernut) slightly deformed or rather fattened above. Some pignuts very large and regularly obovate, one and a quarter inches in diameter.

November 7, 1853. I shook two mockernut trees, one just ready to drop its fruit, and most came out of the shells; but the other tree was not ready—only a part fell, and those mostly in the shells. This is the time for our best walnuts, the smallest or pignuts, say the last of October. Got a peck and a half shelled. I did not wish to slight any of Nature's gifts. I am partial to the peculiar and wholesome sweetness of a nut, and I think that some time is profitably spent every autumn in gathering even such as our pignuts. Some of them are a very sizeable, rich-looking, and palatable fruit. How can we expect to understand Nature unless we accept like children these her smallest gifts, valuing them more as her gifts than for their intrinsic value. I love to get my basket full, however small and comparatively worthless the nut. It takes very severe frosts, and sun and wind thereafter, to kill and open the shells so that the nuts will drop out. Many hold on all winter. I climbed to the tops of the trees and then found that shaking would not do, only jarring the limbs with my feet. It is remarkable how these nuts are protected, some with an outer shell about quarter of an inch thick and an inner nearly as thick as the other, and when cracked open the meat is still hard to extract. I noticed, however, that the nuts on one tree (the second) notwithstanding these thick shells, were now full of fine cracks, as if now that they were ripe they had made themselves ready to be cracked by man or squirrels or the frost. They really crack much easier. It is a hard, tough tree, whose fruit is stones, fit to have been the food of man in the Iron Age. I should like to see a man whose diet was berries and nuts alone. Yet I would not rob the squirrels who, before any man, are the true owners.

September 26, 1855. The squirrels have already begun on the mockernuts, though the trees are still covered with yellow and brown leaves, and the nuts do not fall.

December 5, 1856. There are a great many walnuts on the trees, seen black against the sky, and the wind has scattered many over the snow-crust. It would be easier gathering them now than ever.

December 10, 1856. Gathered this afternoon quite a parcel of walnuts on the hill. It has not been better picking there this season. They lie on the snow, or rather sunk an inch or two into it, and sometimes the trees hang quite full. I see squirrel tracks leading straight from tree to tree.

December 16, 1856. Mrs. Moody very properly calls eating nuts "a mouse-like employment." It is quite too absorbing. You cannot read at the same time, as when you are eating an apple. It is a social employment.

June 12, 1857. Michaux says that mockernuts are of various sizes and forms—some round, some oblong—and so I have found them.

September 24, 1857. Squirrel buries pignuts.

October 20, 1857. I meet the hunter with his game-bag full of nuts and barberries.

August 20, 1854. I hear a sound (on hill) as of green pignuts falling from time to time, and see and hear the chickaree thereabouts!!

March 6, 1853. Gather a pocketful of pignuts from a tree on Lee's Hill, half of them still sound.

I can almost excuse a man's intemperance if it was a walnut tree he fell from and so broke his back—he was so well employed.

Michaux says the mockernut is "odorous" and of remarkably various forms. "The shell is very thick and extremely hard"; that is, the cover. "The kernel is sweet but minute, and difficult to extract, on account of the strong partitions which divide it; hence, probably, is derived the name of Mockernut, and hence, also, this fruit is rarely seen in the markets."

Shellbark hickory is "ripe about the beginning of October. . . . The entire separation of the husk, and its thickness disproportioned to the size of the nut, form a character peculiar to the shell-bark hickories. . . . Contains a fuller and sweeter kernel than any American walnut except the Pacanenut."

Pignut hickory nuts vary in form more than the other kinds. "Some are oval and when covered with their husks, resemble young figs, others are wider than they are long, and others are perfectly round." And they are of as various sizes.

October 2. I observed that many pignuts has fallen yesterday though quite green.

October 14. At Baker's wall two of the walnut trees are bare but full of green nuts (in their green cases) which make a very pretty sight as they wave in the wind. So distinct you could count every one against the sky, for there is not a leaf on these trees, but other walnuts nearby are yet full of leaves. You have the green nut contrasted with the clean gray trunks and limbs. These are pignuts.

November 18. Now is the time to gather mockernuts.

November 19. A-mockernutting. Those long mockernuts appear not to have got well ripe this year. They do not shed their husks, and the meat is mostly skinny, soft, and flabby. May have been too *cold*. I shook the trees. It is just the time to gather them. How *hard* they rattle down, like stones! There is a harmony between this stony fruit and these hard, tough limbs which beat it.

November 20. When walnut husks are fairly opened, showing the white shells within (the trees being either quite bare or with a few withered leaves at present), a slight jar with the foot on the limbs causes them to rattle down, and on bare pasture ground it is very easy picking them up.

September 14. Even the tough-twigged mockernut, yet green, is blown off in some places by this strong wind. I bring home a twig with three of its great nuts together, as big as small apples, and children follow and eye them, not knowing what kind of fruit it is.

CEDAR

Cedar berries, October fourteenth.

October 19. How long? Fourteenth at least.

November 16, 1853. Admire the fine blue color of the cedar berries.

November 30, 1853. What a heavenly blue have the cedar berries (in Mason's pasture) a peculiar light blue whose bloom rubs off, contrasting with the green or purplish-brown leaves.

CHECKERBERRY

Checkerberry, October fifteenth.

June 3, 1851. An abundance of very large checkerberries on Asnebumskit Hill in Paxton, said to be the highest land in Worcester County except Wachusett. Such I thought must be the bluets. Whence are brought those which we see in the markets.

November 16, 1851. Plenty of ripe checkerberries now.

September 11, 1853. Full-grown but green.

October 26, 1853. Have now a fine, clean, fresh tint—a peculiar pink.

March 4, 1854. Are revealed, many of them somewhat shrivelled.

March 6. See children checkerberrying.

September 6, 1854. Just beginning to redden.

May 15, 1856. Very abundant on the south side of Pine Hill by the pitch-pine wood. Now is probably the last time to gather them.

August 19, 1856. Green; about grown.

October 8, 1856. Find many checkerberries on Smith's Hill (near chestnuts) which appear to be just ripe, a lighter pink color with two little checks on the stem side, the marks of what I suppose are the two outer calyx leaves.

October 15, 1856. An abundance of checkerberries by the hemlock at Viola Muhlenbergii Brook. A remarkable year for berries—even this, too, is abundant like the rest. They are tender and more palatable then ever now. I find a little pile of them, maybe fifteen or twenty, on the moss with each a little indentation or two on it, made by some bird or quadruped.

April 1, 1857. Checkerberries very fine and abundant, now near Viola Muhlenbergii Brook, contrasting with the red-brown leaves. They are not commonly touched by the frost.

May 21, 1857. I find checkerberries still fresh and abundant. Last year was a remarkable one for them. They lurk under the low leaves (often), scarcely to be detected when you are standing up almost below the level of the ground, dark scarlet berries, some of them half an inch in diameter, broad, pear-shaped, of a pale or hoary pink color beneath. The peduncle curves downward between two leaves. There they lurk under the glossy dark-green brown-spotted leaves, close to the

ground. They make a very handsome nose-gay. (Thus, meeting strawberries soon, they fetch the berry year about.)

September 18, 1859. See them not yet fully grown nor ripe, somewhat pear-shaped, and whitish at the blossom end.

Loudon says *Gaultherii procumbens*, "Partridge Berry, Mountain Tea, Spring Winter Green. . . . A little shrubby plant somewhat resembling seedling plants of *Kalmia latifolia*."

August 19, 1852. They never bloom, looking almost like snow-white berries.

August 19, 1852. What are the checkerberry-scented plants? Checkerberry, black and yellow birch, *Polygala* (caducous and cross-leaved and whorled at root), *Chiogenes hispidula*.

March 17, 1858. How indulgent is Nature, to give to a few common plants like checkerberry this aromatic flavor (we have all the scent of orange and lemon and cinnamon here) to relieve the general insipidity. Perhaps I am most sensible of the presence of these plants when the ground is first drying up this season, and they are fairly out.

October 14, 1858. The roots of the red-pine sapling have not only a sweet, earthy but a decidedly checkerberry scent. Digging under a tuft in the fall you find this thick white shoot in the earth ready to rise up in the spring (as October 19, 1860).

September 23, 1860. The root of the *freshest* red-pine sapling has a decided checkerberry scent and for a long time, a week after in my chamber the bruised plant has a very pleasant earthy sweetness. It then passes into an earthy sweetness. This shows how innate this fragrance is in the soil.

According to Bigelow the aromatic flavor of the checkerberry is also perceived in the *Gaultheria hispidula*, in *Spiræa ulmaria*, in the root of *Spiræa lobata*, and in birches.

Manasseh Cutler, LL.D., 1785, says that the fruit is not ripe till the following spring. "Common in pine and shrub oak land." The berries "are sometimes eaten by children in milk."

THE FALL

As long ago as September fourteenth, all things suggested fruit and the harvest, and flowers looked late, and for some time the sound of the flail had been heard in the barns. Like the fruits, when cooler weather and frosts arrived, and we shifted from the shady to the sunny side of the house and sat there in an extra coat for warmth—we too were braced and ripened. Our green, leafy, and pulpy thoughts acquired color and flavor, and perchance a sweet *nuttiness* at last, worth your cracking. It is somewhat cooler and more autumnal, and a great many leaves have fallen, and the trees begin to look thin. You incline to sit in a sunny and sheltered place.

This season, the fall, which we have now entered on, commenced, I may say, as long ago as when the first frost was seen and felt in low ground in August. From that time, even, the year has been gradually winding up its accounts. Cold, methinks, has been the great agent which has checked the growth of plants, condensed their energies, and caused their fruits to ripen—in September *especially*. Perchance man never ripens within the tropics.

October 4. Now the year duly begins to be ripe—ripened by the frost, like a persimmon.

October 11. There was a very severe frost this morning. Ground stiffened; probably a chestnut-opening frost—a season-ripener—opener of the burrs that enclose the Indian Summer. Such is the cold of early or *mid-*October.

October 16. This cold refines and condenses us. Our spirits are strong, like that pint of cider in the middle of a frozen barrel.

October 11, 1857. The seventh day of glorious weather. These might be called Harvest Days. Within a week most of the apples have been gathered, potatoes are being dug, corn is still left in the fields.

BLACK WALNUT

Black walnut, October fifteenth.

November 12, 1853. Tasted today a black walnut, a spherical and corrugated nut with a large meat, but of a strong oily taste.

October 28. Walnuts commonly fall, and the black walnuts at Smith's are at least half fallen. They are of the form and size of a small lemon, and, what is singular, have now taken moist from the ground a rich *nutmeg* fragrance. They are now turning dark brown. Gray says it is rare in the eastern but very common in the western states. Emerson says that though rare, it is found in Massachusetts. It is much the most remarkable nut that we have, then.

Michaux says our black walnut most resembles the European, is more round.

October 28, 1860. Say half fallen.

YELLOW BIRCH

Yellow birch, October fifteenth.

October 15, 1859. The yellow birch are bare, revealing the fruit; the short, thick, brown catkins now ripe and ready to scale off. How full the trees are!—almost as thick as the leaves were.

ALDER

Alder, October fifteenth.
Falling all winter.

SHAGBARK

Shagbark, October twentieth.

November 15. In Worcester, gathered half a pocketful of shagbarks, of which many still hung on the trees, though most had fallen.

December 18, 1856. Am told that they sometimes get a dozen bushels of shelled shagbarks from one tree. Shagbarks hanging on the trees on the Souhegan River, where they have not been gathered.

September 1, 1859. You must be careful not to eat too many nuts. I one winter met a young man whose face was all broken out into large pimples (or sores) who, when I inquired what was the matter, announced that he and his young wife being fond of shagbarks, he had bought a bushel of them in the fall, and they spent their winter evenings eating them—and this was the consequence.

October 20, 1854. For the most part shagbarks do not rattle out yet (at Wachusett), but it is *time to gather them* on account of squirrels.

ARTICHOKE

Artichokes, October twentieth.

Gookin says that the Indians used artichokes in their pottage.

October 20, 1859. Dug some. Now is the time to begin to dig them, the plant being considerably frost-bitten. Tried two or three plants. The largest tuber was about one inch in diameter. The main root ran down straight about six inches and then terminated abruptly thus: . They have quite a nutty taste eaten raw.

Hind sees them in the northwest in the richest profusion.

GOLDENROD

Goldenrods fuzzy October twenty-first.

Almost all were fuzzy about October 10, 1860.

WHITE AND BLACK BIRCHES

White birch, November first.

November 4, 1860. Has but recently begun to fall. I see a quarter of an inch of many catkins bare. May have begun a week.

December 4, 1856. I see where the pretty brown bird-like birch scales have been blown into the numerous hollows of the thin-crusted snow. So bountiful a table is spread for the birds. For how many thousand miles this grain is scattered over the earth under the feet of all walkers, in Boxboro and Cambridge alike, and rarely an eye distinguishes it.

January 14, 1856. The white-birch catkins appear to have their seeds first at the base, though they may be the uppermost. They are blown or shaken off, leaving a bare thread-like cone

May 12, 1858. I notice that birches near meadows where there is an exceedingly gentle inclination (over which water has flowed and receded) grow in more or less parallel lines, apparently the seed having been dropt there either by a freshet or else lodged in the parallel waving hollows of the snow.

February 18, 1854. This is a common form of the black-birch scale: ♡.

February 21, 1854. The difference between the white- and black-birch scales is that the wings of the first are curved backwards like a real bird's ⅓. The seeds of this also are broadly winged, like an insect with two little antennæ.

The birch seed is also blown far over the snow like the pine seed. Walking up our river on the second of March 1856—by Mr. Prichard's land, where the shores and neighboring fields were comparatively bare of trees—I was surprised to see on the snow over the river a great many birch scales and seeds, though the snow had but recently fallen and there had been but little wind. There was one seed or scale to a square foot; yet the nearest birches were a row of fifteen along a wall thirty rods off. When, leaving the river, I advanced toward these, the seeds became thicker and thicker, till at half a dozen rods from the trees, they quite discolored the snow; while on the other side, or eastward of the birches, there was not one. These trees appeared not to have lost a quarter part of their seeds yet. As I returned up the river, I saw some of their seeds forty rods off, and perhaps in a more favorable direction

I might have found them much further; for, as usual, it was chiefly the scales which attracted my attention, and the fine winged seed which it is not easy to distinguish had probably been winnowed from them. It suggested how unwearied Nature is in spreading her seeds. Even the spring does not find her unprovided with birch—aye, and alder and pine—seed. A great proportion of the seed that was carried to a distance lodged in the hollow above the river, and when the river broke up, was carried far away to distant shores and meadows. For, as I find by experiment, though the scales soon sink in water, the seeds float for many days.

It is stated in Loudon's *Arboretum* that the small white birch is "rarely found in groups; and single trees are met with only at considerable intervals."

Loudon, speaking of the European variety of the common white birch, says, "According to Pallas, the birch is more common than any other tree throughout the whole of the Russian Empire; being found in every wood and grove from the Baltic Sea to the Eastern Ocean." Loudon also learns from a French author that "in Prussia, the birch is planted everywhere; and it is considered to afford security against a dearth of fuel, and to insure the prosperity of the woods by the dissemination of its seeds, which fill up every blank that occurs."

PITCH PINE

Pitch pine, November fourteenth.

November 9, 1851. Pitch-pine cones are very beautiful—not only the fresh leather-colored ones, but especially the dead gray ones, covered with lichens, the scales so regular and close, like an impenetrable coat of mail. These are very handsome to my eye. Also these which have long since opened regularly and shed their seeds. I live where the *Pinus rigida* grows, with its firm cones, almost as hard as iron, armed with recurved spines.

August 29, 1854. Squirrels have stripped some pitch-pine cones.

December 28, 1854. Some Cape Cod man told Gardiner that it took eighty bushels of pitch-pine cones to make one bushel of seeds with the wings on. Yet European or French pine seeds cost not quite two hundred dollars per bushel delivered at New York.

April 29, 1857. On the pitch pines beyond John Hosmer's I see old gray cones within two feet of the ground on the trunk, sometimes a circle of them around it, which must have been formed on the young tree some twenty-odd years ago—so persistent are they.

November 14, 1857. Squirrels have carried the cones to walls, and the scales are strewn all along beneath.

February 28, 1858. I see twenty-four cones brought together under one pitch-pine tree in the side of an open field, gnawed off but not opened. Evidently gathered from this tree ready to be transported, but left behind.

April 2, 1859. Two hundred thirty-nine pitch-pine cones left in one heap.

Michaux says "Wherever these trees grow in masses the cones are dispersed singly over the branches, and, as I have learned by constant observation, they release the seeds the first autumn after their maturity; but on solitary stocks, exposed to the buffeting of the winds, the cones are collected in groups of four, five, or even a larger number, and remain closed for several years."

January 25, 1855. A pine cone blossoms out now fully in about three days in the house. They begin to open about halfway up. They are exceedingly regular and handsome; the scales with shallow triangular crescent-shaped extremities, the prickles pointing downward are most open above, and are so much recurved at the base of the cone that they lie close together and almost flat there, or at right angles with the stem, like a shield of iron scales making a perfectly regular figure of thirteen curved rays, thus: —only far more regular. There are just thirteen rays in each of the three I have. These vary in their roundness or the flatness of the cone. So the white-pine cones in their length. End of scale on side of cone: .

February 22, 1855. Pitch-pine cones must be taken from the tree at the right season else they will not open or *blossom* in a chamber. I have one which was gnawed off by squirrels, apparently of full size, but which does not open. Why should they thus open in the chamber or elsewhere? I suppose that under the influence of heat or dryness the upper side of each scale expands while the lower contracts, or perhaps only the one expands or the other conracts. I notice that the upper side is a lighter, almost cinnamon color, the lower a darker (pitchy?) red.

March 3, 1855. A few rods from the broad pitch pine beyond Hubbard's Grove, I find a cone which was probably dropt by a squirrel in the fall, for I see the marks of its teeth where it was cut off; and it has probably been buried by the snow till now, for it has apparently just opened, and I shake its seeds out. Not only is this cone resting upright on the ground fully blossomed, a very beautiful object, but the winged seeds which half-fill my hand—small triangular black seeds with thin and delicate flesh-colored wings—remind me of fishes, alewives perchance, their tails more or less curved: . (I do not show the curve of the tail.)

I see in another place under a pitch pine many cores of cones which the squirrels have completely stript of their scales, excepting about three at the extremity which cover no seeds, cutting them off regularly at the seeds or close to the core, leaving it in this form: —or more regular. From some partially stript I see that they begin at the base. These you find left on and about stumps where they have sat and under the pines. Most fallen pitch-pine cones show the marks of squirrels' teeth—and that they were cut off.

November 14, 1855. Heard today in my chamber about 11 A.M. a singular, sharp crackling sound by the window, which made me think of the snapping of an insect (with its wings or striking something). It was produced by one of three small pitch-pine cones which I gathered on the seventh of this month and which lay in the sun on the window-sill. I noticed a slight motion still in the scales at the apex, when suddenly with a louder crackling it, or the scales, separated with a snapping sound on all sides of it. It was a general and sudden bursting or expanding of all the scales, with a sharp crackling sound and a motion of the whole cone as by a force pent up within it. I suppose the strain only needed to be relieved in one point for the whole to go off.

November 20, 1855. Again I hear that sharp crackling, snapping sound and hastening to the window find that another of the pitch-pine cones gathered November seventh, lying in the sun or which the sun has reached, has separated its scales very slightly at the apex. It is discoverable only on a close inspection; but while I look, the whole cone opens its scales with a smart crackling, and rocks and seems to bristle up, scattering the dry pitch on the surface. They all thus fairly loosen and open, though they do not at once spread wide open. It is almost like the disintegration of glass. As soon as the tension is relaxed in one part it is relaxed in every part.

Unlike the white pine, the pitch pine is opening its cones and dispersing its seed gradually *all winter,* and it is not only blown far through the air, but slides yet further over the snow and ice. It has often occurred to me that it was one value of a level surface of snow, especially a crusted snow, that by its smoothness it favored the distribution of such seeds as fell on it. I have many times measured the direct distance on a snowy field from the outmost pine seed to the nearest pine to windward, and found it equal to the breadth of the widest pasture. I have seen that the seed thus crossed one of our ponds, which is half a mile wide, and I see no reason why it should not be blown many miles in some cases. In the fall it would be detained by the grass, weeds, and bushes, but the snow having first come to cover up all and make a level surface, the restless pine seeds go dashing over it like an Esquimaux sledge with an invisible team until, losing their wings or meeting with some insuperable obstacle, they lie down once for all, perchance to rise up pines. Nature has her annual sledding to do, as well as we. In a region of snow and ice like ours, this tree can be gradually spread thus from one side of the continent to the other.

By the middle of July, I notice on the shore of the above-mentioned pond, just below the high-water line, many little pitch pines which have just sprung up amid the stones and sand and muck, whose seed has been blown or drifted across. There are some places for a row of pines along the water's edge, which at length, after fifteen or twenty years, are tipped over and destroyed by the heaving of the frozen shore.

March 22, 1856. At Walden, near my old residence, I find that since I was here on the eleventh, apparently within a day or two, some gray or red squirrel or squirrels have been feeding on the pitch-pine cones extensively. The snow under one young pine is covered quite thick with the scales which they have dropped while feeding overhead. I count the cores of thirty-four cones in the snow there, and that is not all. Under another pine there are more than twenty and a well-worn track from this to a fence-post three rods distant, under which are the cores of eight cones and a corresponding amount of scales. The track is like that of a very small rabbit going up the page: . They have gnawed off the cones, which were perfectly closed. I see where one has taken one of a pair and left the other partly off. He had first sheared off the needles that were in the way, and then gnawed off the sides or cheeks of the twig in order to come at the stem of the cone, which as usual was severed by successive cuts, as with a knife, while bending it. One or two small—perhaps dead (probably still last summer, when little over a year old), certainly unripe—ones were taken off and left un-opened.

I find that many of these young pines are now full of unopened cones, which apparently will be two years old next summer—and these the squirrels now eat. There are also some of them open, perhaps on the most thrifty twigs.

February 27, 1853. A week or two ago I brought home a handsome pitch-pine cone, which had freshly fallen and was closed perfectly tight. It was put into a table drawer. Today I am greatly surprised to find that it has there dried and opened with per-fect regularity, filling the drawer; and from a solid, narrow, and sharp cone 🔘 has become a broad, rounded, open one 🔘 —has in fact expanded with all the regularity of a flower's petals into a conical flower of rigid scales and has shed a remarkable quantity of delicate winged seeds. Each scale, which is very elaborately and perfectly constructed, is armed with a short spine pointing downward, as if to protect its seed from squirrels and birds. That hard closed cone, which defied all violent attempts to open it and could only be cut open with a knife, has thus yielded to the gentle persuasion of warmth and dryness. The expanding of the pine cones—that, too, is a season.

March 6. Part of the pitch-pine cones are still closed.

March 27, 1853. The base of the pitch-pine cone which, closed, was semi-circular, after it has opened becomes more or less flat and horizontal by the crowd-ing of the scales backward upon the smaller and imperfect ones next the stem; and, viewed on this flat end, they are handsomely arranged in curving rays 🌀 . We can perhaps imagine how the primitive wood looked to William Wood, the author of *New England's Prospect*, who left New England August fifteenth, 1633, from the sample still left in Maine. He says, "The timber of the country grows strait, and tall, some trees being twenty, some thirty foot high, before they spread forth their branches; generally the trees be not very thick, tho' there be many that will serve for mill-posts, some being three foot and an half over." One would judge from accounts that the woods were clearer than the primitive wood that is left on account of Indian fires, for he says you might ride a-hunting in most places. "There is no underwood, saving in swamps," which the Indian fires did not burn. "Here no doubt might be good done with saw mills;

for I have seene of these stately high grown trees [he is speaking of pines partic-ularly] ten miles together close by the river [probably Charles River] side."

JUNIPER REPENS

Juniper repens, March first.

April 2, 1853. Those in shade green; in light, turning purplish.

September 4, 1853. Now a hoary green, but full-grown.

April 30, 1855. I now see many *Juniper repens* berries of a handsome light blue above, being still green beneath, with three hoary, pouting lips.

September 29, 1859. Quite green yet. See some of last year's dark-purple ones at the base of the branchlets.

October 19. Though the dark-blue or ripe are chiefly on the lower part of the branches, I see fresh green ones on old wood as big as a pipe stem, and often di-rectly opposite to purple ones! They are strangely mixed up. I am not sure but some of this year's berries are already ripe.

Pliny speaks of a wine made by boiling the juniper berries (Bohn says it is the *Juniper communis* of Linnæus) in must.

Loudon says of the berries of the *Juniper communis*, "They continue on the bush two years," and "The berries are, however, the most useful product of the ju-niper. Many kinds of birds feed on them, and when burnt, they were formerly

thought to possess the power of preventing infection. They are, however, now principally used in making gin"; that is, to flavor it.

I surveyed for a man one winter who was continually going into the juniper bushes to see if the berries were ripe, for he used them to flavor some liquor which he made. He got so thirsty in the meanwhile, perhaps by anticipation, that he would exclaim with emphasis, "I wish I had a barrel of rum up here." Yet he went by the purest springs as if they were useless.

WINTER FRUITS

Berries that hold on into winter are to be enumerated and perhaps deserve a separate notice—as sumac, rose hips and so on, dogwood and so on, *winterberry* above *all*, cat-tail, haws, two-leaved Solomon-seal, barberry, shrivelled pyrus, cranberries, sweet gale, green briar, pitch pine and so on, witch hazel, panicled andromeda, bayberry, hemlock, spruce, larch, cedar, juniper, checkerberry, walnuts, birches, and alders.

How little we insist on truly grand and beautiful natural features. There may be the most beautiful landscapes in the world within a dozen miles of us, for aught we know—for their inhabitants do not value nor perceive them, and so have not made them known to others—but if a grain of gold were picked up there or a pearl found in a fresh-water clam, the whole state would resound with the news. Thousands annually seek the White Mountains to be refreshed by their wild and primitive beauty, but when the country was discovered a similar kind of beauty prevailed all over it—and much of this might have been preserved for our present refreshment if a little foresight and taste had been used.

I do not believe that there is a town in this country which realizes in what its true wealth consists. I visited the town of Boxboro only eight miles west of us last fall, and far the handsomest and most memorable thing which I saw there was its noble oak wood. I doubt if there is a finer one in Massachusetts. Let it stand fifty years longer and men will make pilgrimages to it from all parts of the country, and for a worthier object than to shoot squirrels in it. And yet I said to myself, Boxboro would be very like the rest of New England if she were ashamed of that woodland. Probably, if the history of this town is written, the historian will have omitted to say a word about this forest—the most interesting thing in it—and lay all the stress on the history of the parish.

It turned out that I was not far from right, for not long after I came across a very brief historical notice of Stow, which then included Boxboro, written by the Reverend John Gardner in the *Massachusetts Historical Collections* nearly a hundred years ago—in which Mr. Gardner, after telling us who was his predecessor in the ministry and when he himself was settled, goes on to say, "As for any remarkables, I am of the mind there have been the fewest of any town of our standing in the Province. . . . I can't call to mind above one thing worthy of public notice, and that is the grave of Mr. John Green" who it appears, when in England, "was made clerk of the exchequer" by Cromwell. "Whether he was excluded from the Act of Oblivion or not I cannot tell," says Mr. Gardner. At any rate, he returned to New England and, as Mr. Gardner tells us, "lived and died, and lies buried in this place."

I can assure Mr. Gardner that he was not excluded from the act of oblivion.

It is true, Boxboro was less peculiar for its woods at that date, but they were not less interesting absolutely.

I remember talking a few years ago with a young man who had undertaken to write the history of his native town, a wild and mountainous town far up-country, whose very name suggested a hundred things to me, and I almost wished I had the task to do myself, so few of the original settlers had been driven out, and not a single clerk of the exchequer buried in it. But to my chagrin I found that the author was complaining of want of materials, and that the crowning fact of his story was that the town had been the residence of General C——and the family mansion was still standing. Around this all the materials of this history were to arrange themselves.

You can't read any genuine history, as that of Herodotus or the Venerable Bede, without perceiving that our interest depends not on the subject but on the man—on the manner in which he treats the subject and the importance he gives it. A feeble writer and without genius must have what he thinks a great theme, which we are already interested in through the accounts of others, but a genius— a Shakespeare, for instance—would make the history of his parish more interesting than another's history of the world. Wherever men have lived, there is a story to be told, and it depends chiefly on the story-teller or historian whether that is interesting or not.

I have since heard, however, that Boxboro is content to have that forest stand, instead of the houses and farms that might supplant it, not because of its beauty, but because the land pays a much larger tax now than it would then. Nevertheless it is likely to be cut off within a few years for ship-timber and the like. It is too precious to be thus disposed of. I think that it would be wise for the state to purchase and preserve a few such forests. If the people of Massachusetts are ready to found a professorship of Natural History, do they not see the importance of preserving some portions of Nature herself unimpaired?

I find that the rising generation in this town do not know what an oak or a pine is, having seen only inferior specimens. Shall we hire a man to lecture on botany—on oaks, for instance, our noblest plants—while we permit others to cut down the few best specimens of these trees that are left? It is like teaching children Latin and Greek while we burn the books printed in those languages. It is my own way of living that I complain of as well as yours, and therefore I trust that my remarks will come home to you. I hope that I am not so poor a shot, like most clergymen, as to fire into a crowd of a thousand men without hitting somebody, though I do not aim at any one.

Thus, we behave like oxen in a flower garden. The true fruit of Nature can only be plucked with a fluttering heart and a delicate hand, not bribed by any earthly reward. No hired man can help us to gather that crop. Among the Indians the earth and its productions generally were common and free to all the tribe, like the air and water, but among us who have supplanted the Indians, the public retain only a small yard or common in the middle of the village, with perhaps a graveyard beside it, and the right of way, by sufferance, by a particular narrow route, which is annually becoming narrower, from one such yard to another. I doubt if you can ride out five miles in any direction without coming to where some individual is tolling in the road, and he expects the time when it will all revert to him or his heirs. This is the way we civilized men have arranged it.

I am not overflowing with respect and gratitude to the fathers who thus laid out our New England villages, whatever precedents they were influenced by, for I think that a 'prentice hand liberated from Old English prejudices could have done much better in this New World. If they were in earnest seeking thus far away "freedom to worship God," as some assure us, why did they not secure a little more of it, when it was so cheap and they were about it? At the same time that they built meetinghouses, why did they not preserve from desecration and destruction far grander temples not made with hands?

What are the natural features which make a township handsome and worth going far to dwell in? A river with its waterfalls, meadows, lakes, hills, cliffs, or individual rocks, a forest and single ancient trees. Such things are beautiful. They have a high use which dollars and cents never represent. If the inhabitants of a town were wise, they would seek to preserve these things, though at a considerable expense. For such things educate far more than any hired teachers or preachers, or any at present recognized system of school education. I do not think him fit to be the founder of a state or even of a town who does not foresee the use of these things, but legislates, as it were, for oxen chiefly. It would be worth the while if in each town there were a committee appointed to see that the beauty of the town received no detriment. If here is the largest boulder in the country, then it should not belong to an individual nor be made into doorsteps. In some countries precious metals belong to the crown; so here more precious objects of great natural beauty should belong to the public. Let us try to keep the New World new, and while we make a wary use of the city, preserve as far as possible the advantages of living in the country.

I think of no natural feature which is a greater ornament and treasure to this town than the river. It is one of the things which determine whether a man will live here or in another place, and it is one of the first objects which we show to a stranger. In this respect we enjoy a great advantage over those neighboring towns which have no river. Yet the town, as a corporation, has never turned any but the most purely utilitarian eyes upon it and has done nothing to preserve its natural beauty. They who laid out the town should have made the river available as a common possession forever. The town collectively should at least have done as much as an individual of taste who owns an equal area commonly does in England. Indeed, I think that not only the channel, but one or both banks of every river should be a public highway, for a river is not useful merely to float on. In this case, one bank might have been reserved as a public walk and the trees that adorned it have been protected, and frequent avenues have been provided leading to it from the main street. This would have cost but few acres of land and but little wood, and we should all have been gainers by it. Now it is accessible only at the bridges, at points comparatively distant from the town, and there there is not a foot of shore to stand on unless you trespass on somebody's lot; and if you attempt a quiet stroll down the bank, you soon meet with fences built at right angles with the stream and projecting far over the water, where individuals—naturally enough, under the present arrangement—seek to monopolize the shore. At last we shall get our only view of the stream from the meetinghouse belfry. As for the trees which fringed the shore within my remembrance—where are they? and where will the remnant of them be after ten years more?

So, if there is any central and commanding hilltop, it should be reserved for the public use. Think of a mountaintop in the township, even to the Indians a sacred place, only accessible through private grounds. A temple, as it were, which you cannot enter without trespassing—nay, the temple itself private property and standing in a man's cow-yard, for such is commonly the case. New Hampshire courts have lately been deciding, as if it was for them to decide, whether the top of Mount Washington belonged to A—— or B——, and it being decided in favor of B——, I hear that he went up one winter with the proper officers and took formal possession. That area should be left unappropriated for modesty and reverence's sake—if only to suggest that the traveller who climbs thither in a degree rises above himself, as well as his native valley, and leaves some of his grovelling habits behind.

I know it is a mere figure of speech to talk about temples nowadays, when men recognize none and associate the word with heathenism. Most men, it appears to me, do not care for Nature and would sell their share in all her beauty for as long as they may live for a stated and not very large sum. Thank God, they cannot yet fly and lay waste the sky as well as the earth! We are safe on that side for the present. It is for the very reason that some do not care for these things that we need to combine to protect all from the vandalism of a few.

It is true, we as yet take liberties and go across lots in most directions, but we naturally take fewer and fewer liberties every year, as we meet with more resistance, and we shall soon be reduced to the same straights they are in England, where going across lots is out of the question, and we must ask leave to walk in some lady's park. There are a few hopeful signs. There is the growing *library*, and then the town does set trees along the highways. But does not the broad landscape itself deserve attention? We cut down the few old oaks which witnessed the trans-fer of the township from the Indian to the white man, and perchance commence our museum with a cartridge box taken from a British soldier in 1775.

I think that each town should have a park, or rather a primitive forest, of five hundred or a thousand acres, either in one body or several, where a stick should never be cut for fuel, nor for the navy, nor to make wagons, but stand and decay for higher uses—a common possession forever, for instruction and recreation. All Walden Wood might have been reserved, with Walden in the midst of it, and the Easterbrooks Country, an uncultivated area of some four square miles in the north of the town, might have been our huckleberry field. If any owners of these tracts are about to leave the world without natural heirs who need or deserve to be spe-cially remembered, they will do wisely to abandon the possession to all mankind and not will them to some individual who perhaps has enough already—and so correct the error that was made when the town was laid out. As some give to Har-vard College or another institution, so one might give a forest or a huckleberry field to Concord. This town surely is an institution which deserves to be remem-bered. Forget the heathen in foreign parts, and remember the pagans and salvages here. We hear of cow commons and ministerial lots, but we want *men* commons and *lay* lots as well. There is meadow and pasture and woodlot for the town's poor; why not a forest and huckleberry field for the town's rich? We boast of our system of education, but why stop at schoolmasters and schoolhouses? We are all school-masters, and our schoolhouse is the universe. To attend chiefly to the desk or schoolhouse while we neglect the scenery in which it is placed is absurd. If we do not look out we shall find our fine schoolhouse standing in a cow-yard at last.

It frequently happens that what the city prides itself on most is its park, those acres which require to be the least altered from their original condition.

Live in each season as it passes; breathe the air, drink the drink, taste the fruit, and resign yourself to the influences of each. Let these be your only diet-drink and botanical medicines. In August live on berries, not dried meats and pemmican, as if you were on shipboard making your way through a waste ocean or on the Darien Grounds. Be blown on by all the winds. Open all your pores and bathe in all the tides of Nature, in all her streams and oceans, at all seasons. Miasma and infection are from within, not without. The invalid brought to the brink of the grave by an unnatural life, instead of imbibing the great influence that Nature is, drinks only of the tea made of a particular herb, while he still continues his unnatural life—saves at the spile and wastes at the bung. He does not love Nature or his life, and so sickens and dies, and no doctor can cure him. Grow green with spring, yellow and ripe with autumn. Drink of each season's influence as a vial, a true panacea of all remedies mixed for your especial use. The vials of summer never made a man sick, only those which he had stored in his cellar. Drink the wines, not of your own, but of Nature's bottling—not kept in a goat- or pig-skin, but in the skin of a myriad fair berries. Let Nature do your bottling, as also your pickling and preserving. For all Nature is doing her best each moment to make us well. She exists for no other end. Do not resist her. With the least inclination to be well, we should not be sick. Men have discovered, or think that they have discovered, the salutariness of a few wild things only, and not of all Nature. Why, Nature is but another name for health. Some men think that they are not well in spring or summer or autumn or winter; (if you will excuse the pun) it is only because they are not indeed *well*; that is, fairly *in* those seasons.

RELATED PASSAGES

EDITOR'S NOTE: *The following ten passages relate to* Wild Fruits *with decreasing directness based on their sequence here. Thoreau clearly intended to use the alternate beginning of* Wild Fruits *near the beginning of the book, but he never indicated where or precisely how to situate the passage in relation to the current beginning. He wrote the beginning and ending of his essay "Wild Apples" to frame the section of that name, which is at once the essay's body and the "Wild Apples" section in the book. The remaining passages are from* The Dispersion of Seeds, *a manuscript Thoreau began writing largely as a consequence of his autumn 1860 field work for and revisions of the sections of* Wild Fruits *dealing with acorns and nuts, not to mention his reading earlier in the year of Charles Darwin's great treatise* On the Origin of Species, *two central chapters of which deal with the "Geographical Distribution" of seeds and other biota. (Thoreau approvingly quotes Darwin's treatise in* The Dispersion of Seeds *and points out that the "development theory"—the theory of evolution—"imples a greater vital force in Nature, because it is more flexible and accommodating, and equivalent to a sort of constant new creation.") All but the final passage from* The Dispersion of Seeds *below are incorporated here so that the reader can compare them to the earlier drafts in* Wild Fruits. *The final section, the alternate beginning for* The Dispersion of Seeds, *is included here merely because I had earlier, and I now believe erroneously, represented it as the beginning of* Wild Fruits, *whereas it now seems clear that Thoreau in fact wrote that passage as an alternate beginning for* The Dispersion of Seeds.

WILD FRUITS:
ALTERNATE BEGINNING

Agrestem tenui meditabor arundine musam
I am going to play a rustic strain on my slender reed,

non injussa cano.
but I trust that I do not sing unbidden things.

Moralists say of men, "By their fruits ye shall know them," but botanists have commonly said of plants, "By their flowers ye shall know them." This is very well generally, but they should make an exception when the *fruit* is fairer than the flower. They are to be compared at that stage when they are most significant to man. I say that sometimes by their fruits ye shall know them, though I here use the word "fruit" in the popular sense.

It may be worth the while to consider for a moment what a fruit is. The mystery of the life of plants is kindred with that of our own lives, and the physiologist must not be in too much haste to explain their growth according to mechanical laws, or as he might explain some machinery of his own making. We must not presume to probe with our fingers the sanctuary of any life, whether animal or vegetable; if we do we shall discover nothing but surface still, or all fruits will be apples of the Dead Sea, full of dust and ashes. (Science is often like the grub, which, though it has nestled in the very germ of the fruit, and so perhaps blighted or consumed it, has never truly tasted it.)

The ultimate expression or *fruit* of any created thing is a fine effluence, which only the most ingenuous worshipper perceives at a reverent distance from its surface even. The cause and the effect are equally evanescent and intangible, and the former must be investigated in the same spirit and with the same reverence with which the latter is perceived. Only that intellect makes any progress toward conceiving of the essence which at the same time perceives the effluence. The rude and ignorant finger is ever probing in the rind still, for in this case, too, the angles of incidence and excidence are equal, and the essence is (so to speak) as far on the other side of the surface (or matter) as reverence detains the worshipper on this, and only reverence can find out this angle. Shall we presume to alter the angle at which the Maker chooses to be seen?

Accordingly, I reject Carpenter's explanation of the fact that a potato vine in a cellar grows toward the light, when he says, "The reason obviously is, that, in consequence of the loss of fluid from the tissue of the stem, on the side on which the light falls, it is contracted, whilst that of the other side remains turgid with fluid; the stem makes a bend, therefore, until its growing point becomes opposite to the light, and then increases in that direction." In the same manner he might undertake to show *why* I grow toward the light, and with the same success, for he would no doubt find me *bending* my steps thither according to human laws of locomotion.

There is no ripeness which is not, so to speak, something ultimate in itself, and not merely a perfected means to what we believe to be a higher end. In order to be ripe it must serve a transcendent use. The ripeness of a leaf being perfected (for aught we know), it leaves the tree at that point and never returns to it. It has nothing to do with any other fruit which the tree may bear, and only genius can pluck it. The fruit of a tree is neither in the seed, nor the timber—nor is it the full-grown tree itself—but I would prefer to consider it for the present as simply the highest use to which it can be put. As Mrs. Lincoln says in her *Botany*, "The maturity of the seed marks the close of the life of annual plants, and the suspension of vegetation in woody and perennial ones."

When La Mountain and Haddock dropped down into the Canada wilderness the other day, they came near starving or dying of cold, wet, and fatigue, not knowing where to look for food nor how to shelter themselves. Thus far we have wandered from a simple and independent life. I think that a wise and independent, self-reliant man will have a complete list of the edibles to be found in a primitive country or wilderness—a bill of fare in his waistcoat pocket, at least, to say nothing of matches and warm clothing, so that he can commence a systematic search for them without loss of time. They might have had several frogs a piece if they had known how to find them. Talk about tariffs and protection of home industry, so as to be prepared for hard times and wars! Here we are deriving our bread stuffs from the west, our butter stuffs from Vermont, and our tea and coffee and sugar stuffs (and much more that we stuff ourselves with) from the other side of the globe. Why, a truly prudent man will carry such a list as the above in his mind, at least, even though he walk through Broadway or Quincy Market.

He will know what are the permanent resources of the land and be prepared for the hardest of times. He will go behind cities and their police; he will see through them. Is not the wilderness of mould and dry rot forever invading and threatening them? They are but a camp abundantly supplied today, but gnawing their old shoes tomorrow. Why, a merely æsthetic philosopher, who soars higher than usual in his thoughts, from time to time drops down into what is just such a wilderness to him as that was to La Mountain and Haddock, where he finds scarcely one little frog gone into winter quarters, to sustain himself, and runs screaming toward the climes of the sun.

Accordingly, I have been taking an account of stock in good season. Bigelow says, "No botanist, even if in danger of starving in a wilderness, could indulge his hunger on a root or fruit taken from an unknown plant of the natural order *Luridæ*, of the *Multisiliquæ*, or the umbelliferous aquatics. On the contrary, he would not feel a moment's hesitation in regard to any of the *Gramina*, the fruit of the *Pomaceæ*, and several other natural families, which are known to be uniformly innocent in their effects."

"WILD APPLES":
BEGINNING AND ENDING
The History of the Apple Tree

It is remarkable how closely the history of the apple tree is connected with that of man. The geologist tells us that the order of the *Rosaceæ*, which includes the apple, also the true grasses, and the *Labiatæ*, or mints, were introduced only a short time previous to the appearance of man on the globe.

It appears that apples made a part of the food of that unknown primitive people whose traces have lately been found at the bottom of the Swiss lakes, supposed to be older than the foundation of Rome, so old that they had no metallic implements. An entire black and shrivelled crab apple has been recovered from their stores.

Tacitus says of the ancient Germans, that they satisfied their hunger with wild apples (*agrestia poma*), among other things.

Niebuhr observes that "the words for a house, a field, a plough, ploughing, wine, oil, milk, sheep, apples, and others relating to agriculture and the gentler way of life, agree in Latin and Greek, while the Latin words for all objects pertaining to war or the chase are utterly alien from the Greek." Thus the apple tree may be considered a symbol of peace no less than the olive.

The apple was early so important, and generally distributed, that its name traced to its root in many languages signifies fruit in general. Μῆλον, in Greek, means an apple, also the fruit of other trees, also a sheep and any cattle, and finally riches in general.

The apple tree has been celebrated by the Hebrews, Greeks, Romans, and Scandinavians. Some have thought that the first human pair were tempted by its fruit. Goddesses are fabled to have contended for it, dragons were set to watch it, and heroes were employed to pluck it.

The tree is mentioned in at least three places in the Old Testament, and its fruit in two or three more. Solomon sings—"As the apple-tree among the trees of the wood, so is my beloved among the sons." And again—"Stay me with flagons, comfort me with apples." The noblest part of man's noblest feature is named from this fruit, the "apple of the eye."

The apple tree is also mentioned by Homer and Herodotus. Ulysses saw in the glorious garden of Alcinoüs "pears and pomegranates, and apple-trees bearing beautiful fruit" (καὶ μηλέαι ἀγλαόκαρποι). And according to Homer, apples were among the fruits which Tantalus could not pluck, the wind ever blowing their boughs away from him. Theophrastus knew and described the apple tree as a botanist.

According to *The Prose Edda*, "Iduna keeps in a box the apples which the gods, when they feel old age approaching, have only to taste of to become young again. It is in this manner that they will be kept in renovated youth until Ragnarök" (or the destruction of the gods).

I learn from Loudon that "the ancient Welsh bards were rewarded for excelling in song by the token of the apple spray"; and "in the Highlands of Scotland the apple tree is the badge of the clan Lamont."

The apple tree (*Pyrus malus*) belongs chiefly to the northern temperate zone. Loudon says that it "grows spontaneously in every part of Europe except the torrid zone, and throughout Western Asia, China, and Japan." We have also two or three varieties of the apple indigenous in North America. The cultivated apple tree was first introduced into this country by the earliest settlers, and it is thought to do as well or better here than anywhere else. Probably some of the varieties which are now cultivated were first introduced into Britain by the Romans.

Pliny, adopting the distinction of Theophrastus, says, "Of trees there are some which are altogether wild (*sylvestres*), some more civilized (*urbaniores*)." Theophrastus includes the apple among the last; and, indeed, it is in this sense the most civilized of all trees. It is as harmless as a dove, as beautiful as a rose, and as valuable as flocks and herds. It has been longer cultivated than any other, and so is more humanized; and who knows but, like the dog, it will at length be no longer traceable to its wild original? It migrates with man, like the dog and horse and cow: first, perchance, from Greece to Italy, thence to England, thence to America; and our Western emigrant is still marching steadily toward the setting sun with the seeds of the apple in his pocket, or perhaps a few young trees strapped to his load. At least a million apple trees are thus set farther westward this year than any cultivated ones grew last year. Consider how the Blossom Week, like the sabbath, is thus annually spreading over the prairies; for when man migrates, he carries with him not only his birds, quadrupeds, insects, vegetables, and his very sward, but his orchard also.

The leaves and tender twigs are an agreeable food to many domestic animals, as the cow, horse, sheep, and goat; and the fruit is sought after by the first, as well as by the hog. Thus there appears to have existed a natural alliance between these animals and this tree from the first. "The fruit of the Crab in the forests of France" is said to be "a great resource for the wild-boar."

Not only the Indian, but many indigenous insects, birds, and quadrupeds, welcomed the apple tree to these shores. The tent-caterpillar saddled her eggs on the very first twig that was formed, and it has since shared her affections with the wild cherry; and the canker-worm also in a measure abandoned the elm to feed on it. As it grew apace, the blue-bird, robin, cherry-bird, king-bird, and many more, came with haste and built their nests and warbled in its boughs, and so became orchard-birds, and multiplied more than ever. It was an era in the history of their race. The downy woodpecker found such a savory morsel under its bark, that he perforated it in a ring quite round the tree, before he left it—a thing which he had never done before, to my knowledge. It did not take the partridge long to find out how sweet its buds were, and every winter eve she flew, and still flies, from the wood, to pluck them, much to the farmer's sorrow. The rabbit, too, was not slow to learn the taste of its twigs and bark; and when the fruit was ripe, the squirrel half-rolled, half-carried it to his hole; and even the musquash crept up the bank from the brook at evening, and greedily devoured it, until he had worn a path in the grass there; and when it was frozen and thawed, the crow and the jay were glad to taste it occasionally. The owl crept into the first apple tree that became hollow, and fairly hooted with delight, finding it just the place for him; so, settling down into it, he has remained there ever since.

My theme being the wild apple, I will merely glance at some of the seasons in the annual growth of the cultivated apple, and pass on to my special province.

The flowers of the apple are perhaps the most beautiful of any tree's, so copious and so delicious to both sight and scent. The walker is frequently tempted to turn and linger near some more than usually handsome one, whose blossoms are two-thirds expanded. How superior it is in these respects to the pear, whose blossoms are neither colored nor fragrant!

By the middle of July, green apples are so large as to remind us of coddling, and of the autumn. The sward is commonly strewed with little ones which fall stillborn, as it were—Nature thus thinning them for us. The Roman writer Palladius said—"If apples are inclined to fall before their time, a stone placed in a split root will retain them." Some such notion, still surviving, may account for some of the stones which we see placed to be overgrown in the forks of trees. They have a saying in Suffolk, England—

> At Michaelmas time, or a little before,
> Half an apple goes to the core.

This is "The word of the Lord that came to Joel the son of Pethuel":

Hear this, ye old men, and give ear, all ye inhabitants of the land! Hath this been in your days, or even in the days of your fathers? . . .

That which the palmer-worm hath left hath the locust eaten; and that which the locust hath left hath the canker-worm eaten; and that which the cankerworm hath left hath the caterpillar eaten.

Awake, ye drunkards, and weep! and howl, all ye drinkers of wine, because of the new wine! for it is cut off from your mouth.

For a nation is come up upon my land, strong, and without number, whose teeth are the teeth of a lion, and he hath the cheek-teeth of a great lion.

He hath laid my vine waste, and barked my fig-tree; he hath made it clean bare, and cast it away; the branches thereof are made white. . . .

Be ye ashamed, O ye husbandmen! howl, O ye vine-dressers! . . .

The vine is dried up, and the fig-tree languisheth; the pomegranate-tree, the palm-tree also, and the apple-tree, even all the trees of the field, are withered: because joy is withered away from the sons of men.

T H E   D I S P E R S I O N   O F   S E E D S :
T O U C H - M E - N O T
(Compare earlier draft, p. 64 above.)

Touch-me-not seed vessels, as all know, go off like pistols on the slightest touch, and so suddenly and energetically that they always startle you, though you are expecting it. They shoot their seed like shot. They even explode in my hat as I am bringing them home. De Candolle says that this *Impatiens fulva* is perfectly naturalized in England from America—escaped from gardens.

T H E   D I S P E R S I O N   O F   S E E D S :
H O U N D ' S - T O N G U E
(Compare earlier draft, p. 99 above.)

A few years ago I knew of but one place in the town where the hound's-tongue was naturalized. I put a handful of its nutlets into my pocket with my handkerchief, but it took me a long time to pick them out of the handkerchief when I got home, and I pulled out many threads in the process. I afterward spent twenty minutes in clearing myself of them after having brushed against the plant. But I do not mind such things; and so, the next spring, not intending any harm, I gave some of the above-named seeds, gathered the previous August, to a young lady who cultivates a flower garden and to my sister, wishing to spread it, it is so rare. Their expectations were excited and kept on the *qui vive* for a long time, for it does not blossom till the second year. The flower and peculiar odor were sufficiently admired in due time, but suddenly a great hue and cry reached my ears on account of its seeds adhering to the clothes of those who frequented these gardens. I learned that that young lady's mother, who one day took a turn in the garden in order to pluck a nose-gay just before setting out on a journey, found that she had carried a surprising quantity of this seed to Boston on her dress, without knowing it; for the flowers that invite you to look at and pluck them have designs on you, and the railroad company charged nothing for freight. So this plant is in a fair way to be dispersed, and my purpose is accomplished. I shall not need to trouble myself further about it.

THE DISPERSION OF SEEDS:
LILIES
(Compare earlier draft, p. 172 above.)

So too the yellow lily (*Nuphar advena*) is now curved back in the same manner, ripening its seed September first in the water and mud beneath the surface. This fruit is of an oblong conical form, and ribbed, with a sort of straight beak to it, and is full of yellow seeds. The white-lily fruit, having lost its blackened and decayed leaves, is of a handsome shallow, vase-like form. The seeds are about a quarter as big as apple seeds, and of a similar color or rather more purplish. The white-lily seeds last longer and, when first taken out of the pods, which are now all withdrawn under water, will float—but as soon as the peculiar slimy or mucilaginous matter which envelopes them is washed off, they sink to the bottom and plant themselves. Saint Pierre says that he is so entirely convinced of the perfect adaptation and harmony that reigns throughout all the works of Nature "as to conclude that the time when the seeds of aquatic plants drop is regulated, in most cases, by that of the overflowing of the rivers where they grow."

THE DISPERSION OF SEEDS:
ACORNS
(Compare earlier draft, pp. 183–86 above.)

I have now examined many dense pine woods, both pitch and white, and several oak woods in order to see how many and what kind of oak seedlings there were springing up in them, and I do not hesitate to say that seedlings under one foot high are *very* much more abundant under the pines than under the oaks.

They prevail and are countless under the pines, while they are hard to find under the oaks, and what you do find have commonly (for whatever reason) very old and decayed roots, and feeble shoots from them.

Notwithstanding that the acorns are produced only by oaks and not by pines, the fact is that there are comparatively few seedling oaks (one foot or less in height) under the oaks but thousands under the pines. I would not undertake to get a hundred oaks of this size suitable to transplant under a dense and pure oak wood, but I could easily get thousands from under pines.

Indeed, it appears not to be known that the pine woods are a natural nursery of oaks, from whence we might easily transplant them to our grounds and thus save some of those which annually decay, so long as we let the pines stand. These oaks, at any rate, will bear exposure to the light, for such is their destiny.

This is the reason, then, why oaks and pines commonly grow together, or in the same region. If I am not mistaken, our oaks and pines (pitch and white) are nearly identical in their range. Or perhaps the former extend beyond the latter southward where there is less danger of frost, as the latter extend beyond the former northward where even their shelter cannot defend the oaks from the extreme cold. Perhaps the oak will be found to flourish best, and make the best wood, where the climate is so cold that it requires the shelter of the pines at first, yet not cold enough to kill it in spite of this defense. Nuttall, in his *North American Sylva*, says that "oaks . . . are confined to the Northern Hemisphere. . . . The Old World contains sixty-three species, and North America, including New Spain, about seventy-four. Of these the United States possesses about thirty-seven, and New Spain the same number."

I have also noticed these little oaks abundant in birch woods, which afford a dense covert to jays, squirrels, and other animals which transport the acorns. In short, hereabouts a pine wood or even a birch wood is no sooner established than the squirrels and birds begin to plant acorns in it.

But it is remarkable that, for the most part, there are no seedling oaks in the midst of open grassy fields or pastures. Most kinds of acorns are but little likely to succeed if dropped there. Those springing up in such places appear to have been dropped or buried by birds and quadrupeds when on their way with them from one covert to another. For, depend on it, every such tree comes from a seed. When I examine these little oaks only two or three years old in native localities, I invariably find there the empty acorn from which they sprung.

So far from the seed having lain dormant in the soil since oaks grew there be-fore, as many believe, it is well known that it is difficult to preserve the vitality of acorns long enough to transport them to Europe; and it is recommended in Loudon's *Arboretum*, as the safest course, to sprout them in pots on the voyage. The same authority states that "very few acorns of any species will germinate after having been kept a year," that beech mast "only retains its vital properties for one year," and the black walnut "seldom . . . more than six months after it has ripened." I have frequently found that in November almost every acorn left on the ground had sprouted. Cobbett says of the white oak that "if warm rains come in the month of November, which they very frequently do in America, the acorns still clinging to the tree actually begin to sprout before they are shaken down by the winds." On the eighth of October, 1860, I found a great many white-oak acorns already sprouted, although they had not half fallen, and I could easily be-lieve that they sometimes sprout before they fall. Yet it is stated by one botanical writer that "acorns that have lain for centuries, on being plowed up, have soon vegetated." It is remarkable how soon and unaccountably they decay. Many which I took from the tree and cut open, though they look sound without, are discolored and decaying on one side or throughout within, though there is no worm in them. What with frost, drought, moisture, and worms, the greater part are soon de-stroyed.

Mr. George B. Emerson, in his valuable *Report on the Trees and Shrubs of the State*, says of the pines: "The tenacity of life of the seeds is remarkable. They will remain for many years unchanged in the ground, protected by the coolness and deep shade of the forest above them. But when the forest is removed, and the warmth of the sun admitted, they immediately vegetate." Since he does not tell us on what observation his remark is founded, I must doubt its truth. Besides, the experience of nurserymen makes it the more questionable. According to Loudon, the vitality of the seed of very few of the *Coniferæ* can be preserved more than three or four years by any *artificial* means known, though he says that the seeds of the *Pinus pinaster* often do not come up till the third year.

THE DISPERSION OF SEEDS:
WHITE PINE

(Compare earlier draft, pp. 187–90 above.)

As for the white pine, you have all observed its clusters of sickle-shaped green cones at the top chiefly of the tallest trees, well nigh inaccessible to man. About the middle of September these turn brown and open in the sun and wind, and, as in the case of the pitch pine, away go the seeds of future forests flying far and wide.

How little observed are the fruits which we do not use! How few attend to the ripening and dispersion of the white-pine seed! In the latter part of September in a fruitful year, the tops of high trees for six or ten feet are quite browned with the cones, hanging with their points downward and just opened. They make a great show even sixty rods off, and it is worth the while to look down from some favorable height over such a forest—to observe such evidence of fertility in this which commonly we do not regard as a fruit-bearing tree. I occasionally go to the white-pine woods merely to look at their crop of cones, just as a farmer visits his orchards in October.

These seeds all fall in September, except a few which are left glued to the cones by the pitch. They have one advantage at least over the pitch pine, that growing commonly in the tops of lofty trees they will be wafted to a greater distance by the wind in proportion as they fall further.

The white pine bears much more sparingly than the pitch, and one would say that the latter, though more difficult to transplant, was more likely, both on account of the abundance of its seeds and their falling all winter, to disperse itself and maintain its ground here. Yet it is to be remembered that the white pine has a wider range, since it not only grows well in open ground, but springs up in the midst of the woods far more readily than the pitch pine.

However, in the fall of 1859 the white pines bore a peculiarly abundant crop, as I observed not only in this town but in all this part of the country and as far off as Worcester. I could see its burden of brown cones half a mile distant.

You may often see amid or beside a pine grove, though it may be thirty or forty years old, a few yet larger and older trees from which their seed came, rising above them like patriarchs surrounded by their children, while a third generation shows itself yet further off.

Short, and on some accounts unfavorable, as the season is during which the white-pine seed is falling, it appears to be blown to no less distance than that of the pitch pine. I frequently pass by some wet and bushy meadow in the midst of open land, which is being rapidly filled with little white pines whose seeds must have been blown fifty or sixty rods at least. They are now rapidly spreading over the northeast part of Fair Haven hillside, though the nearest seed-bearing pines are across the river from thirty to sixty rods off. Also, I notice for a quarter of a mile along the Corner Road beyond Abiel Wheeler's, where it runs through a broad, open tract, quite a number of white pines springing up against the south wall, which must have come from seed blown from Hubbard's Grove, some fifty rods east; and I observe the same thing in other parts of the town. They run forward and entrench themselves like the French soldiers in Sevastopol, and ere long we begin to see the plumes waving there.

The last is a single line of trees of various sizes and much interrupted, from seeds which have gradually been caught and protected by the wall; for I find that, however few they may be, they drift according to the same law with snow. Indeed, I am quite satisfied that there is no part of this town so remote from a seed-bearing pine but its seed may be blown thither, and so a pine spring up there. These which we see springing up thus in distant and neglected meadows and by fences show what would happen over all the intervening space if it were not for our cultivation—that there is nothing to prevent their springing up all over the village in a few years but our plows and spades and scythes. They grow slowly at first, but after they get to be four or five feet high they will frequently increase seven feet in the next three years.

For many years the daily traveller along these roads—nay, the proprietor himself—does not notice that there are any pines coming up there, and still less does he consider whence they came; but at last his heir knows himself to be the possessor of a handsome white-pine lot, long after the wood from which the seed came has disappeared.

We need not be surprised at these results when we consider how persevering Nature is and how much time she has to work in. It does not imply any remarkable rapidity or success in her operations. A great pine wood may drop many millions of seeds in one year, but if only half a dozen of them are conveyed a quarter of a mile and lodge against some fence, and only one of these comes up and grows there, in the course of fifteen or twenty years there will be fifteen or twenty young trees there, and they will begin to make a show and betray their origin.

In this haphazard manner Nature surely creates you a forest at last, though as if it were the last thing she were thinking of. By seemingly feeble and stealthy steps—by a geologic pace—she gets over the greatest distances and accomplishes her greatest results. It is a vulgar prejudice that such forests are "spontaneously generated," but science knows that there has not been a sudden new creation in their case but a steady progress according to existing laws, that they came from seeds—that is, are the result of causes still in operation, though we may not be aware that they are operating.

It is a boy's statement, and does not imply much wisdom, to discover that "little strokes fall great oaks," for the sound of the axe invites our attention to such a catastrophe. We can easily count each stroke as it is given, and all the neighborhood is informed by a loud crash when the deed is consummated; but they are few who consider what little strokes, of a different kind and often repeated, *raise* great oaks or pines. Scarcely a traveller hears these or turns aside to communicate with that Nature which is steadily dealing them.

Nature works no faster than need be. If she has to produce a bed of cress or radishes, she seems to us swift; but if it is a pine or oak wood, she may seem to us slow or wholly idle, so leisurely and secure is she. She knows that seeds have many other uses than to reproduce their kind. If every acorn of this year's crop is destroyed, or the pines bear no seed, never fear. She has more years to come. It is not necessary that a pine or an oak should bear fruit every year, as it is that a pea vine should.

However, Nature is not always slow in raising pine woods even to our senses. You have all seen how rapidly, sometimes almost unaccountably, the young white pines spring up in a pasture or clearing. Small forests thus planted soon alter the face of the landscape. Last year perhaps you observed a few little trees there, but next year you find a forest.

In an account of Duxbury in the *Massachusetts Historical Collections* written in 1793, it is said: "Capt. Samuel Alden, who died twelve years since, recollected the first white pine in the town. Now the eighth part, perhaps, of the woodland is covered with this growth." Pigeons, nuthatches, and other birds devour the seed of the white pine in great quantities, and if the wind alone is not enough, it is easy to see how pigeons may fill their crops with pine seed and then move off much faster than a locomotive to be killed by hundreds in another part of the county, and so plant the white pine where it did not grow before.

If you set out for the first time in your life to collect white-pine seed here-abouts, you will probably be indebted for every one you will get to the labor of the red squirrel. As I have said, this seed ripens in September, when the cones open, and the seed is quickly blown out; but the cones hang on all winter, only falling from time to time in high winds. If you wait till a cone may chance to fall thus, you will surely find it empty. I think that I may venture to say that every white-pine cone that by good rights falls to the earth naturally in this town before open-ing and losing its seeds (and almost every pitch pine that falls at all) is cut off by a squirrel; and they begin to pluck them long before they are ripe, and when the crop is a small one, as it commonly is, they cut off thus almost every one before it fairly ripens. I think, moreover, that their design, if I may so speak, in cutting them off green is partly to prevent their opening and losing their seeds, for these are the ones for which they dig through the snow in the winter and the only white-pine cones which contain anything then. Most of these cones appear to be soon carried off by them—fresh to holes in the earth.

Though the seed of pines cannot otherwise be relied on commonly when it is more than a year or two old, it is stated in Loudon that "the seeds of most species, when allowed to remain in the cone, preserve their vegetative power for several years." So few sound seeds as there appear to be in these cones, the squirrel may occasionally plant a pine tree, as well as lay up food for itself, and this might ex-plain a pine's springing up where no seed had fallen for several years—for I often see white-pine cones which have been transported a considerable distance. If you walk through a white-pine wood in the latter part of September, you will find the ground strewn with green cones that have been thus dropped, while those left on the trees are all open. In some woods, every one will be on the ground.

In August and early in September, they are exceedingly busy cutting off cones in all white-pine woods, for they know well the nature of the tree. Perhaps they also store up the seeds separately, for by the middle of September a great part of those left on the ground will have been already stripped by them, they beginning at the base, as with the pitch-pine cone. Many of these, however, cut off late, open of themselves on the ground and shed their seeds there.

The first season that I set out to gather white-pine seed, I was as green at the business as the cones before they have opened and put it off too late. The next year, every one that I got had been gathered for me by the squirrels, but many of these were immature. The third year, I tried to compete with the squirrels and climbed the trees in good season myself. Hear my experience:

September 9th, 1857

To the woods for white-pine cones. Very few trees bear any, and they are on their tops. I can easily manage small trees, fifteen or twenty feet high, climbing till I can reach the dangling green pickle-like fruit with my right hand, while I hold to the main stem with my left; but I am in a pickle when I get one. The cones are now all flowing with pitch, and my hands are soon so covered with it that I cannot easily cast down my booty when I would, it sticks to my fingers so; and when I get down at last and have picked them up, I cannot touch my basket with such hands but carry it on my arm, nor can I pick up my coat which I have taken off unless with my teeth—or else I kick it up and catch it on my arm. Thus I go from tree to tree, rubbing my hands from time to time in brooks and mudholes in the hope of finding something that will remove pitch, as grease does, but in vain. It is the stickiest work I ever did; yet I stick to it. I do not see how the squirrels that gnaw them off and then open them, scale by scale, keep their paws and whiskers clean. They must possess some remedy for pitch that we know nothing of, for they can touch it and not be defiled. What would I not give for their recipe! How fast I could collect cones if I could only contract with a family of squirrels to cut them off for me!—or what if I had a pair of shears eighty feet long and a derrick to wield them with!

At length, after two or three afternoons, I get a bushel of them home, but I have not got at the seeds yet. They are more effectually protected than a chestnut in its burr. I must wait till they please to open and then get pitched once more.

These green cones collected in my chamber have a strong spirituous scent, almost rummy, or like a molasses hogshead, which would probably be agreeable to some.

In short, I found the business far from profitable, for commonly the trees do not bear more than enough for the squirrels.

THE DISPERSION OF SEEDS:
BIRCH

(Compare earlier draft, pp. 224, 226–27 above.)

Birch seed begins to fall in October and continues to fall all winter. It is similar in all our species. The fruit of our commonest kind, the small white birch, consists of numerous pendulous cylindrical aments, composed of imbricated scales, with three winged seeds under each. It is remarkable that it so much resembles the fruit of a very different family of trees, the *Coniferæ*, that it is often called by the same name, namely, a strobile or cone (*strobos* from *στρεφω*); and I find that as the scales of the pitch-pine cone are arranged always in just thirteen spiral lines around it, so are the scales of the white-birch cone, making about one turn—as you may easily prove by counting the fine lines made by the projecting points of the middle lobes of the scales. It might be worth the while to inquire why Nature loves the number thirteen in these cases.

The scales of all our birch cones are three-lobed, like a typical spearhead (or *fléur de luce*); but those of this species are peculiarly interesting, having the exact form of stately birds with outspread wings, especially of hawks sailing steadily over the fields, and they never fail to remind me of them when I see them under my feet.

Volatile as these appear and are, the seeds which they cover, and for which they are often mistaken, are practically far more bird-like and are wafted much further by the wind. Indeed, they can easily be separated from the scales by winnowing. They are much smaller and of a livelier brown, with a very broad transparent wing on each side and two little dark brown persistent styles in front, just like an insect with its antennæ. They may pass for tiny brown butterflies.

When the cones are perfectly ripe and dry, these scales and seeds, being blown or shaken, begin to flake off together like so much chaff or bran, commencing commonly at the base of the cone, and falling gradually throughout the winter, leaving a bare, thread-like core. Thus, unlike the pines, the whole cone loses its cohesion and is disintegrated.

Each catkin, one inch long by a quarter of an inch wide, contains about one thousand seeds, which would suffice to plant an acre of land with birches seven feet apart each way. No doubt many single trees contain seed enough to plant all the old fields in Concord several times over. At this rate you could carry the seed for a thousand acres in a box of three inches cubed.

The seed is so small, and so exceedingly light and chaffy, that it does not fall to the earth in a perfect calm without many gyrations; and when there is considerable wind, it floats on it almost like a mote—disappearing at once from your sight like those little insects which the Indians call "no-see-'ems."

Some falls at the slightest jar, and some is left tossing about incessantly on the light spray till the latest gales of spring. In sudden gusts of wind such seeds as these, and even much heavier ones, must be carried over our highest hills, not to say mountains, and it is evidently one of the uses of such winds, which occur especially in the fall and spring, to disseminate plants. Alphonse De Candolle quotes Humboldt as saying that M. Bousringault had seen seeds (*graines*) elevated 5,400 feet (*pieds*) and fall back in the neighborhood (apparently among the Alps). I think that I could arrange a trap by which I could catch some of the birch seed which might be floating in the air, in very windy weather in the winter or spring in any part of this county.

This is eminently one of those northern "grains" which Nature sows broadcast on the snow and with it—as man does with some seeds occasionally. No sooner has the first snow fallen than I begin to see where these pretty brown bird-like scales and winged seeds have been blown into the numerous hollows of the thin-crusted surface. Indeed, all this part of New England is dusted over with them, throughout almost all woods and many fields, as if they had been regularly sifted on it; and each successive snow is newly covered with them—furnishing ever fresh and accessible repasts to the birds. It would not be easy to find a considerable area in the woodland of this county which is completely clear of them. For how many hundreds of miles this grain is scattered over the earth—under the feet of all walkers, in Boxboro and in Cambridge and the like, and rarely an eye distinguishes it.

Whoever faithfully analyzes a New England snowbank will probably report a certain percentage of birch seed. Where a birch has been bent down and jarred, or run over by a sleigh in a woodland path, you will often see the snow perfectly browned with its fruit so as to be conspicuous a long way off.

It is also blown far over the snow like the pine seed. Walking up our river on the second of March, 1856, by Mr. Prichard's land, where the shores and neighboring fields were comparatively bare of trees, I was surprised to see on the snow over the river a great many birch scales and seeds, though the snow had but recently fallen and there had been but little wind. There was one seed or scale to a square foot; yet the nearest birches were a row of fifteen along a wall thirty rods off. When, leaving the river, I advanced toward these, the seeds became thicker and thicker, till at half a dozen rods from the trees, they quite discolored the snow; while on the other side, or eastward of the birches, there was not one. These trees appeared not to have lost a quarter part of their seeds yet. As I returned up the river, I saw some of their seeds forty rods off, and perhaps in a more favorable direction I might have found them much further; for, as usual, it was chiefly the scales which attracted my attention, and the fine winged seed which it is not easy to distinguish had probably been winnowed from them. It suggested how unwearied Nature is in spreading her seeds. Even the spring does not find her unprovided with birch—aye, and alder and pine—seed. A great proportion of the seed that was carried to a distance lodged in the hollow above the river, and when the river broke up, was carried far away to distant shores and meadows. For, as I find by experiment, though the scales soon sink in water, the seeds float for many days.

I notice accordingly that near meadows where there is a very gentle inclination over which water has flowed and receded, birches often grow in more or less parallel lines, the seed apparently having been left there by a freshet, or else lodged in the parallel waving hollows of the snow.

I observed last summer that the seeds of a few black birches, which grow near one side of one of our ponds (which contains sixty acres), had been drifted to other shores and had just sprung up at high-water mark there.

It is evident that the seeds which are dropped on the surface of a pond or lake, by the wind or any other agent, will be drifted to the shore unless they sink, and thus collected into a comparatively small area—whence their progeny, if fitted for it, may at length spread inland. I have no doubt that if such a pond were to be now dug in the midst of our woods, the willow, birch, alder, maple, and so on would from these and similar causes soon be found skirting its shores, even though none of these trees grew near it before.

Alphonse De Candolle says that M. Dureau "cites a fact according to which seeds of mustard and of birch preserve their vitality after twenty years' immersion in fresh water."

You will often see white birches growing densely in perfectly straight rows in the ruts of old woodpaths now grown up, the seed having been blown into the long hollows in the snow above the ruts.

Birch seed being thus scattered over the country like a fine grain or a shower of dust, which most do not distinguish for seed, suggests how still more impalpable seeds, like those of fungi, are diffused through the atmosphere—and enables us to realize that truth.

No wonder, then, that the white birch is so prevalent and characteristic a tree with us and that the seedling birches spring up every year on so many neglected spots, but especially where the surface has been cleared or burned.

I noticed the other day a little white birch a foot high which had sprung up in the gutter on the main street in front of my house, and it looked about as strange there as it would in State Street in Boston. It had perhaps been wafted thither in some gale or blown out of a woodman's cart. It suggested how surely and soon the forest would prevail here again if the village were deserted.

Yet it is stated in Loudon's *Arboretum* that the small white birch is "rarely found in groups; and single trees are met with only at considerable intervals." This is not true of this part of the country. As a consequence of its seeds being almost universally dispersed, and the soil being adapted to it, it not only forms peculiarly dense and exclusive thickets in open land but is pretty generally distributed throughout pine and oak woods. So that it is very common hereabouts to cut out all the birches when they begin to decay, and leave the longer-lived trees, which are only one-fourth or half grown and are still as dense as they ought to be. If the seeds fall on water, they are drifted to the shore and spring up there, though they are very often killed by the water standing long around them.

It is generally observed that the canoe birch is one of the first and commonest trees to spring up when an evergreen forest is burned, in Maine and elsewhere in the north, forming dense and extensive woods as if by magic where, as is stated, this tree was "not before known." But it is forgotten, or not known, how abundant and volatile the seeds of the birch are, and that these trees are almost universally distributed throughout those woods. Within the last fifteen years I have had occasion to make a fire out of doors in the wilds of Maine about a hundred times, in places wide apart, and I do not remember that I ever failed to find birch bark at hand for kindling. It is the common kindling stuff.

Blodget, in his *Climatology*, says, "The birch abounds in such forests as exist at the Arctic Circle, and for all the distance southward to the 41st parallel it is common in the woodlands, both of the general surface and of the highest mountains." It appears that the same is true of the north of Europe and of Asia.

Loudon, speaking of the European variety of the common white birch, says, "According to Pallas, the birch is more common than any other tree throughout the whole of the Russian Empire; being found in every wood and grove from the Baltic Sea to the Eastern Ocean." Loudon also learns from a French author that "in Prussia, the birch is planted everywhere; and it is considered to afford security against a dearth of fuel, and to insure the prosperity of the woods by the dissemination of its seeds, which fill up every blank that occurs."

Seedling white birches can easily be obtained for transplanting. They are one of the earliest shrubs to leaf out, and so are easily detected. In a walk in the spring of 1859, coming across a bed of them, seedlings of the previous year, in the grass by the side of an old grain field, and knowing that a neighbor wanted to get a quantity of birches, I pulled up just a hundred of them, to see what I could do, and bound them in moss at the next swamp I came to. The next time I met my neighbor, I took this package out of my pocket and presented him with one hundred birch trees for his plantation. I could have collected a thousand thus in an hour or two; but I would recommend to let them grow two or three years before transplanting, when they will bear the drought better. In August 1861 I found sixty of these birches alive and from two to five feet high.

As it comes up commonly in open land and in exhausted soil, this is in some places called old-field birch.

I frequently see a young birch forest springing up very densely over a large tract which has been neglected only a year or two, tingeing it pink with their twigs, and I have been surprised when the owner, as if he had never noticed this godsend, has concluded that he will skim that pasture once more, get one more crop of rye from it, before he lets it lie fallow—and so destroyed some such two-year-old birch wood, in which I could not help taking an interest, though he knew nothing about it. Having in the meanwhile cut down the seed trees, he will now wait twenty years perhaps in the expectation of seeing a forest spring up; whereas, if he had let them alone he would have had a handsome birch wood, ready to be cut, in two-thirds that time. In 1845 or 1846 I pulled up a white birch some two and a half feet high in the woods, brought it home in my hand, and set it out in my yard. After ten years it was much larger than most birches when they are set. It is now ———— inches in circumference at one foot from the ground.

If the winds are not amply sufficient, we may be indebted to the various birds which feed on the birch seed and shake down ten times as much as they consume. When this seed is most abundant, great flocks of lesser redpolls come down from the north to feed on it and are our prevailing winter bird. They alight on the birches and shake and rend the cones, then swarm on the snow beneath, busily picking up the seed in the copses. Though there may be but few birches, white or black, in the midst of a wood, these birds distinguish their tops from afar. When I hear their notes, I look round for a birch and generally descry them on its top. Mudie says, "It is very pretty to watch one picking the catkins on the long pendulous twigs of a weeping birch over a mountain stream. These twigs are often twenty feet long, and little thicker than packthread. On the points of these the little birds may sometimes be seen, swinging backwards and forwards like the bobs of pendulums, busy feeding, and never losing their perch."

I also see the goldfinch, which the last so much resemble, eating the birch seed in the same manner.

But, to say nothing of these cones on the trees, we have seen what a bountiful table is already spread for the birds, and is kept spread for them all winter, on the snow beneath, all over the country.

THE DISPERSION OF SEEDS:
PITCH PINE

(Compare earlier draft, pp. 227–32 above.)

All my readers probably are acquainted with its rigid conical fruit, scarcely to be plucked without a knife—so hard and short that it is a pretty good substitute for a stone. Indeed, this is the use to which the Romans once put their kind. They called it the pine nut, and sometimes the apple of the pine, whence pine-apple. It is related that "when Vatinius gave a show of gladiators to conciliate the people, by whom he was much hated, they pelted him with stones. The ediles made an order forbidding the people to throw anything but apples within the arena; and on this the people pelted Vatinius with the apples of the pine tree. The question was, then, whether this was to be considered as a defiance of the law; and the celebrated lawyer Cascellius being consulted, replied, 'The pine nut, if you throw it at Vatinius, is an apple.' "

If not plucked, these cones hold on all winter and often many years. You see old gray cones, sometimes a circle of them (which the Romans appear to have called *azaniæ*) within two feet of the ground on the trunks of large trees, having been formed there when the tree was young twenty or thirty years before—so persistent are they.

Within this strong, prickly, and pitchy chest are contained about a hundred dark brown seeds in pairs, each pair occupying a separate apartment behind its prickly shield. A very thin membrane or wing about three-fourths of an inch long extends from one end of each seed, which it clasps in its divided extremity like a caged bird holding the seed in its bill and waiting till it shall be released that it may fly away with and plant it.

For already some rumor of the wind has penetrated to this cell, and preparation has been made to meet and use it. According to Darwin, Alphonse De Candolle has remarked that winged seeds are never found in fruits which do not open. They were designed for flight. This wing is so independent of the seed that you can take the latter out and spring it in again, as you do a watch crystal.

The sun and wind, which have the key to these apartments, begin to unlock them with a crackling sound in the second or third fall and continue to do so here and there all winter long, and there they lie exposed with their thin, curved handles upward and outward to the wind, which ever and anon extracts them and conveys them away. If they chance to be released in calm weather, they fall directly to the earth, rapidly whirling all the way; but if there is any wind, they are borne more or less to one side. They remind me most, after all, of some deep-bellied fish—an alewife or shad—with their flanks and a tail curving to this side or that, the whole of whose flexible body is a sort of wing or fin fitted not for the varied and prolonged flight of birds, but to steer and assist its course in the stronger or grosser current in which it floats. Schools of brown fishes which perform this short migration annually.

Nature always adopts the simplest modes which will accomplish her end. If she wishes one seed to fall only a little to one side from a perpendicular line, and so disseminate its kind, perhaps she merely flattens it into a thin-edged disk—with some inequality—so that it will "scale" a little as it descends. In course of time, when it contemplates a more distant and wider flight from the pine-tree tops to the earth, moveable edges, called fins or wings, may be added to this simple form.

The pitch pine is a very seedy tree and is peculiarly bent on extending its domains. It begins to bear when very small—sometimes when less than two feet high.

I have noticed that where, on account of the poverty or rockiness of the soil, these trees find it hard to live at all, they bear the more fruit. I have counted on a solitary pitch pine, which was only three feet high and as broad as high, spreading flat over a rock on a hilltop, more than one hundred cones of different ages. Having scaled this rocky citadel, its first care, though in a crippled state, was to call a hundred followers about it and so get undisputed possession.

Michaux observes that "wherever these trees grow in masses, the cones are dispersed singly over the branches, and . . . they release the seeds the first autumn after their maturity; but on solitary stocks, the cones are collected in groups of four, five, or even a larger number, and remain closed for several years."

Not only is it the outside trees that bear the most seed, where it is most required, but only a considerable wind, which can transport the seed to a distance, is able commonly to set it free, so that it does not fall at once to the ground, where it would be wasted. All have noticed the dense groves of pitch pine of uniform height, which were perhaps planted in a single gale, and you can often tell what tree the seed came from. In my mind's eye, and sometimes partially with my bodily eye, I see the seeds from which they sprang falling in a dense shower which reaches twenty or thirty rods on one side, like grain scattered by the hand of the sower.

Sometimes a man cuts off a lot of young pitch pines, leaving only the old parent tree to seed the ground again. They are not commonly noticed till half a dozen years old.

As I went by a pitch-pine wood the other day, I saw a few little ones springing up in the pasture from these seeds which had been blown from the wood. There was a puny one which came from the seed this year, just noticeable in the sod, and I came near mistaking it for a single sprig of moss. It was, as it were, a little green star with many rays, half an inch in diameter, lifted an inch and a half above the ground on a slender stem. What a feeble beginning for so long-lived a tree! By the next year it will be a star of greater magnitude, and in a few years, if not disturbed, these seedlings will alter the face of Nature here. How ominous the presence of these moss-like stars to the grass, heralding its doom! Thus, from pasture this portion of the earth's surface becomes forest—because the seeds of the pine, and not of moss and grass alone, fell on it. These which are now mistaken for mosses in the grass will perhaps become lofty trees and endure two hundred years.

Unlike the white pine, the pitch pine is opening its cones and dispersing its seed gradually *all winter,* and it is not only blown far through the air, but slides yet further over the snow and ice. It has often occurred to me that it was one value of a level surface of snow, especially a crusted snow, that by its smoothness it favored the distribution of such seeds as fell on it. I have many times measured the direct distance on a snowy field from the outmost pine seed to the nearest pine to windward, and found it equal to the breadth of the widest pasture. I have seen that the seed thus crossed one of our ponds, which is half a mile wide, and I see no reason why it should not be blown many miles in some cases. In the fall it would be detained by the grass, weeds, and bushes, but the snow having first come to cover up all and make a level surface, the restless pine seeds go dashing over it like an Esquimaux sledge with an invisible team until, losing their wings or meeting with some insuperable obstacle, they lie down once for all, perchance to rise up pines. Nature has her annual sledding to do, as well as we. In a region of snow and ice like ours, this tree can be gradually spread thus from one side of the continent to the other.

By the middle of July, I notice on the shore of the above-mentioned pond, just below the high-water line, many little pitch-pines which have just sprung up amid the stones and sand and muck, whose seed has been blown or drifted across. There are some places for a row of pines along the water's edge, which at length, after fifteen or twenty years, are tipped over and destroyed by the heaving of the frozen shore.

I noticed lately a little pitch pine which had come up on the sandy railroad embankment in our meadows, just sixty rods by pacing from the nearest pine tree; nor is this uncommon. I have seen a single pitch pine spring up spontaneously in my yard in this village, about half a mile from the nearest of its kind, with a river and its deep valley, and several roads and fences between, and it grows there yet. This tree would soon sow itself in all our yards if they were neglected.

Every year the seed of the pines is blowing thus from our pine woods and falling on all sorts of ground, favorable and unfavorable. When the circumstances are propitious, a forest of pines springs up, especially if the land to leeward is open or has been lately cleared, or plowed, or burned over.

One man accordingly tells me, and there are countless cases like it, that he had a lot of pines, which being cut, shrub oaks came up. He cut and burned and sowed rye, and, it being surrounded by pine woods on three sides, the next year a dense growth of pines filled the ground.

Squirrels also help to disperse the pitch-pine seed.

I notice every fall, especially about the middle of October, a great many pitch-pine twigs or plumes, which have evidently just been gnawed off and left under the trees. They are from one-half to three-fourths of an inch in thickness, and often have three or four branches. I counted this year twenty under one tree, and they were to be seen in all pitch-pine woods. It is plainly the work of squirrels. As I had not chanced to detect their object, I resolved last fall to look into the matter.

Accordingly, thinking it over one night, I said to myself, "Anything so universal and regular, observed wherever the larger squirrels and pitch pines are found, cannot be the result of an accident or freak, but must be connected with the necessities of the animal." I have found that the necessaries of my life are food, clothing, shelter, and fuel; but the squirrels use only food and shelter. I never see these twigs used in constructing their nests; hence, I presume that their motive was to obtain food, and as its seeds are all of the pitch pine that I know them to eat, my swift conclusion was that they cut off these twigs in order to come at the cones, and also to make them more portable. I had no sooner thought this out than I as good as knew it.

A few days after, as I was passing through a pitch-pine wood, where as usual, the ground was strewn with twigs, I observed one eleven inches long and about half an inch thick, cut off close below two closed cones, the stem of one cone also being partly cut. Also in open land three or four rods from this grove, I saw three twigs which had been dropped near together. One was just two feet long and cut off more than a foot below three cones which were still left on it, two on one branch and one on another. One of the others was longer still.

Thus, my theory was confirmed by observation. The squirrels were carrying off these pine boughs with their fruit to a more convenient place either to eat at once or store up. You would be surprised to see what great limbs they carry, and to what distances sometimes. They are stronger than we suppose. A neighbor tells me that he had a gray squirrel which would take a whole and large ear of corn, run out of a broken window of his corn barn and up the side and over the roof, or perhaps high into an elm with it.

Most of the twigs which you see in the woods, however, are smaller, mere single plumes, which have been sheared off above the cones, whether to lighten the load or to come at the cone. They were so generally cut off last fall, when comparatively few pitch pines bore any cones, that I commonly detected the fertile trees when going through a grove by seeing these green twigs strewn on the brown ground beneath them.

It is surprising how rudely the squirrels strip and spoil the trees on which they depend. I often thought what a hue and cry I should have made about it, if they had been orchard trees and belonged to me. Even the pitch pines thus get *trimmed* after a fashion, and perhaps for their benefit.

In most cases, evidently, they carry off the cone alone; but perhaps a strong squirrel prefers to carry three cones, twig and all, at one trip than come three times after single cones. I frequently see where they have dropped the bare cones, having been interrupted, and I once counted twenty-four such cones quite fresh and unopened brought together under a solitary pine in a field, evidently ready to be transported to another place.

It chanced that I did not see last October where any of these cones had been eaten or stripped, as I often do. I conclude therefore that most of them must have been collected into holes in trees or in the earth, where the squirrels live, and possibly some are buried singly as nuts are.

Think how busy the squirrels are in October, in every pitch-pine grove all over the state, cutting off the twigs and collecting the cones. While the farmer is digging his potatoes and gathering his corn, he little thinks of this harvest of pine cones which the squirrel is gathering in the neighboring woods still more sedulously than himself.

In this way even the squirrels may spread the pine seed far over the field. I frequently see a pitch-pine cone far out in an open field, where it was dropped by a squirrel when on its way toward some tree or wall or stump—or oftener by the side of a fence on which the squirrel travelled at a considerable distance from the woods; and there it will sometimes lie covered by the snow all winter, and not expand and shed its seeds till the snow goes off and it feels the heat of the sun.

The pitch-pine cones have very stout and tough stems, the woody part alone being often a quarter of an inch in diameter; and they are scarcely so long as wide, which makes them hard to come at. But rigid and unmanageable as they are, almost every fresh cone of this kind which you see on the ground was cut off by a squirrel, and you can plainly see the marks of its teeth on the stem. He cuts it as he bends it, and a very few cuts suffice to separate it from the branch.

When he has thus plucked it, sitting on a fence-post or other perch, he begins at the base of the cone and gnaws off the scales one after another, devouring the seeds as he goes, leaving only half a dozen empty scales at the extremity. The close-shaven cone presents thus a pretty flower-like figure, which it would take a long time to produce with a knife.

This plucking and stripping a pine cone is a business which he and his family understand perfectly. It is their forte. I doubt if you could suggest any improvement. After ages of experiment perhaps, their instinct has settled on the same method that our reason would, finally, if we had to open a pine cone with our teeth; and they were thus accomplished long before our race had discovered that the pine cone contained an almond.

Observe more particularly how this one proceeds. He does not prick his fingers, nor pitch his whiskers, nor gnaw into the solid cone, any more than is necessary. Having sheared off the twigs and needles that may be in his way (sometimes even the cheeks of the twig, for like the skillful woodchopper he first deliberately secures room and verge enough), he neatly cuts off the stout stem of the cone with a few strikes of his chisels, and it is his. To be sure, he may let it fall to the ground and look down at it for a moment curiously, as if it were *not* his, but probably he is taking note where it lies and adding it to the heap of a hundred like it in his mind, and it is only so much the more his for his seeming carelessness. When he comes to open it, he holds it in his hands, a solid embossed cone so hard it almost rings at the touch of his teeth, pausing for a moment, perhaps, not because he does not know how to begin, but only to hear what is in the wind. He knows better than to try to cut off the tip and work his way downward against a *chevaux-de-frise* of advanced scales and prickles. If there ever was any age of the world when the squirrels opened their cones wrong-end foremost, it was not the golden age, surely. He knows better than to gnaw into the side for three-fourths of an inch in the face of many armed shields. But he does not have to think what he knows. Having heard the last Æolian rumor, he whirls the cone bottom upward in a twinkling, and beginning where the scales are smallest, and the prickles slight or none, and the short stem is cut so close as not to be in his way—for the same strokes which severed it from the twig have exposed its weak side—he proceeds to cut through the thin and tender bases of the scales, and each stroke tells, laying bare at once a couple of seeds. Thus, the strips it as easily as if the scales were chaff, and so rapidly, twirling it as he advances, that you cannot tell how he does it till you drive him off and inspect his unfinished work. Dropping this, he resorts to the pines for another, till quite a pile of scales and of these interesting cores is left on the snow there.

In April of last year I found under one small pitch pine in a little grove of these trees on the top of Lee's Cliff, a very large heap of cones which had been thus cut off and stripped evidently by the red squirrel the previous winter and fall, they having sat upon some dead stubs a foot or two above the while. Probably there was a hole in the ground there where they lodged. I counted 239 cores of cones under this tree alone, and most of them lay within an area of two feet square upon a mass of the scales one to two inches deep and three or four feet in diameter; showing that these had been stripped by but few squirrels, possibly only one. They had brought them all to this stub to be eaten, in order that they might be near their hole in case of danger. There were also many similar cores of cones under the surrounding pines. They appeared to have devoured all the fruit of that pitch-pine grove; and who had a better right to it?

The red squirrel thus harvests the fruit of the pitch pine annually. His body is about the color of its cone, and he who can open them so dexterously is welcome to what he can find in them. The cones to him who can open them. As for the seed of new plantations, Nature will be contented with the crumbs which fall from his table.

THE DISPERSION OF SEEDS:

ALTERNATE BEGINNING

Agrestem tenui meditabor arundine musam
I am going to play a rustic strain on my slender reed,

non injussa cano.
but I trust that I do not sing unbidden things.

Many public speakers are accustomed, as I think foolishly, to talk about what they call *little things* in a patronizing way sometimes, advising, perhaps, that they be not wholly neglected; but in making this distinction they really use no juster measure than a ten-foot pole and their own ignorance. According to this rule, a small potato is a little thing, a big one a great thing. A hogshead full of anything, the big cheese which it took so many oxen to draw, a national salute, a state-muster, a fat ox, the horse Columbus, or Mr. Blank, the Ossian Boy—there is no danger that anybody will call these *little things*. A cartwheel is a great thing, a snowflake a little thing. The *Wellingtonia gigantea*, the famous California tree, is a great thing, the seed from which it sprang a little thing. Scarcely one traveller has noticed the seed at all, and so with all the seeds or origins of things. But Pliny said, *"In minimus Natura præstat"*—Nature excels in the least things.

In this country a political speech, whether by Mr. Seward or Caleb Cushing, is a great thing, a ray of light a little thing. It would be felt to be a greater national calamity if you should take six inches from the corporeal bulk of one or two gentlemen in Congress than if you should take a yard from their wisdom and manhood.

I have noticed that whatever is thought to be covered by the word "education"—whether reading, writing, or 'rithmetic—is a great thing, but almost all that constitutes education is a little thing in the estimation of such speakers as I refer to. In short, whatever they know and care but *little* about is a little thing, and accordingly almost everything good or great is little in their sense and is very slow to grow any bigger.

When the husk gets separated from the kernel, almost all men run after the husk and pay their respects to that. It is only the husk of Christianity that is so bruited and wide spread in this world; the kernel is still the very least and rarest of all things. There is not a single church founded on it. To obey the higher law is generally considered the last manifestation of littleness.

I have observed that many English naturalists have a pitiful habit of speaking of their proper pursuit as a sort of trifling or waste of time—a mere interruption to more important employments and "severe studies"—for which they must ask pardon of the reader. As if they would have you believe that all the rest of their lives was consecrated to some truly great and serious enterprise. But it happens that we never hear more of this, as we certainly should if it were only some great public or philanthropic service, and therefore conclude that they have been engaged in the heroic and magnanimous enterprise of feeding, clothing, housing, and warming themselves and their dependents, the chief value of all which was that it enabled them to pursue just these studies of which they speak so slightingly. The "severe study" they refer to was keeping their accounts. Comparatively speaking, what they call their graver pursuits and severer studies was the real trifling and misspense of life, and were they such fools as not to know it? It is, in effect at least, mere cant. All mankind have depended on them for this intellectual food.

A THOREAU CHRONOLOGY

1817   Born July 12 in Concord, Massachusetts, to John and Cynthia (Dunbar) Thoreau.

1828–33   Attends Concord Academy.

1833–37   Attends Harvard College.

1837   Teaches briefly at Concord Center School (public).

1838–41   Conducts a private school in Concord with his elder brother John.

1839   Goes on boating excursion on Concord and Merrimack Rivers with his brother John.

1840   Poems and essays published in *The Dial.*

1841–43   Lives with Ralph Waldo Emerson and his family in Concord.

1842   John Thoreau, Jr. (brother), dies suddenly of lockjaw; "Natural History of Massachusetts" published.

1843   "Walk to Wachusett" and "A Winter Walk" published; tutors William Emerson's children on Staten Island, New York.

1844   Accidentally sets fire to woods in Concord with Edward Hoar.

1845–47   Lives in small house he built himself on shore of Walden Pond.

1846   Travels to Maine and climbs Mt. Katahdin; spends a night in jail for refusing to pay poll tax.

1847–48   Lives in Emerson household while Ralph Waldo Emerson lectures in England.

1848   Begins career as professional lecturer; "Ktaadn and the Maine Woods" published.

1849   *A Week on the Concord and Merrimack Rivers* and "Resistance to Civil Government" published; travels to Cape Cod; elder sister Helen dies, apparently of tuberculosis.

1850   *June:* Travels to Cape Cod.
       July: Travels to Fire Island, New York, in search of Margaret Fuller-Ossoli's remains.

August 29: Moves into third-floor attic of parents' house on Main Street in Concord.

September–October: Travels to Quebec.

November: Begins dating journal entries regularly; stops cutting pages from journal volumes as part of his writing process.

December 18: Elected corresponding member of the Boston Society of Natural History.

1851 *April 23:* First delivers "Walking, or the Wild" lecture.

Summer: Begins commonplace book for natural history readings; begins compiling phenological lists and charts.

September 7: Notes in journal that his profession is "to find God in nature."

1852 *April 18:* Notes in journal that he first perceives that "the year is a circle."

July 2: Notes in journal that this is his "year of observation."

1853 Travels to Maine woods; portions of "A Yankee in Canada" published.

1854 *Walden; or, Life in the Woods* and "Slavery in Massachusetts" published; delivers early "Life without Principle" lecture for first time in Providence, Rhode Island.

1855 Portions of "Cape Cod" published; travels to Cape Cod.

1856 Surveys Eagleswood Community near Perth Amboy, New Jersey.

1857 Travels to Cape Cod and Maine Woods; "Chesuncook" published.

1858 Travels to White Mountains in New Hampshire.

1859 *February 3:* John Thoreau (father) dies.

February 22: Delivers "Autumnal Tints" in Worcester, Massachusetts.

October: Begins writing *Wild Fruits*; delivers "A Plea for Capt. John Brown" in Concord.

1860 *February 8:* Delivers "Wild Apples" in Concord and receives "long, continued applause" at end of lecture.

June–September: Works on third draft of *Wild Fruits*.

September–October: Delivers "The Succession of Forest Trees" in Concord, Massachusetts; publishes same in *New-York Weekly Tribune*.

October–November: Visits local woodlots almost daily; works on both *Wild Fruits* and *The Dispersion of Seeds*.

December: Works on both *Wild Fruits* and *The Dispersion of Seeds*.

December 3: While researching tree growth, contracts a severe cold, which rapidly worsens into bronchitis and keeps him housebound.

December 11: Delivers last lecture, "Autumnal Tints," in Waterbury, Connecticut.

1861 *January–early May:* Works on both *Wild Fruits* and *The Dispersion of Seeds*.

May 12–July 14: Travels to Minnesota with Horace Mann, Jr., in effort to regain health.

1862   *February 20:* Sends "Autumnal Tints" manuscript, culled from *The Fall of the Leaf,* to *The Atlantic Monthly.*

February 28: Sends "Life without Principle" manuscript to *The Atlantic Monthly.*

March 11: Sends "Walking" manuscript to *The Atlantic Monthly.*

April 2: Sends "Wild Apples" manuscript, culled from *Wild Fruits,* to *The Atlantic Monthly.*

Dies May 6 in Concord, Massachusetts.

GLOSSARY OF
BOTANICAL TERMS

Ament A catkin or scaly spike.

Anther The pollen-bearing organ of a flower.

Axil The angle formed by a leaf or branch with the stem.

Branchlet Except for the twig, the youngest and smallest division of a branch.

Calyx The outer part (perianth) of the flower, usually green, formed of several divisions called sepals, protecting the bud.

Corymb A flat-topped or convex open flower cluster, the outer flowers opening first.

Corymbose In corymbs or corymblike.

Culm The peculiar aerial stem which bears flowers, found in grasses, sedges, and rushes.

Cyme A usually broad and flattish determinate inflorescence (flowering portion of plant); that is, with its central or terminal flowers blooming earliest.

Fascicle A close bundle or cluster.

Glaucous Bluish white; covered or whitened with a very fine, powdery substance.

Imbricated Closely overlapping each other like the tiles of a roof.

Involucre A circle or collection of bracts (modified leaves) surrounding a flower cluster or head, or a single flower.

Mucronate Having the midvein prolonged beyond the pinnule, forming a point; tipped with a mucro or short, small, suddenly narrowed or cutoff tip.

Pedicel A tiny stalk; the support of a single flower.

Peduncle A primary flower stalk, supporting either a cluster or a solitary flower.

Pericarp Fruit wall; the wall of a matured ovary.

Raceme A simple inflorescence of pediceled flowers upon a common more or less elongated axis.

Radicle Rootlet springing from the sides and base of a stem.

Samara Key; a dry, one-seeded, indehiscent or persistently closed winged fruit.

Spadix A flower spike with a fleshy axis, usually enclosed in a spathe.

Spathe A sheathing bract (modified leaf) or pair of bracts enclosing an inflorescence (flowering portion of plant); a spadix on the same axis.

Stomate Covered with a surface of fine pores, such as breathing pores.

Strobile Cone; an often scaly, imbricated fruit of pines, firs, and other trees.

Style The usually attenuated or tapered portion of the pistil (seed-bearing organ) connecting the stigma and ovary.

Umbel An inflorescence (flowering portion of plant) in which the peduncles or pedicels of a cluster spring from the same point.

A NOTE ON THE PROVENANCE
OF THE MANUSCRIPT

WILD FRUITS WAS EDITED from Henry David Thoreau's original manuscript, cataloged under the nonauthorial title "Notes on Fruits" in the Henry W. and Albert A. Berg Collection of English and American Literature. The Berg Collection acquired the *Wild Fruits* manuscript in 1940, but before then it had passed through successive hands: the W. T. H. Howe collection (1934–40), the William Bixby collection (1905–34), New York manuscript dealer George S. Hellman (1904–5), Worcester high-school principal and one-time Thoreau acquaintance E. Harlow Russell (1898–1904), Thoreau's Worcester friend H. G. O. Blake (1876–98), and Thoreau's younger sister, Sophia, who inherited it from her brother at his death in 1862.

The Berg Collection is one of America's most celebrated collections of literary first editions, rare books, autograph letters, and manuscripts. It was assembled and presented to The New York Public Library by Dr. Albert A. Berg, a famous surgeon and trustee of the library, in memory of his brother, Dr. Henry W. Berg. The collection's more than 35,000 printed items and 115,000 manuscripts cover the entire range of two national literatures, with particular emphasis on the nineteenth and twentieth centuries.

A NOTE TO THE READER

IF YOU ENJOY THOREAU'S WRITINGS, you should consider joing the Thoreau
Society and the Walden Woods Project, two nonprofit organizations devoted to
keeping his legacies alive.

The world's oldest and largest American author's organization, the Thoreau
Society exists to stimulate interest in Thoreau's life, works, and philosophy. The
Society has long contributed to the dissemination of knowledge about Thoreau
by publishing articles in its two periodicals; by encouraging the use of its collections at the Thoreau Institute; and by collecting books, manuscripts, and artifacts
relating to Thoreau and his contemporaries. The Society's members gather once
a year in Concord, Massachusetts, on the weekend closest to Thoreau's birthday,
July 12.

The Walden Woods Project is a charitable organization with two primary
missions: to protect land of ecological and historical significance in Walden
Woods, which surrounds Walden Pond; and to manage, operate, and support the
Thoreau Institute, a research and education facility located less than half a mile
from Walden Pond in Lincoln, Massachusetts.

For further information or to become a member of the Thoreau Society or
Walden Woods Project, call (800) 554-3569; visit www.walden.org; or write 44
Baker Farm, Lincoln, MA 01773-3004 U.S.A.

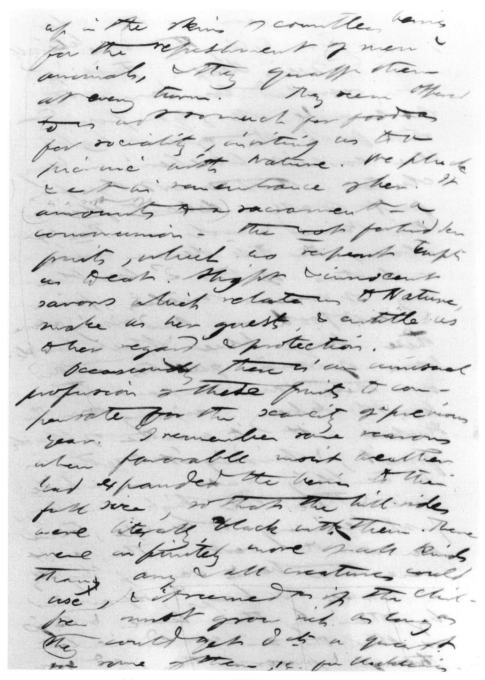

Manuscript page from *Wild Fruits* (see pp. 52–53).
(*Courtesy of Berg Collection, New York Public Library*)

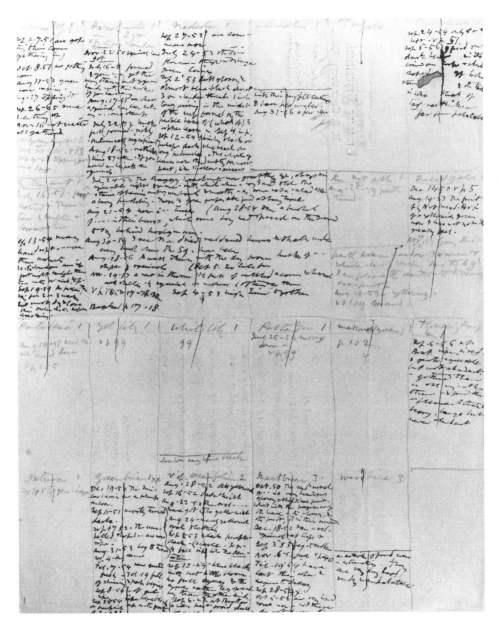

Thoreau's working notes for *Wild Fruits*.
Index of fruits for September 1–3.
(*Courtesy of Berg Collection, New York Public Library*)

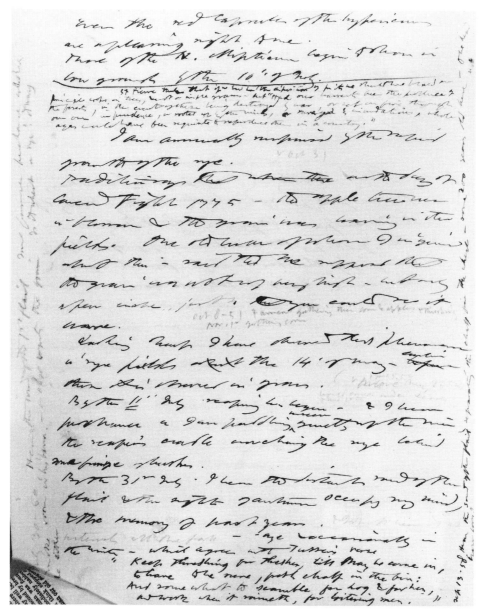

Page 67 in second draft of *Wild Fruits*.
Also used with later additions in third draft, published here (see pp. 63–64).
(*Courtesy of Berg Collection, New York Public Library*)

Page 85 in second draft of *Wild Fruits*.
Also used in third draft, published here (see p. 93).
(*Courtesy of Berg Collection, New York Public Library*)

EDITOR'S NOTES

BEFORE HE DIED, Thoreau wrapped his *Wild Fruits* manuscript in a heavy piece of paper, tied a string around the bundle, and placed it in a wooden chest along-side thousands of pages from other projects he had worked on over the years, including his "Wild Apples" papers. The pages from all of these manuscripts were doubtless in perfect order when Thoreau died in May 1862. But in the seventy-eight years between then and 1940, when his *Wild Fruits* papers came to rest in the Henry W. and Albert A. Berg Collection at the New York Public Library, the wooden chest had disappeared, the *Wild Fruits* manuscript had been unbundled, and its pages had been badly shuffled.

There are compelling reasons why *Wild Fruits* has not been published until now. In addition to the pages at the Berg Collection being out of order, Thoreau's handwriting is notoriously difficult even for experts to read, his method of composition in the latter part of his career had not been sufficiently studied, the sheer bulk of manuscript material from his last years is enormously intimidating, and no one was really sure if the manuscripts from his late projects were complete enough to derive texts from them. The publication in 1993 of Thoreau's previously unpublished *The Dispersion of Seeds* manuscript in *Faith in a Seed: The Dispersion of Seeds and Other Late Natural History Writings* (Shearwater Books, Island Press) changed everything. Not only did it demonstrate that Thoreau's late work can be successfully recovered, the book's commercial success indicated that Thoreau's late work was eminently worthy of being placed before his large and growing number of readers. Moreover, the enthusiastic reception accorded *The Dispersion of Seeds* by well-respected scientists, environmentalists, artists, and scholars established the importance of what Thoreau had to say at the end of his life—and the beauty with which he said it.

This volume presents a clear reading text of *Wild Fruits* and of ten "Related Passages." For ease of reading, I have regularized the idiosyncrasies of Thoreau's manuscript by silently (1) expanding his abbreviations, including his ampersands; (2) writing words for his numerals, except numerals where they appear in sources from which he quoted and dates in the "incomplete" portions of the text; (3) using ellipses within quotations where he employed a series of asterisks, dashes, or similar devices; (4) italicizing book titles and foreign words, including Latin names for plants; (5) correcting misspellings when they were not in his lexicon (see Walker in "Works Cited"); (6) adding internal titles to each of the sections; (8) standardizing on the basis of his most common practice in each instance certain alternate spellings accepted by his lexicon (for instance, "grey" to "gray") and certain inconsistently applied capitalizations (for instance, "nature" to "Nature" and "*vide*" to "*Vide*"); and (7) standardizing the format for his dates. All square brackets in the text are Thoreau's own.

I explain more substantive editorial intrusions in the following notes, which are keyed to page numbers in the text. Sources I refer to in my introduction or that Thoreau quotes from or alludes to are listed in "Works Cited," which follows "Editor's Notes." In those notes I refer to the source by the author's last name only if that is unique in "Works Cited"; otherwise I provide only enough additional information (first name or short title or both) to enable the reader to identify the source in "Works Cited." Also, I have tried to cite in the notes the editions that Thoreau himself consulted. I have in some cases cited book, chapter, section, and so on, rather than or in addition to giving page numbers so that readers can more conveniently locate the material in other editions. Further, on occasion I quote in the notes material, whether from the manuscript or elsewhere, that I deemed relevant to Thoreau's text and therefore interesting or possibly useful to readers. Finally, readers interested in considering any or all of my editorial decisions in more detail can consult my facsimile transcripts of Thoreau's manuscript pages at www.walden.org/thoreau/writings/fruits.

3 **Wild Fruits:** This is Thoreau's title, although it does not appear as a formal title on any of the *Wild Fruits* manuscript (MS) pages; instead, he used the title throughout his late natural history projects when referring to the *Wild Fruits* MS. Most particularly, he employed the title on a heavy-paper wrapper that he used to keep the *Wild Fruits* MS pages together. This wrapper is now at the front of a folder nonauthorially labeled "Notes on Fruits" in the Henry W. and Albert A. Berg Collection at the New York Public Library. Thoreau himself wrote on the wrapper, "Matter to be used in completing Wild Fruits. Journal examined as far as October 19, 1859—only first Common Place book examined." (Thoreau refers throughout the *Wild Fruits* MS to "Common Place Book 1" and "Common Place Book 2." As I point out in the "Works Cited" section at the end of these notes under Thoreau's name, "Common Place Book 1" is at the Widener Library, Harvard University, and "Common Place Book 2" is in the Berg Collection, New York Public Library.) The sources I use to reconstruct *Wild Fruits* are 359 holograph pages in the Berg Collection—13 in a folder labeled "Portion of Holograph Journal, 1853, 1860–1861" and paged with accession numbers 1–13, and the remaining 346 in the aforementioned "Notes on Fruits" folder and paged with accession numbers 1–9, 9a, 10–77, 128, 128a, 129–32, 134–59, 164–70, 170a–c, 171, 173, 173b–c, 174–76, 176a–c, 177–95, 195a–95b, 196–229, 229a, 230–38, 240–41, 241a–b, 242–48, 248a, 249–60, 262–74, 276–77, 277a, 278–81, 281a, 282–97, 297a, 298–301, 301a–b, 302–5, 305a–b, 306–21, 322a, 323, 323a, 324–30, 334, 403–20, 435–40, 574–89, 589a–b, 590, 590a, 591–92, 596, 598–600. (The letter after a page number indicates that the page is unnumbered but is either affixed with sealing wax to the parent page or is laid into the MS next to the parent page. For instance, 590a is affixed with sealing wax to 590, and 323a is laid into the MS next to 323.) Other sources of text are cited in the notes that follow below.

3 **Most of us:** Thoreau left the *Wild Fruits* MS with two beginnings but left no indication of which should take precedence over the other. Had he lived, he might

have integrated the two beginnings or perhaps used one before the other. I decided to begin this reconstruction of *Wild Fruits* with this particular beginning simply because its tone and subject seem to me better than the other's. I place the other beginning to *Wild Fruits* in the section titled "*Wild Fruits*: Alternate Beginning" in "Related Passages," pp. 242–44. I also place under "Related Passages" a section titled "*The Dispersion of Seeds*: Alternate Beginning" (pp. 270–71), which I had earlier represented as a beginning to *Wild Fruits* but which I am now convinced Thoreau intended to use as one of two possible beginnings to *The Dispersion of Seeds* (see Thoreau, *The Dispersion of Seeds*, pp. 23–24, for the other beginning).

3   **Ceram and Amboyna:** Exotic locations mentioned several times in Saint Pierre. Ceram is an island in the Moluccas, Indonesia, west of New Guinea; Amboyna is the chief city and commercial center of the Moluccas on Amboina Island in the northern Banda Sea. Both locations were critical to the economy of what were then called the Spice Islands.

5   **"several hundred . . . of turpentine":** Thoreau's source for this quotation has not been located.

5   **fit us to live here:** Thoreau originally wrote "fit us to live in New England" but he later interlined "here" in pencil above "New England" without deleting the latter two words or "in." I emend to reflect what appears to have been Thoreau's final intention for this clause.

6   **the saying of Cyrus . . . valiant in war":** Quoted in Herodotus, bk. 9, chap. 122.

6   **About the same time . . . their crispy stems:** Thoreau drew a single vertical line through this paragraph, an indication that he considered deleting the passage.

6   **boys are wont . . . do not want them:** "When three puffs of breath failed to blow all the tufted seeds from a dandelion globe, the shout arose, 'Your mother wants you!' " (Botkin, p. 331).

7   **seventh of June:** Thoreau interlined "(and May 30, 1860)" in the MS here.

7   **Gerarde . . . silk intermixt":** Gerarde, p. 46.

7   **inmost tender leaf:** Thoreau originally wrote "also" after "leaf" in the MS, but he later enclosed "also" in parentheses. Thoreau often enclosed within parentheses words or passages that he considered deleting from his working text.

8   **Gerarde . . . this root therein":** Gerarde, p. 47.

8   **Sir John Richardson . . . a glass of water":** Sir John Richardson, *Fauna Boreali-Americana*, 3:263. Thoreau originally wrote the clause beginning "that the Indians of British America" first and followed it immediately with the clause beginning "that 'the Cree name of this plant," although in the MS this latter clause begins, "The Cree name of this plant. . . ." Later Thoreau transposed these two clauses without inserting transition words, so I emend by adding the words "and that," and by changing "The" to "the" before "Cree."

8   **About the twentieth of May . . . open to the sun":** This paragraph has a single vertical line drawn through it, which indicates that Thoreau considered deleting the passage.

8   **Gerarde . . . open to the sun":** Gerarde, p. 638.

9   **Gerarde's account . . . grasshoppers":** Gerarde, p. 1485.

10   **now . . . a swamp:** Identified in the journal source as May 16, 1860, and Beck Stow's Swamp, respectively (entry of that date; see *Journal*, 13:296–97).

10   **Tusser . . . prove excellent good:** Tusser, p. 24. This is stanza 15 in Tusser's poem, "September's Husbandry"; the first line in later editions reads, "Wife, into thy garden, and set me a plot. . . ."

10   **The old herbalist Gerarde . . . nourishment is naught:** Gerarde, pp. 997, 998.

12   **Virgil . . . growing on the ground":** Virgil, *Eclogues*, bk. 3, line 93.

12   **This bug, as you know . . . to it" its peculiar odor:** Emmons, p. 203. The *Scutellaridæ* is more popularly known by its common name, the stink bug.

12   **dog in the manger:** An allusion to Aesop's fable "The Dog in the Manger," the moral of which is "People often grudge others what they cannot enjoy themselves."

12   **little knolls or swells:** After this phrase in the MS Thoreau wrote "(protuberances or warts on the slopes of the hills)," which I omit on the assumption that Thoreau placed it in parentheses to indicate deletion rather than to incorporate into the text as parenthetical information.

12   **the ancients speak:** Pliny the Elder wrote of the earth exuding a "divine odor" to which "there is no perfume, however sweet, that can possibly be compared" (*Natural History*, bk. 17, chap. 3). Thoreau copied the passage into his "Common Place Book 2," pp. 133–34, under the heading "Odor of the Earth."

13   **weeded:** I expanded "weeded" from "wed" in the MS.

15   **"a native . . . to the Greeks":** Thoreau's source for this quotation has not been located.

15   **as I am told:** Thoreau was probably told this by his cousin, George Thatcher, who lived in Bangor, Maine.

15   **Hearne . . . Churchill River":** Hearne, pp. 452–53. The clause Thoreau puts in brackets appears in a footnote in Hearne. Churchill River is in Manitoba, its mouth on the west coast of Hudson Bay.

15   **Sir John Franklin . . . *Otei-meena*:** Franklin, p. 78.

15   **Tanner . . . Lake Superior:** Tanner, p. 296.

15   **Dakotahs . . . strawberry is red":** Quotation marks added. A possible source is Eastman, p. 221, where she writes, however, "The month of June" is "the 'moon for strawberries.' "

15   **William Wood's . . . bushel in a forenoon":** William Wood, p. 16.

16   **Roger Williams . . . food for many days":** Williams, p. 221. The "chiefest doctor of England" was William Butler, called "the Æsculapius of our age" in Fuller, p. 387.

16 **Boucher . . . raspberries and strawberries:** Boucher, p. 64.

16 **Loskiel's . . . fine scarlet cloth":** Loskiel, p. 79.

16 **Mr. Peters . . . for poetic description":** Peters, p. 238. The passage in the source reads, in part, "mountains on its borders, would have furnished. . . ." Thoreau correctly transcribed the passage in his MS, but when he wrote the bracketed phrase, he interlined "the" over "its" without deleting the latter word or placing "the" in brackets.

16 **historians of New Hampshire towns:** Seward, p. 48.

16 **as one reads, the gray rocks . . . summer palace of Tsazkoy Chèlè:** "A Winter Underground," p. 3. The newspaper's type for this passage was so badly battered that "Tsazkoy" is unclear, which is no doubt why Thoreau in the *Wild Fruits* MS wrote "(?)" after that word. According to an appended note of attribution, this article was reprinted from *Chamber's Journal.* Tsazkoy Chèlè, now more often Anglicized to Tsarskoye Selo or simply translated "Czar's Village," is a small town outside St. Petersburg and was the imperial summer residence prior to the Russian Revolution.

17 **sluggish and mephistic . . . was a boy":** Identified in Thoreau's journal entry of May 20, 1856, as "Haynes the carpenter" (*Journal,* 8:350).

17 **their:** I emended "their" from "its" in the MS.

18 **according to Loudon . . . Traubenbirne, Ger.":** Loudon, 2:874.

19 **Assabet River:** I emend by adding "River."

19 **as if I were . . . between me and the village:** Based on his use of "batteaus" and "banks of the Saskatchewan," Thoreau almost certainly has in mind here his reading in Hind, *Northwest Territory,* 1:248, 252–53.

19 **One said, "Well . . . heard of them":** This person has not been identified.

19 **July thirtieth, 1860, one . . . Martial Miles's Swamp:** In his journal entry of this date, Thoreau does not identify the person who he says led him to the frosty hollow, and in fact his use of "he" suggests that he was walking that day with his neighbor and usual walking companion, the poet William Ellery Channing (*Journal,* 13:426–28). I emend by adding "Swamp."

20 **"Josh Pears," . . . corruption of "juicy":** Thoreau's source for this quotation, assuming it is in fact a quotation, has not been located.

20 **Richardson says . . . Zante currant":** Sir John Richardson, *Arctic Searching Expedition,* 1:126. *"La Poire"* is French for "the pear."

20 **Mr. George B. Emerson . . . feet from the ground:** Thoreau almost certainly refers to Emerson, *Report on Trees,* where the shad bush is treated on pp. 443–45, but I have been unable to locate this particular quotation in Emerson.

21 **Monadnock mountain:** Mount Monadnock (elevation 3,165 feet) is in southwestern New Hampshire between Troy and Petersborough, about nine miles north of the Massachusetts border and forty-six miles northwest of Concord Center. Thoreau climbed the mountain several times, usually camping overnight on or near the summit. See Harding, pp. 171, 216, 294–95, 397–98, 431–33.

21 **The earlier European . . . her tobacco trade:** Van der Donck, p. 138, writes, "Some persons who are not well informed, name all North-America *Virginia,* because Virginia from her tobacco trade is well known." Thoreau extracted this remark into his "Common Place Book 1," p. 13.

22 **pailsful to sell at their doors:** After this sentence Thoreau originally wrote, "The girl that has Indian blood in her veins and picks berries for a living will find them out as soon as they turn," but he deleted this sentence in very light, possibly erased pencil.

22 **still, fresh green of oaks and hickory sprouts:** The MS reads "still fresh green" with a continuous pen stroke between the last two words. Thoreau occasionally kept his pen on the paper between two words when he clearly intended to hyphenate them, but I do not believe the context here supports the construction "still fresh-green." Another option, likelier than the former, would be "still-fresh green." Also, after "hickory sprouts" in the MS Thoreau wrote the following passage, a portion of which he later drew a single vertical pencil line through, apparently to indicate deletion: "and George B. Emerson says that 'They are particularly suited to be preserved by drying, and, when prepared in that way, are equal in value to the imported currants as an ingredient in cakes and puddings.' He but repeats what the very earliest explorers of this country affirmed, having learned it from the Indians. But in my opinion they are chiefly valuable before they are dried or even plucked. He also says it 'feeds immense flocks of wild pigeons' and other animals." The quotations here are from Emerson, *Report on Trees,* p. 404.

22 **"bluet," adapting . . . the Canadians:** Thoreau read very widely in the early travel literature of North America, particularly of New England and Canada (Sattelmeyer, pp. 92–99). Most of the early travelers, particularly the French, but also the English, referred to the "bluet" frequently in the accounts of their travels.

22 **Many years ago . . . milk for supper:** Thoreau made a four-day trip to Mount Wachusett with Margaret Fuller's brother, Richard, in mid-July 1841 and wrote the

excursion up into essay form and published it in the January 1843 *Boston Miscellany of Literature* as "A Walk to Wachusett" (Harding, pp. 131–33). He writes in the essay, "The blueberries which the mountain afforded, added to the milk we had brought, made our frugal supper, while for entertainment, the even-song of the wood-thrush rung along the ridge" (p. 34). Mount Wachusett (elevation 2,006 feet) is twenty-eight miles west of Concord.

23   **On September seventh:** I emend by adding "On."

25   **Mr. Blood . . . winter before last?:** Thoreau originally wrote "Stow" and "Fair Haven" where he later interlined "Blood" and "Pomciticut," respectively. On April 18, 1859, he surveyed a woodlot in "the south part of Acton" for Stedman Buttrick, who planned to sell the lot to Sumner Blood. Pomciticut Hill was actually just over a mile south of the Acton-Sudbury line in northern Sudbury. That part of Sudbury is now part of Maynard, and Pomciticut Hill is now called Summer Hill.

25   **an ill wind . . . any good:** Bartlett states that this common proverb was first listed in John Heywood's *Proverbs* (1546), and shortly thereafter was used in Thomas Tusser's *Description of the Properties of Winds* and Shakespeare's *Henry IV, Part II* (act 5, scene 3, line 87).

25   **grow there!:** After this sentence in the MS Thoreau interlined in pencil "*Vide* more under Huckleberries," almost certainly indicating that he planned to insert at this point in the MS more text on the subject of berries growing after a cutting. The "Black Huckleberry" section does in fact have text on that subject—beginning "If you look closely you will find" on p. 44 and extending perhaps as far as "small fruits of the Algonquin and Iroquois Families" on p. 46. But the MS containing the latter material (in the "Black Huckleberry" section) has nothing that might indicate how much of that material Thoreau may have intended to incorporate here in the "Early Low Blueberry" section. For this reason, and because Thoreau has integrated the "Black Huckleberry" material so well into that section, I opt not to move any text to this location.

25   **"bluets" by the voyageurs:** See the note above for p. 22.

25   **St. John and Penobscot Rivers in Maine:** Thoreau visited the Maine woods on three occasions, in 1846, 1853, and 1857, penetrating to the headwaters of these rivers only on the last trip. The St. John River flows in a northeasterly direction out of Maine, eventually emptying into the Bay of Fundy at Saint John, New Brunswick; the Penobscot River flows in a generally southeasterly direction past Bangor, Maine, and empties into Penobscot Bay just south of Bucksport, Maine.

26   **The traveller Mackenzie . . . in great numbers:** Mackenzie, 1:181.

26   **Red Hill in New Hampshire:** Thoreau and fellow Concordian Edward Hoar rode in a horse-drawn buggy to the White Mountains of New Hampshire in early July 1858, stopping on the way to climb and botanize on Red Hill, which is in east-central New Hampshire, just north of Lake Winnipesawkee (Harding, pp. 398–99).

Thoreau noted in his journal for July 5, 1858, the day he and Hoar climbed Red Hill, "Dr. Jackson says that Red Hill is so called from the uva-ursi on it turning red in the fall" (*Journal*, 11:8–9).

26 **bog bilberry . . . produce a headache:** Loudon, 2:1158.

26 ***Rubus triflorus* . . . (or *rubus*):** Thoreau enclosed each of these pairs of words in parentheses and may have intended to delete one or the other or both pairs. I emend by omitting the parentheses enclosing the former pair.

26 **Gray says . . . hill sides:** Gray (1848), p. 125.

27 **Family tradition . . . June, 1775:** Thoreau's grandmother was Mary Jones Dunbar Minott, who in 1775 lived with her father, Colonel Elisha Jones, on an estate in Weston, Massachusetts, six and a half miles south of Concord. She died in 1830, when Thoreau was thirteen years old, the only one of his grandparents he knew. In the MS there is a blank space after "brother," obviously left so that Thoreau could later insert the first name of the great-uncle who had been confined in Concord Jail. Thoreau had recounted this story in more detail in an undated journal entry (ca. 1848), where he also points out that Simeon is the great-uncle's first name (Thoreau, *Journal*, Volume 3, p. 15).

27 **Pliny, writing . . . to Britain":** Thoreau translated these passages from Pliny, *Historiæ Mundi*, bk. 15, chap. 30. The Bohn edition, *Natural History*, which Thoreau also read, translates the last clause thus: the cherry "has travelled beyond the Ocean, and arrived in Britannia even" (*Natural History*, 3:322).

27 **Saint Pierre says . . . 42ᵈ degree":** Saint Pierre, 3:223.

27 **Some, however, think . . . indigenous in Europe:** Loudon points out that "Some writers assert that the cherries introduced by the Romans were lost during the period that the country was under the dominion of the Saxons, till they were reintroduced by Richard Harris, gardener to Henry VIII . . ." (2:696).

27 **Pliny names one . . . to bear transporting":** Thoreau translated these passages from Pliny, *Historiæ Mundi*, bk. 15, chap. 30. The Bohn edition, *Natural History*, refers to the "Junian" in its translation of this sentence, and the translators state in a footnote, "It is most generally thought that this is the Cerasus avium of botanists, our morello, which is a very tender cherry" (*Natural History*, 3:322 n. 79). Loudon, who also provides a translation of this sentence from Pliny, agrees with Thoreau in calling this the "Julian" (2:696).

27 **fifteenth:** After this word in the MS Thoreau wrote, "(or 20th?)"; I interpret the parentheses here as indicating that Thoreau intended to delete this date.

27 **One European species . . . "*Idæus*":** As Thoreau mentions in his journal entry of January 8, 1861, "the common English raspberry is called *Rubus Idæus* from the old Greek name" for Mount Ida (*Journal*, 14:309).

28 **recent stories . . . foundation of Rome:** Thoreau uses a version of this passage, altered to apply to apples instead of raspberries, at the beginning of his posthumously

published essay, "Wild Apples," reprinted in the "Wild Apples" section of "Related Passages" (see p. 244). Newspaper reports appeared throughout the 1850s and into the 1860s on the discovery and careful excavation of "lake-dweller" communities that had been built about 4000 B.C. upon piles driven into the shallow areas of lakes in Switzerland, particularly Lake Leman (at least twenty-four communities), the Lake of Constance (thirty-two communities), and the Lake of Neuchâtel (forty-six communities). Lake-dweller communities were also discovered in Germany and Italy during this period.

28 **The English botanist Lindley . . . been questioned:** Thoreau's source is a footnote in Alphonso Wood, p. 61 n. I have not found where the correctness of Lindley's statement has been questioned.

28 **Pliny . . . layers and quicksets":** Pliny, *Natural History*, bk. 17, chap. 21 (3:476). Multiplying by layers involves bending shoots or twigs to the ground and covering them partly with earth so that they may strike root and propagate; multiplying by quicksets involves setting slips or cuttings of plants in the ground to grow.

29 **Pliny . . . size of the fruit":** Pliny, *Natural History*, bk. 15, chap. 27 (3:320).

30 **They are said . . . and Quebec:** Gray (1856), p. 250.

30 **Pursh . . . black, insipid":** Pursh, p. 429.

30 **it is said . . . of the cranberry":** Thoreau's source was Loudon, 2:1161. Enghien is located a few miles southwest of Brussels, Belgium.

32 *redeemed:* A swamp is said to be "redeemed" after it has been drained and suitably prepared for cultivation.

32 **"touched my trembling ears" . . . "mortal soil":** John Milton, "Lycidas," lines 77, 78. Thoreau was able to recite this entire 193-line poem from memory.

32 **Perhaps you press:** Thoreau wrote, "Perhaps (as at Martial Miles's Swamp) you press," so I emend by deleting the parenthetical phrase.

33 **Gerarde . . . between the teeth":** Gerarde, p. 1417.

33 **Mithridates:** The ancients believed that Mithridates the Great had saturated his body with poisons so that no one could murder him. When the Romans captured him, he tried in vain to poison himself; then he ordered a Gallic mercenary to kill him.

34 **variety:** In the MS Thoreau wrote, "*var.* (or species)," so I emend by omitting the parenthetical phrase.

34 *pennsylvanicum:* Thoreau interlined "(see July 23, 1854)" in the MS here, referring to two sentences in his journal entry of that date (*Journal*, 6:409). These two sentences form the basis for the observations in this paragraph.

34 **damages being allowed . . . were burnt:** I have not been able to locate any information on the legal action Thoreau alludes to here.

34 **"blueberry hollow":** I have been unable to locate any other mention of this dish.

35 **I climbed up . . . season for berries:** After this paragraph in the MS Thoreau wrote and placed extended parentheses around the following one-sentence paragraph, the

parentheses apparently indicating deletion: "There is a clump within ten feet of this consisting of twenty-three stems whose average diameter at three feet from the ground is about two inches, and there are many other clumps of large ones thereabouts."

36 **cut down the woods:** After the sentence ending here, Thoreau wrote and placed extended parentheses around the following sentence, apparently indicating deletion: "This is the largest of the *Vacciniæ* which grow here or is described in the botanies of the northern United States."

36 **before the writer was born:** Thoreau interlined in the MS here *"Vide* (if necessary) how they bear snow about February 16, 1860," referring to the following passage from his journal entry of that date:

When we descend on to Goose Pond we find that the snow rests more thickly on the numerous zigzag and horizontal branches of the high blueberries that bend over it than on any deciduous shrub or tree, producing a very handsome snowy maze, and can thus distinguish this shrub, by the manner in which the snow lies on it, quite across the pond. It is remarkable also how very distinct and *white* every plane surface, as the rocks which lie here and there amid the blueberries or higher on the bank,— a place where no twig or weed rises to interrupt the pure white impression. In fact, this crystalline snow lies up so light and downy that it evidently admits more light than usual, and the surface is more white and glowing for it. It is semitransparent, like alabaster. Also all the birds' nests in the blueberry bushes are revealed, by the great snow-balls they hold. (*Journal*, 13:148)

36 **begins to be ripe:** The original version of the sentence ending here read, "The late or second kind of low blueberry, the common low blueberry *(Vaccinium vacillans)*, the firm berry which is generally found with huckleberries on a bush of the same size, begins to be ripe from the second to the fifth of July." And after this sentence in the MS Thoreau wrote, "They are thick enough to pick about the twentieth of July, at their height the third of August, and last till the latter part of that month, or, in a half-dried state, two or three weeks later. I notice the green berries about the nineteenth of June." When revising Thoreau placed extended parentheses around the passage beginning "from the second to the fifth of July" and ending "about the nineteenth of June," apparently indicating deletion.

36 **The earlier low blueberry . . . time more earthy:** In the MS Thoreau drew a vertical line in the margin beside these two sentences, which may indicate that he planned to delete them.

37 **By the first . . . still vegetable food:** In the MS Thoreau drew a vertical line in the margin beside these two sentences, which may indicate that he planned to delete them.

37 **Black huckleberries:** Thoreau apparently deleted the word "Black" in the MS here when he decided to separate this section, the "Late Whortleberry" section (see

p. 111), and the "Hairy Huckleberry" section (see p. 113) from the larger *Wild Fruits* MS; combine them; and make them a single, independent lecture-essay titled "Huckleberries"—almost precisely what he had done with the "Wild Apples" section as well, although "Wild Apples" appears never to have been more than a single section of *Wild Fruits*. Thoreau never lived to complete his revisions of "Huckleberries." I restore the original name for the "Black Huckleberry" section because I split out and reintegrate into the larger *Wild Fruits* MS the pages making up each of the three "Huckleberries" sections.

37 **It is said . . . not found at all:** Thoreau's source for this allusion has not been located.

37 **celebrated French chemist:** Thoreau interlined here the following query: "(Gaylussacia being the name of the genus which is without a representative in Europe?)?" I do not include the query in the text because Thoreau appears not to have resolved the truth of the assertion. Gray (1856), p. 247, says of the *Gaylussacia* or huckleberry, "Named for the distinguished chemist, *Gay-Lussac.*"

37 **daguerreotype had . . . The-Wind-that-Blows:** The daguerreotype was invented in 1838 by the French painter and physicist Louis-Jacques-Mandé Daguerre. I have located no reference to a Chippeway named The-Wind-that-Blows.

37 **By another it has . . . huckleberries and milk:** Thoreau's source is Loudon, 2:1163, where "Andrómeda baccàta" is listed as a "*Synonyme*" of *Vaccinium resinosa*. Loudon cites his source as "*Wangh. Amer.*, t. 30. f. 69.," which is expanded in his "List of Books Referred to" as "Wangenheim (F.A.G.), Anpflanzung nord-americanischer Holzarten. Göttingæ, 1787. 3 vols. folio" (1:ccxxv).

38 **Nagog Pond:** A large pond in the town of Acton, about six miles west of Concord.

39 **I once did some . . . have heard of it:** On January 11 and 12, 1853, Thoreau surveyed two farms and a woodlot near the Acton line for John LeGrosse, who pointed out to Thoreau at that time that "both red and white huckleberries" grew near his house (*Journal*, 4:462–63). In his journal entry for August 2, 1853, Thoreau mentions that John LeGrosse had the previous day brought him a "quart of red huckleberries" (*Journal*, 5:352; but this differs slightly from Thoreau's MS journal, vol. 15, p. 461, which is the source of my quotation here).

39 **when I should . . . I was perfectly that:** Directly below the word "when" in the MS is the word "that," and what I interpret as Thoreau's crossing of the initial *t* in "that" could be interpreted as the underlining of "when."

40 **so are spoiled:** I emend from "are so spoiled" in the MS.

40 **dog-days . . . ten of them):** The *Oxford English Dictionary* defines *dog-days* as "The days about the time of the heliacal rising of the Dog-star; noted from ancient times as the hottest and most unwholesome period of the year." Most almanacs define the dog-days as beginning July 3 and ending August 11, a period which encompasses the forty days preceding the cosmical rising of Sirius, the greater Dog Star.

40 **Plants of this order . . . in a fossil state:** Thoreau's source for this allusion has not been located.

41 **George B. Emerson . . . calyx segments":** Emerson, *Report on Trees*, p. 397.

41 **etymology . . . is in dispute:** Loudon writes that "Vaccinium" is "An ancient Latin name, but whether of a berry or a flower, has been a point in dispute among critics, as well as its etymology" (2:1156).

41 **word "whortleberry" . . . the hart's berry:** Emerson, *Report on Trees*, p. 398.

41 **"Hurts" is an old . . . resembling hurtleberries":** Bailey, p. 398.

41 **The Germans say . . . "heath berry":** Loudon, 2:1156.

41 **"Huckleberry," this . . . Lawson in 1709:** Thoreau mistakenly wrote "1609" in the MS, which I have corrected. He refers to the first printing of Lawson.

41 **According to the . . . cluster of grapes:** Oswald, p. 86.

41 **The Englishman Lindley . . . Sandwich Islands":** Lindley, p. 222. The Sandwich Islands are now called the Hawaiian Islands.

41 **as George B. Emerson . . . more of use":** Emerson, *Report on Trees*, p. 397.

41 **According to the last . . . seasons and localities):** Thoreau originally wrote "According to Gray's arrangement" and later interlined "the last" after deleting "Gray's." He refers to Gray (1856), where on pp. 247–50 Gray describes each species of the Whortleberry Family; however, I count not fourteen but the following fifteen: (1) G. *brachycera* (box-leaved huckleberry), (2) G. *dumosa* (dwarf huckleberry), (3) G. *frondosa* (blue tangle or dangleberry), (4) G. *resinosa* (black huckleberry), (5) V. *oxycoccus* (small cranberry), (6) V. *macrocarpon* (common American cranberry), (7) V. *erythrocarpon* (unnamed), (8) V. *vitis-idæa* (cowberry), (9) V. *stamineum* (deerberry or squaw huckleberry), (10) V. *cæspitosum* (dwarf bilberry), (11) V. *uliginosum* (bog bilberry), (12) V. *pennsylaticum* (dwarf blueberry), (13) V. *canadense* (Canada blueberry), (14) V. *vacillans* (low blueberry), and (15) V. *corymosum* (common swamp-blueberry).

42 **I gather from Loudon . . . and in Scotland:** Loudon, 2:1156–58. Emerson, *Report on Trees*, p. 398, mentions these two as being "European species" and "of Europe." Gray (1848), p. 261, states that the *Vaccinium uliginosum* is found on "Alpine tops of the White Mountains, New Hampshire, Green Mountains, Vermont, and Essex Mountains, New York."

42 **of the thirty-two . . . found in Europe:** Loudon, 2:1156–67. The three species that Loudon mentions as native to Europe are V. *arctostaphylos* (2:1163–64), V. *padifolium* (2:1164), and V. *vitis idæa* (2:1164–65). He does not mention the origin of V. *canadense* (2:1166–67).

42 **Loudon says . . . an astringent quality":** Loudon, 2:1158, 2:1157. Thoreau adds the article "a" between Loudon's words "into jelly."

42 **Coleman in his . . . pictorial subjects:** Coleman, pp. 91–92.

43 **Jonathan . . . John Bull:** Generic names for Americans and Englishmen, respectively.

43 **Dr. Manasseh Cutler . . . with their milk:** Cutler writes of the white and red whortleberries, "The fruit of these species are agreeable to children, either eaten by themselves, or in milk, or in tarts and jellies" (p. 439).

43 **put in his thumb . . . Doctor am I?":** An allusion to the nursery rhyme: "Little Jack Horner sat in the corner, / Eating a Christmas pie. / He put in his thumb, and pulled out a plum, / And said, 'What a good boy am I!' "

43 **One botanist says . . . of its vegetation":** Thoreau's source is Loudon, 2:1157, where this quotation is attributed to H. C. Watson, *Outlines of the Geographical Distribution of British Plants* (London, 1832), p. 201. I emend both Thoreau and Loudon by italicizing the two Latin plant names in order to conform to the practice used throughout the text.

44 **According to Loudon . . . and very good:** Thoreau's comparison is based on Loudon, 2:735–747; and Gray (1848), pp. 124–26. Loudon refers to *R. affinis, R. suberectus, R. idæus, R. cæsius, R. hirtus, R. corylifolius,* and *R. fruticosus* as indigenous to Britain, of which the latter two are common. Gray lists *R. hispidus, R. chamæmorus, R. triflorus, R. occidentalis, R. odoratus, R. stigosus, R. villosus,* and *R. canadensis* as indigenous to New England, of which the latter four he classifies as common and "often cultivated," "finely flavored," "pleasant," and "sweet," respectively.

44 **The Englishman Coleman . . . much importance":** Coleman, p. 105.

44 **the sandal wood . . . who cuts it:** Thoreau's source for this allusion has not been located.

44 **the three hills . . . among the rest:** The three hills of Boston are Pemberton Hill, Beacon Hill, and Mount Vernon. Bunker Hill is across the Charles River in Charlestown.

44 **My mother . . . church now stands:** Doubtless a reference to the Unitarian minister Charles Lowell, who preached from 1806 to 1861 at West Church (now Old West Church) on the corner of Cambridge and Lynde Streets in Boston. The church was designed by Asher Benjamin and built in 1806 (Whitehill, p. 177).

45 **The small berry-bearing . . . turf and earth:** Crantz, p. 139.

45 **somebody in this neighborhood . . . cutting up huckleberry bushes for fuel:** I have not been able to locate any reference to a machine such as Thoreau describes here.

45 **It is stated . . . cohesive nature":** Loudon, 2:1076.

46 **walking behind . . . tasting before:** Thoreau doubtless refers to Joseph Polis, the Penobscot Indian whom he secured as a guide for his last excursion into the Maine woods, July 20 to August 3, 1857. Thoreau admired Polis a great deal and made him the hero of the last section of *The Maine Woods,* "The Allegash and East Branch" (pp. 155–297).

46 **In the year 1615, Champlain . . . huckleberry cake that I know of:** From about the time of his residence at Walden Pond in 1845 to the end of his life almost seventeen years later, Thoreau transcribed into eleven MS notebooks extracts from his wide-ranging reading on Native American Indians. These "Indian Notebooks" are now in the J. Pierpont Morgan Library in New York City and, unfortunately, have not yet been published; when they are finally published, they will show us yet another facet of this extraordinarily multifaceted man. His extracts from Champlain (see "Works Cited") are in MS vol. 4 of his Indian Notebooks, and on one page (the notebook is unpaged, but this would be p. 36 if the pages were numbered) he writes, "In the country of the Algonquins far up the Ottawa he [Champlain] finds a kind of small fruit or berry which he calls bluës, as well as *framboises*, both which the people dry for the winter. The Indians made a business of collecting and drying the bluës." Thoreau footnotes the first use of "bluës" here as follows: *"Vide* plate [illustration] and account of this in 2d volume of Charlevoix Histoire; he calls it *Vitis idæa Canadensis; Mystifolio."* I also list Charlevoix's book in "Works Cited" below.

47 **Gabriel Sagard . . . dry and green":** Sagard, *Le Grand Voyage*, pp. 326–27.

47 **Le Jeune . . . full of *bluets*":** Le Jeune, p. 46.

47 **Roger Williams . . . to the English":** Williams, p. 221. Thoreau placed a question mark in the margin adjacent to each of the words *"Sautaash"* and *"Sautauthig."*

47 **Nathaniel Morton . . . no doubt whortleberries:** Morton, p. 136.

48 **John Josselyn . . . into water gruel":** Josselyn, *New-Englands Rarities Discovered*, pp. 59, 60.

48 **The largest Indian . . . substantial provisions:** Josselyn, *New-Englands Rarities Discovered*, pp. 49–51.

48 **La Hontan . . . chase fails them":** La Hontan, 1:124.

48 **Father Rasles . . . blueberries are ripe":** Rasles, p. 417.

48 **Father Hennepin . . . imported currants:** Hennepin, p. 225.

48 **The Englishman John . . . the word "huckleberry":** Lawson, p. 110.

49 **The well-known natural . . . children was tending":** Bartram, p. 87.

49 **Kalm, in his travels . . . plumb pudding":** Kalm, 1:339.

49 **The Moravian missionary . . . but not boiled":** Heckewelder, p. 186.

49 **Lewis and Clarke . . . berries extensively:** Lewis and Clarke, 1:366, 1:391.

49 **Owen's *Geological* . . . article of food":** Owen, p. 204.

50 **pearl-ash or alum into it:** Thoreau originally wrote "soda or pearl-ash into it," but he later deleted "into it" and interlined "alum or arsenic or potash into it." Then he deleted "arsenic or potash." So "or alum" is an editorial transposition of "alum or." The *Oxford English Dictionary* defines *pearl-ash* as "The potassium carbonate of commerce, so called from its pearly hue."

50 **The last Indian . . . his last days:** Thoreau had visited the island of Nantucket, which is located south of Cape Cod, in late December 1854 to deliver a lecture at

the Nantucket Athenæum. He wrote in his journal entry of December 28, 1854, "The last Indian, not of pure blood, died this very month, and I saw his picture with a basket of huckleberries in his hand" (*Journal*, 7:96). This Indian was Abram Quary, who actually died on November 25, 1854, and the "picture" Thoreau saw still hangs in the Nantucket Athenæum.

50 **Tanner . . . terminal syllable:** Tanner, p. 296. In the MS Thoreau interlined "words" above Tanner's "all which," and I silently incorporate Thoreau's interlineation into Tanner's sentence here ("all words which").

50 **side of the Atlantic:** Thoreau originally followed these words with the phrase "with a reference to Mount Ida." Later he deleted "reference to Mount" and, apparently at the same time, placed a period after "Atlantic"—both of which actions I interpret to mean he wanted to end the sentence at "Atlantic" and was simply hasty in his deletion, neglecting to delete all six words in the concluding phrase.

50 **It is still in doubt . . . berry or a flower:** See the note above to p. 41.

50 **Tourneforte . . . Mount Ida":** Duhamel du Monceau, p. 38. Thoreau queries this statement in the margin of the MS. Also, he underlines "Vine of Mount Ida" in the MS, but he appears to have done so only to call attention to the phrase as such, a purpose for which I use quotation marks, so I add quotation marks and do not italicize.

50 **Mount Monadnock . . . Bad rock":** According to Nutting, who cites *"United States Geological Survey Bulletin no. 259,"* Monadnock derived its name from "the Indian *m'an* meaning 'surpassing,' *adn*, 'mountain,' and *ock*, 'place'—place of the surpassing (unexcelled) mountain" (p. 3). For other information on the mountain, see the note above to p. 21.

51 **This was written . . . pockets with the fruit:** The journal source of Thoreau's comparison of the pear crop to the huckleberry crop was his entry of September 19, 1856 (*Journal*, 9:86). Ralph Waldo Emerson's pear orchard began bearing prodigiously in the autumn of 1860, as Thoreau mentions and meditates upon in the "Pear" section, pp. 126–28.

51 **some of the inhabitants . . . huckleberries in 1856:** I have not been able to locate Thoreau's source for this reference. Ashby, Massachusetts, is twenty-eight miles northwest of Concord, near the New Hampshire border.

52 **Mahometans:** A common spelling of the time for Muhammadans or followers of Islam.

52 **General Court:** The legislature of the Commonwealth of Massachusetts is officially known as the "General Court."

52 **men live like birds:** Thoreau may allude here to the Sermon on the Mount, "Behold the fowls of the air: for they sow now, neither do they reap, nor gather into barns; yet your heavenly Father feedeth them" (Matthew 7:26).

52 **refreshment of animals:** Thoreau originally wrote "for the refreshment of men and animals"; later he deleted "of men," interlined "his" above "the," and then erased "his." So I emend by restoring "of" before "animals."

52 **We pluck . . . remembrance of her:** This brief sentence clearly echoes two well-known accounts of critically significant events: the Fall of the Judeo-Christian tradition, which "Brought Death into the World, and all our woe, / With loss of Eden," as John Milton phrased it in *Paradise Lost*, bk. 1, lines 2–3; and the Eucharist of the Christian tradition, which commemorates the death of Christ, the Son of God, through whom paradise can be regained and everlasting life achieved. The first half of the sentence echoes Milton's *Paradise Lost*, bk. 9, lines 781–84, where the Fall is recounted: Eve's "rash hand in evil hour / Forth reaching to the Fruit, she pluck'd, she eat; / Earth felt the wound, and Nature from her seat, / Sighing through all her Works, gave signs of woe, / That all was lost." The last half of the sentence echoes Luke 22:19 and I Corinthians 11:24, the latter of which reads, "And when [the Lord] had given thanks, he brake [the bread], and said, 'Take, eat: this is my body, which is broken for you: this do in remembrance of me.'"

52 *not* **forbidden . . . tempts us to eat:** In the Judeo-Christian tradition, Adam and Eve were forbidden to eat the fruit of the tree that grew in the center of the Garden of Eden, the Tree of the Knowledge of Good and Evil, but Satan in the form of a serpent tempted them to eat of the fruit, which occasioned the Fall of Mankind (see preceding note).

52 **now:** The journal source of this passage is the entry of August 7, 1853, where Thoreau points out that he was climbing Fair Haven Hill (*Journal*, 5:360–61).

53 **One such year:** The journal source of this passage is the entry of August 4, 1856 (*Journal*, 8:444–45).

53 **those who had . . . of it before:** In the journal source of this passage (see preceding note), Thoreau mentions that he had a party of "two ladies" a-berrying with him, but he does not identify either one or them.

54 **I once carried . . . from time to time:** Thoreau refers here to the "two ladies" mentioned in the preceding note.

54 **Delectable Hills:** John Bunyan's *The Pilgrim's Progress* (1678) mentions the Delectable Mountains.

54 **a land flowing with milk and huckleberries:** The Promised Land of the Old Testament flowed with milk and honey (Exodus 3:8, 33:3; Jeremiah 11:5).

54 **O *fortunatos* . . . their own happiness:** Thoreau's source for this quotation has not been located.

54 **The First of August . . . in New England:** In antebellum New England the First of August, or the anniversary of Emancipation in the West Indies, was celebrated by

abolitionists almost as widely and in much the same fashion as the Fourth of July or Independence Day.

54 **masculine, wild-eyed woman of the fields:** Thoreau queries this passage in the left margin of the MS. The passage may be an allusion to the woman in John Keats's poem "La Belle Dame sans Merci," who is described as "a lady in the meads" whose "eyes were wild" (stanza 4). Compare with the note to p. 84, however.

54 **that far off Elysium . . . any person:** Elysium is the abode of the blessed after death in classical mythology. The Old Testament prophet Zechariah might be said to *see all* because his prophecies are eschatological. Also, there is a sort of refrain in the Book of Zechariah involving an angel asking the prophet what he sees and the prophet responding that he sees particular visions. Here, for instance, are the first two verses of Chapter 5: "Then I turned, and lifted up mine eyes, and looked, and behold a flying roll. And he said unto me, What seest thou? And I answered, I see a flying roll; the length thereof is twenty cubits, and the breadth thereof ten cubits." Zechariah See-all may also be a literary character in a work I have been unable to locate.

55 **Theodore Parker . . . huckleberry field:** According to Weiss, "With the proceeds of a whortleberrying campaign in 1822, [Parker] bought his first book. He had to carry the berries to Boston for sale . . ." (1:44). Commagher points out that "It was on one of these trips [to Boston] that Theodore bought his first book, with his own money earned from endless hours of huckle-berry picking. It was Ainsworth's 'Latin Dictionary,' the cornerstone of the greatest private library in America" (p. 12). Parker died in 1859, the year before the heaviest period of Thoreau's work on the *Wild Fruits* MS, and left his enormous library to the city of Boston.

55 **Story and Warren and Ware:** Joseph Story, John C. Warren, and the Reverend Henry Ware taught law, medicine, and theology, respectively, at Harvard University during the time Thoreau attended the university (1833–37).

55 **a mantua-maker:** A mantua is a loose-fitting gown, particularly associated with seventeenth- and eighteenth-century fashion.

55 **had been decided on:** After this phrase in the MS Thoreau wrote, "(by the authorities)," which I omit on the presumption that the parentheses indicate deletion.

56 **Dutch House:** This house derived its name, according to Franklin B. Sanborn, Thoreau's friend and neighbor, "from the Dutch 'stoop' along its front, with that peculiar curve in its roof, which identified it as of Holland origin" (quoted by Leslie Wilson, curator of Special Collections at the Concord Free Public Library, Concord, Massachusetts, in a letter of February 9, 1999, to Bradley P. Dean from an unidentified newspaper article dated 1914).

56 **Young America:** An economic, political, and philosophical movement in the United States from the early 1840s to the mid-1850s, Young America was characterized by enthusiasm for free-market principles, support for republican ideas abroad, and territorial expansionism.

57 **ah, we have fallen on evil days!:** Milton, *Paradise Lost*, bk. 7, lines 23–26: "Standing on Earth, not rapt above the Pole, / More safe I Sing with mortal voice, unchang'd / To hoarse or mute, though fall'n on evil days, / On evil days though fall'n, and evil tongues. . . ."

57 **pickers ordered out of:** I add the word "of" here on authority of the journal source of this passage, entry of August 6, 1858 (*Journal*, 11:78).

57 *Sic transit gloria ruris:* Latin for "So the glory of the countryside passes away," playing on the Latin aphorism *"Sic transit gloria mundis,"* translated "So the glory of *the world* passes away."

57 **your old fellow laborer Bright:** Bright was a generic name for a cow, rather like Fido or Spot for a dog, a relic that survives in the name Brighton, a suburb of Boston where slaughterhouses were located prior to and perhaps during Thoreau's time.

58 **labor naturally tend:** Thoreau enclosed the words "—to make all things venal" in parentheses here, apparently to indicate deletion.

58 **It has come to this, that A——:** Thoreau deleted "It has come to this, that" at the beginning of this paragraph, but he queried the deletion in the left margin.

58 **patent huckleberry horse-rake:** I have not been able to locate any record of this patent or of this machine.

58 **dog-in-the-manger:** Another allusion to Aesop's fable, "The Dog in the Manger," the moral of which is "People often grudge others what they cannot enjoy themselves."

58 **I do not know . . . ringing dumb-bells:** Thoreau drew a pencil mark in the left margin beside this passage, a mark that he occasionally drew to indicate larger passages of text that he considered deleting or intended to delete.

59 **not that I . . . Rome more:** Shakespeare, *Julius Cæsar*, act III, scene 2, line 22.

59 **Many old writers . . . abundant here then:** After this sentence in the MS, Thoreau wrote, "—(Josselyn, e.g.)," referring to Josselyn, *An Account of Two Voyages*, p. 72.

59 **Red currants, like . . . Island of Anticosti:** James Richardson, p. 51. The 3,200 square-mile Anticosti Island is situated between the St. Lawrence River and the Gulf of St. Lawrence.

59 **Roger Williams . . . and whortleberries:** Williams, p. 221.

59 **Loudon and Canterbury, New Hampshire:** On July 4, 1858, while on their way to the White Mountains, Thoreau and fellow Concordian Edward Hoar botanized along Hollow Road between Loudon and Canterbury, small towns north of Concord, New Hampshire, in the Saucook River and Merrimack River valleys, respectively (*Journal*, 11:6).

59 **Monadnock:** See the note above to p. 21.

59 **White Mountains:** Thoreau and Edward Hoar visited the White Mountains of New Hampshire, and were joined there by several friends, between July 5 and 16, 1858 (*Journal*, 11:6; Harding, pp. 398–402).

60 **Loudon and Canterbury:** See the note above to p. 59.

60 **Worcester County:** This large county stretches across the breadth of central Massachusetts.

60 **Monadnock:** See the note above to p. 21.

60 **Fitchburg and Troy:** Fitchburg, Massachusetts, is twenty-five miles west-northwest of Concord Center and twenty-five miles southeast of Troy, New Hampshire.

61 **"There is a delicious . . . a pleasant tartness":** Gosse, *Canadian Naturalist*, p. 244.

61 **On the sand thrown . . . nobody any good:** According to Bartlett, "an ill wind that blows nobody any good" is a proverb first recorded in 1546 by John Heywood, *Proverbs*. Moll Pitcher was, as Hawthorne explains in *Blithedale Romance,* a "renowned old witch of Lynn," Massachusetts (actually a noted fortune teller), made particularly famous after the publication in 1832 of John Greenleaf Whittier's poem, "Moll Pitcher." In his journal entry of November 5, 1854, Thoreau explains the story of the money-diggers, who dug along the Sudbury River just south of Clamshell Hill, near where Emerson Hospital is now located:

> Passing the mouth of John Warner's hollow near the river, was hailed by him and Anthony Wright, sitting there, to come and see where they [the money-diggers] had dug for money. There was a hole six feet square and as many deep, and the sand was heaped about over a rod square. Hosmer said that it was dug two or three weeks before, that three men came in a chaise and dug it in the night; they were seen about there by day. Somebody dug near there in June, and then they covered up the hole again. He said they had been digging thereabout from time to time for a hundred years. I asked him why. He said that Dr. Lee (who hid where Joe Barrett did) told him that old Mr. Wood who lived in a house very near his (Hosmer's) told him that one night in Capt. Kid's day three pirates came to his house with a pair of old-fashioned deer-skin breeches, both legs full of coin, and asked leave to bury it in his cellar. He was afraid and refused them. They then asked for some earthen pots and shovels and a lantern, which he let them have. A woman in the house followed the pirates at a distance down the next hollow on the south and saw them go along the meadowside and then up this hollow, and then, being alone and afraid, she returned. Soon after the men returned with the tools and an old-fashioned hat full of coin (holding about a quart) which they gave to Wood. He, being afraid, buried it in his cellar, but afterward, becoming a poor man, dug it up and used it. A bailiff made some inquiry hereabouts after the pirates.
>
> Hosmer said that one thing which confirmed the diggers in their belief was the part that when he was a little boy, plowing one day with his father on the hillside, they found three old-fashioned bottles bottom upward but empty under the plow. Somebody consulted Moll Pitcher, who directed to dig at a certain distance from an apple tree on a line with the bottles, and then they would find the treasure. (*Journal,* 7:69–70)

61 **spiritualist's:** I emend from "spiritist's" in the MS on authority of this usage in the journal source, entry of July 19, 1856 (*Journal,* 8:419). Kerr, pp. 3–21, provides a good survey of the spiritualist fervor in America during the 1850s and the 1860s.

61 **Looking up, I . . . not yet spread over it:** The journal source of this passage is the entry of July 19, 1856 (*Journal*, 8:419).

62 **strong-tasted berries:** After this phrase in the MS Thoreau originally wrote "now ripe," but he later enclosed the phrase in parentheses, which I interpret to indicate deletion.

62 **clusters generally drooping:** Thoreau interlined in the MS here the following passages in very light, possibly erased pencil: "Picked seventy-three cymes, four without moving my hand, where a fine, dense wood now" and "What the English blackberry."

62 **this open pine grove:** After "pine grove" in the MS Thoreau wrote "(under Fair Haven) Hill," apparently using the parentheses to indicate deletion but misplacing his closing parenthesis, which should have been placed after "Hill."

62 **Josselyn says . . . color when ripe":** Josselyn, *An Account of Two Voyages*, p. 72. Thoreau modernizes and Americanizes Josselyn's spelling; the original reads, "The Gooseberry-bush, the berry of which is called Grosers or thorn Grapes, grow all over the Countrie, the berry is but small, of a red or purple colour when ripe."

63 **Lindley says . . . particularly abundant":** Lindley, p. 26.

63 **rapid growth of the rye:** Thoreau interlined in the MS here, "*Vide* October 31," almost certainly referring to his journal entry of that date in 1860, where he writes, "I hear the sound of the flail in M. Miles's barn, and gradually draw near to it from the woods, thinking many things. I find that the thresher is a Haynes of Sudbury, and he complains of the hard work and a lame back. Indeed, he cannot stand up straight. So all is not gold that glitters. This sound is not so musical after I have withdrawn. It was as well to have heard this music afar off." The page on which this passage is written contains many interlined passages—so many, in fact, that Thoreau appears to have written some of them where he did on the basis of there being space to write there rather than for the usual reason of establishing the sequence of passages. Based on the assumption that this was in fact the case and on Thoreau's usual practice (during the earliest stages of his composition process) of adding secondary sources after his own extracts, I move the paragraph interlined in the MS and beginning "Saint Pierre thinks" so that it follows all of the extracts from Thoreau's journal on this page.

63 **day of Concord Fight, 1775:** The Battle of Concord between British troops and American minutemen took place at the Old North Bridge on April 19, 1775.

63 **observed in the grass:** In the MS here Thoreau interlined in pencil "(*Vide* more May 26, 1854, and June 5, 1852, would come under Leaves, and June 1st, 1855.)" He refers to passages in his journal for each of those three dates, passages he very likely intended to insert into the text here. The passage of June 1, 1855, reads, "Rye, to my surprise, three or four feet high and glaucous" (*Journal*, 7:401). The passage for May 26, 1854, reads as follows:

[R]ye four feet high. The luxuriant and rapid growth of this hardy and valuable grass is always surprising. How genial must Nature be to it! It makes the revolution of the seasons seem a rapid whirl. How quickly and densely it clothes the earth! Thus early it suggest the harvest and fall. At sight of this deep and dense field all vibrating with motion and light, looking into the mass of its pale(?)-green culms, winter recedes many degrees in my memory. This the early queen of grasses with us(?). (*Journal*, 6:303) The passage from his journal entry of June 5, 1852, reads, "White clover now. Some rye fields are almost fully grown where it appears to have sown itself. It is commonly two feet high" (*Journal*, 4:81). This passage appears within the context of Thoreau writing at some length about the colors of plants in the landscape, with a suggestion that the muted colors of late spring anticipate the much more vibrant autumnal colors to come. For instance, he writes of the silvery cinquefoil that it is a "spring-yellow, sunny-yellow . . . flower [with] none of the fire of autumnal yellows in it" (*Journal*, 4:80). Thoreau's note that the passage about white clover in rye fields "would come under Leaves" is almost certainly an indication that he planned to use or was using this passage (and the longer passage it is a part of) in his work about leaves, which he most often called *The Fall of the Leaf*.

63   **Tusser's verse . . . for loitering men:** Tusser, p. 112. This is stanza 7 in Tusser's poem "May's Husbandry." The *Oxford English Dictionary* defines "scamble" thus: "To scatter (money, food) for a crowd to scramble for" and cites this verse of Tusser's as an example.

64   **It may be either:** Affixed with red sealing wax to the bottom of the MS page that ends here is a newspaper clipping titled "Curious Experiment in Botany," attributed in type at the end of the article to *"Chambers's Journal"* and with Thoreau's note of attribution as "Standard, July 28, 1855," probably the *National Anti-Slavery Standard*, which was published in Boston as an organ of the National Anti-Slavery Society:

IN Sicily there grows a wild grass, which, when ripe, at the end of summer, is gathered by the peasantry, tied in bundles, and set on fire; not, however, to be consumed, but for a mere scorching. The flame flies rapidly through the light husks and beard of the plant, and leaves the seeds slightly roasted, in which state they are eaten with considerable relish by numbers of the rural population. What the Sicilians do with their grass might be done with other grasses, and in other countries, were it not that the seeds generally are too small to repay the trouble of producing them for food. If all were but as large as those of the maize, or even wheat and barley, we should hear but few complaints of dear bread. Instances, indeed, are on record of grass-seeds having been largely eaten in times of scarcity, and with the desired effect of sustaining life, for all are more or less floury.

The botanical name of the Sicilian grass above mentioned is *Ægilops*, or goat's-eye—the Greeks having believed it to be a remedy for a disease that appears in one corner of the eye. There are three or four species growing all around the Mediter-

ranean, as well as in the islands, chiefly in the hot, dry, sandy plains near the sea. They flourish even on the scorched volcanic soils, in strange contrast to the prevalent aridity, showing the vital principle to be in them unusually energetic, and proof against extremes of heat. Moreover, the *Ægilops ovata,* as though sporting with its powers, shoots out another species, the *Triticoides,* or wheat-like, from one and the same root; not by artificial cultivation, be it understood, but spontaneously. Clearly, these goat-eyes are remarkable plants, and as we shall see presently, they have been experimented on with remarkable results.

M. Fabre, an enlightened agriculturalist, of Agde, in the South of France, considering these grasses to belong to the cerealia, began a series of careful experiments on the *Ægilops ovata,* with a view to ascertain what effect would be produced upon it by cultivation. A plot of ground, sheltered by high walls, and sufficiently distant from the fields of grass and other gramina, was prepared, and in this he sowed a few seeds in 1838. The plants grew from twenty to twenty-four inches high, and ripened by the middle of July in the following year; and though with but few fertile spikelets, the yield was in the proportion of *five* to *one.* Here was already a difference, best understood when we remember that in its wild state the *Ægilops* seldom grows higher than from six to nine inches with curved stalks, bearing a small flat rudimentary ear containing one or two grains. The stalks are extremely brittle, and when fully ripe the ears turn black and fall off, like the leaves from a tree. In these latter respects, M. Fabre's crop of 1839 retained its original habit, for the ears were deciduous, and the stalks broke easily; but we see a marked difference in height, and in amount of produce. The seeds were again sown; and in 1840, the spikelets were more numerous, scarcely an ear without two seeds, and these more floury than before, approaching the character of wheat. In 1841, the resemblance to wheat was still more observable; the ears, which were less flat, had from two to three grains, and the awns or beard had almost disappeared. In the next year, the plants stood still, being slightly attacked by rust; the number of grains, however, was not diminished. But in 1843, the delay was made up: the stalks grew three feet high, and stronger than in any previous season; the ears could not be easily broken off; the grains were plump; and one of the plants yielded 380 for 1; another 450 for 1. In 1844, every ear was full, and the grains not so densely coated as before; and in 1845, M. Fabre considered the transformation into wheat *(triticum)* complete: all the plants were true representatives of cultivated wheat.

Here, then, in seven years, we have a change effected by artificial means, which may be regarded as one of the most extraordinary phenomena of cultivation. The brief account we have given of the history of the experiments, shows by what a gradual progress a wild and comparatively useless grass was converted into one of our most valuable cereals; and more than this, the question as to the origin of wheat may now be considered as settled. Botanists have long repeated the statements, that our cultivated wheat once grew wild in Sicily, Babylonia and Persia; and here we have the explanation. No need now to assume the existence of a distinct variety; and already the first scientific agriculturists of France have come to the conclusion, that cultivated wheat, *tritica*, are only races of *Ægilops*.

Since 1845, M. Fabre has sown the seed, obtained with so much care, in an open field among vineyards by the roadside, and with a return of six or eight fold. The stems are straight and strong; the ears are round and beardless; the grains very floury; and in no single instance has there been any return to the form of the original *Ægilops ovata*. After this, who shall say what may or may not be effected by cultivation? The bearded wheat of Egypt is known to lose its beard when cultivated in England; and in some places the country people have a notion that our own wheat is changed into rye-grass in wet summers. This may be an error; but one thing is certain, that the more wheat is treated as a biennial, the better is the result.—*Chambers's Journal*.

64 **Saint Pierre thinks . . . them in a country":** Saint Pierre, 3:319.

64 **Alphonse De Candolle . . . and Mesopotamia:** De Candolle, 2:172.

64 **Touch-Me-Not [section]:** Compare this section with the later revision from *The Dispersion of Seeds* in "Related Passages," p. 248.

64 *(noli-me-tangere)*: "Touch-me-not" in Latin.

65 **Raw turnips. July fifteenth:** Thoreau wrote in the MS here *"Vide* scrap" and also (with a horizontal caret) "Turnips." The scrap he refers to is in the Berg Collection, "Miscellaneous Holograph Fragments" folder, no accession number, but reads, "Pulling turnips 329," which refers to p. 329 in his MS journal vol. 32, and which contains the paragraph following here in the text ("Another finger-cold evening . . . have not sown too many"). My source for the paragraph in the text is, in fact, Thoreau's MS journal vol. 32, p. 329. I add the date here, July fifteenth, on authority of the dating scheme of the other sections in which Thoreau entered nothing more than the name of the plant and the date.

65 **July fifteenth.** *Scheuchzeria*: After these words in the MS Thoreau noted, "See July 3, 1860, still green; and see January 10, 1855, and June 13, 1858, going to seed?" He appears to have intended to transcribe these passages from his journal into the MS at this location so that he could later work the passages up or otherwise revise them (a common technique of Thoreau's composition process, quite obvious later in this MS), so I omit what I take to be his note and incorporate in sequence and with their dates each of the three passages he refers to (*Journal*, 13:384, 7:111, 10:493, respectively).

65 *Scheuchzeria palustris*: When he first wrote this passage in his journal, Thoreau appears not to have been able to identify this species, but later he interlined its name in the passage without identifying where the name should be placed. I arbitrarily place the interlineation in this location.

66 **stale early in September:** Thoreau wrote in the MS here, "In prime August 28, 1856 or say the latter part of August. July 30, 1860 not yet in prime."

66   **time with the blueberries:** Thoreau wrote in the MS here, "(or the first week of August? or later? or say the 20th August? *Vide* below)," apparently referring by the last remark to one of the dated entries that follow in the text.

66   **In some swamps:** After this phrase in the MS Thoreau wrote, "(as Hubbard's)."

68   **emitting a different fragrance:** Thoreau interlined in the text here "laid bare by mowers July 30, 1860."

68   **has anything ripe or:** I add the word "or" here.

69   **attracted our attention:** Thoreau wrote "(whenever found)" after this phrase, the parentheses apparently indicating deletion.

69   **perchance like a banana:** After this phrase Thoreau wrote, "(or bread fruit)," the parentheses apparently indicating deletion.

69   **I suspect by mice:** After this clause Thoreau wrote, "(as April 1st, 1853)."

69   **eighteenth of July:** Thoreau wrote the following note after this date: "(July 26, 1860 turning)."

69   **some call it "eatable":** Emerson, *Report on Trees*, p. 453.

69   **Emerson and Gray . . . in this state:** Emerson, *Report on Trees*, p. 453; Gray (1848), p. 115 ("dark red"); Gray (1856), p. 128 ("rare"); Bigelow, *American Medical Botany*, 2:96.

69   **Hind, in *Report* . . . of the Savages":** Hind, *Narrative*, 1:101. About a third of Lake of the Woods falls within Minnesota, a small portion makes up the southeastern corner of the Canadian Province of Manitoba, and the largest portion of the lake is in the southwestern corner of the Province of Ontario. Hind found the *Cerasus pumila* abundant on a "sandy shore" of Garden Island, which lies within the Minnesota portion of Lake of the Woods between the Red Lake Indian Reservation and Big Island.

70   **the edges of swamps:** Thoreau wrote in the MS here, "(as C. Hubbard's and E. Hubbard's and Loring's)."

70   **some say "Amethystine blue":** I have not been able to locate the source of this quotation.

70   **size of large peas:** After "peas" Thoreau wrote and then enclosed in parentheses for deletion the phrase "—dark spotted."

70   **still perfect in form . . . checker the ground:** After "still" and "ground" Thoreau wrote, and then enclosed in parentheses for deletion, the phrases "the last 24th of July" ("24th" inserted in pencil) and "as if it were some select square in Nature's patch-work," respectively.

70   **twentieth—or how long?:** Thoreau interlined in the MS here "Beginning about August 12, 1860," and penciled in the left margin "N.B.," the abbreviation for *nota bene*, Latin for "note well."

70   **A month later . . . say September first:** Thoreau originally wrote this and the preceding sentence immediately after "how long?" in the preceding (*"Gnaphalium uliginosum"*) section, but Thoreau drew a circle around these two sentences and careted

them for insertion directly after *"Polygonatum pubescens"* (that is, before "is seen"), a location that makes no sense syntactically. I emend by moving the two sentences to this location.

70 **axils of the leaves:** After this phrase in the MS Thoreau wrote "(pendulous from the axil of the recurved stem)," the parentheses apparently indicating deletion.

71 **an inch in diameter:** Thoreau interlined in the MS here "July 27, 1860, green yet on island; hardly ripe August 12," apparently referring to the island in Fair Haven Bay, which he christened Witch Hazel Island in his journal entry of February 9, 1852 (*Journal*, 3:292).

71 **and you come . . . roadsides, but in some moist:** Thoreau originally wrote, "and you find these in some moist," but he later deleted "find" and interlined "come across these not by dusty roadsides, but. . . ." I therefore emend by omitting the undeleted "these."

72 **peculiar light pink:** Thoreau interlined in the MS here, *"Vide perhaps* August 27, 1857," a reference to the following passage, which is his entire journal entry for that date:

> P.M.—To Conantum, high blackberrying.
>
> Detected a, to me, new kind of high blackberry on the edge of the cliff beyond Conant's wall on Lee's ground—a long-peduncled (or pedicelled), leafy-racemed (somewhat panicled), erect blackberry. It has the aspect of *Rubus canadensis* become erect, three or four feet high. The racemes (or panicles?) leafy, with simple ovate and broad-lanceolate leaves; loose, few flowered (ten or twelve); peduncles (or pedicels) one to two or more inches long, often branched, with bracts midway, in fruit, at least, drooping. Perhaps the terminal flowers open first. Stem angular and furrowed much like that of *Rubus villosus,* leaf-stalks more prickly; leaves broader, thinner, and less pointed, smooth above; beneath, as well as young branches, much smoother than *Rubus villosus;* lower leaves ternate and, if I remember, sometimes quinate. Berries of good size, globular, of very few large grains, very glossy, of a lively flavor, when young of a peculiar light pink; sepals less recurved when ripe than those of *villosus*. It is apparently Bigelow's *Rubus frondosus* made a variety by Gray; but see flowers.

Thoreau refers to Bigelow, *Florula Bostoniensis,* pp. 199–200, and Gray (1848), pp. 125–26. Bigelow, p. 200, points out that *R. frondosus* "has probably been confounded with" *R. villosus,* and cites the differing petals (flowers) as one way to distinguish between the two, with those of the latter being "lance-ovate with wide intervals when expanded" and those of the former being "orbicular-ovate, much larger, and nearly in contact with each other when expanded."

72 **Gerarde says . . . to be eaten":** Gerarde, p. 1274.

72 **Wood, in his *New* . . . wild as the Indians":** William Wood, p. 19. Thoreau wrote this passage following in the left margin of the MS and careted it for insertion be-

tween the first and second lines of the MS (first line ends "to be ripe"). I emend by placing the passage after the opening, date-oriented paragraph.

72 **This is said . . . dried and bruised":** Although Thoreau apparently identifies his source for this quotation by interlining in the MS here "(*Vide* Disc. on Northwest Coasts, p. 311)," I have not been able to locate the source.

73 **blasted into a puff:** Thoreau interlined in pencil here, "(*Vide apples* elsewhere)." He later interlined "Wild" before *"apples."* Later still (probably when writing the "Lindley" extract, which is written in the same ink and appears on the MS page, for lack of space elsewhere, *under* the note about apples), Thoreau used a pen to draw a line under the *"apples"* note. It was after writing the *"apples"* note and the Lindley extract, I surmise, that he transcribed the "Yew" section onto the MS page from another MS page. Also, in faint and perhaps erased pencil at the very bottom of the MS page appears the note "Next comes Wild Apples." Further, the first page of the four-page folio sheet that these materials appear on is numbered "81," and the three sections immediately following the "Apples" section are on (in one instance keyed to be on) a MS page numbered "85." In sum, the available textual evidence indicates that the "Choke Cherry" section should precede the "Yew" section, to be followed by the "Apples" section, which should itself be followed by the "Alternate Cornel," *"Rubus sempervariens,"* and "Staghorn Sumac" sections, respectively.

73 **Lindley says . . . dangerous" to cattle:** Lindley, p. 147.

73 **The yew . . . September twelfth, at least:** After "twelfth" in the MS Thoreau interlined "(1858)," and after "at least" he interlined, "August 1st, 1860 say one week—or July 25." I emend by adding the article "The" and the Latin name, basing these emendations on an earlier draft of this passage, which reads, "The yew, *Taxus americana,* is ripe by August fifth and lasts till September twelfth at least."

74 **Wild Apples [section]:** I derive the text for this entire section from Thoreau's "Wild Apples" essay as published in *The Atlantic Monthly Magazine* for November 1862, pp. 515–26. The editors of *The Atlantic Monthly* applied their own house style to the MS Thoreau submitted to them on April 2, 1862, just over a month before his death; likewise, I have silently modified nonsubstantive elements of *The Atlantic Monthly* text to conform to the style I employ throughout this volume and describe in the headnote to "Editor's Notes" above, p. 286. I also silently omit the essay's internal section headings, which I do not think Thoreau would have used when incorporating "Wild Apples" back into *Wild Fruits.* Finally, based on evidence indicating that Thoreau wrote the first seventeen and last eight paragraphs of the essay specifically to serve as the published essay's introduction and conclusion (see MS drafts of those paragraphs, Houghton Library, Harvard University, call number bMS Am 278.5, folders 9a–9g), I omit those twenty-five paragraphs from *Wild Fruits* and place them in the "Wild Apples" section of "Related Passages" (see pp. 244–48).

74 **Pomona:** The Roman goddess of fruits.

75 **Pliny says . . . a load of them:** Pliny, *Historiæ Mundi*, bk. 13, chap. 55.

75 **Iduna's apples . . . destruction of the gods:** Sturluson, *Prose Edda*, p. 54. Thoreau also read about this Norse myth in Loudon as follows:

> In the *Edda*, we are told that the goddess Iduna had the care of apples which had the power of conferring immortality; and which were, consequently, reserved for the gods, who ate of them when they began to feel themselves growing old. The evil spirit Loke took away Iduna and her apple tree, and hid them in a forest, where they could not be found by the gods. In consequence of this malicious theft, every thing went wrong in the world. The gods became old and infirm; and, enfeebled both in body and mind, no longer paid the same attention to the affairs of the earth; and men, having no one to look after them, fell into evil courses, and became the prey of the evil spirit. At length, the gods finding matters get worse and worse every day, roused their last remains of vigour, and, combining together, forced Loke to restore the tree. (2:897)

According to translator Jean I. Young, "Iduna" is Icelandic for "One-who-renews"; Thjazi (Thjassi), a giant who appears in the form of an eagle, was an accomplice of Loki's in the abduction of Iduna; Thrymheim (Jötunheim) is the location of Thjazi's house; and "Ragnarök" is Icelandic for "Twilight of the Gods" (pp. 54, 54 n, 98).

75 **an ill wind . . . any good:** Bartlett states that this common proverb was first listed in John Heywood's *Proverbs* (1546), and shortly thereafter was used in Thomas Tusser's *Description of the Properties of Winds* and Shakespeare's *Henry IV, Part II* (act 5, scene 3, line 87).

75 **one year in a neighboring town:** On October 24, 1852, Thoreau and the poet William Ellery Channing, his neighbor and most regular walking companion, visited the town of Stow, which is about three miles southwest of Concord Center. While there they saw the apple trees, which Thoreau remarked upon in his journal entry of that date (*Journal*, 4:398).

75 **As an old English . . . to the folk":** I have not been able to locate a reference to the Old English manuscript Thoreau quotes from here.

76 **I talk with one . . . qualities leave it:** Thoreau identifies this person in his journal entry for October 16, 1856, as Wright (*Journal*, 9:115), possibly Anthony Wright, a local farmer whom he mentions a few times elsewhere in his journal.

76 **Some old English . . . full, too! / Huzza!:** Even though Thoreau appears to cite "Brand's *Popular Antiquities*" as his source for this material, he actually derived the material from Loudon, 2:899–900, who in turn cites two sources for the material that Thoreau quotes: the first (from "on Christmas eve" to "toast on the branches") is from "*Mrs. Bray's Borders of the Tamar and the Tavy*, vol. i, p. 335"; the other (from "encircling one of" to "Huzza!") is from "Hone's *Every Day Book*." In his "List of Books Referred To," Loudon expands these two sources thus: "Description of the Part of Devonshire bordering on the Tamar and Tavy; its Nat[ural] Hist[ory], &c. London,

1836. 3 vols. 8vo" (1:cxciv); and "Hone's (W.), Every-Day Book and Year Book. London, 1826. 3 vols. 8vo." (1:ccv). Based on this ascription of Loudon as Thoreau's source and on the difficulty of distinguishing the letters *r* and *z* in Thoreau's handwriting—a difficulty I have experienced and believe the compositors at *The Atlantic Monthly* experienced as they set Thoreau's manuscript in print after his death—I emend my source's (*Atlantic Monthly*) "Hurra!" to Loudon's "Huzza!" and follow Loudon's formatting of the poetry rather than my source's.

77 **Also what was called . . . sacrifice to Pomona":** Thoreau's source for this quotation has not been located. As mentioned above (note to p. 74), Pomona was the Roman goddess of fruits.

77 **Herrick sings . . . give them wassailing":** Herrick, 2:65, where the poem is titled "Another" and follows three poems titled (in order) "Ceremonies for Christmasse," "Christmas-Eve, Another Ceremonie," and "Another to the Maids." In this edition of Herrick, the last line of this poem reads "As you doe give them Wassailing."

77 **sing better than English Phillips did:** Thoreau refers here to the minor English poet John Philips (1676–1709), whose last poem, "Cyder, in Two Books" (1708), was a didactic imitation in Miltonic blank verse of Virgil's *The Georgics*. Thoreau read extracts of Philips's poem in Henry Phillips (no relation), 1:7, 1:53, and in Loudon, 2:901; in both of these sources the poet's name is spelled "Phillips."

77 *urbaniores,* **as Pliny calls them:** Pliny, *Historiæ Mundi*, bk. 16, chap. 32.

78 **The owners of this tract:** In his journal entry of October 20, 1857, Thoreau writes, "Warren Brown, who owns the Easterbrooks place, [on] the west side [of] the road, is picking barberries. Allows that the soil thereabouts is excellent for fruit, but it is so rocky that he has not patience to plow it. That is the reason this tract is not cultivated" (*Journal*, 10:111). I emend my source's (*Atlantic Monthly*) "plough" to "plow" even though Walker, p. 402, accepts "plough" as the proper spelling and, in fact, does not have the spelling "plow," because after the mid-1850s Thoreau consistently used the form "plow," as evidenced by his usage throughout the *Wild Fruits* MS.

78 **Going up . . . young apple tree:** Thoreau's journal source of this passage is actually his entry of September 14, 1859, which reads in part, "This wind has strewn the Fair Haven Hill-side with apples. I think that fully three quarters of all are on the ground. Many trees are almost entirely stripped, the whole crop lying in a circular form beneath, yet hard and green. Others on the hillside have rolled far down" (*Journal*, 12:325).

79 **not simply carried but:** I emend by deleting "as I have said" from my source, the *Atlantic Monthly* printing of the essay "Wild Apples," because I dropped the introductory portion of the essay, where Thoreau mentions that the wild apple "migrates with man, like the dog and horse and cow" ("Wild Apples," p. 180). For my rationale in dropping the introductory portion of the essay, see my note to p. 74.

79 **Wilder still, as I have said:** Interestingly, Thoreau does in fact *not* say this or anything similar to this earlier in the text or in his essay "Wild Apples," a clear indication that he did not have sufficient time in the weeks before his death to revise this material closely. An analogous instance occurs in his essay "Autumnal Tints," which he also hastily worked up and submitted to *The Atlantic Monthly* on February 20, 1862, just two and a half months before his death. In that essay he points out that "the two Aspens and the Sugar Maple come nearest to [the Scarlet Oak] in date," but nowhere previous to that mention of "the two Aspens" does he refer to an aspen ("Autumnal Tints," p. 399).

79 **"whose nature . . . modified by cultivation":** Michaux, 2:67, 68.

79 **Michaux says . . . of its perfume":** Michaux, 2:67, 68.

80 **I never saw . . . its northern limit:** Michaux, 2:68, explains that the crab apple "abounds above all, in the *Glades,* which is the name given to a tract fifteen or eighteen miles wide, on the summit of the Alleghanies, along the road from Philadelphia to Pittsburg." Thoreau left Concord on May 13, 1861, and traveled by rail and riverboat to Minnesota in a vain effort to regain his failing health. On May 23, en route from Chicago to Dunleith (now East Dubuque), Illinois, he glimpsed from his rail car what he thought might have been a crab-apple tree, *Pyrus coronaria* (*Minnesota Notebook*, p. 3); but he did not actually find it until June 11, when he was staying at a boarding house operated by one Mrs. Hamilton between Lake Calhoun and Lake Harriett, about three miles southwest of downtown Minneapolis. Thoreau that evening jotted in his notebook the following account of his day's discovery, which I edit slightly from the source (*Minnesota Notebook*, pp. 17–18):

She [Mrs. Hamilton] said the wild apple grew about her premises. Her husband first saw it on a ridge by the lake shore. They had dug up several and set them out, but all died. (The settlers also set out the wild plum and thimble berry and so on). So I went and searched in that very unlikely place, but could find nothing like it, though [Mrs.] Hamilton said there was one there three feet higher than the lake. But I brought home a thorn in bloom instead and asked if that was it. She then gave me more particular directions, and I searched again faithfully and this time I brought home an Amelanchier [shad-bush] as the nearest of kin, doubting if the apple had ever been seen there. But she knew both these plants. Her husband had first discovered it by the fruit. But she had not seen it in bloom here. Then called on Fitch and talked about it. [He] said it was found—the same they had in Vermont (?) and directed me to a Mr. [Jonathan T.] Grimes as one who had found it. He was gone to catch the horses to send his boy six miles for a doctor on ac[count] of the sick child. Evidently a [word] and enquiring man. The boy showed me some of the trees he had set out this spring. But they had all died, having a long tap root and being taken up too late. But then I was convinced by the sight of the just expanding though withered flower bud to analyze. Finally stayed and went in search of it with the father in his pasture, where I found it first myself, quite a cluster of them.

80 **those backwoodsmen among the apple trees:** Thoreau is thinking here, in his reference to "backwoodsmen," of men such as James Beckworth and James Bridger, men we now more commonly refer to as "mountain men."

80 **Nobscot Hill, in Sudbury:** The summit of Nobscot Hill is actually just over the southern border of Sudbury in Framingham, about nine miles south-southwest of Concord Center.

80 **In two years' time 't had thus . . . And cut it down a span:** I have not been able to locate the source of these lines.

81 **the scrubby fir . . . than anything else:** Thoreau is thinking here of his experience on Mount Katahdin (elevation 5,268 feet) in central Maine on September 6, 1846, which he describes in the "Ktaadn" chapter of *The Maine Woods* as follows:

> Leaving this [a "torrent" or mountain spillway] at last, I began to work my way, scarcely less arduous than Satan's anciently through Chaos, up the nearest, though not the highest peak. At first scrambling on all fours over the tops of ancient black spruce-trees (*Abies nigra*), old as the flood, from two to ten or twelve feet in height, their tops flat and spreading, and their foliage blue, and nipt with cold, as if for centuries they had ceased growing upward against the bleak sky, the solid cold. I walked some good rods erect upon the tops of these trees. . . . Here the principle of vegetation was hard put to it. There was apparently a belt of this kind running quite round the mountain, though, perhaps, nowhere so remarkable as here. . . . This was the sort of garden I made my way over, for an eighth of a mile, at the risk, it is true, of treading on some of the plants, not seeing any path through it,—certainly the most treacherous and porous country I ever travelled. (*Maine Woods*, pp. 60–61)

82 **the numerous varieties . . . Van Mons and Knight:** Jean-Baptiste Van Mons and Thomas Andrew Knight were famous pomologists from Belgium and England, respectively.

83 **Porter and the Baldwin:** These were the two principal varieties of apples grown in southern New England during Thoreau's time.

83 **The celestial fruits . . . to pluck them:** In Greek and Roman mythology, Hercules had to perform twelve labors to atone for killing his children, and the eleventh labor was to retrieve golden apples from a walled garden owned by nymphs called the Hesperides and guarded by the dragon Ladon. Hercules enlisted the assistance of Atlas, who plucked the apples of the Hesperides while Hercules temporarily held the world aloft.

83 **As Palladius says, "*Et injussu . . .* fruit of an unbidden apple tree:** Thoreau's source for Palladius is known to be *Scriptores Rei Rusticæ*, but I have not been able to identify the page where this quotation appears.

83 **"inteneration":** The *Oxford English Dictionary* defines this as a synonym of "soften-ing" and quotes Evelyn's *Pomona*, which is doubtless where Thoreau came across the word, as follows: "The pleasanter or plumper or larger Apple being the effect of some Inteneration."

83 **highest plot / To plant the Bergamot:** The bergamot pear, a popular winter pear cul-tivated in Britain since the time of the Romans, is a large, round fruit with a yellowish-green skin that has russet markings. Thoreau's source for this quotation has not been located.

84 **wild-eyed woman . . . after all the world:** The passage may be an allusion to the woman in John Keats's poem "La Belle Dame sans Merci," who is described as "a lady in the meads" whose "eyes were wild" (stanza 4), but Thoreau may also allude to the most famous gleaner, Ruth. (Compare with the note above to p. 54).

84 **"the custom of . . . to collect them":** Loudon, 2:901.

84 *Fruits and Fruit Trees of America:* I emend by italicizing this, the title of Down-ing's book.

84 **An old farmer . . . bow-arrow tang":** Thoreau does not identify who this "old farmer" is, but on a few occasions he makes much in his journal of George Minott's abilities to tell a good story and select the right word (see, for instance, his journal entries of October 4, 1851, and January 28, 1858; *Journal,* 3:40–43 and 10:264–66, respectively). Just over a month after a long talk with Minott, Thoreau uses the phrase "bow-warrow tang" to describe the speech of a Chippeway lecturer he had heard, equating "bow-arrow tang" with an "unsubdued Indian accent" (entry of March 5, 1858; *Journal,* 10:291). He also uses the phrase in "The Allegash and East Branch" chapter of *The Maine Woods,* p. 169, where he attributes the phrase to "my neighbor."

85 **Loudon quotes . . . sweet and insipid":** Loudon, 2:897. As usual, Thoreau Ameri-canizes the spelling of "flavour." Loudon quotes from John Duncumb, *General View of the Agriculture of the County of Hereford . . .* (London, 1805), p. 84.

85 **Evelyn says . . . their cider-vat":** Evelyn reprints Dr. John Newburgh's article "Ob-servations Concerning the Making and Preserving of Cider" on pp. 390–95, and this quotation is from p. 395.

85 **when Tityrus, seeing . . . *poma, castaneæ molles:*** Virgil, *Eclogues,* bk. 1, lines 80–81. The Loeb Classical Edition of *Eclogues* translates the phrase "ripe apples, mealy chestnuts" (p. 9).

86 **Peter Whitney . . . parts of the tree:** Whitney actually writes, "The apples are fair, and, when fully ripe, of a yellow colour, but, evidently, of different tastes—sour and sweet. . . . Two apples growing side by side, on the same limb, will be often of these different tastes, the one all sour, and the other all sweet. And, which is more re-markable, the same apple will frequently be sour on one side, end or part, and the

other sweet, and that not in any order or uniformity nor is there any difference in the appearance of the one part from the other" (p. 386).

86 **a kind of plum tree in Provence . . . eaten them, from their sourness":** Loudon, 2:687. Although Loudon does not italicize "prunes sibarelles," I do because of my policy to italicize foreign words. Also, I emend my source (*Atlantic Monthly*), which has *"Prunes sibarelles,"* almost certainly capitalizing the first word because the editor thought this was the Latin name of the plant rather than a French name. The word *sibarelles* was apparently derived from the Latin *sibilus*, which means "a hissing" or "a whistling."

87 **Nor is it every apple I desire . . . an apple from the tree of life!:** I have not been able to locate the source of these lines.

87 **apples not of Discord, but of Concord!:** In Greek legend, Eris, the goddess of Discord, tossed a golden apple inscribed "to the fairest" amongst the guests at a wedding celebration to which she had not been invited. Although claimed by three of the goddesses in attendance, it eventually ended up in the hands of Aphrodite, the goddess of Love. Thoreau, of course, is playing on the name of his hometown.

88 **In 1836 there were in the garden . . . fourteen hundred distinct sorts:** Loudon, 2:895.

89 **the Wood Apple (*Malus sylvatica*) . . . numerous to mention—all of them good:** Thoreau lists twenty-seven apple species here, twelve with their Latin names. In his journal entries of May 23 and 29, 1851 (*Journal, Volume 3*, pp. 232–33, 241), he lists an additional forty-nine species. These listings are for the most part fanciful. In his comment on the Saunterer's Apple, he may intend an echo to the sentence in "The Village" chapter of *Walden*, "Not till we are lost, in other words, not till we have lost the world, do we begin to find ourselves, and realize where we are and the infinite extent of our relations" (p. 171). The Native American name for the Concord River was Musketaquid. The Latin *"Cholera morbifera aut dysenterifera,"* refers to the gastrointestinal disorders, cholera morbus and dysentery, while *"puerulis dilectissima"* means "esteemed by young boys." The compound word *"pedestrium-solatium"* translates to "solitary-walker." On August 8, 1851, Thoreau saw "three scythes hanging on an apple tree" (*Journal*, 2:381–82); Senator Daniel Webster, who was extremely well known during Thoreau's time, told a story that became widely known of better appreciating the form of a scythe hanging in an apple tree than the form of one grasped in his own hand (*The New England Farmer*, p. 315). For information on Iduna and Loki, see the note above to p. 75.

89 **Bodæus exclaims . . . these *wild apples*:** Theophrastus, p. 398. Johannes Bodæus, the Latin commentator of this volume, adapts Virgil's *Georgics*, bk. 2, lines 42–44, which reads, *"Non ego cuncta meis amplecti versibus opto, / Non mihi si linguæ centum sint oraque centum, / Ferrea vox,"* and which the Loeb Classic Edition translates, "Not mine the wish to embrace all the theme within my verse, not though I had a

hundred tongues, a hundred mouths, and a voice of iron!" (p. 119). Bodæus adapts Virgil by omitting the first clause, slightly modifying the second clause, and adding a clause of his own: "*Non mihi si linguæ centu essent, oraque centum, / Ferrea vox omnes malum comprendere formas, / Omnia pomorum percurrer nomina possem*" (p. 398). Thoreau translates Bodæus directly, but where Thoreau uses "*wild apples,*" Bodæus wrote, "fruits" (*pomorum*).

90 **with a leaf . . . mouldy cellar):** In March 1837 Curzon visited the library of the Souriani monastery in the Nitrian Desert near the Natron Lakes (*Wadi an Natrun*), sixty miles northwest of Cairo, Egypt. A blind abbott showed him an oil cellar filled knee-deep with rotting fragments of ecclesiastical manuscripts, some of which the monks occasionally used to cover pots of preserves. Curzon purchased many of the manuscripts and returned with them to England, where they are now in the British Museum (Curzon, p. 88).

90 **Topsell's *Gesner* . . . time to come":** Topsell, p. 278.

92 **I have heard of . . . made into cider:** Thoreau wrote in his journal entry of November 13, 1857, about Stedman Buttrick telling him about this orchard, which was "in the town of Russell" (*Journal*, 10:177). Russell, Massachusetts, is a small community on the Westfield River fourteen miles west of Springfield.

92 **apples in a barrel:** I drop the final paragraph and offset quotation from my source, the *Atlantic Monthly* printing of "Wild Apples," because the existence of an early-draft MS of this passage in the Houghton Library at Harvard University (call number bMS Am 278.5, folder 9G) suggests that Thoreau did not include this passage in *Wild Fruits* but instead composed it solely as a conclusion for the essay.

92 **Alternate cornel:** After this phrase in the MS Thoreau wrote, "July 26, 1854, a day or 2," and in the margin beside this he wrote, "N.B.," which is the Latin abbreviation for "note well" (*nota bene*).

92 **drop off. It:** I emend by adding the word "It."

92 **witch-like nevertheless:** I emend by omitting from after the paragraph ending here the following passage, which is redundant: "August 2, 1854. How interesting the small alternate cornel trees with often a flat top, a peculiar ribbed and green leaf, and pretty red stems supporting its harmless blue berries, inclined to drop off."

93 **The *Rubus* . . . say the twenty-fifth:** Thoreau wrote in pencil at the top of the MS page that begins with this sentence, "Next after apple." After "*sempervariens*" he interlined "ripe 26, 1860" in pencil. Also, I emend by adding "the" before "twenty-fifth."

93 **hollows in the woods:** Thoreau wrote in the MS here, "(for example, at Lincoln hard by Walden)."

94 **Staghorn sumac:** After this phrase in the MS Thoreau wrote, "(ours are injured by worms?)."

95 **poisonous to eat?:** In the margin beside this phrase in the MS Thoreau wrote, "*Are not.*"

95   **Gerarde thus describes . . . heal the hurt places:** Gerarde, pp. 349–50. In this instance Thoreau spelled Gerarde's name without the terminal *e*, a common alternate spelling, so I emend by adding it to conform with Thoreau's usual spelling.

97   **Perhaps fruits . . . attracts birds to them:** Thoreau wrote *"Vide* thorn" here, apparently as a reminder to himself that he used this same sentence in the "Thorn" section (see p. 137), but he deleted the sentence in neither location.

97   **Sagard in his . . . there were any here":** Sagard, *Le Grand Voyage,* p. 327. Thoreau appears not to have translated the French phrase *"viennent quasi contre terre"* because the verb *"viennent"* is here used in an unusual manner. The phrase could be translated more literally as "comes almost on the ground" but more accurately means "grows almost on the ground."

98   **Michaux says . . . American forests":** Michaux, 2:205.

98   **appear silent and deserted:** After this paragraph Thoreau wrote, "(if necessary *Vide* August 29, 1854 or *Miscellaneous p. 48—and September 1, 1859).*" Thoreau refers in the first of these notes to his journal entry for August 29, 1854, which contains the following sentence: "Many birds nowadays resort to the wild black cherry tree, as here front [*sic*] of Tarbell's. I see them continually coming and going directly from and to a great distance—cherry-birds, robins, and kingbirds." The passage about cherries on p. 48 of Thoreau's 112-page "Miscellaneous" draft (Berg Collection, "Notes on Fruits" folder, accession number 375) is simply a transcript of the journal sentence and reads, "Many birds now-a-days resort to the wild black cherry trees. I see them (behind Tarbell's) continually coming and going directly from and to a great distance—cherry birds, robins, and kingbirds." In a penciled note at the end of this passage on Miscellaneous, p. 48, Thoreau wrote, *"Vide* below," referring to a sentence from his entry of August 30, 1854, transcribed onto Miscellaneous, p. 48, and revised to read as follows: "No berries to pluck in my walk, unless black cherries and apples mainly—the huckleberries being dried up or wormy." Thoreau's last note, *"September 1, 1859,"* refers to the following paragraph from his journal entry of September 1, 1859:

> If you would study the birds now, go where their food is—that is, the berries— especially to the wild black cherries, elderberries, poke berries, mountain-ash berries, and ere long the barberries, and for pigeons the acorns. In the sproutland behind Britton's Camp, I came to a small black cherry full of fruit, and then, for the first time for a long while, I see and hear cherry birds—their shrill and fine seringo—and the note of robins, which of late are scarce. We sit near the tree and listen to the now unusual sounds of these birds, and from time to time one or two come dashing from out the sky toward this tree, till, seeing us, they whirl, disappointed, and perhaps alight on some neighboring twigs and wait till we are gone. The cherry birds and robins seem to know the locality of every wild cherry in the town. You are as sure to find them on them now, as bees and butterflies on the thistles. If we stay long, they

go off with a fling to some other cherry tree, which they know of but we do not. The neighborhood of a wild cherry full of fruit is now, for the notes of birds, a little spring come back again, and when, a mile or two from this, I was plucking a basketful of elderberries (for which it was rather early yet), there too, to my surprise, I came on a flock of golden robins and of bluebirds, apparently feeding on them. Excepting the vacciniums, now past prime and drying up, the cherries and elderberries are the two prevailing fruits now. We had remarked on the general scarcity and silence of the birds, but when we came to the localities of these fruits, there again we found the berry-eating birds assembled,—young (?) orioles and bluebirds at the elderberries.

99 **first of August:** I emend the MS from "tenth of August" because Thoreau indicates that this section should be moved from that date to August first.

99 **"red and black currants":** Josselyn, *New-Englands Rarities,* p. 51.

99 **Hound's-Tongue [section]:** Compare the "Hound's-Tongue" section in "Related Passages," pp. 248–49, for a later version of this passage that Thoreau used in *The Dispersion of Seeds* (pp. 98–99).

99 **the nutlets in:** After "nutlets" in the MS Thoreau originally began writing "with my handkerchief," but he stopped, deleted the first few letters of "handkerchief," wrote "pocket" instead, and then continued by writing "with" again; but he failed to change his first "with" to "in." I therefore emend by changing "with" after "nutlets" to "in."

99 **a young lady . . . on her dress:** The young lady was Edith Emerson, Thoreau's sister was Sophia Thoreau, and Edith's mother was Lydia Emerson, wife of Ralph Waldo Emerson (Thoreau, *Journal* 11:149; entry of September 6, 1858).

100 **thenceforward till winter:** Thoreau interlined in the MS here "(as November 20)." In none of his journal entries for 20 November between 1850 and 1860 does Thoreau mention thistledown, but in the entry for 22 November 1860 he wrote, "Every plant's down glitters with a silvery light along the Marlborough Road—the sweet-fern, the *Lespedeza,* and bare blueberry twigs, to say nothing of the weather-worn tufts of *Andropogon scoparius*" (*Journal,* 14:258).

100 **pulling them to pieces:** Thoreau interlined in his MS here "(as September 4, 1860)."

100 **The Romans . . . with this genus:** Pliny, *Natural History,* bk. 10, chap. 57.

100 **Mudie . . . species are soon added":** Mudie, 2:54.

100 **one afternoon last year:** Thoreau interlined in the MS here "(1860, also Fair Haven Pond, August 19 another year)." The journal source of the passage in the text is the entry of August 26, 1860; the other reference is to his entry of August 19, 1858, where he writes about seeing thistledown sailing over Fair Haven Pond (*Journal,* 11:114).

101 **a wise balloonist for you, crossing its Atlantic:** Readers of Thoreau's time may have recognized the pun here. The era's most famous balloonist was John Wise, who by the fall of 1859 had completed about five hundred ascensions in balloons and who

was soon thereafter to achieve even greater fame by his aeronautical contributions during the American Civil War. According to "Balloons" (see "Works Cited"), Wise's most famous voyage before the fall of 1859 was "from St. Louis to the lakes, a distance of 1,200 miles"; he felt that "the certain existence of a current to the East [would] enable him to cross the Atlantic in a balloon."

101 **Theophrastus . . . a very high wind":** Theophrastus, bk. 3, chap. 27.

101 **Phillips . . . the approaching tempest!":** Henry Phillips, 1:6–7.

102 **Maine earlier than here:** Thoreau inserted in the MS at the end of this sentence: "Sophia found red cohosh berries in New Hampshire July 9th in 1860."

102 **Cornutus evidently . . . *niveis et rubris"*:** Cornut, p. 76. The Latin sentence may be translated, "Aconitum berries snowy and red," aconitum being any plants of the genus of that name, which are usually bluish-flowered poisonous herbs of the buttercup family, including the monkshood, once used as a sedative.

102 **sixth in some places:** Thoreau interlined in the MS here "some full grown August 10, 1860."

103 **the latter part of:** Thoreau interlined in the MS here "(August 23rd, 1858)."

103 **Some think it . . . much they are injured:** Loudon, 2:911.

103 **into which he rakes:** After "rakes" Thoreau wrote, "(hauling)." I interpret his parentheses as an indication that he intended to delete this word.

103 **Some regard the pear- . . . from the round ones:** Thoreau writes in his journal entry for September 5, 1854, "[Samuel] Barrett shows me some very handsome pear-shaped cranberries, not uncommon, which may be a permanent variety different from the common rounded ones" (*Journal*, 7:15).

103 **one picking over . . . apart from the others:** Identified in Thoreau's journal of November 20, 1850, as Horace Hosmer (*Journal*, 8:105).

104 **I once came near . . . them at in Boston:** Thoreau explains in his journal source for this passage, his entry of November 20, 1853 (*Journal*, 5:512), that it was the commercial failure of his first book, *A Week on the Concord and Merrimack Rivers*, published in 1849 at his own expense, that prompted him to consider speculating in cranberries. He also points out that he went to New York City during the fall of 1849 to sell a thousand dollars worth of pencils that he had manufactured in his family's pencil shop so that he could "pay an assumed debt of a hundred dollars." Quincy Market was and still is a shopping district in downtown Boston.

105 **Old Foster:** *Concord Births, Marriages, and Deaths* mentions a son born to "Asa-F. Foster & Almira his wife" in Concord on September 15, 1828 (p. 301), which is approximately the time this incident took place, for Thoreau would have turned twelve years of age on July 12, 1829.

105 *Geological Survey* . . . **formation of the ice":** Thoreau extracted this passage into his "Common Place Book 2," p. 203, from an unidentified copy of *Geological Survey of Canada* owned by his neighbor and friend, Franklin Sanborn. Apparently San-

born's volume contained reports of the surveys that had been conducted for the four years Thoreau lists. In any case, immediately after writing this passage in "Common Place Book 2," Thoreau writes, "In James Richardson's Report on the Island of Anticosti for 1856, p. 199—(with a complete map in it)." I include a later version of Richardson's *Report* in "Works Cited" below because Thoreau alludes to that work once in *Wild Fruits* and quotes from it another time in *Wild Fruits* (see the notes for pp. 59 and 177, respectively). Probably an earlier version of Richardson's *Report* was included as a monograph or essay in the larger *Geological Survey of Canada* volume that Thoreau quotes from here. In "Common Place Book 2," Thoreau writes, "the only *difficulties . . . were* the small amount their canoes were capable of conveying at a time" (p. 203, my emphases and ellipsis). Lake Nipissing is in Ontario, about 160 miles north of Toronto.

105 **cleared in March:** After "March" in the MS, Thoreau wrote, "(19–22)."

106 **for this salad or:** Thoreau interlined in the MS here, "March 22d, 1854 shores stream with cranberries."

106 **afford in the spring:** Thoreau interlined in the MS here "May 7, 1852."

106 **Harwich and Provincetown on Cape Cod:** Two towns that Thoreau visited during trips to Cape Cod on (as he notes interlinearly on his MS) "July 5, 1855, and June 17, 1857." Provincetown is at the tip of Cape Cod, and Harwich is located just west of Chatham, which is at the southeastern extremity of Cape Cod.

106 **set in the coarse white:** After this phrase in the MS Thoreau wrote, "(? sometimes)."

107 **uniform green bed, very striking and handsome:** This phrase appears on two MS pages in the Berg Collection's "Notes on Fruits" folder, accession numbers 164 and 307. Of these two pages, the former, 164, is the later draft. After the "uniform green bed" phrase on the earlier draft, 307, Thoreau penciled in the notes *"Vide* account of running from Foster—October 19, 1859" and *"Vide* back Hops September 6." After the "uniform green bed" phrase on the later draft, 164, is the note *"Vide* account of my running away from Old Foster written since October 19th 1859." The notes about "Old Foster" are clearly Thoreau's reminders to incorporate that paragraph into this section ("Common Cranberry"). Although the note about hops on the earlier draft, 307, suggests that Thoreau may have intended to move that section (see p. 177) to this location, I believe the note is instead a reminder from the earlier draft to move the section from this location to where it is now located; however, I have not found any evidence to indicate that the "Hop" section was located here in an earlier draft of *Wild Fruits.*

107 **John Josselyn . . . admixed when ripe":** Josselyn, *New-Englands Rarities Discovered,* pp. 52, 57.

107 **their third winter . . . preserved meats:** Thoreau wrote "(?)" after "Parry," querying his recollection of a book he had read in 1844, some seventeen years earlier. His

actual source for this image was Kane, p. 146. Thoreau had used the same image of piling empty cans of preserved meats as a "sign" in the second paragraph of *Walden's* "Conclusion" (p. 321).

108 **root, as the oldest:** At the end of this sentence Thoreau interlined, "August 31, 1852. Methinks I am in better spirits and physical health now that melons are ripe—that is, for three weeks past." He may have intended this sentence to be inserted here.

108 **like a mildew:** Thoreau had originally written "fresh mildew," but he later enclosed the adjective in parentheses, apparently to indicate deletion.

108 **through and through:** I emend from "through and through and through."

108 **quirl:** The *Oxford English Dictionary* cites *quirl* as a variant of *querl*, which it defines as "A curl, twist, twirl." Here, presumably, it is the base of the twisting stem.

108 **One man told me . . . father's dominions:** In his journal source of this passage (entry of August 27, 1859; *Journal*, 12:298–99), Thoreau does not identify this man or any of his children. Thoreau probably derived the phrase "father's dominions" from Sturluson (*Heimskringla*, 2:48, bk. 13), who writes, "The priest Are Frode says that Earl Hakon was thirteen years earl over his father's dominions in Throndhjem district before the fall of Harald Grafeld. . . ."

108 **convicted himself out of his own mouth:** "Daniel had convicted them of false witness by their own mouth" (*Aprocrypha*, Susanna, 61).

108 **not fit to be . . . Confucius's standard:** In *The Great Learning*, Confucius says, "In order rightly to govern the state, it is necessary first to regulate the family."

108 **had designed on it:** After this paragraph in the MS Thoreau penciled the note, " 'You can't carry two melons under one arm.' Miss Minot," which I omit from this location because the sentence is clearly a reminder to include the saying somewhere in this section, which he does later in the section (see note after next).

108 **today:** Identified by the journal source as September 2, 1859 (*Journal*, 12:312).

108 **you cannot carry . . . under one arm:** On another MS page Thoreau attributes this saying to "Miss [Mary] Minot," a tailoress who lived with her brother George on Lexington Road in Concord.

108 **a lady who had . . . streets of Concord:** Likely this lady was Mary Minot, who spoke of the difficulty of carrying watermelons (see previous note), but I have located no other evidence to identify her as the protagonist of this story.

109 **said to be unknown to the Greeks and Romans:** Thoreau's source for this allusion has not been located.

109 **one of those fruits . . . name of *abbattichim*:** A reference to Numbers 11:5, "We remember the fish, which we did eat in Egypt freely; the cucumbers, and the melons, and the leeks, and the onions, and the garlick." The Hebrew word for *melons* is usually transliterated as *"ha'avatichim."*

109 **The nearest that Gerarde . . . bark is eaten":** Gerarde, p. 914. In this instance Thoreau spelled Gerarde's name without the terminal *e*, a common alternate spelling, so I emend by adding it to conform with Thoreau's usual spelling. I also emend by supplying terminal punctuation and the close-quotation mark.

109 **In Spense's *Anecdotes* . . . very little value":** Spence, p. 76. Ludovico Ariosto's romantic epic, *Orlando Furioso* (1532), was widely admired in nineteenth-century America.

109 **Montaigne says . . . in my garden' ":** Montaigne, p. 63 (set. 1, cap. 41). At the bottom of the MS scrap containing this sentence, Thoreau wrote, "*N.B.* These must have been muskmelons." This scrap is affixed with sealing wax to another MS scrap (which is in turn affixed with sealing wax to a full-size MS page) that reads on one side "Gerarde says of the Bramble common 'the ripe fruit is sweet and containeth in it much juice of a temperate heat, therefore it is not unpleasant to be eaten' " (Gerarde, p. 1274). The other side of this scrap reads, "raw, but more commonly boiled,' & even Loudon tells us that 'This fruit should be eaten by Europeans with great caution' and he describes some of the bad causes [word] which follow after the eating of it." I have not yet located this quotation in Loudon.

109 **Gosse, in his *Letters* . . . conserve for winter:** Gosse, *Letters from Alabama*, pp. 195, 196. Thoreau wrote this extract on a loose scrap in the MS and did not indicate where in the text the extract should be placed. I place the material here based on the MS scrap's position following the MS leaves containing the preceding several paragraphs. Also, I emend by omitting and altering quotation marks to accommodate the offset format, by adding "it" in the clause beginning "but it is abundant," and by omitting "says," which Thoreau had inserted in the quotation (but outside quotation marks) to serve as a transition between the sentences ending "specimens than their masters" and beginning "it may be considered."

110 **ripe by August seventh:** Thoreau wrote "August 19, 1860 just beginning" above this date in the MS.

110 **twenty-second of August:** Thoreau wrote "(1852)" after this date in the MS.

110 **seen the elderberry:** I emend by expanding "elder" to "elderberry" here.

111 **They are said to make a good dye:** Loudon, 2:1029.

111 **About the first of . . . late to gather them:** Thoreau drew a vertical pencil line through this paragraph, which likely indicates that he intended to delete the entire paragraph.

111 **assembled where they grow:** Thoreau wrote in the MS here, "(as September 1, 1859)."

112 **say August eighth:** Thoreau interlined the following notes in the MS here: "*Vide* Scrap on Michaux; *Vide* January 24, 1855; July 26, 1860 green—August 10 begins to be ripe." I have not located the scrap on Michaux, and the latter two notes are

two more of many such indications that Thoreau returned from his daily walks during the July–September 1860 period and interlined his observations directly into his burgeoning *Wild Fruits* MS, which he worked on regularly during that time, as well as later. Usually during that time he did not even bother to mention these observations on fruits in his journal entries. In his entry of January 24, 1855, he quotes William Wood's "plumbs of the country" passage, which follows in the MS here, and then writes, "Yet Emerson has not found the yellow plum, that is, Canada, growing wild in Massachusetts" (*Journal*, 7:134), a reference to Emerson, *Report on Trees*, p. 449–50.

112 **William Wood . . . reasonable good taste":** William Wood, p. 19.

112 **Cartier speaks . . . as the French do:** Thoreau's source for Cartier is known (see "Works Cited"), but I have not been able to identify the page where this quotation appears.

112 **Josselyn found round . . . those in England:** Josselyn, *New-Englands Rarities Discovered*, p. 51.

112 **Nuttall, in his *North* . . . mixture of both colors:** Nuttall, 2:29.

113 **ripe about August eighth:** After this sentence in the MS Thoreau wrote, "August 26, 1860 ripe, how long?"

113 **August tenth in 1854 . . . August twelfth in 1853:** I emend by adding both instances of "in" here.

114 **Theophrastus speaks . . . the seed in milk:** Theophrastus, bk. 7, chap. 3. Theodore Gaza (ca. 1400–75) is best known for his translations of Aristotle.

114 **Columella adds . . . the seed in *musa*:** Thoreau's source for Columella is known to be *Scriptores Rei Rusticæ*, but I have not been able to identify the page where this quotation appears.

114 **(the *cucumis*):** Thoreau interlined in ink the two words in parentheses here without deleting "it," so I emend by adding the parentheses.

114 **Palladius says . . . dry rose leaves:** Thoreau's source for Palladius is known to be *Scriptores Rei Rusticæ*, but I have not been able to identify the page where this quotation appears.

114 **these verses of Columella's . . . teach to swim:** Thoreau's source for Columella is known to be *Scriptores Rei Rusticæ*, but I have not been able to identify the page where this quotation appears.

115 **De Candolle, speaking . . . likens it to women:** De Candolle, 2:906. The words "writing in" added. Emended from ". . . bad indeed.' & in this. . . ."

115 **Gerarde writes . . . *Muschatellini,* or musk melons":** Gerarde, p. 918. In this instance Thoreau spelled Gerarde's name without the terminal *e*, a common alternate spelling, so I emend by adding it to conform with Thoreau's usual spelling. I also emend by adding "Of" and "writes" to the clause introducing the quotation.

115 **Saint Pierre . . . among a neighborhood":** Saint Pierre, 3:311–12.

115 **before they are sweet:** At the end of this section in the MS Thoreau wrote, *"Vide* (if necessary) how they bear snow about February 16, 1860," but in his journal Thoreau does not mention either muskmelons or melons or potatoes in this context anywhere near this date.

115 **eleventh of August:** Thoreau wrote, "begin about July 20, 1860" in the MS here, another of many such indications that he was working on this MS at that time.

115 **My neighbor . . . covered them up again:** Thoreau does not identify the neighbor in his journal source (*Journal,* 2:309).

116 **the rapid increase of the population of New York:** During the 1850s the growth of New York City was so dramatic that it made national headlines on a regular basis and caused massive problems with a continually stressed urban infrastructure. I omit from here the sentence, enclosed in parentheses apparently to indicate deletion, "(I am the more contented with the place where any lives have fallen.)."

116 **A man:** Thoreau does not identify this man in his journal source (*Journal,* 13:425).

117 **the shade of his ancestral trees:** According to Bartlett, in "The Homes of England," the early nineteenth-century poet Felicia Dorothea Hemans wrote of how beautifully English homes stood "Amidst their tall ancestral trees, / O'er all the pleasant land!"

117 **Potatoes are so abundant this year . . . Davis seedlings as big as robins:** Thoreau wrote this sentence hastily in pencil, making the words difficult to recover. I feel confident that I recovered all of them correctly except "smarter" and "robins," both of which should be regarded as conjectural. According to "American Institute Farmers Club" (see "Works Cited"), a Davis seedling is "a red potatoe [*sic*], very white inside," and is an "abundant yielder . . . one of the most valuable potatoes in cultivation."

117 **a field *d'or* or *d'argent*:** In heraldry, the field is the background of the shield, which is the principal vehicle for displaying heraldic devices. Fields of gold (*d'or*) and of silver (*d'argent*) are often displayed in yellow and white, respectively.

117 **An Irishman . . . seventy-five bushels apiece:** I have not been able to identify this Irishman.

117 **see me going across-lots:** By "going across-lots" Thoreau means that he did not stay on established paths or roads but instead cut across the lots owned by his neighbors. After this sentence he mistakenly careted for insertion here the passage below dated "October 16, 1859," which I move to its proper location, after the following sentence.

118 **owner . . . this farmer:** I have not been able to identify this farmer.

118 **It is commonly stated . . . correctly referred to:** Thoreau read a very detailed history of the "potatoe" (this is also Thoreau's spelling throughout the MS, but I emend it to our modern spelling) in Henry Phillips, 2:78–89, who prefaces his account with the following observations:

Peter Cicca, in his Cronical [*sic*], printed in 1553, tells us, that the inhabitants of Quito and its vicinity have, besides maize, a tuberous root which they eat and call Papas. . . . In Italy, where it was then [1598] in use, no one knew whether it originally came from Spain or from America; but as the Spaniards were at that period sole possessors of South America, there can be little doubt but that they procured it from the mountainous parts of that country, and particularly in the neighbourhood of Quito, and from thence sent it to Spain. (2:78, 79)

Quito, the capital city of Ecuador, is in the mountainous north-central part of the country.

118 **Charles Darwin . . . any bitter taste":** Darwin, 2:23. The spine title of the volume is *Voyage of a Naturalist round the World*.

118 **Gerarde says: . . . own native country:** Gerarde, pp. 926–27. As usual when Thoreau quotes from Gerarde, he silently modernizes and Americanizes the spelling in several instances. I omit from the text the following two sentences in the MS, which I interpret as Thoreau's notes to himself: "Did not he originate the blunder?" and "The figure is said, in Gerarde, to be from Clusius." The former sentence is almost certainly a query about Gerarde being the first person to misinterpret historical sources indicating that the potato came from South America rather than North America; the latter sentence is puzzling, for "figure" in a context like this is usually used by Thoreau and his botanical sources as a synonym of "drawing" or "etching." Gerarde refers throughout his book to Carolus Clusius (Latin for Charles de L'Écluse [1526–1609]), who was a botanist who developed new garden cultures and cultivated plants from other parts of the world, and who from 1573 to 1587 was director of the Holy Roman emperor's garden in Vienna. A footnote in Gerarde to the last paragraph Thoreau quotes from (the one mentioning Clusius) reads, "*Clusius* questions whether it be not the *Arachidna* of *Theophrastus*. *Bauhine* hath referred it to the Nightshades, and calleth it *Solanum tuberosum Esculentum*, and largely figures and describes it in his *Prodromus*, pag. 89" (p. 927).

119 **single cyme presents:** Thoreau interlined in the MS here, "August 8, 1852. Greenish white."

120 **one evening:** Thoreau's journal source for this passage is his entry of August 31, 1856 (*Journal* 9:49).

120 **one afternoon:** Thoreau's journal source for this passage is his entry of August 19, 1854 (*Journal* 6:456–57).

120 **Perth Amboy . . . neighboring school:** Thoreau visited the Eagleswood Community, located one mile west of Perth Amboy, New Jersey, from October 25 to November 25, 1856. While there he surveyed the property for the owner, wealthy Quaker abolitionist Marcus Springs, and read three lectures to the communitarians, who lived in a large phalanstery on the property (Harding, pp. 370–76; Dean and Hoag, pp. 273–79).

120 *(Viburnum prunifolium):* Thoreau queried this name in the MS. Gray (1848), p. 174, uses both the English and the Latin names, so Thoreau apparently queried his identification of the plant rather than one or another of the names.

120 **called "Nanny berries" about New York:** The original version of this paragraph ends with "ornaments." Thoreau later added in ink the note "(*Vide* perhaps Torrey, July 20, 1857)," referring to his reading about "Nanny berries" in Torrey, 2:87, during a visit on July 20, 1857, to the Natural History Library in Boston (*Journal* 9:484–85).

120 **thickets of it:** Thoreau originally wrote this sentence without "in this region," which he later interlined in ink. In that original version Thoreau ended the sentence with "there," but when he added "in this region" he did not delete "there," which I delete as redundant.

120 **swampy sproutlands—and:** After "sproutlands" Thoreau wrote "(as at Shadbush Meadow)" and interlined "and by path in Hubbard's rear wood." I emend by adding the word "and."

120 **September 3. Now is . . . asters in their turn:** Thoreau drew a pencil line in the margin beside this paragraph and penned along the line, "Beautiful Berrying."

121 **you, as you wind:** Thoreau originally wrote "pass" and then wrote "wind" above "pass" without deleting "pass."

121 **them with each other:** After this phrase in the MS Thoreau wrote, "September 4, 1853 rather stale."

121 **about August twelfth:** After these words in the MS Thoreau wrote, "(July 26, 1860 not yet ripe but reddish)."

121 **last through September:** At the end of this sentence in the MS Thoreau wrote, "(many in 1859—very few in 1860)."

121 **robins and cherry birds:** Beginning with "cherry birds" there is a single pencil line through the remainder of this paragraph, which Thoreau may have used to indicate deletion of that material.

121 **Loudon says . . . when ripe, as fruit":** Loudon, 2:917.

122 **August second:** Thoreau first wrote "August 8" in the MS, but then he penciled in a "2" and did not delete the "8."

122 **are eaten by birds:** At the end of this sentence Thoreau wrote, "(before they are fairly ripe)."

123 **Silky cornel with . . . and fill its crevices:** In the MS this sentence reads, "(Hazelnut husks fully formed—richly, autumnally significant—*viburnum dentatum*, elder, and) silky cornel—(all) with abundance of green berries help clothe the bank of the Assabet and fill its crevices." Thoreau placed in parentheses the material he apparently intended to delete.

123 **dangling over the . . . reflected in it:** Thoreau put an open parenthesis before the word "dangling," which suggests he may have considered deleting the remainder of the sentence.

123 **nearly blue green:** After "nearly" in the MS Thoreau wrote, "(pearly? amethystine?)."

123 **kinnikinnik of the Indians:** As the next note makes clear, Thoreau read about kinnikinnik, which he occasionally spells "kinnikinnic," in Hind, *Northwest Territory*, p. 47. Almost all the other early French voyageurs Thoreau read or read about also mention kinnikinnik, its ingredients, how it is made, and so on.

123 **Hind writes . . . tobacco was exhausted:** After "Fairly begin to be ripe" in the MS Thoreau wrote, "*Vide* Common Place Book no. 2, p. 191 for account of kinnikinnic," a reference to the passage from Hind, *Northwest Territory*, p. 47, that I incorporate into the text here from pp. 193–94 of Thoreau's "Common Place Book 2," not from "p. 191." I emend by adding "Hind writes about the" to the introductory clause and by omitting "[sic]" after "smoke bark."

124 **The smooth sumac . . . about August thirteenth:** At the top of the MS page that begins with this passage, Thoreau wrote two notes in pencil. The first note, "*Vide* last page," refers to the paragraph about Kalm's *Travels*, which I place at the end of this section in the text. The other note, "put this August 13," is Thoreau's instruction to move this section from where he had earlier placed it, at "the nineteenth of July" in the chronological structure, to its present location. Based on Thoreau's instructional note, I emend by supplanting "the nineteenth of July" in the MS with "August thirteenth." At the end of the sentence in the MS, Thoreau wrote, "say after August 13th" and "July 26, 1860 still in bloom, far from fruit" and "August 17, 1860 now fairly handsome but not long."

124 **crimson or vermillion?:** After these words in the MS Thoreau wrote, "September 24, 1859, probably past beauty."

124 **and probably mice:** After this sentence in the MS Thoreau wrote, "found some on the snow."

124 **plenty still in April:** Between "plenty" and "still" in the MS Thoreau interlined "and red still April 22, 1856" in pencil.

124 **Loudon, apparently . . . that same color":** Loudon, 2:552. Earlier in the "*Rhus glabra*" section of his book, Loudon paraphrases Kalm by beginning a sentence, "According to Kalm" (2:551). After an intervening sentence, Loudon has a long quotation that, within the context of the section and particularly given his earlier paraphrase of Kalm, appears to be a quotation from Kalm. This long quotation—and particularly the last sentence of that quotation, which is what Thoreau quotes here ("The berries are eaten . . . that same color.")—is what Thoreau refers to when he writes, "Loudon, apparently quoting Kalm." Curiously, though, at the end of the long quotation Loudon cites his source not as Kalm but as "(*Martyn's Miller*)," which Loudon expands in his "List of Books Referred To" section (1:ccx) as Professor Martyn's four-volume "improved edition" (London, 1807) of Philip Miller's *Gardener's Dictionary; or, a Complete System of Horticulture*, 3 vols. (London, 1759). So the

quotation Thoreau uses here is not actually from Kalm via Loudon—a conclusion Thoreau himself may have arrived at because of the similarities between the *"Martyn's Miller"* quotation from Loudon and the actual Kalm quotation that Thoreau uses later in this "Smooth Sumac" section, for which see the note below to p. 125.

125 **Professor Rogers . . . economy and medicine":** Thoreau's source is Loudon, 2:552; Loudon cites the source as *"Silliman's Journal,* vol. xxvii, p. 294."

125 **creamy incrustation:** After "creamy" Thoreau wrote, "(for consistence)."

125 **From Kalm's . . . they are very sour":** *Travels into North America,* 1:75, part of which Thoreau just quoted from Loudon (see p. 124). I emend by adding the word "From" to the introductory phrase and by moving the entire introductory phrase from the end to the beginning of the quotation.

125 **depressed, globular, and scarlet:** After these words in the MS Thoreau wrote, "(Is not the other?)."

126 **Manasseh Cutler . . . London dispensatory":** Cutler, p. 451.

126 **December 14, 1850 . . . thick as winterberries:** At the end of this sentence in the MS here Thoreau wrote, *"Vide* Miscellaneous p. 5 (late rose?)," referring to p. 5 of his 112-page "Miscellaneous" draft (Berg Collection, "Notes on Fruits" folder, accession number 334), which is the source of paragraph that follows in the text ("December 14, 1850 . . . thick as winterberries"). Note that Thoreau uses this same passage in his section on "Late Rose" (see p. 194 and the note below to p. 194), a duplication that reflects Thoreau's difficulty distinguishing, in this case at least, between the early and late roses.

126 **Loudon quotes Pliny . . . well boiled or baked":** Loudon, 2:882.

126 **Gerarde says . . . mention the poorer ones:** Gerarde, p. 1455.

126 **September 9, 1853 . . . good there, in prime:** Thoreau wrote these two paragraphs in the margin of the MS and did not indicate an insertion point. I place them at this location somewhat arbitrarily. In the MS Thoreau began the second paragraph "September 22, 1854," which I emend to "September 23, 1854," for that is the entry where he actually recorded the second observation in his journal (*Journal,* 7:52, where he writes, "I gather pretty good wild pears near the new road—now in prime").

126 **Sophia:** Thoreau's younger sister.

127 **Ralph Waldo Emerson's:** I expand from "R.W.E.'s" in the MS.

127 **darker-green rust:** Thoreau wrote after this phrase in the MS, "(or fungi?)."

127 ***plum* weight of the carpenter . . . *poire* or "pear" of the weigher:** The weight of the carpenter and mason is actually a *plumb,* a word derived from the Latin word for lead, *plumbum.* "Pear" in French is *poire,* and Thoreau mentions later in the "*Asclepias cornuti*" section on p. 196 a "steelyard *poire,*" a pear-shaped object of some kind. The *Oxford English Dictionary* does not list "poire," nor does it list a definition for *pear* suggesting that the word was ever used to denote a weigher's weight. Thoreau's apparent confusion may have resulted from his having read "The Weight and Culture

of Dwarf Pears" (see "Works Cited"), which contains the following passage loosely associating steelyards and pears: "It has often been asserted, and as frequently denied, that dwarf pears weighing above three-quarters of a pound are commonly raised. The Worcester (Mass.) Horticultural Society have settled the question by the aid of steelyards. They took the fairest specimens of several varieties shown at the Fairs of 1859 and 1860, and found a marked difference in their weight in the two years." I italicize *"poire"* in the text on the presumption that it is, in fact, a foreign word.

127 *glout-morceaux:* The *Oxford English Dictionary* states that the French translates literally to "tit-bit" and quotes Robert Thompson, *Gardener's Assistant* (1859), p. 483, "Glou-Morceau [sic] . . . a dessert pear of the finest excellence." In an article titled "Fruits, Nuts, and Wine," Marshall P. Wilder of Boston lists the "Glout Morceau" under the subheading "Pears, For Cultivation on Quince Stocks" (in *Report of the Commissioner,* p. 230).

128 **The Romans are said . . . it came to Britain:** Loudon, 2:681. After this sentence in the MS Thoreau interlined the note, *"Vide* somewhere my account of their coming to Lincoln," but I have not been able to locate any such account, in the MS or otherwise.

128 **the Smiths:** Likely C. Smith, who lived on the Cambridge Turnpike in Lincoln, just north of Flint's Pond, as well as his relations.

128 **Evelyn says . . . before Pliny's time":** Evelyn, p. 119. Galen of Pergamum (A.D. 129–216) was a Greek physician, writer, and philosopher. Pliny the Elder lived from A.D. 23 to 79.

128 **Lincoln in New England:** The town of Lincoln, Massachusetts, abuts the town of Concord on the south. In fact, a small portion of Walden Pond's southeastern shoreline is in Lincoln. According to a report delivered to the Legislative Agricultural Society by Massachusetts State Representative and Concord resident Simon Brown, "before 'the yellows' destroyed the peach crop [in Middlesex County], the town of Lincoln alone realized from $8,000 to $9,000 from this crop" (*The New England Farmer,* p. 120).

128 **In Lawson's *Carolina* . . . wilderness of peach trees":** Lawson, p. 115.

129 **in Beverly's *Virginia* . . . purposely for their hogs":** Beverly, *The History and Present State of Virginia,* ed. Louis B. Wright (Chapel Hill: University of North Carolina Press, 1947), p. 315. Thoreau's source was Robert Beverly, *The History of Virginia, in Four Parts . . .* (London: F. Fayram and J. Clarke, and T. Bickerton, 1722).

129 **I see the carrion . . . say September fourth:** I emend by deleting "The Carrion flower" at the beginning of this sentence as redundant with "it" in the sentence itself, which I here changed to "the carrion flower." I also emend by changing Thoreau's original "August 15" to "August seventeenth" based both on this MS page's location in the chronological structure of *Wild Fruits* and on Thoreau's having noted after the original date "(1854, say then 17th)."

129 **and on moist banks:** Thoreau wrote after these words in the MS, "(as by Violet Wood-Sorrel Wall)."

129 **cone-shaped mass:** Thoreau interlined in ink "conical or ovate" above "cone-shaped" without indicating which word or phrase should supplant the other.

130 **leaves, and it is:** I add the word "is."

131 **by some creatures:** Thoreau wrote "(apparently birds?) in the MS here, the parentheses apparently indicating deletion.

131 **one year:** Thoreau's journal entry of September 21, 1859, indicates that the year was 1859 (*Journal*, 12:339).

131 **August nineteenth:** Thoreau wrote above the line ending here in the MS, "September 21, 1860 some time."

131 **generally till September:** I keep this sentence before the following paragraph, which Thoreau had written in ink vertically in the left margin and had careted for insertion, apparently, before this sentence. My assumption in doing so is that his caret was hastily placed before this "dating" sentence, which in virtually every other instance immediately follows the section-plant name.

131 **Cornutus evidently . . . called ivy today:** Cornut, p. 387.

132 **hills in sproutlands:** After this phrase in the MS Thoreau wrote, "(as at Lee's Cliff, and in the Sproutland east, red huckleberry, and E. Hubbard hill-side)."

132 **green even in November:** Thoreau wrote "(as 2d, 1853)" after this sentence in the MS.

133 **of the largest plants:** I add the word "of." Thoreau initially wrote, "half-dozen plants" and later interlined "the largest."

133 **one tells me:** Thoreau identifies this person as Minot Pratt in his journal entry of October 15, 1859 (*Journal*, 12:385).

133 *one year:* Thoreau interlined in pencil after this sentence, *"Vide if worthwhile Tribune* January 24, 1860," referring to the following extract from the report of a January 16, 1860, meeting of the American Institute Framers' Club in the *New-York Weekly Tribune:*

The Ground-Nut.—Solon Robinson read a letter from G. F. Waters of Waterville, Maine, giving his opinion about the Ground-Nut, that grows so common all over this country, in which he says:

"A few words reported from your Club, last year, on the 'Apios Tuberosa,' or 'American Ground-Nut,' directed my attention to the same. The plant has been growing in a wet corner of my garden for years. I have obtained tubers two inches in diameter. I send inclosed a few slices from one of the large tubers, dried. You will find it rich in gums, starch, etc., with a taste like 'Snake Root.' There are two kinds of this plant indigenous hereabouts. I have not as yet distinguished them from each other by the flower. The tuber in one kind is quite round, and has a sweet taste, yellowish meat, etc. The other, which is the most common, tapers toward the ends, one being blunter than the other; meat white, sweetish, and quite gummy. It was recommended in your Club to use rotten wood as a manure for this plant. I have found the 'Apios Tuberosa' to thrive best when well dressed with a rich compost. And so tenacious is it of life, that, when once well under way in a rich soil, it will be found quite difficult to eradicate it.

"I have been told by one of our oldest inhabitants that many people lived upon this Ground-Nut during the Winter 1817 and 1818, the nuts having been collected in the Fall for food. The flower of this plant is quite showy and fragrant—the odor strongly resembles that or Orris Root. This plant would thrive in swampy lands, where boys might harvest the crop."

The specimen inclosed was tasted, and the flavor and food-like taste of it in this dried condition much admired by members. Mr. Robinson alluded to the fact of the attention of people having been called to it by our fellow-member, Andrew S. Fuller of Brooklyn, who is a practical, and reading, thinking horticulturalist and botanist.

ANDREW S. FULLER—This nut may be cultivated to advantage anywhere in this country. It is very nutritious, and will grow in great abundance in any rich soil. It grows very common upon Western prairies and timber land. Undoubtedly many of the people of whom we have had accounts of their starving on the route to Pike's Peak, and in Minnesota, might, without doubt, have found this food-plant if they had only known where to look and how to designate it. It grows something like the small running pea vine. Its blossom is fragrant and pretty. It is a plant really worthy of more attention by the American people, notwithstanding it has grown wild and neglected so long.

133 **foot, you come to:** I emend by adding the word "to" on authority of the journal source of this passage, the entry of September 29, 1859 (*Journal*, 12:358).

134 **about which historians . . . Britain from Virginia:** After "Virginia" Thoreau wrote and did not delete "(where it did not grow," leaving the parenthesis unclosed. For information on the history of the potato, see the note above to p. 118.

134 **September in sunny places:** Thoreau interlined "in sunny places" in pencil, with his caret positioned after the "——" in the construction "Sep—— I see them," which means that he may have intended the interlineation to *begin* the next sentence rather than to *end* the preceding one, as I have here. The only reason I use the interlineation at the end of the preceding sentence is that the *i* in "in" is clearly lower case.

135 **end of the month:** After "month" Thoreau wrote, "(23d)." His journal source, entry of October 10, 1857, establishes the year (*Journal*, 10:82).

135 **late as March seventh:** After this phrase in the MS Thoreau wrote, "(1854)."

136 **one year:** Thoreau interlined "1858" in the MS here.

136 **of varnished mahogany:** Thoreau wrote in the MS here, "(In rather swampy land)," after which he intelined in pencil, "not edible. Just ripe September 4, 1856."

136 **say August twenty-first:** After these words in the MS Thoreau penciled the note "*Vide* no. 15, p. 43," referring to the paragraph about cat-tail down that follows in

the text and that appears on pp. 43–44, 47 of his MS journal vol. 15, entry of March 23, 1853 (*Journal*, 5:43–44).

136 **like an eruption:** In the MS journal source here (see preceding note) Thoreau wrote, "*Vide* amount of seed *Tribune*, March 16, 1860," referring to the following extract from the report of a meeting of the American Institute Framers' Club in the *New-York Semi-Weekly Tribune*, March 16, 1860:

> HOW MUCH SEED TO THE ACRE.—This, one of the questions of the day, was called up, and Robert L. Pell, who is a very large farmer in Ulster County, up the river, read a very interesting and valuable paper, detailing his method of seeding various crops, which we commend to an attentive perusal. It is as follows:
>
> > "To answer this question understandingly, we require to know the number of seed contained in a pound and the number of pounds in a bushel. . . .
> >
> > ["]The amazing number of seeds which many plants produce much facilitates their reproduction and wonderful multiplication. A single capsule of the common poppy contains no less than 7,500 seeds, a single stalk of corn 2,100, a single spike of the cat's-tail, typha major, 11,000, a single tobacco plant 370,000, and a single stalk of spleenwort 1,100,000. If, by any accident, all these seeds were placed where they could develop themselves, under circumstances favorable to their growth, the twelfth generation of any of them would seed the world. The structure of nearly all seeds is similar, every one is provided by nature with an external covering suited to its nature, which protects it from the excesses of moisture or dryness, and there is no seed with which I am acquainted that is devoid of this covering, usually called pericarp."

137 **Lindley writes . . . substitute for it":** Lindley, p. 366. I emend by adding the word "writes."

137 **Perhaps fruits . . . attracts birds to them:** See note above to p. 97.

138 **mass of red fruit:** Thoreau wrote after these words in the MS, "(Bears none in '59)."

138 **Nawshawtuct Hill:** I add the word "Hill."

138 **William Wood's . . . pleasantness to the taste":** William Wood, p. 21. I emend by expanding this introductory clause from "Wᵐ. Woods N E's Prospect London ed. 1639."

138 **Measured a thorn . . . in circumference:** This entire sentence is derived from the journal passage Thoreau refers to when he writes in the MS here, "Large thorn *Vide* March 6, 1859" (*Journal*, 12:18).

138 **Mrs. Lincoln . . . sign of severe winter":** Phelps (Mrs. Lincoln), pp. 207–8.

139 **middle of October:** Expanded from the MS's "*mid*. Oct." Thoreau often underscores his abbreviations, as he does with "mid." (italicized here), so I am confident he did not intend "mid-October."

139 **hills and rocky places:** Thoreau interlined in pencil after these words, "Hill, and Tupelo Cliff." His "Hill" here, as it almost always is, is Fair Haven Hill.

139 **semi-lucent red:** Thoreau interlined here in pencil, "August 26, 1860 just beginning to be ripe or red."

139 **Go a-berrying . . . twenty-fourth, 1859:** Thoreau may have planned to extract each of these barberrying excursions from his journal and add them to *Wild Fruits*.

140 **middle of the barberry season:** Thoreau interlined the following two penciled notes here: "September 28, 1852, just right time" and "*Vide* next page but one for beauty— Few objects &c." Thoreau careted the passage he refers to in the second note (the paragraph beginning "Few objects," which in the MS appears two pages forward) for insertion after this passage. Thoreau wrote the first of the two notes in order to confirm for himself the "October first or September twenty-fifth" dates in the text.

140 **the cedar hill . . . Easterbrook's Country:** I add the word "hill."

140 **Sophia:** Thoreau's younger sister.

141 **than the apple crop:** Thoreau had written "cultivated" before "apple," but he enclosed the word in parentheses to indicate deletion.

142 **end of September:** Thoreau interlined here "(as September 24, 1859)."

142 **Parker's:** Built in 1855 at the corner of School and Tremont Streets, and perhaps best known as the place where Boston Cream pies and Parker House rolls originated, the Parker House restaurant was Boston's premier dining establishment for decades. Soon after it opened it began offering lodging accomodations and meeting rooms.

142 **rocks by the mice:** Thoreau wrote at the end of this sentence, "(as November 14, 1857)."

142 **crows and even partridges:** Thoreau's interlined "(January 22, 1856)" after "crows." After "partridges" he wrote "(?)" and interlined "(January 14, 1854)" above that word ("partridge").

142 **the poet says . . . red berries be:** Very, 1:131.

143 **chiefly), and in May:** After "May," Thoreau wrote, "(as May 29, 1858)."

143 **Loudon says . . . increasing much in size":** Loudon, 1:301–2. Thoreau emends Loudon's "berberry" to "barberry," "4 ft. or 5 feet," to "4 or 5 feet," and "30 ft." to "30 feet."

143 **much higher than four or five feet:** Between these words and the following section Thoreau wrote these three notes: "for age *Vide* journal about 1858"; "*Vide* no. 17, p. 12, February 18"; and "also March 6, 1859." I have not located in Thoreau's journal of the late 1850s a passage referring to the age of barberries, but the last two notes refer to the following journal passages:

[Entry of February 18, 1854] Barberries still hang on the bushes, but all shrivelled. I found a bird's nest of grass and mud in a barberry bush filled full with them. It must have been done by some quadruped or bird. (*Journal*, 6:128–29)

[Entry of March 6, 1859] Measured a thorn which, at six inches from the ground, or the smallest place below the branches,—for it branches soon,—was two feet three inches in circumference. Cut off a barberry on which I counted some twenty-six rings, the broadest diameter being about three and a half inches. Both these were on the west side the Yellow Birch Swamp. (*Journal,* 12:18)

143 **perhaps August thirty-first:** Thoreau wrote after this passage, "(1854)."

143 **I see it in . . . Brook Swamp and elsewhere:** I expand from the MS, which reads, "*Vide* Sawmill Brook Swamp and elsewhere."

144 *cincinnata,* **August twenty-seventh:** Thoreau's interlined pencil note: "not August 11, 1860."

144 **and *paniculata:*** Thoreau wrote in ink after this phrase, "Find account of by Cornel Rock," which almost certainly refers to the passage about Cornel Rock that follows in the text, which begins "September 4, 1857."

145 **I went up-country a week ago:** From September 5 to 12, 1856, Thoreau visited the vicinities of Brattleboro, Vermont, and Walpole, New Hampshire, which are on the Connecticut River fifteen and thirty miles north of the Massachusetts border, respectively (*Journal* 9:61–80).

145 **October 13, 1860 . . . but not so long:** Thoreau penciled this sentence in the left margin vertically and did not indicate where it should be inserted.

145 **crimson berries before this is in bloom:** After these words in the MS Thoreau interlined in pencil, "September 7, 1860, begun, and probably the first." He does not mention sumac in his journal of September 1860 until September 18, when he wrote the following sentence, which appears in the "Smooth Sumac" section: "Smooth sumach berries are about past their beauty and the white creamy incrustation mostly dried up."

145 **It appears to bear quite sparingly here:** Thoreau wrote after this sentence, "(*Vide* Knoll below Cliff—at Sunset Interval and so on)."

145 **the next April:** Thoreau wrote after this phrase, "(22d 1856)."

146 **August twenty-eighth:** Thoreau interlined in pencil here, "(1859)."

146 **August 31, 1852. From Israel Rice's hill:** This small hill is in Sudbury, Massachusetts, just west of the Sudbury River and a quarter of a mile north of the mouth of Pantry Brook, or a mile and a half south of Fair Haven Bay.

146 **In the spring of 1857 . . . Pumpkin (or Squash):** According to *Report of the Commissioner,* beginning in 1852 a "considerable share of the money appropriated by Congress for Agricultural purposes has been devoted to the procurement and distribution of seeds, roots, and cutting" (p. [v]). These were procured "from every quarter of the globe" and were distributed through the mails in "smaller packages" (p. vii). Later in this same volume, in an article titled "Report on the Seeds and Cuttings Recently Introduced into the United States," and under the subtitle "Plants Cultivated for Their Berries or Fleshy Fruits," is listed the "*Large Yellow-fleshed Pumpkin, or Squash,* (Potiron jaune gros,) from France; the fruit of which is very heavy, of a gold yellow within, and grows to an enormous size" (p. xxi). *Potiron jaune gros* is French for "large yellow pumpkin." I have emended "*Poitrine*" in the MS to "*Potiron*"

on authority of both the listing in *Report of the Commissioner* and the fact that *poitrine* is French for "chest" (ribs and breastbone).

146 **pumpkin which weighed:** I add the word "weighed."

146 **together 186¼ pounds:** I add the word "pounds." Thoreau wrote this sentence, the preceding sentence, and the following sentence in such a way that he was able to line up the three numerals vertically with a horizontal line under the second numeral, like the line under an addend in an addition problem. Thoreau wrote the correct sum, "309¾," under the horizontal line, but he also rounded that sum off to "310," which appears in the correct location in the following sentence. I emend by not underlining or italicizing "186¼" and by omitting the sum of the two weights, "309¾."

147 **The big squash . . . ten cents apiece:** Thoreau originally wrote, "The big squash took a premium at the Middlesex Show, and I understand that the man who bought it intends to sell the seeds for ten cents apiece." Later he revised the sentence in preparation for use in "The Succession of Forest Trees," which he delivered as a lecture during the Middlesex County Agricultural Fair (often called the "Cattle Show") on September 20, 1860, and published just over two weeks later, on October 6, 1860, in the *New-York Weekly Tribune.* The revised version of the sentence in both the MS and in the lecture-essay as published in the *Tribune* is identical to the one here, except that I emend by omitting the words "your fair" and using in their stead the words "Middlesex Show" from the MS. (Thoreau originally wrote the phrase "Middlesex Show," later interlined "your fair that fall" above the phrase, but never deleted the original phrase.)

147 **Signor Blitz:** I have not been able to locate any reference to this person or character.

147 **men love darkness rather than light:** An echo, possibly, of Psalms 139:12, which reads, "The darkness and the light are both alike to thee."

147 **As for pumpkins . . . and "Acorn" squashes:** This passage is an expansion of Thoreau's interlineation, "Pumpkins and squashes. *Vide* Harris in *Patent Office Reports* for 1854, p. 208." Harris's remarks about pumpkins and squashes appear under the title "Pumpkins" in *Report of the Commissioner* (spine title: "Patent Office Reports, 1854, Agriculture"), p. 208, with the following introductory remarks: "The common field pumpkin, (*Cucurbita pepo,*) as well as the squashes, properly so called, is believed to be of American origin, as will appear from the following remarks by Dr. T. W. Harris, of Harvard University, in Cambridge, Massachusetts."

148 **White ash begins:** After "ash" Thoreau interlined in pencil, (*black* September 2d)," which note was likely used as the basis for Thoreau distinguishing between the two ashes and giving each a separate section (see "Black Ash" section, p. 175).

149 **It is whitening:** Thoreau interlined in pencil the note, "Handsome as soon as leaves fell about middle of October."

149 **the end of December:** I emend by adding "the" before "end."

149 **broken, and are:** I emend by using "are" rather than "is" in the MS, which disagrees with the subject, "berries."

149 **pearly or waxen:** After both "pearly" and "waxen," Thoreau wrote "(?)." Also, he interlined here, with a caret after "waxen," "what is its color?"

149 **beautiful as Satan:** Although this sentiment may at first seem peculiar, it agrees with John Milton's portrayal of Satan at the beginning of *Paradise Lost.* Milton had to portray God's and mankind's arch-adversary as an extremely attractive character, albeit fundamentally evil, for to diminish Satan too much (particularly at the outset of the epic) would risk portraying God and mankind very unflatteringly as omnipotent bully and dependent dupes, respectively.

149 **With its long . . . against the snow:** The MS reads, "With its long fruit stems scored is an agreeable object seen against the snow," but the journal source of this sentence reads, "The poison sumac with its stems hanging down on every side is a very agreeable object now seen against the snow" (entry of January 27, 1852; *Journal,* 3:239). I therefore emend the MS by adding "and" and changing what appears to be "scored," which makes no apparent sense, to "hanging," which most closely agrees with the journal source.

149 **now in mid-winter:** Thoreau wrote at the end of this sentence, "(January 5, 1858)."

150 **any bird eats them:** At the end of this section in the MS Thoreau penciled the following notes: "Leaves begin to fall September 29, 1859," "appear handsome as soon as the berries begin to fall," and "Odor of, *Vide* no. 18, p. 281." The latter of these three references is to a passage in his MS journal entry of March 9, 1855 (*Journal,* 7:236), "The heart-wood of the poison dogwood, when I break it down with my hand, has a singular rotten, yellow look and a spirituous or apothecary odor."

150 **(on trees), August thirtieth:** I delete from the end of this line the query "or earlier?"

151 **Theophrastus includes . . . refers it to Asia.}** Thoreau's source for the observations on Theophrastus and Columella is a footnote in Pliny, *Natural History,* bk. 14, chap. 3 (3:218 n. 11) by the translators, Bostock and Riley, who point out in another footnote, "It was generally known in very early times in Egypt and Greece, and it is now generally considered that [the grape vine] is indigenous throughout the tract that stretches to the south, from the the [*sic*] mountains of Mazandiran on the Caspian to the shores of the Persian Gulf and the Indian Sea, and eastward through Khorassan and Cabul to the base of the Himalayas" (*Natural History,* bk. 14, chap. 3; 3:215 n. 2). Henry G. Bohn was the publisher. I emend by pluralizing "translator" in the MS.

151 **Pliny complains . . . climbing the trees"):** Pliny, *Natural History,* bk. 14, chap. 1 (3:217).

151 **Pliny says further . . . day, for instance:** Pliny, *Natural History,* bk. 14, chap. 3 (3:219).

151 **Pliny says of the . . . blood of the earth . . .' ":** Thoreau translated these passages from Pliny, *Historiæ Mundi*, bk. 14, chaps. 3, 7; Bostock and Riley's translation of these passages (again, Henry G. Bohn was the publisher) is substantively the same as Thoreau's. I emend by using an ellipsis at the end of the final passage here (after "blood of the earth") rather than "&c" in the MS. Thoreau may have intended to include the remainder of the paragraph, which in the Bostock-Riley translation reads (immediately after "blood of the earth"), " 'hemlock is a poison to man, wine a poison to hemlock.' And if Alexander had only followed this advice, he certainly would not have had to answer for slaying his friends in his drunken fits. In fact, we may feel ourselves quite justified in saying that there is nothing more useful than wine for strengthening the body, while, at the same time, there is nothing more pernicious as a luxury, if we are not on our guard against excess" (*Natural History*, bk. 14, chap. 7; 3:238–39).

152 **the Vineland of the North men?:** The early Norse explorers referred to undetermined portions of the New World as "Vineland."

152 **hanging over the water:** Thoreau interlined in the MS here, "Minot's green grape shooting."

152 **Early in September:** Thoreau wrote after this phrase, "(as 6th, 1851)."

153 **September twentieth:** Thoreau originally wrote "September 8, 1854" but later deleted "8, 1854" and interlined "20," which my policy is to alter by spelling out, as I do here.

154 **we rowed along:** Thoreau does not identify his companion in the journal source of this passage, his entry of September 13, 1856, but he most often was joined on his daily excursions by his neighbor, the poet William Ellery Channing.

154 **Billerica . . . Jug Island . . . Grape Island:** Jug Island is on the Concord River about half a mile north of Hill's Bridge (also called Nashua Road Bridge) in Billerica, a town two miles northeast of Concord, on the other side of the town of Bedford.

154 **memorable:** Thoreau interlined the following two notes in the MS here, the first in pencil and the other in ink: "*Vide* September 18, 1858 in Autumnal Tints for graping," and "Grapes are singularly various for a wild fruit—in color, size, and flavor— purple, red, and green—and so on and so forth." His reference to "Autumnal Tints" may be either to his lecture-essay of that title or to the larger work, still unpublished, that his lecture-essay formed a part of, but Thoreau usually referred to that larger work as *The Fall of the Leaf*. The passage from his journal entry of September 18, 1858, reads as follows: "Finding grapes, we proceeded to pluck them, tempted more by their fragrance and color than their flavor, though some were very palatable. We gathered many without getting out of the boat, as we paddled back, and more on shore close to the water's edge, piling them up in the prow of the boat till they reached to the top of the boat,—a long sloping heap of them and very handsome to

behold, being of various colors and sizes, for we even added green ones for variety. Some, however, were mainly green when ripe. You cannot touch some vines without bringing down more single grapes in a shower around you than you pluck in bunches, and such as strike the water are lost, for they do not float. But it is a pity to break the handsome clusters." The "we" of this passage is Thoreau and "C.," the poet William Ellery Channing, who lived across the street from Thoreau in Concord.

155 **Eagleswood grape:** Thoreau's name for the grape he found in the vicinity of the Eagleswood Community, for which see the note above to p. 120.

155 **one and a half wide:** I emend by adding "wide."

155 **my mother:** I emend by adding "my."

155 **leaf of peculiar form such as described by Michaux:** I have not been able to locate the passage in Michaux that Thoreau alludes to.

155 **Brattleboro:** A city in southeastern Vermont on the Connecticut River, as Thoreau points out, and fifty-eight miles west-northwest of Concord, Massachusetts.

155 **About the tenth . . . Eagleswood, New Jersey . . . eaten in France:** Thoreau's host while at the Eagleswood Community was Marcus Springs, a wealthy Quaker, avid abolitionist, and fervent reformer. For Eagleswood, see the note above to p. 120.

156 **to *Vitis æstivalis*:** Thoreau wrote in the MS after this sentence, "(*Vide* date if necessary)," apparently referring to the following remaining material in the journal source of this paragraph: "*Vide* fruit and leaves. One I opened has only two seeds, while *one* of the early ones at Brattleboro has only two, but one of the late ones of Brattleboro has only two, which also I have called *Vitis æstivalis*" (*Journal*, 9:138).

156 **Torrey . . . vicinity of New York":** Torrey, 1:147.

156 **Naushon:** The largest of the Elizabeth Islands off the southeastern point of Cape Cod, between Martha's Vineyard and New Bedford.

157 **Dr. Carpenter says . . . resist moisture":** Carpenter, p. 217.

157 **Pursh says . . . called Fox-grape":** Pursh, p. 169.

157 **Beverly . . . called fox grapes":** Beverly, p. 133.

158 **say September fifteenth:** Thoreau interlined in ink below this line in the MS, "notice cluster July 24."

159 ***woods* not ripe:** After "ripe" in the MS Thoreau wrote, "*Vide* September 5, 1860 or same in Dispersion of Seeds," referring to a journal passage in his journal entry of that date (*Journal*, 14:74), a passage which he includes later in this section and which begins "One afternoon, having landed far down the river. . . ." This passage also appears in Thoreau's *The Dispersion of Seeds*, p. 97.

159 **One afternoon . . . a companion:** Thoreau interlined "(September 5, 1860)" in the MS after "One afternoon," and he interlined "(at Ball's Hill)" after "down the river." The companion is identified from Thoreau's journal entry of September 5, 1860, as William Ellery Channing (*Journal*, 14:74).

159 **walked about through:** The MS reads "walked about there through," so I emend by omitting "there" to avoid redundancy. Thoreau had added the words "by the shore there" later and had neglected to delete the first occurrence of the word "there."

159 *lemna* **on a ditch:** The *Oxford English Dictionary* defines *lemna* as "A genus of aquatic plant" and "Duckweed."

159 **By August second I see it yellowing:** Thoreau originally wrote "August ninth," but he later deleted "ninth" and inserted "second, 1853." I emend by dropping the year. After "yellowing" Thoreau interlined in pencil, "September 20, 1860 yellow but not red."

159 **reveals the red inside:** Thoreau interlined in pencil after this sentence, "How it is dipped in hot water." I have found nothing in Thoreau's writings, including his journal, where he writes about dipping the fruit of wax-work in hot water.

160 **burrs make a show:** Thoreau penciled into the margin beside this observation, "June 29, 1854."

160 **Loudon says . . . a different interpretation:** Loudon, 3:2016. Thoreau renders Loudon's "*korus*" as "*κόρυς*."

160 **shaggy fruit now:** Thoreau interlined in ink here, "(July 24, 1852)."

160 **Thomson . . . an ardent brown:** Thomson, p. 88. I emend by correcting Thoreau misspelling in the MS, "Thompson."

160 **Indeed, you cannot . . . not worked yet:** Thoreau drew a single light-pencil use mark through these passages, which may indicate that he intended to delete them.

161 **not worked yet:** Thoreau interlined the following note in the MS here: "(*Vide* August 29 and September 3d and 13, 1858 for squirrel) *Vide* Dispersion of Seeds." He refers first to the three journal passages, which he intended to transcribe for use here, and then to his revised version of those passages in *The Dispersion of Seeds*, pp. 145–46 (Berg Collection, "Dispersion of Seeds" folder, accession numbers 330–31), which I incorporate into the text here, from "The striped squirrels begin" to "show that they are empty."

162 **Assabet River:** I add the word "River" here.

162 **red-edged:** Thoreau wrote in the MS after this word, "(*Vide* perhaps Wordsworth's lines on savaging hazel-nut bushes—Loudon p. 2022—or put it with stoning chestnut trees)," referring in the latter case to his own passages in the "Chestnut" section of *Wild Fruits* about jarring chestnut trees with stones to make the nuts fall (see pp. 211, 212, 215), and in the former case to Loudon, 3:2022, where an early version of Wordsworth's well-known poem "Nutting" is quoted as follows:

> ———"Among the woods
> And o'er the pathless rocks I forced my way;
> Until at length I came to one dear nook,
> Unvisited, where not a broken bough
> Droop'd with its wither'd leaves, ungracious sign

Of devastation! But the hazels rose
Tall and erect, with milk-white clusters hung,—
A virgin scene! A little while I stood,
Breathing with such suppression of the heart
As joy delights in; and with wise restraint,
Voluptuous, fearless of a rival, eyed
The banquet. Then up I arose,
And dragg'd to earth each branch and bough with crash,
And merciless ravage; and the shady nook
Of hazels, and the green and mossy bower,
Deform'd and sullied, patiently gave up
Their quiet being: but, unless I now
Confound my present feelings with the past,
Even then, when from the bower I turn'd away
Exulting, rich beyond the wealth of kings,
I felt a sense of pain when I beheld
The silent trees, and the intruding skies."

162 **I sometimes see . . . has left them:** Thoreau drew a single vertical use mark through this paragraph, which may indicate that he intended to delete it from the text.

162 **brazen tipt):** It was a common practice of the time to place bronze caps, often in the shape of balls, on the tips of oxen horns to blunt the damage of getting gored.

162 **Loudon . . . inhabitants as shot":** Loudon, 3:2030.

163 **common September twenty-seventh:** I emend by omitting the year, "1852," from the end of this sentence.

163 **dark blue-black berries on slender peduncles:** In the MS the modifiers to "berries" are unhyphenated. They could be hyphenated either as I have them here or as "dark-blue, black"—or could even be placed in a series, as "dark, blue, black." Also, after "slender" Thoreau wrote, "(threads)," the parentheses apparently indicating deletion.

164 **Phillips . . . Dr. Holland 'pease' ":** Henry Phillips, 2:45. After "Tusser," Thoreau quietly omits the clause in Phillips, "(who wrote in the reign of Queen Mary)." Phillips points out that "Gerard spells ["peason"] in the same manner, in the succeeding reign" and that "In the time of Charles the First, Dr. Philemon Holland spells it 'peas,' since which it has been abbreviated into 'pea.' "

164 **Phillips . . . beans for vulgar fare' ":** Henry Phillips, 2:68.

164 **Gerarde . . . to be taken away":** Gerarde, p. 1216.

164 **Emerson says . . . commerce there:** Emerson, *Report on Trees*, p. 406. Thoreau quotes what Emerson says of the European cranberry, which Emerson calls *Oxycoccus palustris*. Emerson also states, "Its berries are applied to the same purposes as our cranberry, and great quantities are sent from Russia to the more southern countries" (*Report on Trees*, p. 406). Of "our cranberry," the common cranberry, which he clas-

sifies *Oxycoccus marcocarpus*, Emerson writes, "The berries are gathered in great quantities, and [are] used for making tarts and sauce, for which purpose they are superior to any other article, especially as they have the advantage of being kept without difficulty throughout the winter. . . . Great quantities of the berries are exported to Europe" (*Report on Trees*, p. 406).

164 **sphagnum mountains:** I expand "mountains" from "*mts.*" in the MS. Thoreau commonly underlined (here, italicized) his abbreviations, as well as placed a period after them. In addition to using the abbreviation here, he uses it in his journal twice elsewhere in the same context ("*mts.*" of sphagnum): in his entry of December 25, 1858 (*Journal*, 11:378), and in the journal source of this passage (October 17, 1859; *Journal*, 12:396–97). The abbreviation could be expanded to "mounts" or perhaps to "mounds," but in the latter journal entry Thoreau actually writes about these sphagnum mounds coming up to his "idea of a mountainous country better than many actual mountains" he had seen (*Journal*, 12:396). Finally, although the editors of the 1906 edition of Thoreau's journal read "sphagnous" before "mountains" in the journal source to this passage, the *Wild Fruits* MS (Berg Collection, "Notes on Fruits," accession number 248) clearly reads "sphagnum."

165 **Thanksgiving dinner:** After this phrase in the MS, Thoreau writes, "*Vide* Journal August 30 (and September 2d and 3d), 1856 for account of picking them—*Vide* account also of eating them—where? *Vide* Loudon extract Common Place Book, vol. 1, p. 346." Four of these five sources have been incorporated into the text in the order indicated and are separately noted below; the remaining one, the account of eating European cranberries, I have been unable to locate, although Thoreau probably confused this species with the mountain cranberry, *Vaccinium vitis-idæa*, which he gathered while visiting Mount Monadnock in early August 1860 and about which he wrote in his journal entry of August 5, 1860, "We stewed these berries for our breakfast the next morning, and thought them the best berry on the mountain, though, not being quite ripe, the berry was a little bitterish—but not the juice of it. It is such an acid as the camper-out craves" (*Journal*, 14:15). He mentions in a footnote to this passage that he "Brought some home, and stewed them the 12th, and all thought them quite like, and as good as, the common cranberry" (*Journal*, 14:15 n. 1).

165 **I have come out . . . matter of public rejoicing [p. 169]:** The source for these eight paragraphs is Thoreau's journal entry of August 30, 1856 (MS vol. 15, pp. 35–42, 46–48; The Pierpont Morgan Library, New York; accession number MA 1302:15). As with Thoreau's *Wild Fruits* MS, I have emended accidentals in this source to conform to the editorial standards for this volume (*Wild Fruits*) and have noted substantive emendations. See the preceding note for Thoreau's MS note providing the rationale for including this material here. At the end of the sixth of these eight paragraphs in his journal, Thoreau wrote, "*Vide* 4 pages forward." The fourth page after

that note contains the end of a sentence from one paragraph, another full paragraph, and the beginning of a long paragraph—with no indication in the journal MS if Thoreau would have continued his *Wild Fruits* text with the full paragraph or with the beginning of the long paragraph. I have opted to continue the text here with the beginning of the long paragraph; the full paragraph, which Thoreau may have intended to incorporate in the text between the sixth and seventh paragraphs here, reads, "Those small gray sparrow-egg cranberries lay so prettily in the recesses of the sphagnum, I could wade for hours in the cold water gazing at them, with a swarm of mosquitoes hovering about my bare legs—but at each step the friendly sphagnum in which I sank protected my legs like a buckler—not a crevice by which my foes could enter" (MS vol. 15, p. 46; compare *Journal*, 9:44).

165 **small cranberry, *Vaccinium oxycoccus*:** Following "*oxycoccus*" in Thoreau's source, his journal entry of August 30, 1856, he wrote, "which Emerson says is the common cranberry of the north of Europe" (MS vol. 15, p. 35; The Pierpont Morgan Library, New York; accession number MA 1302:15; compare *Journal*, 9:35). I emend by deleting this clause, which is redundant because Thoreau previously quoted this passage from Emerson (see p. 164 in the text and note above for p. 164). Thoreau's source in Emerson is *Report on Trees*, p. 405.

165 **Beck Stow's Swamp:** I add the word "Swamp" here.

165 **drives Kansas . . . border ruffians:** The Kansas-Nebraska Act of 1854 resulted in proslavery Missourians or "border ruffians" crossing the Kansas-Missouri border in 1855 to intimidate antislavery settlers and elect a proslavery legislature by stuffing ballot boxes. Fierce resistance from antislavery forces throughout the spring and summer of 1856 led to widespread guerilla warfare, and the nation's newspapers had columns almost daily about what soon came to be called "Bleeding Kansas."

166 **go consul to Liverpool . . . dollars for it:** In 1852 Nathaniel Hawthorne lived in Concord and wrote the campaign biography of his college friend and Democratic presidential nominee, Franklin Pierce, in return for which the following year he was awarded a consulship in Liverpool, which "was deemed the most lucrative in the foreign service" because in addition to the regular salary, "the consul received 'emoluments'—a percentage on all American shipping in the busy English port" (Mellow, p. 415). Mellow suggests that the consulship gave Hawthorne the "prospect of clearing $5000 to $7000 a year during a four-year term," an enormous sum at the time.

166 **sphagnum—their:** I emend by changing "its" to "their" to agree with the antecedent, "cranberries."

168 **good genius seemed to:** I add the word "to."

168 **Slocum:** Although this is a popular surname in New England today, as well as in Thoreau's time, *Concord Births, Marriages, and Deaths* lists no one by that name; and I have found no indication of what connotations the surname might have suggested, if any.

168 **wild vine of the Assabet:** At this point in his MS journal (vol. 15, p. 42) Thoreau wrote *"Vide 4 pages forward,"* referring to the passage (on p. 46) beginning "I see that all is not garden. . . ." But see the note above to p. 165 ("Thanksgiving dinner") for another possible reference on p. 46.

168 **Middlesex County:** The town of Concord is located almost precisely in the geographic center of Middlesex County, which extends from the New Hampshire border (north) to the town of Holliston (south), and from the town of Cambridge (east) to the town of Ashby (west). Cambridge is the seat of the county.

168 **the moon, supposing it to be uninhabited:** The following portion of a dialogue between a newspaper reporter and a professional astronomer appeared in March 1861 (for source, see "Night Notes" in "Works Cited") and suggests what moderately well-educated people of Thoreau's time thought about the issue of life on the moon:

> *Astronomer*—The moon's surface presents every appearance of a chaotic world, whose surface is all scarred over with the effects of the struggle of mighty interior forces.
>
> *Reporter*—Rather a wild place for a residence.
>
> *Astronomer*—Pythagoras and Orpheus, and perhaps Herodotus also, believed the moon to be inhabited by giants, though modern glasses [telescopes] detect no traces whatever of any creature living, or having ever lived, upon its surface. Some astronomers claim to have detected evidences of vegetation—tracks of forest, leafy or leafless, according to the season. But this remarkable conclusion is of too profound an interest and significance to be received without a far greater mass of evidence than has yet been adduced in its support. No; the moon seems to be a world unborn—a mass of matter not yet called to take its place in the retinue of living, habitable globes.

168 **healthily attract:** I emend by deleting an ampersand between these words, obviously an oversight on Thoreau's part.

168 **Hodge's wall as good as the ærolite at Mecca:** *Concord Births, Marriages, and Deaths* does not list a Hodge as having lived in Concord during Thoreau's time, but Thoreau may have been thinking of Maine geologist James Thacher Hodge, whose 1838 report on the geology of Maine and Massachusetts Thoreau read and occasionally quoted. The *Oxford English Dictionary* defines *ærolite* as "A stone . . . which has fallen to the earth from, or rather through, the atmosphere," and Thoreau's reference is probably to the so-called "Black Stone of Mecca," a Muslim object of veneration that is built into the eastern wall of the Ka'bah, the principal shrine within the Great Mosque of Mecca.

169 **makes two blades . . . is a benefactor:** Jonathan Swift, *Gulliver's Travels*, "Voyage to Brobdingnag," chap. 7: "And [the King of Brobdingnag] gave it for his opinion, that whoever could make two ears of corn or two blades of grass to grow upon a spot of ground where only one grew before, would deserve better of mankind, and do more essential service to his country than the whole race of politicians put together."

169 **The botanist refers . . . than an eastern one!:** The source for this paragraph is Thoreau's journal entry of September 2, 1856 (MS vol. 15, pp. 55–56; The Pierpont Morgan Library, New York; accession number MA 1302-15). See the note above for p. 165 ("Thanksgiving dinner") for Thoreau's MS note providing the rationale for including this material here. The selection of this particular paragraph from Thoreau's entry of September 2, 1856, is based solely on my judgment that none of the other material in that entry would be appropriate for inclusion here.

169 **So many plants . . . there it is at home:** The source for this paragraph is Thoreau's journal entry of September 3, 1856 (MS vol. 15, pp. 59–60; The Pierpont Morgan Library, New York; accession number MA 1302-15). See the note above for p. 165 ("Thanksgiving dinner") for Thoreau's MS note providing the rationale for including this material here. The selection of this particular paragraph from Thoreau's entry of September 3, 1856, is based solely on my judgment that none of the other material in that entry would be appropriate for inclusion here.

169 **Loudon writes . . . harnessing horses:** Loudon, 2:1168, 1169. I emend the source, Thoreau, "Common Place Book 1," pp. 346–47, by adding square brackets and ellipses as necessary to accommodate the offset format; by adding to the introductory clause the words "Loudon writes of"; and by deleting an ellipsis before the close-parenthesis in *"(Don's Mill.)."* Where Thoreau completes a sentence by writing, "[that is, of England and in America]," Loudon writes, "as in Lincolnshire and the neighbouring part of Norfolk" (2:1168). Interestingly, in the left margin beside the assertion about Russian cranberries being better than American ones, Thoreau drew a heavy, bold exclamation mark. In Loudon, *"Eng."* means "English"; *"Smith* and *Withering"* refers to "English Botany. By Sir J. E. Smith and Messrs. Sowerby. Lond[on] 1790–1814, 36 vols. 8vo." (1:cxcix) and to *"Withering's Botany.* A Systematical Arrangement of British Plants. By W. Withering . . . ed. 7. with additions, London, 1830, 4 vols., 8vo." (1:ccxxvi); and *"Don's Mill."* refers to *"Don's Miller's Dictionary*[:] A general System of Gardening and Botany . . . founded on Miller's Dictionary . . . By George Don . . . 3 vols. published in 1837" (1:cxcviii).

170 **Of "Marish Worts . . . or Moore berries":** Gerarde, p. 1419. This paragraph is written on a scrap affixed with red sealing wax to a leaf with the preceding MS source material on the European cranberry. Thoreau left no indication where he wanted the text placed, so its placement here is conjectural. I emend by adding the words "Of" and "Gerarde says" to the clause introducing the quotation. After the sentence ending "taste rough and astringent" in the MS Thoreau drew a horizontal line, and just above that line he wrote, "This all," which I have not been able to interpret. The complete sentence in Gerarde that Thoreau abbreviates in the MS reads, *"Valerius Cordus* nameth them *Oxycoccon:* wee have called them *Vaccinia palustria,* or Marish Wortleberries, of the likenesse they have to the other berries: some also call them Mosse-Berries, or Moore-berries."

170 **Gray . . . ripen in September:** Gray, (1848), p. 394, says, "the dark blue fruit borne on a red stalk, ripe in September."

170 **On Hill and trees northwest of P. Dudley's:** Thoreau appears to be referring here to the unusual sassafras he saw on August 15, 1854, about which he wrote in his journal of that date: "A mile and a half northeast of Strawberry Hill, two or three large and very healthy and perfect sassafrass trees (three large at least), very densely clothed with dark-green lemon (?) or orange (?) tree shaped leaves, singularly healthy. This half a mile or so west of the [Paul] Dudley House. Comparatively few of the leaves were of the common form, *i. e.* three-lobed, but rather simple" (*Journal*, 6:443–44).

171 **According to Loudon . . . middle of September:** Loudon, 3:1439. "In America, in the neighborhood of New York, the nuts are ripe about the middle of September, a fortnight earlier than those of the other species of walnut."

171 **Alcott:** The reference is to the educator Amos Bronson Alcott, Thoreau's good friend and the father of Louisa May Alcott.

171 **Thornton and Campton:** Two small towns in north-central New Hampshire between eight and eleven miles north-northwest of Squam Lake, and between seventeen and twenty miles south of Franconia Notch.

171 **Michaux . . . species of walnut":** Michaux, 1:162–63.

171 **About the first . . . come to get them:** I derive the text of this paragraph from a later version of this passage (Berg Collection, "Dispersion of Seeds" folder, accession number 228) because the earlier, *Wild Fruits* MS version (Berg Collection, "Notes on Fruits" folder, accession number 252) has a single vertical pencil line through it, which may indicate that Thoreau intended to delete the passage from *Wild Fruits* but may just as well indicate that he transcribed the earlier version for use in one or both of these later manuscripts.

172 **Curving down August tenth, 1860:** Thoreau wrote this sentence between the lines that compose the preceding sentence without indicating where to place the interlineation, so my placement of this sentence here is conjectural.

172 **lily (*Nuphar advena*):** In the MS Thoreau wrote the Latin name after the date, "September first," so I emend by moving the Latin name to this location.

173 **Brattleboro:** See the note above for p. 155.

173 **Marblehead:** A town on the coast of Massachusetts eighteen miles north of Boston and twenty-seven miles east of Concord Center.

173 **Gerarde . . . thro' this land":** Gerarde, p. 347. I emend by adding both the material in square brackets and the brackets themselves.

174 **of *Viburnum acerifolium*:** I emend by adding these two words, which are clearly implied in the MS.

175 **Brattleboro:** See the note above for p. 155.

175 **Loudon calls them "black":** Loudon, 2:1034.

176 **Gerarde says . . . rich man's mouth":** Gerarde, pp. 1269, 1271. In this instance Thoreau spelled Gerarde's name in the MS without the terminal *e*, a common alternate spelling but contrary to Thoreau's usual spelling, which I here restore.

177 **Woodbine, September third:** I emend by omitting "1858" after "third."

177 **Old Gerarde . . . ripe "in August":** Gerarde treats "the Ash tree" on pp. 1471–72 and under "The Time" writes, "The leaves and keyes come forth in April and May, yet is not the seed ripe before the fall of the leafe" (p. 1472). He treats "the wilde Ashe, otherwise called Quicke-Beame or Quicken tree" on pp. 1473–74 and under "The Time" writes, "The wild Ash floures in May, and the berries are ripe in September" (p. 1473). In neither chapter does Gerarde use the word "August."

177 **days—say sixth:** I emend by deleting as redundant after this line the line "August 25, 1859 partly turned," which Thoreau copied from the preceding MS page.

177 **"The mountain ash . . . North America":** Nuttall, 2:63. I emend by adding "says" and by moving "Nuttall" from the end of this quotation to the beginning.

177 **In the *Geological* . . . forty feet high:** James Richardson, p. 51.

177 **Petersboro:** Also spelled "Petersborough." A town in south-central New Hampshire eleven miles north of the Massachusetts–New Hampshire border, and forty-three miles northwest of Concord Center.

177 **Brattleboro:** See the note above for p. 155.

178 **Osterman . . . seeds and roots":** Pulteney, pp. 420–21, where "M. G. Osterman" is the author of a brief essay on *Culina mutata.*

178 **"Oak corn, that is ac-corn, or acorn":** In the MS Thoreau cites his source with the note, "Burnet quoted by Loudon, p. 1721," referring to Loudon's remark: " 'Little as we now depend for sustenance on the fruits of our forest trees,' Burnet observes, 'and great as is the value of their wood, the reverse was formerly the case: oak corn, that is, ac-cern, or acorns, some centuries ago, formed an important food both for man and beast.' (*Amœn. Quer.*, fol. 1.)" (3:1721). The citation "*Amœn. Quer.*, fol. 1" is expanded in Loudon's "List of Books Referred to" as "*Amœnitates Querneæ.* 1722. By the late Professor Burnet, published in Nos. 5. and 6. of Burgess's Eidodendron. 1833. folio" (1:cxci). Thoreau seems to have regarded Loudon's "ac-cern" as a typographical error, for he clearly writes "ac-corn" in the MS.

178 ***all kinds* are green yet:** I derived the last three words here, "are green yet," from the journal source (*Journal*, 12:324).

179 **Michaux . . . upon their hind feet":** Michaux, 1:83. Thoreau wrote this quotation in the upper-right corner of the MS page at a later time and did not indicate where it should be inserted in the text. I insert it, based solely on its position at the top of the page, into the text before the other material on the MS page.

179 **When Gosnold . . . grew on the mainland:** Both Archer (for Gosnold) and Pring mention oaks several times in their relations, but not the shrub specifically. I have

not been able to determine if Champlain mentions shrub oaks specifically in his relation.

180 **Emerson's Lot:** Of the various lots around Concord that Ralph Waldo Emerson owned in the early 1860s, it is not clear which this might be. His holdings were especially extensive in the Walden Woods, particularly around Walden Pond.

181 **on the trees still:** In the MS Thoreau continued this sentence with the words, "and in some places," which is the beginning of another clause in his journal source, the whole of which reads, "and in some places at least half the shrub-oak acorns" (*Journal*, 12:384). I emend by deleting "and in some places."

182 **Michaux . . . are "rarely abundant":** Michaux, 1:20.

183 **When the Lacedæmonians . . . will hinder thee":** Herodotus, p. 27. This passage is written on a scrap affixed with wax to a full MS page, but Thoreau did not indicate where in the text on the full page he wanted to insert the passage. My insertion at this location is arbitrary.

183 **Dodonean fruit?:** Dodona in Epirus, Greece, was in ancient times regarded as the sanctuary of Zeus, the chief Greek god, and the Dodonean oaks were reputed to be the source of oracles, presumably from the rustling of their leaves.

183 **The Indians used to boil them in a log:** Thoreau source for this observation has not been located.

183 **nuts abstracted:** After these words in the MS Thoreau wrote, "(*Vide* perhaps date)," referring to the remainder of his journal passage for October 11, 1859, which reads as follows:

> Looking under large oaks (black and white), the acorns appear to have fallen or been gathered by squirrels, and so on. I see in many distant places stout twigs (black or scarlet oak) three or four inches long which have been gnawed off by the squirrels, with four to seven acorns on each, and left on the ground. These twigs have been gnawed off on each side of the nuts in order to make them more portable, I suppose— the nuts all abstracted and sides of the cups broken to get them out.

183 **wholesome, shining, dark-chestnut color:** The MS reads, "wholesome shining dark chestnut (?) color," so the hyphenation is editorially supplied and the query omitted. Note that Thoreau later extracted this same passage from his journal as the first extract after the end of his earlier, 188-page draft of *Wild Fruits* (see notes below to p. 186 and p. 186).

184 **twenty-sixth, 1853):** I emend by moving Thoreau's note of the year, "1853," from the beginning of this sentence to its current location.

184 **all kinds have fallen:** Thoreau wrote after this sentence in the MS, "(No)."

184 **1852. I find an:** I add the word "an" here.

184 **What proportion sound:** Thoreau wrote *"Vide date"* in the MS here, referring to the remainder of the journal passage, which I include in the text ("In about five quarts . . . whatever you can get"; *Journal*, 12:157).

184 **How oak woods are produced, if necessary:** Thoreau's note: "(that is, May 13, 1856, no. 21, and June 3d.)" By "no. 21" he means vol. 21 of his MS journal, which contains the two entries referred to, which are as follows:

[From entry of May 13, 1856 (*Journal*, 8:335)] I suspect that I can throw a little light on the fact that when a dense pine wood is cut down oaks, etc., may take its place. There were only pines, no other tree. They are cut off, and, after two years have elapsed, you see oaks, or perhaps a few other hard woods, springing up with scarcely a pine amid them, and you wonder how the acorns could have lain in the ground so long without decaying. There is a good example at Loring's lot. But if you look through a thick pine wood, even the exclusively pitch pine ones, you will detect many little oaks, birches, etc., sprung probably from seeds carried into the thicket by squirrels, etc., and blown thither, but which are overshadowed and choked by the pines. This planting under the shelter of the pines may be carried on annually, and the plants annually die, but when the pines are cleared off, the oaks, etc., having got just the start they want, and now secured favorable conditions, immediately spring up to trees. Scarcely enough allowance has been made for the agency of squirrels and birds in dispersing seeds.

[From entry of June 3, 1856 (*Journal*, 8:363)] While clearing a line through shrub oak, which put his eyes out, [John Hosmer] asked, "What is shrub oak made for . . . ?" Hosmer says he had a lot of pine in Sudbury, which being cut, shrub oak came up. He cut and burned and raised rye, and the next year (it being surrounded by pine woods on three sides) a dense growth of pine sprang up. As I have said before, it seems to me that the squirrels and so on disperse the acorns and so forth amid the pines, they being a covert for them to lurk in, and when the pines are cut the fuzzy shrub oaks and so on have the start. If you cut the shrub oak soon, probably pines or birches, maples, or other trees which have light seeds will spring next, because squirrels and so forth will not he likely to carry acorns into open land. If the pine wood had been surrounded by white oak, probably that would have come up after the pine.

These two journal passages were the first articulations of Thoreau's theory on forest succession, later formalized in his lecture-essay "The Succession of Forest Trees" and expanded in his book-length MS, *The Dispersion of Seeds*.

184 **Michaux . . . is peculiarly downy:** Michaux, 1:44.
184 **Michaux . . . those of the other species":** Michaux, 1:96.
184 **Scarlet-oak acorn *figured*:** In the MS after these words Thoreau wrote, "*Vide* date and also perhaps p. 54," by which he means that the drawing in his journal entry of September 19, 1854 (*Journal*, 7:47), should be inserted in the *Wild Fruits* text at this point and that he considered placing the following text from p. 54 of his MS journal vol. 18 (*Journal*, 7:51) into *Wild Fruits* at this location as well:

I am surprised to see balls on the scarlet oak. Its acorn and cup are peculiarly top-shaped, the point of the acorn being the bottom. The cup is broader than in the black oak, making a broader shelf about the acorn, and is more pear-shaped or prolonged at top. The acorn is not so rounded, but more tapering at point. And some scarlet oak leaves which I see have their two *main* veins and diverging ribs nearly opposite, while in a black-oak leaf these veins, and hence lobes, are not nearly opposite.

In his journal Thoreau wrote "Not general" in the left margin next to this passage, and I emend his journal text for this passage by adding the word "see" in the last sentence.

185 **November 10, 1858:** Thoreau wrote after this citation in the MS, "Jays plucking and *Vide* p. 90 for form," which refers first to the remainder of the paragraph in the text after this citation, which I derive from MS journal vol. 28, pp. 9–10 (*Journal*, 11:308), and second to the "form" or drawing of the scarlet-oak acorn, which is derived from MS journal vol. 28, p. 90 (*Journal*, 11:347).

185 **November 10, 1856:** Although the MS reads "November 10, *1857*" (my emphasis), it should read as I here emend it, for the journal entry for November 10, *1856*, is the source from which Thoreau drew this passage (*Journal*, 9:138).

185 **Perth Amboy:** I emend by adding the word "Perth" here. For information on Perth Amboy, see the note above for p. 120.

185 **November 2, 1856:** Although the MS reads "November 2, *1857*," (my emphasis), it should read as I here emend it, for the journal entry for November 2, *1856*, is the source from which Thoreau drew this passage (*Journal*, 9:137).

185 **Michaux says *Quercus* . . . is very fertile:** Michaux, 1:47, 51.

185 **Melvin:** George Melvin was one of Concord's ne'er-do-wells who, as Harding points out, "spent all their time hunting and fishing, living their lives from one day to the next and enjoying every minute" (p. 328). As such, Thoreau liked him and referred to him often in his journal.

185 **Assabet River:** I add the word "River."

185 **Wood . . . every third year":** William Wood, p. 18. This passage is the last one in Thoreau's 188-page second draft of *Wild Fruits*.

186 **wholesome, shining, dark-chestnut color:** The MS reads, "wholesome shining dark chestnut (?) color," so the hyphenation is editorially supplied and the query omitted. Note that Thoreau had earlier extracted this passage from his journal as the second extract in the "Acorns Generally" section (see note above to p. 183).

186 **April 29, 1852:** Thoreau wrote along the left margin in the MS next to this passage, "or in Dispersion of Seeds," indicating that he had revised this passage for use in *The Dispersion of Seeds* and that the revised version of this passage could supplant this early version. Rather than use the revised version of the passage here, however, I include it (as well as relevant surrounding passages) in the "The Dispersion of Seeds: Acorns" section of "Related Passages," pp. 249–51.

186 **Sagard . . . thickened their broth":** Sagard, *Histoire du Canada*, p. 976. The translation is Thoreau's.

186 **And *Trillium*:** I add the word *"Trillium"* here.

186 **large red berry:** After this line in the MS Thoreau wrote, *"Vide* two last trips to Monadnock." He had last visited Mount Monadnock on June 2–4, 1858, and August 4–9, 1860 (*Journal*, 10:452–80 and 14:8–52). While on the first of these two trips he mentioned the trillium in his journal twice, as follows: "There, too, the *Trillium erythrocarpum*, now in prime, was conspicuous—three white, lanceolate, waved-edged petals with a purple base. This the handsomest flower of the mountain, coextensive with the wooded sides" (entry of June 2, 1858; *Journal*, 10:454); and "Beneath them [the trees on Monadnock] grew the *Trillium pictum* and *clintonia*, both in bloom" (entry of June 4, 1858; *Journal*, 10:480). He did not mention the trillium at all in his journal during his last trip to Mount Monadnock.

186 **Michaux . . . food for "red-breasts":** Michaux, 3:37.

187 **Gray calls it "blackish-blue":** Gray (1848), p. 397.

187 **Staples's meadow wood:** The reference is to Sam Staples, the one-time town constable who locked Thoreau in the Concord Jail for refusal to pay taxes, an incident which occasioned Thoreau's enormously influential essay "Civil Disobedience," sometimes titled "Resistance to Civil Government."

187 **White Pine [section]:** See the later revision of this material in "Related Passages," the passage titled *"The Dispersion of Seeds:* White Pine," pp. 252–56.

187 **handsome grove?:** Thoreau identifies this in his journal source as "the white-pine grove behind Beck Stow's" Swamp (*Journal*, 7:489).

188 **June 1850 . . . strewn with:** Thoreau wrote these passages vertically in the left margin and did not indicate where he wanted them inserted. I insert them here arbitrarily.

188 **Michaux says open about first of October:** Michaux, 3:159.

188 **September 9, 1857 . . . almost entirely:** Thoreau transcribed these passages from his journal for use in *Wild Fruits*, of course, but he then revised them for use (whether simultaneous use or exclusive use, it is not possible to determine at this stage of composition) in *The Dispersion of Seeds*. In the revision process Thoreau inserted transposition lines and other marks, but I do not here incorporate Thoreau's revisions as indicated by those marks because he made those marks when revising for *The Dispersion of Seeds* rather than for *Wild Fruits*.

188 **Emerson's Heater-Piece trees:** Thoreau's journal entry of October 8, 1856 (*Journal*, 9:105), which is the source of this passage, suggests that Emerson's Heater Piece was just off or near the Cambridge Turnpike near Smith's Hill. The *Oxford English Dictionary* defines a *heater-piece* as "a gore or triangular piece of land."

188 **be agreeable to some:** Thoreau originally wrote in pencil after this paragraph, "Next perhaps the chestnut." But later he wrote the passage beginning "September 16, 1860" over the pencil and the remaining blank space. It is likely that he considered following this section on white pines with a section on the chestnut when he was

drafting this passage for an early draft of *The Dispersion of Seeds*, where this passage
is used. In the draft of *The Dispersion of Seeds* that Thoreau left at his death, however, the analogous passage about the white-pine cones is followed by a passage on
the seeds of the hemlock and larch" (Thoreau, *Dispersion of Seeds*, pp. 39–40).

189 **cones beneath branches:** This word ("branches") added. Note that Thoreau's journal entry for that day contains no mention of this phenomenon, another of many
indications that Thoreau was revising *Wild Fruits* at this time (*Journal*, 14:88).

189 **October 29, 1858 . . . hard to come off:** Thoreau put this line in parentheses,
which might indicate that he intended to delete it.

189 **How little observed . . . half a mile distant:** In the *Wild Fruits* MS containing the
early version of this passage (Berg Collection, "Notes on Fruits" folder, leaf paged
with accession number 289), Thoreau wrote, "*Vide* Dispersion [of] Seeds for corrected version," referring to the later revision of this passage in the Berg Collection,
"Dispersion of Seeds" folder, leaf paged with accession number 29. I follow Thoreau's
instructions, of course, and use here the later version of this passage from *The Dispersion of Seeds* MS (see *The Dispersion of Seeds*, pp. 34 and 35).

190 **Worcester:** The second largest city in Massachusetts, about thirty-five miles southwest of Concord. Thoreau visited the city often, for he had several good friends
who lived there, most notably Harrison G. O. Blake and Theophilus Brown.

190 **Coombs:** Beginning in February 1856 Thoreau mentions Coombs (by his last name
only) in his journal a dozen times, all but two times in connection with hunting. In
his journal for March 26, 1860, Thoreau approvingly quoted his neighbor and walking companion William Ellery Channing's description of Coombs as " 'the musquash
hunter and partridge and rabbit snarer" (*Journal*, 13:231).

190 **Found in drill hole:** Thoreau queried this assertion in the MS, but see *The Dispersion of Seeds*, where he writes, "Exploring one of the old limestone quarries in the
north part of Concord one November, I noticed in the side of an upright sliver of
rock, where the limestone had formerly been blasted off, the bottom of the nearly
perpendicular hole which had been drilled for that purpose, two or three inches
deep and about two and a half feet from the ground, and in this I found two fresh
chestnuts, a dozen or more pea-vine (*Amphicarpæa*) seeds, as many apparently of
winterberry seeds, and several fresh barberry seeds, all bare seeds or without the
pericarp, mixed with a little earth and rubbish" (p. 147).

190 **say September tenth:** I add the word "September" here. After this passage in the MS
Thoreau wrote, "*Vide* Dispersion of Seeds—or else Miscellaneous p. 101." He refers
to the paragraph that follows in the text, beginning "One September I gathered," the
source of which is two MS pages in the Berg Collection, "Dispersion of Seeds" folder,
accession numbers 91–92. Thoreau refers in his note to an earlier version of this same
paragraph on p. 101 of his 112-page "Miscellaneous" draft, which is in the Berg
Collection, "Notes on Fruits" folder, accession number 501.

190 **One September:** Thoreau interlined "(18th, 1859)" in the MS here.

191 **Pin-weed:** To Thoreau pin-weed, cistus, and lechea are synonymous.

191 ***nigrum,* September fourteenth:** I add "September" here.

191 **Walpole, New Hampshire:** From September 10 to 12, 1856, Thoreau visited his friend, the educator Amos Bronson Alcott, in Walpole, which is about twenty-five miles north of the Massachusetts border on the Connecticut River (*Journal* 9:76–80).

192 **rattle-pod:** I add this word on authority of the journal source (*Journal,* 14:89–90).

192 **west of the Deep Cut:** I add the word "Deep." This is Thoreau's name for the "Deep Cut" dug in 1844 through the small hill northwest of Walden Pond to accommodate the Fitchburg Railroad.

192 **back and found it:** I delete from this location the following passage, which Thoreau appears to have tried to revise as he transcribed it from his journal and which he placed in parentheses, probably immediately after he transcribed it, to indicate deletion: "(So in the winter (?) I hear the seeds rattling—but more finely in the little black pods of the indigo weed when the wind—and late in the fall I sometimes detect the beans which the farmer has not gathered in some weedy or grassy field—by my feet striking them and causing them to rattle. Perchance these seeds are thus betrayed to those wild creatures that feed on them.)"

192 **when the wind blows:** I add the word "blows."

192 **One year . . . unexpected place:** The journal source of this passage is the entry of October 3, 1858 (*Journal,* 11:194).

193 **ripen September fifteenth:** I emend by drawing the date, "September fifteenth," from Thoreau's interlined note, which reads, "Put this forward to September 15."

193 **amaranth, and so on:** Thoreau first wrote "Roman wormwood and chenopodium" but later interlined "—Amaranth and so on" after "chenopodium," so I emend by standardizing the parallel construction.

193 **hundreds of sparrows:** Thoreau wrote "(chip-birds?)" in the MS following this phrase.

194 **Springer . . . fifty feet in air":** Springer, p. 28. Thoreau identifies his source in the MS as "Common Place Book 1, p. 15."

194 **Red beech ripe . . . according to Michaux:** Michaux, 3:26.

194 **Hips of rose:** I emend by adding the word "rose."

194 **December 14, 1850 . . . thick as winterberries:** Thoreau wrote immediately after this sentence, "(What kind?)." Later he wrote next to this query, "*Vide* same side other rose," a reference to his section on "Early Rose," where he expresses the same difficulty he has here of distinguishing the early from the late rose (see the note above to p. 126).

195 **Loudon . . . food of bears":** Loudon, 2:1123.

195 **a woman on Cape Cod . . . better than cherries:** Thoreau wrote in his journal entry for June 20, 1857, when he was visiting the Highland Light and surrounding area in

Truro, Massachusetts, on the Atlantic side of Cape Cod, just south of Province-town, "Talked with an old lady who thought that the beach plums were better than cherries" (*Journal*, 9:446).

196 ***cornuti*, September sixteenth:** Thoreau wrote in the MS after this sentence, "*Vide* Dispersion [of] Seeds," referring to the text on six MS pages in folder titled "Dispersion of Seeds" at the Berg Collection, accession numbers 209–12, 214–15, which is the source of the remaining text in this section (*The Dispersion of Seeds*, pp. 90–94).

196 **it in the air even in the spring.):** Thoreau originally wrote the sentence this way, but in revising for *The Dispersion of Seeds* he changed "it" to "one kind," a change that I reverse here because "one kind" only makes sense within the context of *The Dispersion of Seeds*. Also, after "spring" Thoreau interlined in the MS here "? (March 20, 1853)," referring to his journal source for this observation.

196 **stem like a flourish:** I emend by deleting the following four sentences, which follow here in the MS but which are only relevant within the larger context (milkweeds generally, as opposed to *Asclepias cornuti*) of *The Dispersion of Seeds*: "The wavy-leaved has slender pods. It is perfectly upright and five inches long. The water milkweed, whose down I begin to see about the 4th of October (1856), has small, slender, straight, and pointed pods—perfectly upright—and large seeds with much margin or wing. But to confine ourselves to the *Asclepias cornuti*."

196 **inside and out, its pod:** Because I deleted the preceding four sentences from the MS (see preceding note), I further emend by moving "Its pod" from the front of this sentence in the MS to this location. My only reason for emending here, however, is stylistic: the preceding sentence here begins "Its pods"; having this sentence also begin "Its pod" would be a stylistic injustice I feel confident Thoreau would not want me to commit.

196 **(or shaped like a steelyard *poire*):** See the note below to p. 127. I italicize *poire* (French for "pear") on the presumption that it is a foreign word.

197 **One of my neighbors:** I have been unable to identify this person.

197 **attic window:** From 1850 until his death in May 1862 Thoreau lived in the attic of his parents' house on Main Street in Concord. His writing desk was in front of the two windows on the western side of the room.

197 **end of September:** Thoreau interlined "(20th, 1860)" in the MS here.

197 **I notice:** I delete "(August 26, 1860)" from the beginning of this sentence.

197 **one afternoon:** Thoreau interlined "(September 24, 1857)" in the MS here.

197 **meadow on Clematis Brook:** Thoreau interlined in the MS here "(near the deserted Abel Minott house)."

197 **now point upward:** Thoreau interlined in the MS here "(Did they before point down?)."

198 **Mr. Lauriat:** According to Crouch, pp. 191–96, Louis Anselm Lauriat emigrated from the French West Indies to Salem, Massachusetts, in 1806. In Boston on July 17, 1835, the forty-nine-year-old Lauriat made the first of nearly fifty ascents in a balloon, the last ascent occurring in 1848. He died ten years later in Sacramento, California.

198 **prophecies of Daniel or of Miller:** The apocalyptic visions or prophecies of the prophet Daniel are recorded in the Old Testament, Book of Daniel, chaps. 7–12. William Miller (1782–1849), whose followers were known as Millerites, founded the Adventist movement in the United States during the 1840s and predicted that the Second Coming of Christ would take place on March 21, 1844.

198 **end of November:** Thoreau interlined "(22d, 1857)" in the MS here.

199 **Hieracium down. September eighteenth:** Thoreau wrote in the margin of the MS beside this phrase, *"Vide* Dispersion of Seeds," referring to the paragraph that follows here, which is derived from a single MS in the folder titled "Dispersion of Seeds" in the Berg Collection, accession number 216 (*The Dispersion of Seeds*, p. 94).

199 **eighteenth of September:** Thoreau interlined "(1860)" in the MS here.

200 **December 14, 1850:** At the top of the MS page that begins with this phrase (Berg Collection, "Notes on Fruits" folder, accession number 251), Thoreau wrote, "Sweet Gale September 1" and "September 22, 1860. Is yet green, but perhaps it is ripe." Then he deleted the "1" after "September," wrote "22" in its stead, and interlined "Move this forward to September 22." I emend by deleting all of these passages as redundant vestiges of Thoreau's composition process.

200 **August 28, 1859. . . . begin to yellow:** I emend by putting the date before the passage here.

200 **Assabet River:** I add the word "River."

200 **Gerarde . . . full of small flowers":** Gerarde, p. 1414. Thoreau adds the word "many" here.

200 **last of September:** Thoreau interlined "(21st, 1860)" in the MS here, but his journal source was actually the entry of September 22, 1860.

201 **It is said . . . part of their supply":** Knapp, p. 118.

201 **This appears . . . (*oxydendron*) of the South:** Cutler, p. 443. I have not been able to locate the "recent *Systema Naturæ*" Thoreau refers to.

201 *Lespedeza,* **September twenty-fifth:** Thoreau wrote in the MS here and then deleted "September 25, 1860," and beside that deleted date he wrote, "Put *here.*" It is unclear what he intended to place here. Perhaps somewhere in his late natural history manuscripts is a scrap with material about the lespedeza. In any case, nowhere in his journal for September 1860 does he mention this plant.

202 **My sister saw much in Princeton:** I emend by replacing "Sophia" in the MS with "My sister," which would conform with Thoreau's practice of not using proper names of individuals in his published writings. Sophia had visited her friend Dora

(Swift) Foster in East Princeton, Massachusetts, about thirty-five miles west of Concord.

202 **Leaves *not* fallen . . . by their greenness:** Expanded from Thoreau's MS note, "Leaves *not* fallen &c &c." I derived the words after "fallen" here from Thoreau's manuscript journal entry of September 24, 1859 (*Journal*, 12:351).

202 **as they will be:** Thoreau wrote after this sentence, "*Vide* perhaps making tallow in New Bedford." From April 2 to April 15, 1857, Thoreau visited his friend Daniel Ricketson in New Bedford, Massachusetts, a coastal city sixty miles south of Concord. While there he wrote the following passages in his journal about making bayberry tallow:

> [From entry of April 7, 1857 (*Journal*, 9:320)] At sundown I went out to gather bayberries to make tallow of. Holding a basket beneath, I rubbed them off into it between my hands, and so got about a quart, to which were added enough to make about three pints. They are interesting little gray berries clustered close about the short bare twigs, just below the last year's growth. The berries have little prominences, like those of an orange, encased with tallow, the tallow also filling the interstices, down to the nut.
>
> They require a great deal of boiling to get out all the tallow. The outmost case soon melted off, but the inmost part I did not get even after many hours of boiling. The oily part rose to the top, making it look like a savory black broth, which smelled just like balm or other herb tea. I got about a quarter of a pound by weight from these say three pints of berries, and more yet remained. Boil a great while, let it cool, then skim off the tallow from the surface; melt again and strain it. What I got was more yellow than what I have seen in the shops. A small portion cooled in the form of small corns ("nuggets" I called them when I picked them out from amid the berries)—flat, hemispherical, of a very pure lemon yellow—and these needed no straining. The berries were left black and massed together by the remaining tallow.
>
> [From entry of April 8, 1857 (*Journal*, 9:321)] I discovered one convenient use the bayberries served: that if you got your hands pitched in pine woods, you had only to rub a parcel of these berries between your hands to start the pitch off. Arthur [Ricketson's son] said the shoemakers at the Head of the River used the tallow to rub the soles of their shoes with to make them shine. I gathered a quart in about twenty minutes with my hands. You might gather them much faster with a suitable rake and a large, shallow basket, or if one were clearing a field he could cut the bushes and thresh them in a heap.

Thoreau used these entries as the basis for the first paragraph of his chapter "VI. The Beach Again" in *Cape Cod*, pp. 80–81. The first four chapters of *Cape Cod* were published serially in 1855, but the full book (including the bayberry-tallow paragraph below) was posthumously published in 1865. The paragraph reads:

Our way to the high sand-bank, which I have described as extending all along the coast, led, as usual, through patches of Bayberry bushes, which straggled into the sand. This, next to the Shrub-oak, was perhaps the most common shrub thereabouts. I was much attracted by its odoriferous leaves and small gray berries which are clustered about the short twigs, just below the last year's growth. I know of but two bushes in Concord, and they, being staminate plants, do not bear fruit. The berries gave it a venerable appearance, and they smelled quite spicy, like small confectionery. Robert Beverley, in his "History of Virginia," published in 1705, states that "at the mouth of their rivers, and all along upon the sea and bay, and near many of their creeks and swamps, grows the myrtle, bearing a berry, of which they make a hard brittle wax, of a curious green color, which by refining becomes almost transparent. Of this they make candles, which are never greasy to the touch nor melt with lying in the hottest weather; neither does the snuff of these ever offend the smell, like that of a tallow candle; but, instead of being disagreeable, if an accident puts a candle out, it yields a pleasant fragrancy to all that are in the room; insomuch that nice people often put them out on purpose to have the incense of the expiring snuff. The melting of these berries is said to have been first found out by a surgeon in New England, who performed wonderful things with a salve made of them." From the abundance of berries still hanging on the bushes, we judged that the inhabitants did not generally collect them for tallow, though we had seen a piece in the house we had just left. I have since made some tallow myself. Holding a basket beneath the bare twigs in April, I rubbed them together between my hands and thus gathered about a quart in twenty minutes, to which were added enough to make three pints, and I might have gathered them much faster with a suitable rake and a large shallow basket. They have little prominences like those of an orange all encased in tallow, which also fills the interstices down to the stone. The oily part rose to the top, making it look like a savory black broth, which smelled much like balm or other herb tea. You let it cool, then skim off the tallow from the surface, melt this again and strain it. I got about a quarter of a pound weight from my three pints, and more yet remained within the berries. A small portion cooled in the form of small flattish hemispheres, like crystallizations, the size of a kernel of corn (nuggets I called them as I picked them out from amid the berries). Loudon says, that "cultivated trees are said to yield more wax than those that are found wild." (See Duplessy, *Végétaux Résineux,* Vol. II. p. 60.) If you get any pitch on your hands in the pine-woods you have only to rub some of these berries between your hands to start it off. But the ocean was the grand fact there, which made us forget both bayberries and men.

202 **Bigelow says . . . in their effects":** Bigelow, *American Medical Botany,* 2:xiii. Thoreau silently omits Bigelow's "of plants" after "other natural families" in the final sentence. He also used this quotation at the end of one of the beginnings of

Wild Fruits (see the end of "Wild Fruits" section in "Related Passages," p. 244, and the note below for p. 244).

202 **umbelliferous aquatics:** Thoreau underscored these two words in MS and spelled the former "umbiliferous," both of which anomalies I correct by restoring to the source (see previous note).

203 **Michaux says about October first:** Michaux, 3:103.

204 **Corn, October first:** Thoreau wrote in the MS here, "*Vide* October 7, and September 18, 1860" and "Harvest home *Vide* Common Place Book 2, p. 174." The first of these notes refers to two passages that Thoreau transcribed from his journal onto a separate MS page and added to the larger *Wild Fruits* MS; those passages appear in their turn (where Thoreau placed them) later in the "Corn" section. The second note, about "Harvest home," refers to a long passage that Thoreau had transcribed into "Common Place Book 2," pp. 174–76, from Brand and that Thoreau clearly planned to insert at some location in the "Corn" section; lacking any indication where he wanted that passage inserted, I have placed it at the end of the "Corn" section.

204 **Early in August:** Thoreau wrote in the MS after this phrase, "(11th, 1852)."

205 **my father:** John Thoreau, who had died peacefully at his Main Street home in Concord, Massachusetts, on February 3, 1859, with his family gathered around him, including Thoreau, who wrote an eloquent tribute to his father in his journal of that date (*Journal*, 11:435–37).

205 **Gerarde says . . . swine than for men:** Gerarde, pp. 82, 83.

205 **stalk be a span long:** After this clause in the MS Thoreau wrote "(branches of sterile part)," which is not in Gerarde and which Thoreau may have intended to be a bracketed comment. I omit the phrase from the text.

205 **Lindley quotes . . . America of Maize":** Lindley, pp. 376, 377. Thoreau wrote at the top of the scrap this quotation appears on, "under corn," with no other indication of its placement, so its placement here is somewhat arbitrary.

206 **Brand in his *Popular* . . . brought home every load:** Brand, 2:16–17, 20, 28, 34. For the placement of this passage here, see the note above to p. 204. In "Common Place Book 2," pp. 174–76, the source of this passage, Thoreau wrote the title "Harvest Home" on p. 174 and transcribed the passage from Brand with no introduction, so the introductory clause ("Brand in his *Popular Antiquities* describes 'Harvest Home' ") before the offset quotation is my own, although Thoreau did ascribe his extracts to "Brand's Popular Antiquities" on p. 173 of "Common Place Book 2."

207 **October 27, 1856. At Perth Amboy . . . scarlet leaves:** I emend by placing the date at the beginning rather than the end of this sentence and by adding "Perth." For information on Perth Amboy, see the note above for p. 120.

208 **Pliny . . . for their fragrance:** Pliny, *Historiæ Mundi*, bk. 15, chap. 10. The translation is Thoreau's.

208 **November 10, 1856:** Emended from "November 10, 1857" in the MS; see journal source in entry of November 10, 1856 (*Journal*, 9:137).

208 **Perth Amboy:** For information on Perth Amboy, see the note above for p. 120.

208 **ticks in the fields:** I emend by deleting "there" after "fields," where it is redundant.

209 **Michaux . . . violet colored instead of green":** Michaux, 3:215.

211 **packed in a little chest:** Thoreau wrote "Nuts placed in the bark—*Vide* March 7, 1859" in the MS here, referring to the passage from his journal entry for that date, which I insert into the MS after this passage (*Journal*, 12:20).

211 **jar down many nuts:** I emend by omitting "yet" from the end of this sentence, where it is redundant.

213 **not only are squirrels:** I derive the words "only are" here from the journal source of this passage (*Journal*, 9:147).

213 **Loudon quotes Pliny . . . any other manner":** Loudon, 3:1897.

213 **Evelyn says, referring . . . beans to boot":** Thoreau's source here is actually Loudon, 3:1994.

213 **In France, according . . . for immediate use":** Loudon, 3:1995. A "sabot" is a wooden shoe or clog worn of old in France and other European countries. The word *sabotage* (etymologically, from *saboter*, "to clatter with sabots") is derived from this word.

213 **Minott tells . . . near Flint's Pond:** The sense of this sentence is difficult because Thoreau used the first "near" in its somewhat rare adverbial sense, as in "finding *nearly* a bushel." I do not emend this usage because Thoreau employs it in his journal source as well as here (entry of September 24, 1857; *Journal*, 10:41).

213 **It has gaped:** After "gaped" in the MS Thoreau wrote "(open)."

214 **infant in the arms:** Before "arms" Thoreau had written "brawny," but he later enclosed the word in parentheses to indicate deletion.

215 **skin enwraps the meat:** Thoreau wrote at the end of this sentence "(with its germ)."

215 **successive concentric circles:** Thoreau wrote at the end of this sentence, "(around the tree)."

216 **I hear the dull thump of heavy stones:** Thoreau originally began this sentence "I hear from time to time the dull thump of heavy stones cast," but he later enclosed "from time to time" and "cast" in parentheses to indicate deletion.

216 **One of the company . . . half a bushel:** Thoreau suggests in the journal source to this passage (*Journal*, 10:173) that he was surveying for Stedman Buttrick and Mr. Gordon when this story was related to him. He also relates a story told him by Jacob Farmer, who was no doubt one of the "company" that day.

216 **Loudon, New Hampshire. First and frequently:** Loudon, New Hampshire, is seven miles northeast of Concord, New Hampshire. Apparently Thoreau means by "First and frequently" that he saw the chestnut when he *first* entered Loudon on the evening of July 3, 1858, and saw it *frequently* thereafter during his visit (*Journal*, 11:6).

216 **Josselyn says . . . twelve pence per bushel:** Josselyn, *New-Englands Rarieties Discovered*, p. 51.

216 **Gathered a few chestnuts:** After this passage in the MS, Thoreau wrote "*q.v.*" (*quod vide* or "which see"), referring to the remainder of the journal passage he had begun with the words "Gathered a few chestnuts." I add hereafter the text referred to, but Thoreau may have meant to include as well (after "and so do a service" in the text) the one-sentence paragraph that follows in the journal source: "I find whitish grubs stretching themselves under the moist chestnut leaves, but they were in the same state in January" (*Journal*, 5:9).

216 **Sophia's:** Thoreau's younger sister.

216 **March 20, 1853:** After this date in the MS, Thoreau wrote, "*q.v.* [*quod vide* or "which see"] p. 26 and 15," referring to passages on those two pages in his MS journal. The first passage referred to, page 26, follows in the text because it is clear that is the passage Thoreau refers to. Page 15 of the same journal volume, however, actually contains the following material from his entry of March 18, 1853—material which has nothing to do with chestnuts and does not seem relevant to the context Thoreau has established in his text:

> The season is so far advanced that the sun—every now and then promising to shine out through this rather warm rain, lighting up transiently with a whiter light the dark day and my dark chamber—affects me as I have not been affected for a long time. I must go forth.
>
> Afternoon to Conantum.
>
> I find it unexpectedly mild; it appears to be clearing up, but will be wet underfoot. Now, then, spring is beginning again in earnest after this short check. Is it not always thus? Is there not always an early promise of spring, something answering to the Indian summer which succeeds the true summer, so an Indian or false spring preceding the true spring? A first false promise, which merely excites our expectations to disappoint them, followed by a short return of winter. Yet all things appear to have made progress even during true wintry days, for I cannot believe that they have thus instantaneously taken a start.

216 **Walnuts, October thirteenth:** Thoreau originally wrote "15" in the MS here and then reformed the "15" to "13." Although this reformation is not immediately apparent in the MS (the "5" still looks very much like a "5"), the placement of the MS page within the sequence of pages in the "Notes on Fruits" folder supports the change from "15" to "13."

216 **the hill):** The journal source makes it clear that Nawshawtuct Hill is meant here (*Journal*, 4:32).

217 **shell. The walnuts:** After "walnuts" Thoreau wrote "(pignuts?)."

217 **with their fine . . . reproving the while):** After the passage ending here, Thoreau interlined the note "(*Vide* perhaps for nuts gnawed and Buster Kendal)," referring to

the remainder of this paragraph in the journal source (entry of November 1, 1853; *Journal*, 5:471), which reads as follows: "It is not true, as I noticed today, that squirrels never gnaw an imperfect and worthless nut. Many years ago I came here nutting with some boys who came to school to me; one of them climbed daringly to the top of a tall walnut to shake. He had got the nickname of Buster for similar exploits, so that some thought he was christened so. It was a true Indian name earned for once." *Concord Births, Marriages, and Deaths*, p. 319, lists the birth on March 16, 1829, of Henry Kendall, who was a student of Thoreau's at the Concord Academy. Thoreau and his brother John, Jr., operated the Concord Academy from the summer of 1838 until the spring of 1841 (Harding, pp. 75–87).

219 **December 16, 1856. Mrs. Moody:** I emend the MS from December "14" because Thoreau's source is actually December 16. The Mrs. Moody that Thoreau refers to has not been identified but may have been the wife of George Barrell Moody, a classmate of Emerson's at Harvard College.

219 **Michaux says that . . . round, some oblong:** Michaux, 1:178.

219 **Michaux says the . . . others are perfectly round":** Michaux, 1:196.

221 **Asnebumskit Hill . . . except Wachusett:** At 1,395 feet, Asnebumskit Hill in Paxton, four miles northwest of the city of Worcester, is indeed the second highest land in Worcester County, which spans the breadth of central Massachusetts. For Wachusett, see the note above to p. 22 ("Many years ago").

221 **March 6:** I add the word "March" here.

221 **Viola Muhlenbergii Brook:** I add the word "Viola" here. Thoreau variously called this brook "Viola Muhlenbergii Brook," "V. Muhlenbergii Brook," and simply "Muhlenbergii Brook."

222 **Loudon . . . seedling plants of *Kalmia latifolia*":** Loudon, 2:1125.

222 **August 19, 1852. They never bloom:** Thoreau inserted the date and journal extract beginning here sometime after writing the one following, which has the same date.

223 **According to Bigelow . . . lobata, and in birches:** Bigelow, *American Medical Botany*, 2:30. Thoreau originally wrote "and the root of *Spiræa lobata*" and ended the sentence there, but he later changed the period to a comma and added "and in birches." So I emend both by deleting "and" and adding "in" before "the root."

223 **Manasseh Cutler . . . children in milk":** Cutler, p. 444.

223 **as September fourteenth:** After this phrase Thoreau wrote "(1859)."

223 **flavor, and perchance:** Thoreau at first wrote these words as they are here, but he then interlined *"now"* after "and." He then enclosed *"now"* in parentheses, which I interpret as indicating deletion.

223 **This season:** I emend by omitting "October 3, 1859" from the beginning of this paragraph.

223 **ripens within the tropics:** Here Thoreau interlined the intriguing sentence *"Vide perhaps more elsewhere in Wild,"* which almost certainly means he considered in-

corporating into this location one or more passages from his lecture manuscript "Walking, or the Wild," which was not published until after his death as the essay "Walking," the last half of which is on "The Wild" and which contains one of his most famous statements: "in Wildness is the preservation of the world." I have found no indication of what material from the last half of Thoreau's lecture he may have considered using in this location.

224 **middle of a frozen barrel:** Thoreau wrote after this paragraph, "*Vide* p. 85 and p. 51 on Frost," but a check of both his journal volumes for the October 1857 and October 1859 periods turns up no passages relating to frost.

224 **Harvest Days:** Although the nature of this holiday period seems clear from the context, as well as the fact that it was a holiday, I have not been able to locate a specific reference to the period as a holiday.

224 **walnut, October fifteenth:** Thoreau wrote "*Vide* last page" after this heading, referring to the passages in this section, which are all on another single MS page.

224 **size of a small lemon:** I delete from this location Thoreau's comment "(R. Rice says these are his brother Israel's)."

224 **Gray says it . . . western states:** Gray (1848), p. 411.

224 **Emerson says that . . . found in Massachusetts:** Emerson, *Report on Trees*, p. 185.

224 **Michaux says our . . . is more round:** Michaux, 1:158, writes, "Though differing widely from the European species [European walnut], [the black walnut] bears a nearer resemblance to it than any other American Walnut."

225 **Shagbark, October twentieth:** After this passage in the MS Thoreau wrote, "*Vide* last page but one," which refers to passages about shagbark hickories on the MS leaf paged with accession numbers 259–60 in the Berg Collection's "Notes on Fruits" folder. I follow Thoreau's instruction by inserting those passages here. However, one of those passages is dated December 18, 1856, and immediately following the note ("*Vide* last page but one") Thoreau transcribed from his journal of that same date another passage, also on shagbark hickories. Both of these passages dated December 18, 1856, are one sentence in length. I emend by inserting the second of these passages into the MS directly after the first of these two passages.

225 **Shagbarks hanging:** I emend by deleting "December 18, 1856" from before this word as redundant.

225 **Souhegan River:** The word "River" added. Thoreau traveled in a buggy along the Souhegan River on his way to Amherst, in south-central New Hampshire, on December 18, 1856, to deliver a lecture in the Congregational Church there.

225 **Wachusett:** See the note above to p. 22 ("Many years ago").

225 **Gookin . . . artichokes in their pottage:** Gookin, p. 10.

225 **Hind . . . in the richest profusion:** Hind, *Rapport sur L'Exploration*, pp. 44–47. In "Common Place Book 2," p. 202, Thoreau wrote, "Hind is translated, 'The earth is covered with the richest profusion [he is on Rainy River] of [among other plants] . . .

de topinambours (artichauts de Jérusalem).' " French *topinambours* are Jerusalem artichokes in English. After "profusion" in the *Wild Fruits* MS Thoreau wrote, *"Vide*
perhaps my extract from Gerarde" and *"Vide* perhaps Common Place Book 2, p.
202." The second note refers to the Hind passage just quoted. The first note, on Gerarde, apparently refers to an unlocated MS containing an extract from Gerarde's
fairly brief chapter on artichokes, Gerarde, pp. 1152–54.

226 **Boxboro and Cambridge:** Boxboro, Massachusetts, is about nine miles west of Concord Center, on the other side of Acton, and Cambridge is about fifteen miles east
of Concord, just across the Charles River from Boston.

226 **black-birch scale:** Thoreau wrote in the MS here, "(?) (not white)."

226 **little antennæ:** At the bottom of the MS page that ends here, Thoreau wrote the following notes: *"Vide* Dispersion of Seeds of March 2, 1856, that is, Behind Pritchard
and Loudon extracts," and "Potatoes—corn and turnips not quite all gathered November 15, 1856." I incorporate into the text here the two specific passages from *The
Dispersion of Seeds* that Thoreau refers to in these notes (Berg Collection, "Dispersion
of Seeds" folder, accession numbers 143–44 and 147, 149; see *The Dispersion of Seeds*,
pp. 44 and 46, 46–47) and, for the sake of comparison, include Thoreau's analogous
section on birches from *The Dispersion of Seeds* in "Related Passages," pp. 257–62.

226 **Mr. Prichard's land:** Moses Prichard lived on Main Street in Concord, but Thoreau
doubtless refers to land elsewhere owned by Prichard.

227 **It is stated in . . . blank that occurs":** Loudon, 3:1691, 1694, 1696. Peter Simon Pallas was a well-known Russian botanist, and Loudon identifies the French author only
as "the author of the article Bouleau, in the *Dictionnaire des Eaux et Forêts."*

227 **Cape Cod man . . . delivered at New York:** Captain Edward W. Gardiner of Nantucket Island was Thoreau's host when Thoreau visited the island to deliver a lecture before the Nantucket Athenæum on December 27–28, 1854. Gardiner's
avocation was the reforestation of the island, a subject he and Thoreau discussed at
length during Thoreau's brief visit. At the end of this passage in the MS Thoreau interlined several notes, all of which he later deleted (probably after transcribing the
passages he lists) except one, which reads, *"Vide* extract from Loudon." I feel confident that the Loudon extract he refers to is the quotation he uses at the beginning
of the section on the pitch pine, just after the exordium of *The Dispersion of Seeds*,
p. 24 (begins "It is related that 'when Vatinius' "; see "Related Passages," pp.
262–63).

228 **persistent are they:** Thoreau wrote at this point in the MS, *"Vide* Pliny's name for
them," a reference to Pliny, *Historiæ Mundi*, bk. 16, chapt. 44, where Pliny names
them *"azaniæ,"* which the translators, Bostock and Riley, say in a footnote means
" 'Dried' nuts" (3:385 n. 11). Thoreau uses this word, *"azaniæ,"* near the beginning
of *The Dispersion of Seeds*, p. 25.

228 **Michaux . . . closed for several years":** Michaux, 3:151–52.

229 **regularly at the seeds:** I emend by omitting the following passage that follows "seeds" in the MS here and that clearly represents Thoreau's extemporaneous attempt to compose one sentence in the midst of transcribing another from his journal: "(If we bungle art a boiled ear of corn—asking a knife to aid us—what think you of a family of young squirrels with each a rigid pitch pine—cone in its paws—not boiled nor salted and no knife)." Later, after this attempt, Thoreau revised this material and was more successful with expressing the idea he attempted here (see "Related Passages," p. 268).

229 **seventh of this month:** Where the words "of this month" appear here, Thoreau actually wrote "ult." (for *ultimo*, which is from the Latin for "before" and was often used during Thoreau's time to mean "last month"). Thoreau regularly used *ult.* when he obviously meant *inst.* (for "instant," or "this month"). I emend by correcting Thoreau's common error, expanding the Latinate abbreviation to its plain-English equivalent ("this month"), and adding the preposition "of."

229 **relaxed in every part:** Thoreau wrote in the MS after these words, *"Vide* scales blown across Walden—in Dispersion [of] Seeds," which I interpret to mean that he wanted the relevant passage from *The Dispersion of Seeds* inserted at his location in *Wild Fruits.* My source for the next two paragraphs (from "Unlike the white pine" to heaving of the frozen shore") is two MS pages in the Berg Collection, "Dispersion of Seeds" folder, accession numbers 12–13 (also see *The Dispersion of Seeds*, pp. 27–28).

230 **one of our ponds:** Identified from the journal source of the next paragraph (entry of July 20, 1860) as Walden Pond.

230 **middle of July:** Thoreau interlined "(July 20, 1860)" in the MS here.

231 **curving rays:** Thoreau wrote at this point in his MS, *"Vide* Miscellaneous January 24, 1855," which is a reference to the passage from William Wood that follows in the MS on a separate page. Thoreau also wrote a draft of this passage on page 52 of his 112-page "Miscellaneous" draft MS in the Berg Collection ("Notes on Fruits" folder, accession number 379).

231 **how the primitive wood . . . Charles River] side":** Wood, p. 57. I add from Thoreau's journal entry of January 24, 1855 (*Journal,* 7:132), the words "to William Wood, the author of *New England's Prospect,* who left New England August fifteenth 1633." On page 52 of his "Miscellaneous" draft (see preceding note) Thoreau had added the following introductory passages before quoting Wood: "From William Wood, *New England's Prospect.* (He left New England in 1633.)"

232 **Pliny . . . *communis* of Linnæus) in must:** Pliny, *Historiæ Mundi,* bk. 14, chapt. 19 (Bohn edition, *Natural History,* 3:260 n. 81).

232 **Loudon . . . gin"—that is, to flavor it:** Loudon, 4:2491, 2493.

233 **a man:** Thoreau refers here to John LeGrosse, whom he surveyed for on January 11 and 12, 1853, and whom Thoreau alluded to in the "Black Huckleberry" section when he said that he had surveyed for a man who neglected to pay for the survey-

ing—or paid only with a quart of red huckleberries (see p. 39 above). Thoreau wrote of LeGrosse in his journal entry of these dates, "This man is continually drinking cider; thinks it corrects some mistake in him; wishes he had a barrel of it in the woods; if he had known he was to be out so long would have brought a jugful; will dun Capt. Hutchinson for a drink on his way home. This, or rum, runs in his head, if not in his throat, all the time. Is interested in juniper berries, gooseberries, currants, etc., whether they will make wine; has recipes for this. Eats the juniper berries raw as he walks" (*Journal*, 4:462–63).

233 **White Mountains:** A range of mountains in northern New Hampshire, extending into Maine, and a popular vacation spot in Thoreau's time because the area was within a day's train ride from Boston and other metropolitan areas in southern New England.

233 **I visited . . . its noble oak wood:** On October 23, 1860, as Thoreau points out in his journal, neighbor Anthony Wright told him "of a noted large and so-called primitive wood, Inches Wood, between the Harvard turnpike and Stow, sometimes called Stow Woods, in Boxboro and Stow" (*Journal*, 14:167). Thoreau visited Inches Wood on November 9 and 16, 1860.

234 **to shoot squirrels in it:** In *The Dispersion of Seeds*, p. 135: "I visited last fall the three principal old oak woods in this vicinity, or that I know of within eight or ten miles, and found accidentally that these were such peculiar resorts for the gray squirrel that several with whom I talked supposed that I had come after these squirrels, and one was able to give me some information about the most distant and interesting wood because he had been accustomed to go there formerly to hunt gray squirrels." The "one" who told Thoreau about the interesting wood (Inches Wood) was Anthony Wright (see preceding note).

234 **a very brief historical notice . . . buried in this place":** Gardner, pp. 83–84. I emend the MS spelling from "Gardiner" to "Gardner" and restore the word "the" in the expression "I am of the mind" on authority of Gardner and Thoreau's journal source (entry of November 26, 1860; *Journal*, 14:274–75), which has the correct spelling of "Gardner" and which also has "the" in the aforementioned expression. Thoreau transcribed correctly from Gardner to his journal but made these two errors when transcribing from his journal to the *Wild Fruits* MS. Gardner's predecessor in the ministry was John Eveleth. Gardner "was ordained to the pastoral office" in Stow on November 26, 1718, and John Green had been "captain of the guard at the king's dock-yard at Deptford" as well as Cromwell's clerk of the exchequer (pp. 83–84). In 1660, with the Restoration of the monarchy after the English Civil Wars, the English Parliament passed the Act of Indemnity and Oblivion, which granted general amnesty to all citizens who had acted against Charles II except those listed in the act as supporters of the Cromwellian regicides, who were excluded from the act and therefore liable to prosecution.

234 **a young man . . . was still standing:** I have located no information on who this young man may have been.

234 **still standing. Around . . . is interesting or not:** After "still standing," which originally ended the paragraph it is part of, Thoreau interlined in pencil the sentence "Around this all the materials of this history were to arrange themselves." At that time he also wrote in the margin of the MS here, *"Vide* March 18th, 1861," which refers to the paragraph in the text beginning "You can't read any genuine history." When selecting this material from his MS journal, I was mindful of a vertical use mark Thoreau had drawn through the material, a clear indication that only the material I present here from his journal (from "You can't read" to "interesting or not") should be incorporated into the text of *Wild Fruits.* I point this out because at the end of the journal version of this paragraph are the following fascinating sentences: "You are simply a witness on the stand to tell what you know about your neighbors and neighborhood. Your account of foreign parts which you have never seen should by good rights be less interesting" (*Journal,* 14:330).

234 **Herodotus or the Venerable Bede:** Saint Bede the Venerable was an Anglo-Saxon historian and the author of *The Ecclesiastical History of the English People,* which records events in Britain from the Roman incursions of 55 B.C. to the arrival of St. Augustine in A.D. 597. Herodotus was a Greek historian and the author of *History,* which records the events leading to Greece's twenty-year war with Persia (499–479 B.C.), as well as the events of the war itself.

235 **I have since heard . . . tax now than it would then:** See the note above to p. 233 ("I visited").

235 **the people of Massachusetts . . . professorship of Natural History:** Dupree points out that "A group of leading Boston citizens in 1805 founded the Massachusetts Professorship of Natural History. . . . While linked with [Harvard] college, the establishment was a community project" (p. 104).

236 **"freedom to worship God," as some assure us:** The First Amendment to the U.S. Constitution reads in part, "Congress shall make no law respecting an establishment of religion, or prohibiting the free exercise thereof. . . ."

236 **New Hampshire courts . . . took formal possession:** I have not been able to locate any report about this incident.

238 **commence our museum with a cartridge . . . from a British soldier in 1775:** In a telephone call on October 7, 1998, David Wood, Curator of the Concord Museum in Concord, Massachusetts, informed me that Thoreau gave Cummings Davis, the founder of the Concord Museum, such a cartridge box.

238 **salvages:** The *Oxford English Dictionary* points out that this word is an archaic form of *savage;* Thoreau uses it, of course, to point to the Latin etymology of the word *silva,* which means "wood" or "forest."

238 **through a waste . . . Darien Grounds:** Darien Grounds was the name for the At-

lantic shelf east of the Isthmus of Darien, now called the Isthmus of Panama. The area had a bad reputation for barrenness among New England mariners who were short of supplies on their returns from the Pacific Ocean. Thoreau originally wrote "through a waste ocean or in a northern desert," but later he interlined "the Darien Grounds" without altering the preposition, "in," which I here emend to "on." Also, after "Darien Grounds" Thoreau had written, "and so die of ship-fever and scurvy. Some will die of ship-fever and scurvy in an Illinois prairie, they lead such stifled and scurvy lives." Later, he enclosed this passage in parentheses, which I interpret to mean that he wished the passage deleted.

239 **saves at the spile and wastes at the bung:** A popular, somewhat homely expression whose meaning is clear if one understands that a barrel is filled through a bung-hole, which is stoppered with a bung and is usually located in the center of the upright barrel, and that one uses the contents of a barrel by drawing small amounts out of the spile, a spigot usually located at the bottom of the upright barrel. Hence, the expression refers to conserving or preserving a resource in one way while squandering or despoiling that same resource in another manner—which is foolishness.

NOTES TO "RELATED PASSAGES"

242 *Wild Fruits:* **Alternate Beginning:** I derived the text for this passage from six MS pages in the folder titled "Notes on Fruits" at the Berg Collection of the New York Public Library, accession numbers 283, 421–24, 594.

242 *Agrestem tenui* . . . **sing unbidden things:** Virgil, *Eclogues*, bk. 6, lines 8–9. The Latin sentence alone appears in the source manuscript; the translation here, apparently Thoreau's, is from a leaf in the Berg Collection of the New York Public Library, "Notes on Fruits" folder, accession number 399.

242 **Moralists:** Thoreau preceded this passage with the date "August 21, 1852," which I emend by deleting.

242 **"By their fruits . . . know them":** Matthew 7:20.

242 **"By their flowers . . . know them":** I have not been able to locate a botanist Thoreau is known to have consulted who wrote this expression.

242 **(Science is often . . . tasted it.):** Thoreau sometimes used parentheses to enclose material he considered deleting; this may be an instance of such a usage, a possibility rendered the more likely by the sentences's position (near the beginning of a section or chapter or perhaps the entire book) and the sentence's caustic tone.

242 **Carpenter's explanation . . . in that direction":** Carpenter, p. 174.

242 **As Mrs. Lincoln says . . . perennial ones":** Phelps (Mrs. Lincoln), p. 37. I supply this clause from Thoreau's "Common Place Book 1," p. 201, on authority of

Thoreau's note in the MS: "Mrs. Lincoln's Botany, [p.] 37; Common Place Book 1, p. 201."

242 **When:** In the MS Thoreau preceded this passage with the date "October 17, 1859," which he enclosed in parentheses, apparently indicating deletion.

243 **When La Mountain and Haddock dropped . . . nor how to shelter themselves:** John La Mountain and John A. Haddock ascended in the balloon *Atlantic* from Watertown, New York, on September 22, 1859, intending to be the first balloonists to cross the Atlantic Ocean; but strong winds blew them on a north-northeasterly course deep into the Canadian wilderness, where for four days they subsisted on "a frog apiece, four clams, and a few wild berries," the latter of which La Mountain identified as "high-bush cranberries" ("The Great Balloon Voyage," see "Works Cited").

243 **Broadway or Quincy Market:** Well-known shopping districts of the time in New York City and Boston, respectively.

244 **in good season:** Thoreau wrote in pencil at the end of this passage in the MS, "*Vide* Bigelow on poisonous Plants and fruits under Cicuta," which I interpret as Thoreau's instruction to move to this location the quotation from Bigelow that he had used under the "*Cicuta maculata*" section of *Wild Fruits* (see p. 202 and see the note that follows here).

244 **Bigelow says . . . in their effects":** Bigelow, *American Medical Botany*, 2:xiii. Thoreau silently omits Bigelow's "of plants" after "other natural families" in the final sentence. Thoreau used this quotation in the "*Cicuta maculata*" section of *Wild Fruits* as well. See the previous note here, p. 202, and the note above for p. 202.

244 **umbelliferous aquatics:** Thoreau underscored these two word in MS and spelled the former "umbiliferous," both of which anomalies I correct by restoring to the source (see previous note).

244 **"Wild Apples": Beginning and Ending:** I derived the text for this passage from Thoreau's "Wild Apples" essay as published in *The Atlantic Monthly Magazine* for November 1862, pp. 513–15, 526. The editors of *The Atlantic Monthly* applied their own house style to the MS Thoreau submitted to them on April 2, 1862, just over a month before his death; likewise, I have silently modified nonsubstantive elements of *The Atlantic Monthly* text to conform to the style I employ throughout this volume and describe in the headnote to "Editor's Notes" above, p. 286. For evidence indicating that Thoreau wrote the material in this passage specifically to serve as the published essay's introduction and conclusion, see MS drafts of those paragraphs, Houghton Library, Harvard University, call number bMS Am 278.5, folders 9a–9g.

244 **The geologist . . . man on the globe:** Hugh Miller points out that "Agassiz, a geologist whose statements must be received with respect by every student of the science, finds reason to conclude that the order of the Rosaceæ . . . was introduced only a short time previous to the appearance of man" (p. 78). Miller himself adds to the list

of such plants "the true grasses" (p. 78) and "the *Labiate* family,—a family to which . . . the mints . . . belong . . ." (p. 79).

244 **It appears that apples . . . recovered from their stores:** Compare the almost identical passage on p. 28, and see the note above for p. 28.

244 **Tacitus says of the ancient Germans . . . (agrestia poma), among other things:** Thoreau's source for Tacitus is known (see "Works Cited"), but I have not been able to identify the page where this quotation appears.

244 **Niebuhr . . . alien from the Greek":** Niebuhr, 1:64.

245 **the first human pair were tempted by its fruit:** Genesis 3:6 reads, "And when the woman saw that the tree was good for food, and that it was pleasant to the eyes, and a tree to be desired to make one wise, she took of the fruit thereof, and did eat. . . ."

245 **at least three places . . . "apple of the eye":** The apple is actually mentioned ten separate times in the Old Testament. Thoreau quotes from the Song of Solomon 2:3 and 2:5, respectively; "apple of the eye" appears at Psalms 17:8; "apple of thine eye" at Proverbs 7:2 and Lamentations 2:18; "apple of my eye" at Deuteronomy 32:10; and "apple of his eye" at Zechariah 2:8. Proverbs 25:11 reads, "A word fitly spoken is like apples of gold in pictures of silver." The Song of Solomon 7:8 and 8:5 read in part, "the smell of thy nose [shall be] like apples" and "I raised thee up under the apple tree," respectively.

245 **Homer and Herodotus . . . away from him:** Homer, *The Odyssey*, bk. 7, line 589 (garden of Alcinoüs), and bk. 11, line 585 (Tantalus). Although Thoreau may have read what Herodotus said about the apple tree in *Herodotus, A New and Literal Version*, p. 427 (bk. 7, chap. 41), he may as well have relied on Loudon, who writes, "The apple tree is mentioned by Theophrastus, Herodotus, and in sacred history" (2:894).

245 **Theophrastus . . . as a botanist:** Theophrastus refers to the apple (tree, fruit, seeds, leaves, wood, and so on) in considerable detail throughout his *Enquiry into Plants*.

245 **the Prose Edda . . . destruction of the gods:** Sturluson, *Prose Edda*, p. 54, and see the note above to p. 75.

245 **Loudon . . . badge of the clan Lamont":** Loudon, 2:899, 2:894. The phrase "the token of the apple spray" is enclosed in quotation marks in Loudon, who cites the source as *"Davies's Welsh Bards,"* which he expands in his "List of Books Referred to" as "Edw. Davies's Celtic Researches; London, 1801, 8vo: and Edw. Davies's Rites of the British Druids; London, 1809, 8vo." (1:cxcvii).

245 **Loudon . . . Western Asia, China, and Japan":** Loudon, 2:894.

246 **Pliny, adopting . . . civilized (urbaniores)":** *Pliny, Historiæ Mundi*, bk. 16, chap. 32.

246 **Theophrastus . . . most civilized of all trees:** Theophrastus, bk. 3, chap. 45.

246 **Blossom Week . . . spreading over the prairies:** Thoreau is probably referring to one or more of the efforts of John Chapman (1774–1847) to encourage the propogation of the apple among early settlers of the American Midwest, efforts that earned Chap-

man the nickname Johnny Appleseed. I have not been able to locate any reference to a Blossom Week as a midwestern holiday.

246 **"The fruit of the Crab . . . resource for the wild-boar":** Thoreau's source for this quotation has not been located.

247 **The Roman writer Palladius said . . . split root will retain them":** Thoreau's source for Palladius is known to be *Scriptores Rei Rusticæ*, but I have not been able to identify the page where this quotation appears.

247 **a saying in Suffolk . . . apple goes to the core:** Thoreau's source for this quotation has not been located.

247 **"The word of the Lord . . . from the sons of men:** Joel 1:1–2, 4–7, 11, 12.

248 *The Dispersion of Seeds:* **Touch-Me-Not:** I derived the text for this passage from a single MS page in the folder titled "Dispersion of Seeds" at the Berg Collection of the New York Public Library, accession number 92. Substantively the same version of this passage appears in *The Dispersion of Seeds*, p. 81.

248 *The Dispersion of Seeds:* **Hound's-Tongue:** I derived the text for this passage from two MS pages in the folder titled "Dispersion of Seeds" at the Berg Collection of the New York Public Library, accession numbers 231–32. Substantively the same version of this passage appears in *The Dispersion of Seeds*, pp. 98–99.

248 **was naturalized:** Thoreau interlined in the MS here "(notice about August 1; at height perhaps middle of August)."

248 **a young lady . . . young lady's mother:** See the note above for p. 99.

249 *The Dispersion of Seeds:* **Lilies:** I derived the text for this passage from three MS pages, two in the folder titled "Dispersion of Seeds" at the Berg Collection of the New York Public Library, accession numbers 227–28, the other from the folder titled "Notes on Fruits" in the Berg Collection, accession number 253. Substantively the same version of this passage appears in *The Dispersion of Seeds*, pp. 99–100.

249 **Saint Pierre . . . where they grow":** Saint Pierre, 3:192.

249 *The Dispersion of Seeds:* **Acorns:** I derived the text for this passage from eight MS pages in the folder titled "Dispersion of Seeds" at the Berg Collection of the New York Public Library, accession numbers 259–62, 339, 351–53. Substantively the same version of this passage appears in *The Dispersion of Seeds*, pp. 110–12.

250 **Nuttall . . . New Spain the same number":** Nuttall, 1:17. This passage is an expansion of Thoreau's interlineation in the MS, "*Vide* Nuttall on Range of Oaks, Common Place Book 1, p. 190," which refers to the following extract: " 'oaks—are confined to the Northern Hemisphere.—The Old World contains sixty-three species, and North America, including New Spain, about seventy-four. Of these the United States possesses about thirty-seven, and New Spain the same number.' Nuttall's North American Sylva. Philadelphia 1853."

251 **it is recommended . . . it has ripened":** Loudon, 3:1728, 1718, 1968, 1437. When Loudon uses the phrase "beech mast," he is using "mast" in the sense of "the fruit of the beech . . . especially as food for swine" (*Oxford English Dictionary*).

251 **Cobbett says . . . down by the winds":** Cobbett, 2:14.

251 **it is stated by one . . . soon vegetated":** Thoreau's source for this quotation has not been located.

251 **Mr. George B. Emerson . . . immediately vegetate":** Emerson, *Report on Trees*, p. 54.

251 **According to Loudon . . . up till the third year:** Loudon, 4:2178, 2224.

252 ***The Dispersion of Seeds: White Pine:*** I derived the text for this passage from fifteen MS pages in the folder titled "Dispersion of Seeds" at the Berg Collection of the New York Public Library, accession numbers 27–41. Substantively the same version of this passage appears in *The Dispersion of Seeds*, pp. 34–39.

252 **Worcester:** The second largest city in Massachusetts, about thirty-five miles southwest of Concord.

253 **French soldiers in Sevastopol:** On September 16, 1854, a large contingent of French soldiers, as well as troops from Britain, Turkey, and Sardinia, landed on the Crimean Peninsula and for a full year laid siege to the Russian fortress at Sevastopol.

253 **few they may be:** Thoreau interlined "other side of wall?" in the MS here.

254 **"spontaneously generated":** During most of the nineteenth century many people believed—and even so great a scientist as Louis Agassiz believed—that plants were capable of growing or being generated spontaneously, without the benefit of progenitors, such as seeds or cuttings. Charles Darwin's great treatise *On the Origin of Species* (published November 1859) was written in part to counter this belief, as was Thoreau's *The Dispersion of Seeds*, which was written during the fall and winter of 1860–61 and which strongly supports Darwin's argument. For a Thoreau-centered discussion of spontaneous generation, see Dean, "Henry D. Thoreau and Horace Greeley Exchange Letters."

254 **"little strokes fall great oaks":** Bartlett points out that John Lyly wrote in *Euphues: The Anatomy of Wit* (1579), "Many strokes overthrow the tallest oaks"; and that in his *Poor Richard's Almanack* for August 1750, Benjamin Franklin wrote, "Little strokes, / Fell great oaks."

254 **In an account of Duxbury . . . this growth":** "Topographical Description of Duxborough," p. 5. Duxbury is on Plymouth Bay, thirty miles south of Boston and forty-five miles southeast of Concord Center.

255 **it is stated in Loudon . . . several years":** Loudon, 4:2131.

256 **for the squirrels:** Thoreau interlined here "Insert Douglas on Lambert getting pine cones," apparently a reference to the botanists David Douglas and Aylmer Bourke Lambert, but the source in Douglas's writings has not been located. Douglas was a

collector for the Horticultural Society of London; Lambert was a fellow of the society. During the nineteenth century the two men were the world's foremost students of conifers.

257 *The Dispersion of Seeds*: **Birch:** I derived the text for this passage from sixteen MS pages in the folder titled "Dispersion of Seeds" at the Berg Collection of the New York Public Library, accession numbers 139–47, 148a–b, 149–53. Substantively the same version of this passage appears in *The Dispersion of Seeds*, pp. 41–48.

258 **Alphonse De Candolle . . . among the Alps):** De Candolle, 2:613. Thoreau cited De Candolle's source in the MS as "(*Tabl. de la Nat.*, ed. 1851, volume 2, page 37, [Alexander] Humboldt)."

258 **Boxboro and in Cambridge:** Boxboro is a small town about twelve miles west-northwest of Concord; Cambridge is across the Charles River from Boston, about eighteen miles east-southeast of Concord.

258 **Mr. Prichard's land:** Moses Prichard lived on Main Street in Concord, but Thoreau doubtless refers to land elsewhere in Concord that Prichard owned.

259 **last summer:** Thoreau interlined "1860" in the MS here.

259 **one of our ponds (which contains sixty acres):** In the journal source of this passage, the entry of August 24, 1860 (*Journal*, 14:61), it is clear that Thoreau refers here to Walden Pond, where birches were springing up on the shore of Deep Cove.

259 **Alphonse De Candolle . . . in fresh water":** De Candolle, 2:985. Thoreau cited De Candolle's source in the MS as "(*Ann. Sc. Nat.*, V[I], page 373)," which appears in "Common Place Book 2," p. 253, " 'Annales des Sciences Naturelles*, 3d series, 1846, VI, page 373[']."

260 **the other day:** There is no journal source for this passage.

260 **State Street in Boston:** In the mid–nineteenth century, Boston's State Street was considered the center of commerce and finance in New England, much as we regard New York's Wall Street the national center today.

260 **Loudon's *Arboretum* . . . considerable intervals":** Loudon, 3:1691.

260 **as is stated . . . before known":** Thoreau's source for this quotation has not been located.

260 **I have had occasion . . . wilds of Maine:** Thoreau traveled three times to the Maine woods—in September 1846, September 1853, and July–August 1857—spending a total of about thirty-five days there. He wrote an essay for each of his three trips; they are collected in his *The Maine Woods*.

260 **Blodget, in his . . . highest mountains":** Blodget, pp. 78–79. Thoreau added the scrap containing this quotation to the larger *Dispersion of Seeds* MS in April 1861. I emend by moving the attribution, "Blodget's *Climatology*," from the end of the quotation to the introductory clause and by adding to the introductory clause the words "in his" and "says."

261 **Loudon, speaking . . . blank that occurs":** Loudon, 3:1694, 1696. In the first quotation Loudon refers to Peter Simon Pallas, a Russian botanist. Loudon identifies the French author referred to in the second quotation as "the author of the article Bouleau, in the *Dictionnaire des Eaux et Forêts.*"

261 **spring of 1859 . . . my neighbor:** In his journal source, the entry for April 30, 1859 (*Journal*, 12:168–69), Thoreau mentions collecting 110 birch seedlings, 10 of which he planted in his own yard, but he does not identify the neighbor to whom he gave the other 100 seedlings.

261 **In August 1861 I:** I add the words "In" and "I" here.

262 **now———inches:** Intending, no doubt, to measure the tree later, Thoreau left a space blank where I place the dash and never measured the tree, although he did insert a query ("?") in the margin of the MS opposite the blank space.

262 **seed is most abundant:** Thoreau interlined "(January 20–24, 1860)" in the MS here.

262 **seed in the copses:** Thoreau interlined "(January 8, 1860)" in the MS here.

262 **Mudie . . . losing their perch":** Mudie, 1:148.

262 **in the same manner:** Thoreau interlined "(January 7, 1860)" in the MS here.

262 *The Dispersion of Seeds:* **Pitch Pine:** I derived the text for this passage from twenty-two MS pages in the folder titled "Dispersion of Seeds" at the Berg Collection of the New York Public Library, accession numbers 7–24, 46–48, 48a. Substantively the same version of this passage appears in *The Dispersion of Seeds*, pp. 24–33.

262 **It is related . . . an apple' ":** Loudon, 4:2112. Thoreau has translated some of Loudon's Latin. According to the *Oxford English Dictionary*, an edile is "an officer who took care of the repair of temples and other buildings."

263 **its prickly shield:** Thoreau interlined in the MS at this point "count seventy-seven *good* in one."

263 **Darwin . . . do not open:** Darwin, *Origin of Species*, p. 146.

263 **little to one side:** I add the word "to" here.

264 **Michaux . . . for several years":** Michaux, 3:151–52.

264 **the other day:** Identified from the source of this passage in Thoreau's journal as November 26, 1860 (*Journal*, 14:269–70).

265 **one of our ponds:** Identified from the journal source of the next paragraph (entry of July 20, 1860) as Walden Pond (*Journal*, 13:410–11), although in that passage Thoreau refers to "little pines" rather than black birches.

265 **middle of July:** Thoreau interlined "(July 20, 1860)" in the MS here.

265 **I noticed lately:** Identified as November 20, 1860, from the journal source of that date (*Journal*, 14:253–54).

266 **last fall . . . one night:** Thoreau mentions in the journal source, the entry for October 30, 1860, that he had "tried the other night while in bed to account for" the phenomenon to which he refers in these two paragraphs (*Journal*, 14:196).

266 **I have found . . . and fuel:** In the "Economy" chapter of *Walden*, Thoreau had written, "The necessaries of life for man in this climate may, accurately enough, be distributed under the several heads of Food, Shelter, Clothing, and Fuel . . ." (p. 12).

267 **A neighbor:** Identified in the journal source (entry of October 20, 1860) as Edmund Hosmer (*Journal*, 14:161).

267 **last October:** Thoreau interlined "1860" in the MS here.

269 **for the same . . . its weak side:** Thoreau originally wrote "for the stem being removed, this becomes the weak side or point of attack," but he later interlined the clause cited here without deleting the original clause.

269 **April of last year:** Thoreau interlined "(1859)" in the MS here.

270 *The Dispersion of Seeds:* **Alternate Beginning:** I derived the text for this passage from three MS pages in the folder titled "Notes on Fruits" at the Berg Collection of the New York Public Library, accession numbers 399–401. Substantively the same version of this passage appears in *The Dispersion of Seeds*, pp. 177–79.

270 *Agrestem tenui . . .* **sing unbidden things:** See note above for p. 242.

270 **horse Columbus:** Reputed in 1860 to be the fastest horse alive.

270 **Mr. Blank, the Ossian Boy:** In his edition of Thoreau's nascent lecture "Huckleberries," Leo Stoller identifies "Mr. Blank" as "John C. Heenan, the Benecia Boy, who had become notorious in 1860—first by boxing the British champion Tom Sayers to a forty-two round draw, then by marrying the famous actress Adah Menken and afterward charging her with bigamy" (p. 40). Stoller, however, misread "Ossian" as "Oinan," which he took to be a play by Thoreau on *oeno* (sometimes spelled *oino*), the Greek root for *wine*. The name Ossian became widely known throughout Europe in 1762, after the Scottish poet James Macpherson "discovered" the poems of Oisín, the Irish warrior-poet of the Fenian cycle, and published the epic *Fingal*, representing the work as his translation of third-century Gaelic manuscripts. The "Poems of Ossian," as they were usually called, contained many similarities to Homer's epics, Milton's *Paradise Lost*, and both the Old and New Testaments. Many people were taken in by Macpherson's hoax, including the famous German writer Johann Wolfgang von Goethe—and the famous American writer Henry D. Thoreau.

270 **Pliny . . . the least things:** I have not located this quotation in Pliny.

270 **Mr. Seward or Caleb Cushing:** After Lincoln's election as president of the United States in November 1860, Senators Caleb Cushing (Democrat, Massachusetts) and William Henry Seward (Republican, New York) debated the issue of secession on the floor of the U.S. Senate and at Newburyport, Massachusetts.

271 **many English naturalists . . . pardon of the reader:** I have not been able to locate even one of the English naturalists Thoreau alludes to here.

WORKS CITED

Alcott, Amos Bronson. *Report of the School Committee of Concord, for the Year Ending April 2, 1860.* Concord, Mass.: Benjamin Tolman, 1860.

———. *Reports of the School Committee, and Superintendent of the Schools, of the Town of Concord . . . on Saturday, March 16, 1861.* Concord, Mass.: Benjamin Tolman, 1861.

———. *Reports of the School Committee, and Superintendent of the Schools, of the Town of Concord . . . on Saturday, March 15th, 1862. Concord, Mass.: Benjamin Tolman, 1861.*

"American Institute Farmers Club." *New-York Semi-Weekly Tribune.* 19 October 1860.

Archer, Gabriel. "The Relation of Captain Gosnold's Voyage to the North Part of Virginia. . . ." In *Collections of the Massachusetts Historical Society,* 3d ser., vol. 8 (1843): 72–81.

Bailey, Nathan. *A New Universal Etymological Dictionary. . . .* London: T. Osgood, J. Snipton, [et al.] 1755.

"Balloons." *New-York Semi-Weekly Tribune.* 11 October 1859.

Bartlett, John. *Familiar Quotations. . . .* Edited by Emily Morison Beck et al. 1882. Reprint, Boston: Little, Brown and Company, 1980.

Bartram, John. *Observations on the Inhabitants, Climate, Soil. . . . Made by Mr. John Bartram, in His Travels from Pennsylvania to Onondago, Onego, and the Lake Ontario, in Canada. . . .* London: J. Whiston and B. White, 1751.

Beverly, Robert. *The History and Present State of Virginia.* Edited by Louis B. Wright. Chapel Hill: University of North Carolina Press, 1947. Thoreau's edition: Robert Beverly. *The History of Virginia, in Four Parts. . . .* London: F. Fayram and J. Clarke, and T. Bickerton, 1722.

Bigelow, Jacob. *American Medical Botany. . . .* 3 vols. Boston: Cummings and Hilliard, 1817–20.

———. *Florula Bostoniensis. A Collection of Plants of Boston and Its Vicinity. . . .* Boston: Cummings, Hilliard, & Co., 1824.

Blodget, Lorin. *Climatology of the United States, and the Temperate Latitudes of the North American Continent. . . . Philadelphia: J. B. Lippincott, 1857.*

Botkin, B. A., ed. *A Treasury of New England Folklore.* New York: Crown Publishers, 1965.

Boucher, Pierre. *Histoire Véritable et Naturelle des Moeurs et Productions du Pays de la Nouvelle France, Vulgairement Dite la Canada*. Paris: F. Lambert, 1664.

Brand, John. *Observations on Popular Antiquities. . . . Arranged and Re., with Additions by Henry Ellis*. 2 vols. London: F. C. and J. Rivington, 1813.

Cameron, Kenneth Walter. "Tracing Scattered Thoreau Manuscripts (1905–1913): Sanborn, Bixby and Harper." *American Renaissance Literary Report* 4 (1990): 333–53.

Carpenter, William. *Vegetable Physiology, and Systematic Botany. . . .* London: H.G. Bohn, 1858.

Cartier, Jacques. *Voyages de Découverte au Canada, Entre les Années 1534 et 1542. . . .* Quebec: W. Cowan et Fils, 1843.

Champlain, Samuel de. *Voyages de la Nuuelle France Occidentale, dicte Canada. . . .* Paris: C. Collet, 1632.

Charlevoix, Pierre-François-Xavier de. *Histoire et Descritpion de la Nouvelle France. . . .* 3 vols. Paris: Veuve Ganeau, Libraire . . . , 1744.

Cobbett, William. *A Year's Residence in the United States of America. . . .* 3 vols. New York: Clayton & Kingsland, 1819.

Coleman, William Stephen. *Our Woodlands, Heaths & Hedges. . . .* London: Routledge, Warnes & Routledge, 1859.

Commagher, Henry Steele. *Theodore Parker*. Boston: Little, Brown, and Company, 1936.

Concord, Massachusetts: Births, Marriages, and Deaths, 1635–1850. Concord, Mass.: printed by the town, n.d.

Cornut, Jacques. *Doctors Medici Parisiensis Canadensium Plantarum . . . Aliarumque Nondum Editarum Historia. . . .* Paris: Venundatur apud Simonem Le Monye, 1635.

Crantz, David. *The History of Greenland. . . .* London: Brethern's Society for the Furtherance of the Gospel among the Heathen, 1767.

Crouch, Tom D. *The Eagle Aloft: Two Centuries of the Balloon in America*. Washington, D.C.: Smithsonian Institution Press, 1983.

Curzon, Robert. *Visits to Monasteries in the Levant*. London: John Murray, 1849.

Cutler, Mannaseh. "An Account of Some of the Vegetable Productions, Naturally Growing in This Part of America, Botanically Arranged." In *Memoirs of the American Academy of Arts and Sciences*, 1st ser., vol. 1 (1785): 396–493.

Darwin, Charles. *Journal of Researches into the Natural History and Geology of the Countries Visited during the Voyage of H.M.S. Beagle round the World. . . .* 2 vols. New York: Harper & Brothers, 1846.

———. *On the Origin of Species by Means of Natural Selection, or The Preservation of Favored Races in the Struggle for Life*. 1859. Reprint, New York: D. Appleton, 1860.

Dean, Bradley P. "Henry D. Thoreau and Horace Greeley Exchange Letters on the 'Spontaneous Generation of Plants.' " *New England Quarterly* 66, no. 4 (December 1993): 630–38.

————. "A Reconstruction of Thoreau's Early 'Life without Principle' Lectures." In *Studies in the American Renaissance, 1987*, edited by Joel Myerson, 285–311. Charlottesville: University Press of Virginia, 1987.

————. "The Sound of a Flail: Reconstructions of Thoreau's Early 'Life without Principle' Lectures." 2 vols. Master's thesis, Eastern Washington University, 1984.

————. "A Textual Study of Thoreau's *Dispersion of Seeds* Manuscripts." Ph.D. diss. University of Connecticut, 1993.

————, and Ronald Wesley Hoag. "Thoreau's Lectures after *Walden*: An Annotated Calendar." In *Studies in the American Renaissance, 1996*, edited by Joel Myerson, 241–362. Charlottesville: University Press of Virginia, 1996.

De Candolle, Alphonse Louis Pierre Pyramus. *Géographie Botanique Raisonnée; ou, Exposition des Faits Principaux et des Lois Concernant la Distribution Géographique des Plants de L'époque Actuelle. . . . 2 vols*. Paris: V. Masson [et al.], 1855.

Downing, Andrew J. *The Fruits and Fruit Trees of America. . . .* New York and London: Wiley and Putnam, 1845.

Duhamel du Monceau, Henri Louis. *Traités des Arbes et Arbustes qui se Cultivent en France en Pleine Terre*. Paris: H. L. Guerin & L. F. Delatour, 1755.

Dupree, A. Hunter. *Asa Gray: American Botanist, Friend of Darwin*. 1959. Reprint, Baltimore: John Hopkins University Press, 1988.

Eastman, Mary (Henderson). *Dahcotah; or, Life and Legends of the Sioux around Fort Snelling. . . .* New York: J. Wiley, 1849.

Emerson, George B. *A Report on the Trees and Shrubs Growing Naturally in the Forests of Massachusetts. . . .* Boston: Dutton and Wentworth, 1846.

Emerson, Ralph Waldo. "Thoreau." In Joel Myerson, "Emerson's 'Thoreau': A New Edition from Manuscript," in *Studies in the American Renaissance, 1979*, 35–55. Boston: Twayne Publishers, 1979.

Emmons, Ebenezer. *Insects of New-York*. Albany, N.Y.: C. Van Benthuysen, 1854.

Evelyn, John. *Sylva, or a Discourse of Forest-Trees . . . To Which Is Annexed Pomona. . . . Also Kalendarium Hortense. . . .* London: Jo. Martyn and Ja. Allestry, 1679.

Franklin, Sir John. *Narrative of a Journey to the Shores of the Polar Sea, in the Years 1819, 20, 21, and 22. . . .* Philadelphia: H. C. Carey [et al.], 1824.

Fuller, Thomas. *The Worthies of England*. Edited by John Freeman. London: George Allen & Unwin, 1952.

Gardner, John. "An Account of the Town of Stow (Mass.) in a Letter from Rev. John Gardner to Rev. Nathan Stone, Dated 'Stow, March 9, 1767.' " In *Collections of the Massachusetts Historical Society*, 1st ser., vol. 10 (1809): 83–84.

Gerarde, John. *The Herball of Generall Historie of Plantes. . . .* London: Adam Islip, Joice Norton and Richard Whitakers, 1633.

Gookin, Daniel. *An Historical Account of the Doings and Sufferings of the Christian Indians in New England in the Years 1675, 1676, 1677*. Boston: Belknap and Hall, 1772.

Gosse, Philip Henry. *The Canadian Naturalist. A Series of Conversations on the Natural History of Lower Canada.* London: John Van Voorst, 1840.

———. *Letters from Alabama (U.S.), Chiefly Relating to Natural History.* London: Morgan and Chase, 1859.

Gray, Asa. *A Manual of Botany of the Northern United States. . . .* Boston: James Munroe and Company, 1848.

———. *A Manual of Botany of the Northern United States. . . .* New York: G. P. Putnam & Co., 1856.

"The Great Balloon Voyage." *New-York Semi-Weekly Tribune.* 7 October 1859.

Harding, Walter. *The Days of Henry Thoreau: A Biography.* 1962. Reprint, New York: Dover Publications, 1982.

Hearne, Samuel. *A Journey from Prince of Wales Fort in Hudson's Bay to the North Ocean . . . in the Years 1769, 1770, 1771, and 1772.* London: A. Strahan & T. Cadell, 1795.

Heckewelder, John. "An Account of the History, Manners, and Customs, of the Indian Natives Who Once Inhabited Pennsylvania and the Neighbouring States." In *Transactions of the Historical & Literary Committee of the American Philosophical Society, Held at Philadelphia, for Promoting Useful Knowledge,* 1st ser., vol. 1, (1819): 3–347.

Hennepin, Louis. *A Description of Louisiana. . . .* Translated by John Gilmary Shea. New York: John G. Shea, 1880. Thoreau's edition: *Description de la Louisiane, Nouvellement Decouverte. . . .* (Paris: Chez la veuve Sebastian Huré, 1683.

Herodotus, A New and Literal Version, From the Text of Bæhr. . . . London: H. G. Bohn, 1854.

Herrick, Robert. *The Poetical Works of Robert Herrick.* Edited by George Saintsbury. 2 vols. London: George Bell & Sons, 1893. Thoreau's source was *The Poetical Works of Robert Herrick.* 2 vols. London: William Pickering, 1825.

Hind, Henry Youle. *Northwest Territory . . . Report on the Assiniboine and Saskatchewan Exploration Expedition. . . .* Toronto: J. Lovell, 1859.

———. *Rapport sur L'Exploration de la Contrée Situé Entre le Lac Supérieur et les Établissements de la Riviére Rouge. . . .* Toronto: S. Derbishire & G. Desbarats, 1858.

Homer. *The Odyssey. Translated from the Greek by Alexander Pope.* Georgetown, D.C., and Philadelphia: Richards & Mallory & Nicklin, 1813.

Howarth, William L. *The Book of Concord: Thoreau's Life as a Writer.* New York: Viking, 1982.

———. *The Literary Manuscripts of Henry David Thoreau.* Columbus: Ohio State University Press, 1974.

Josselyn, John. *An Account of Two Voyages to New England. . . .* 2d ed. London: Giles Widdows, 1675.

———. *New-Englands Rarities Discovered: In Birds, Beasts, Fishes, Serpents, and Plants of that Country. . . .* London: G. Widdowes, 1672.

Kalm, Pehr. *Travels into North America; Containing Its Natural History, and a Circumstantial Account of Its Plantations and Agriculture in General. . . .* 2 vols. Translated by John Reinhold Forster. London: T. Lowndes, 1772.

Kane, Elisha Kent. *The U.S. Grinnell Expedition in Search of Sir John Franklin. A Personal Narrative*. New York: Harper & Brothers, 1853.

Kerr, Howard. *Mediums, and Spirit-Rappers, and Roaring Radicals: Spiritualism in American Literature, 1850–1900*. Urbana: University of Illinois Press, 1972.

[Knapp, John Leonard.] *The Journal of a Naturalist*. Philadelphia: Carey & Lea, 1831.

La Hontan, Louis Armand de Lom D'Arce, Baron de. *Voyages du Baron de La Hontan dans l'Amerique Septentrionale. . . . 2nd éd., Revue, Corigée, & Augmentée*. 2 vols. Amsterdam: F. l'Honoré, 1705.

Lawson, John. *The History of Carolina*. In *A New Collection of Voyages and Travels . . . in All Parts of the World. . . .* edited by John Stevens. London: J. Knapton [et al.], 1708–10.

Le Jeune, Paul. *Jesuit Relations. Relation de ce Qui S'est Passe en la Nouvelle France, en l'Année 1639. . . .* Roven, France: Chez Jean de Boulenger, 1639.

Lewis, Meriwether, and William Clark. *History of the Expedition . . . to the Sources of the Missouri, thence . . . to the Pacific Ocean. . . .* 2 vols. Philadelphia: Bradford and Inskeep, 1814.

Lindley, John. *Natural System of Botany. . . . 2nd Ed. . . .* London: Longman Rees Orme, Brown, Green, and Longman, 1836.

Loskiel, George Henry. *History of the Mission of the United Brethren among the Indians in North America. . . .* Translated by Christian Ignatius Latrobe. London: The Brethren's Society for the Furtherance of the Gospel, 1794.

Loudon, John Claudius. *Arboretum et Fruticetum Britannicum; or, The Trees and Shrubs of Britain. . . .* 2d ed., 8 vols. London: the author, 1844.

Mackenzie, Sir Alexander. *Voyages from Montreal, on the River St. Lawrence. . . .* 2 vols. London: T. Cadell, Jun. et al.; Edinburgh: W. Creech, 1802.

Mellow, James R. *Nathaniel Hawthorne in His Times*. Boston: Houghton Mifflin Co., 1980.

Michaux, Francois Andre. *The North American Sylva, or A Description of the Forest Trees of the United States, Canada, and Nova Scotia. . . .* 3 vols. Paris: printed by C. D'Hautel, 1819.

Miller, Hugh. *The Testimony of the Rocks; or, Geology in Its Bearings on the Two Theologies, Natural and Revealed*. Boston: Gould and Lincoln, 1857.

Montaigne, Michel de. *Essais: Nouvelle Ed. Precedee d'une Lettre de M. Villemain sur l'Eloge de Montaigne par P. Christian*. Paris: Lavigne, 1843.

Morton, Nathaniel. *New-Englands Memoriall*. Boston: Club of Odd Volumes, 1903.

Mudie, Robert. *The Feathered Tribes of the British Islands*. 2 vols. London: Bohn, 1834.

The New England Farmer; A Monthly Journal. . . . Edited by Simon Brown et al. Boston: Nourse, Eaton & Tolman, 1861.

Niebuhr, Barthold Georg. *The History of Rome. . . .* 3 vols. Translated by Julius Charles Hare and Connop Thirwall. Philadelphia: Thomas Wardle, 1835.

"Night Notes." *New-York Semi-Weekly Tribune*. 22 March 1861.

Nuttall, Thomas. *The North American Sylva; or, a Description of the Forest Trees of the United States, Canada, and Nova Scotia. . . .* 3 vols. Philadelphia: J. Dobson, 1842. Thoreau's edition: Thomas Nuttall. *The North American Sylva.* . . . 3 vols. Philadelphia: Robert P. Smith, 1853.

Nutting, Helen Cushing [compiler]. *To Monadnock: The Records of a Mountain in New Hampshire.* . . . New York: Stratford Press, 1925.

Oswald, John. *An Etymological Dictionary of the English Language.* . . . Philadelphia: E. C. Biddle, 1844.

Owen, David Dale. *Report of a Geological Survey of Wisconsin, Iowa and Minnesota.* . . . Philadelphia: Lippincott, Grambo & Co., 1852.

Oxford English Dictionary. 1971. Oxford: Oxford University Press, 1979.

Parry, Sir William Edward. *Three Voyages for the Discovery of a Northwest Passage from the Atlantic to the Pacific.* . . . 2 vols. New York: Harper's Family Library, 1841.

Peters, Richard. "Herbage and Shrubs Spontaneously Produced, after Forest Timber Burnt, by Firing the Woods." In *Memoirs of the Philadelphia Society for Promoting Agriculture*, vol. 1 (1808): 237–39.

Phelps, Mrs. A. Hart Lincoln. *Familiar Lectures on Botany, Practical, Elementary, and Physiological.* . . . 5th ed., Rev. and Enl. . . . New York: F. J. Huntington, 1837.

Philips, John. *The Poems of John Philips.* Edited by M. G. Lloyd Thomas. Oxford: Basil Blackwell, 1927.

Phillips, Henry. *The History of Cultivated Vegetables.* . . . 2 vols. London: H. Colburn and Co., 1822.

Pliny the Elder. *Historiæ Mundi.* . . . 3 vols. [Geneva]: Jacobum Storer, 1593.

———. *The Natural History of Pliny.* Translated by John Bostock and H. T. Riley. 6 vols. London: H. G. Bohn, 1855–57.

Pulteney, Richard. *A General View of the Writings of Linnæus.* . . . 2nd ed. London: J. Mawman, 1805.

Purchas, Samuel. *Purchas His Pilgrimes.* . . . 4 vols. London: W. Stansby for H. Fetherstone, 1625.

Pursh, Frederick. *Flora Americæ Septentrionalis; or . . . Description of the Plants of North America.* . . . 2 vols. London: White, Cochrane, and Co., 1814.

Rasles, Sebastien. "A Dictionary of the Abnaki Language in North America . . . with an Introductory Memoir and Notes, by John Pickering." In *Memoirs of the American Academy of Arts and Sciences*, n.s., vol. 1 (1833): 375–574.

Report of the Commissioner of Patents for the Year 1854, Agriculture. Washington, D.C.: A. O. P. Nicholson, 1855.

Richardson, James. "Extracts from Report for the Year 1856 [on Geological Survey of Anticosti]." In Alfred R. Roche, *Anticosti; Notes on the Resources and Capabilities of the Island of Anticosti.* . . . 45–60. London: G. Smythe & Co., n.d.

Richardson, Sir John. *Arctic Searching Expedition . . . in Search of . . . Sir John Franklin.* . . . 2 vols. New York: Harper & Brothers, 1852.

———. *Fauna Boreali-Americana; or, The Zoology of the Northern Parts of British America.* . . . 4 vols. London: J. Murray, 1829–37.

Richardson, Robert D. *Henry Thoreau, A Life of the Mind.* Berkeley: University of California Press, 1986.

Sagard, Gabriel. *Histoire du Canada et Voyages Que les Freres Mineurs Recollects y ont Faicts pour la Conversion des Infidelles.* . . . Paris: C. Sonnius, 1636.

———. *Le Grand Voyage du Pays des Hurons, Situé en L'Amerique.* . . . Paris: D. Moreau, 1632.

Saint Pierre, Jacques Henri Bernardin de. *Studies of Nature.* . . . Translated by Henry Hunter. 5 vols. London: C. Dilly, 1796.

Sattelmeyer, Robert. *Thoreau's Reading: A Study in Intellectual History with Bibliographical Catalogue.* Princeton: Princeton University Press, 1988.

Scriptores Rei Rusticæ, Rei Rusticæ Auctores Latine Veteres, M. Cato, M. Varro, L. Columella, Pallâdius. . . . [Heidelberg]: Hier. Commelini, 1595.

[Seward, Leonard]. *The History of Dublin, N.H., Containing the Address by Charles Mason, and the Proceedings at the Centennial Celebration, June 17, 1852.* . . . Boston: J. Wilson, 1855.

Spence, Joseph. *Anecdotes, Observations, and Characters, of Books and Men.* London: John Russell Smith, 1858.

Springer, John S. *Forest Life and Forest Trees: Comprising Winter Camp Life . . . of Maine and New Brunswick.* New York: Harper & Brothers, 1851.

Sturluson [also Sturleson], Snorri. *The Heimskringla; or, Chronicle of the Kings of Norway.* Translated by Samuel Laing. 3 vols. London: Longsman, Brown, Green and Longmans, 1844.

———. *The Prose Edda.* translated by Jean I. Young. Berkeley: University of California Press, 1954. Thoreau's edition: Snorri Sturluson. *The Prose Edda.* In Paul Henri Mallet, *Northern Antiquities; or, an Historical Account of the Manners, Customs, Religion, and Laws . . . of the Ancient Scandanavians.* . . . *Tr. from the French of M. Mallet by Bishop Percy.* . . . London: Henry G. Bohn, 1847.

Tacitus. *C. Cornelii Taciti Opera ex Recensione Io. Augusti Ernesti.* . . . 3 vols. Boston: Wells et Lilly, 1817.

Tanner, John. *A Narrative of the Captivity and Adventures of John Tanner . . . during Thirty Years Residence among the Indians.* . . . New York: G. & C. & H. Carvill, 1830.

Theophrastus. *Theophrasti Eresii De Historia Plantarum Libri Decem, Græce et Latine . . . cum Notis, tum Commentariis . . . Ioannes Bodæus a Stapel.* . . . Amsterdam: H. Laurentium, 1644.

Thomson, James. *The Seasons, with a Biographical Sketch of the Author.* London: W. S. Orr & Co., [ca. 1845].

Thoreau, Henry D. "Autumnal Tints." *The Atlantic Monthly Magazine* 10, no. 60 (October 1862): 385–402.

————. *Cape Cod*. Edited by Joseph J. Moldenhauer. 1865. Reprint, Princeton: Princeton University Press, 1988.

————. "Common Place Book 1." MS notebook labeled "Extracts Mostly upon Natural History." Harry Elkins Widener Memorial Library, Harvard University. Facsimile reproduction and partial transcript, with photocopies of most source pages, available in Kenneth Walter Cameron, *Thoreau's Fact Book in the Harry Elkins Widener Collection. . . .* 3 vols. [Hartford: Transcendental Books, 1966.]

————. "Common Place Book 2." MS notebook labeled "Extracts Mostly upon Natural History." Henry W. and Albert A. Berg Collection, New York Public Library.

————. *The Dispersion of Seeds*. In *Faith in a Seed: The Dispersion of Seeds and Other Late Natural History Writings*, 23–173. Edited by Bradley P. Dean. Covelo, Calif.: Shearwater Books/Island Press, 1993.

————. *Huckleberries*. Edited by Leo Stoller. Iowa City and New York: Windhover Press of the University of Iowa and the New York Public Library, 1970.

————. *The Journal of Henry D. Thoreau*. 14 vols. Edited by Bradford Torrey and Francis H. Allen. Boston: Houghton Mifflin Company, 1906.

————. *Journal, Volume 3: 1848–1851*. Edited by Robert Sattelmeyer et al. Princeton: Princeton University Press, 1990.

————. *Journal, Volume 4: 1851–1852*. Edited by Leonard N. Neufeldt and Nancy Craig Simmons. Princeton: Princeton University Press, 1992.

————. *Journal, Volume 5: 1852–1853*. Edited by Patrick F. O'Connell. Princeton: Princeton University Press, 1990.

————. *The Maine Woods*. Edited by Joseph J. Moldenhauer. 1864. Reprint, Princeton: Princeton University Press, 1972.

————. *Minnesota Notebook*. In *Thoreau's Minnesota Journey: Two Documents* (Thoreau Society Booklet no. 16), edited by Walter Harding. [Concord, Mass.]: Thoreau Society, Inc., 1962.

————. "Natural History of Massachusetts." In *The Dial: A Magazine for Literature, Philosophy, and Religion*, 3:19–40. 4 vols. Boston: Weeks, Jordan, and Co., 1841–44.

————. "The Succession of Forest Trees." *New-York Weekly Tribune*, 6 October 1860.

————. *Walden*. Edited by J. Lyndon Shanley. 1854. Reprint, Princeton: Princeton University Press, 1971.

————. "A Walk to Wachusett." In *Boston Miscellany of Literature and Fashion*, vol. 3, no. 1 (January 1843): 31–36.

————. "Walking." *The Atlantic Monthly Magazine* 9, no. 56 (June 1862): 657–74.

————. "Wild Apples." *The Atlantic Monthly Magazine* 10, no. 61 (November 1862): 513–26.

"A Topographical Description of Duxborough, in the County of Plymouth." In *Collections of the Massachusetts Historical Society*, 1st ser., vol. 2 (1793): 3–8.

Topsell, Edward. *The Historie of Four-Footed Beasts and Serpents*. . . . London: W. Iaggard, 1607.

Torrey, John. *Flora of the State of New-York*. . . . 2 vols. Albany, N.Y.: Carroll and Cook, 1843.

Tusser, Thomas. *Some of the Five Hundred Points of Good Husbandry*. . . . Oxford: John Henry Parker, 1848.

Van der Donck, Adriaen. "Description of the New Netherlands." Translated by Jeremiah Johnson. In *Collections of the New York Historical Society*, 2d ser., vol. 1 (1841): 125–242.

Very, Jones. "The Barberry Bush." In *The Dial: A Magazine for Literature, Philosophy, and Religion*, 1:131. 4 vols. (Boston: Weeks, Jordan, and Co., 1841–44).

Virgil. *Eclogues* and *Georgics*. In *Virgil . . . in Two Volumes*. Vol. 1. Rev. ed. Loeb Classical Edition. Cambridge, Mass.: Harvard University Press, 1978. Thoreau's edition: Virgil. *Eclogues*. In *Opera . . . ad Usum Serenissimi Delphini*. . . . Philadelphia: M. Carey & Son, 1817.

Walker, John. *A Critical Pronouncing Dictionary, and Expositor of the English Language*. . . . New York: Collins and Hannay, 1823.

"The Weight and Culture of Dwarf Pears." *New-York Semi-Weekly Tribune*. 19 October 1860.

Weiss, John. *The Life and Correspondence of Theodore Parker*. . . . 2 vols. New York: D. Appleton & Co., 1864.

Whitney, Peter. "An Account of a Singular Apple-Tree. . . ." In *Memoirs of the American Academy of Arts and Sciences*, vol. 1 (Boston, 1785): 386–87.

Williams, Roger. "A Key into the Language of America. . . ." In *Collections of the Massachusetts Historical Society*, 1st ser., vol. 3 (1794): 203–39.

"A Winter Underground." *New-York Semi-Weekly Tribune*, 13 November 1860.

Wood, Alphonso. *A Class-Book of Botany, Designed for Colleges, Academies, and Other Seminaries*. 23d ed., rev. and enl. Boston: n.p., 1851.

Wood, William. *New England's Prospect, Being a True, Lively, and Experimental Description of . . . New England*. 3d ed. London: printed 1639. Reprint, Boston: Thomas and John Fleet, 1764.

ACKNOWLEDGMENTS

FOR PERMISSION TO PUBLISH Thoreau's *Wild Fruits* manuscript, I thank the New York Public Library, Astor, Lenox, and Tilden Foundations. I am grateful to Rodney Phillips, curator of the Henry W. and Albert A. Berg Collection of English and American Literature at the New York Public Library, and to his assistants, Stephen Crook and Philip Milito, for their hospitality during my many visits to their wonderful reading room and for their assistance with many of the tasks associated with preparing Thoreau's manuscript for publication. I also thank the J. Pierpont Morgan Library for allowing me in my notes to refer to and quote from the manuscript volumes of Thoreau's journal. Like all Thoreauvians, I am indebted to Theo Baumann for his fine map of Thoreau country; and I thank Princeton University Press, Elizabeth Witherell, and Daphne Ireland for permission to publish the map and for production assistance. I also thank Bob Stewart and The Virtual Mirror, Inc., for permission to use some of the botanical definitions from the GardenWeb site at www.gardenweb.com. My good friend Thomas Siegman very graciously allowed me to stay at his Manhattan home whenever I visited the Berg Collection, a favor which I appreciate very much because it made my visits a greater joy than they might otherwise have been.

Michael Frederick spent many dozens of hours working with me on this project; he located many of the sources cited in the notes, scrupulously read one of my early drafts of Thoreau's *Wild Fruits* into a dictation machine so that I could proof that text against Thoreau's manuscript pages, culled out of my typescript place names for the map and botanical terms for the glossary, and helped advance this project in many other important ways. I could have completed the project without him, I suppose—but not as quickly and only with a great deal more grief to myself and others. I am enormously grateful for his assistance and enthusiasm, and I thank Stacia Fondulis Frederick, his lovely wife, for agreeing to let him spend so much time working on this project.

In addition to being blessed with living and working at the most estimable place in all the world to conduct Thoreau research—the Thoreau Institute in Lincoln, Massachusetts, a fifteen-minute walk from Walden Pond—I have been blessed with wonderful colleagues. These individuals have quietly, over a long period, performed all the small but invaluable favors of friendship that made working on this project a greater joy to me than it otherwise would have been. I am enormously grateful to each of them for their helpfulness, patience, and encouragement: Kathi Anderson, Margaret Norton, and Juliet Trofi (with the Walden Woods Project); Tom Harris and Karen Kashian (with the Thoreau Society); Helen Bowdoin, Susan Glover Godlewski, and Dan Schmid (with the Thoreau Institute); and Jeanne Barr, Frannie Hodge, and Mark Mosher (with the Thoreau Institute Technology Team of Compaq Services). I must single out Frannie Hodge for added appreciation because she was so wonderful about overseeing many of the activities of the Thoreau Institute Media Center when I was called away to work on this project. She was also gently but firmly insistent that I do my Thoreau work—and very sweet to listen to me as I expressed my enthusiasms for that work. I am also grateful to those staff members and assistants of the Thoreau Society who passed through the Thoreau Institute while I was working on this project and provided me with assistance and encouragement while there: Kelly Basile, Ashleigh Fines, Mike Long, and Chris Nelson.

Many Thoreauvians, both scholars and enthusiasts, provided expertise, assistance, and goodwill during this project, and I thank each of them. The subscribers to the Thoreau electronic-mail distribution list were generously responsive to the queries I addressed to them during this project. Dave Bonney, Phyllis Cole, Robert Galvin, and Ed Zahniser were particularly helpful with information that I included in some of the notes. Ed Meyer helped out with some of Thoreau's drawings. In addition to providing encouragement on two critical occasions, Robert D. Richardson provided translations of and assistance relating to Thoreau's French and Latin, and Kevin Van Anglen generously checked Thoreau's use of Greek in the manuscript and my transcript of those words and phrases. Peter Alden, Raymond Angelo, and Walter Brain helped a great deal with identifications of and information relating to various flora and fauna, particularly as to where in the Concord area a few difficult-to-locate specimens might be located. David Wood, curator at the Concord Museum, and Leslie Wilson, curator of Special Collections at the Concord Free Public Library, generously responded to my queries relating to Thoreau's remarks about Concord history. Also, while working on this project I found very useful and encouraging the scholarship of Michael Berger, Ronald Wesley Hoag, Patrick F. O'Connell, Robert Sattelmeyer, the late Leo Stoller, and Laura Dassow Walls. I am also grateful to Berger, Hoag, Walls, and Elizabeth Witherell for discussing Thoreau's late natural history writings with me during the last few years.

This project also benefitted from the assistance of individuals who, while not Thoreauvians, were nonetheless generous in their responses to my inquiries. M. Rosalie Fisher very kindly helped with translations of Thoreau's French, as did Jean Folly of Compaq Services, who also provided me with valuable technical assistance. Dave Griffin, Ellen Joyce, Carleton C. Lane, Peter M. Lauriat, and Joop de Wilde very graciously helped me locate information that I used in a few of my notes. I very much appreciate the efforts of these generous individuals.

Two good friends deserve special thanks. I got to know them while working on *Faith in a Seed* and was fortunate enough to continue working with them on this project: Howard Boyer, who had great faith in this project, and Abigail Rorer, whose lovely drawings again accompany Thoreau's prose. (Abigail asks that I pass along her gratitude to Roland and Rexine Barnes, Karen Davis, David Foster, Peter and Gloria George, Susan Kelley, Dennis Magee, John O'Keefe, Martha Siccardi, Ralph Tiner, Peter Del Tredici, and Cecily Cookman Westervelt—as well as Ray Angelo and Walter Brain—for the important roles they played in her work on this project.) I owe special thanks as well to those at W. W. Norton & Company who made the business end of this project so pleasant: editor Alane Mason for a welcome blend of patience and encouragement; Ashley Barnes for cheerfulness and many small favors; and Don Rifkin for excellent, even sensitive copyediting.

I have taken the liberty of dedicating my labors on this project to Don Henley and Kathi Anderson of the Walden Woods Project, and to Debra Kang Dean. I have had the great good fortune of working closely with Don and Kathi for almost a decade now. I know how much they care for Thoreau's writings and for the land Thoreau loved. I know as well how much they have sacrificed for that land and that literature. All of us who care deeply about Thoreau and his invaluable legacies owe these two humanitarians an enormous debt, and it gives me a great deal of pleasure to be able to make this small installment on that debt.

As always, I owe by far my greatest debt of gratitude to my wife and best friend, the poet Debra Kang Dean, whose patience, encouragement, and generosity have enabled me for many years now to pursue my work on Thoreau—often, I know and regret, at great disruption to her own important interests and pursuits, not to mention her far more sensible routine. Were it not for Debra's support, more years would have elapsed before readers could savor these wild fruits of Thoreau's final years.

Henry David Thoreau should have the last word in his own book:

I know a blue-pearmain tree growing within the edge of a swamp almost as good as wild. You would not suppose that there was any fruit left there, on the first survey. . . . Nevertheless, with experienced eyes I explore amid the bare alders and the huckleberry bushes and the withered sedge, and in the crevices of the rocks, which are full of leaves, and pry under the fallen and decaying ferns, which, with apple and alder leaves, thickly strew the ground. For I know that they lie concealed, fallen into hollows long since and covered up by the leaves of the tree itself—a proper kind of packing. From these lurking places anywhere within the circumference of the tree I draw forth the fruit, all wet and glossy, maybe nibbled by rabbits and hollowed out by crickets, and perhaps with a leaf or two cemented to it . . . but still with a rich bloom on it, and at least as ripe and well kept, if not better than those in barrels, more crisp and lively than they.

INDEX

DATE DUE			

JAN 11 2000

GAYLORD, FR2

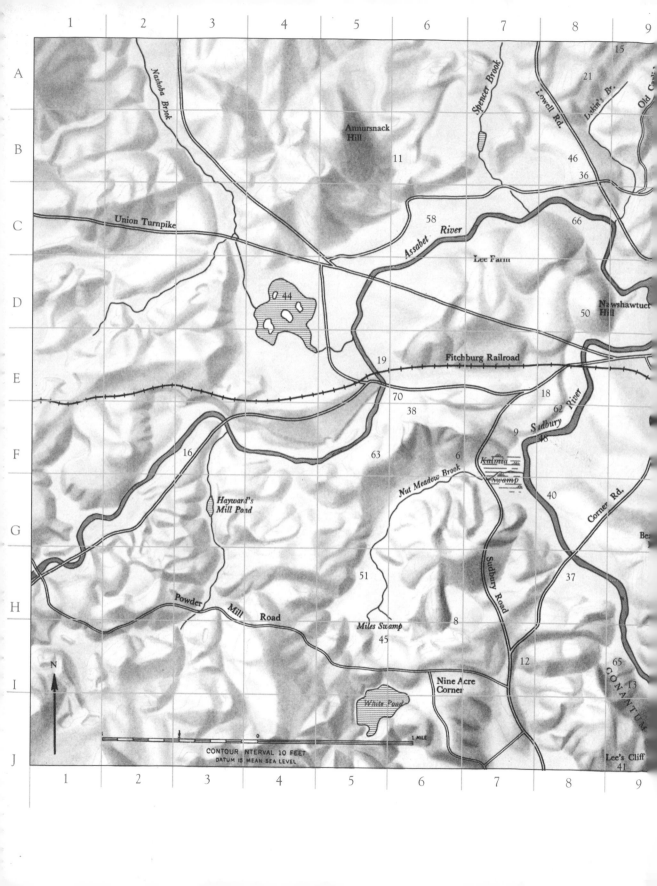